The Bhagavad Gita for Daily Living, Volume 3

भक्त्या मामभिजानाति यावान्यश्चास्मि तत्त्वतः । ततो मां तत्त्वतो ज्ञात्वा विशते तदनन्तरम् ॥ १८-५५॥
सर्वकर्माण्यपि सदा कुर्वाणो मद्व्यपाश्रयः । मत्प्रसादादवाप्नोति शाश्वतं पदमव्ययम् ॥ १८-५६॥

To love is to know me: thus one shares in my glory and enters into my boundless being. All his acts are performed in my service, and through my grace he wins eternal life.

— BHAGAVAD GITA 18:55–56

The Bhagavad Gita for Daily Living

VOLUME 3

A Verse-by-Verse Commentary
Chapters 13–18
To Love Is to Know Me

BY EKNATH EASWARAN

 NILGIRI PRESS

To my Teacher
EKNATH CHIPPU KUNCHI AMMAL
my Grandmother & my Playmate

First published 1984. Second edition 2020

paperback 10 9 8 7 6 5 4 3 2 1 hardback 10 9 8 7 6 5 4 3 2 1

ISBN: 978-1-58638-136-3 (paperback)

ISBN: 978-1-58638-137-0 (hardcover)

ISBN: 978-1-58638-145-5 (ebook) (set of three volumes)

ISBN: 978-1-58638-752-5 (audiobook) (set of three volumes)

This second edition incorporates revisions made in all three volumes
following the author's final instructions.

Publisher's Cataloging-In-Publication Data
(Prepared by The Donohue Group, Inc.)

Names: Eknath, Easwaran, 1910-1999, author.
Title: The Bhagavad Gita for daily living : a verse-by-verse commentary /
by Eknath Easwaran.
Description: Second edition. | Tomales, California : Nilgiri Press, 2020.
| Includes glossary and guide to Sanskrit pronunciation. | v.1.
Chapters 1-6: The end of sorrow -- v.2. Chapters 7-12: Like a thousand
suns -- v.3. Chapters 13-18: To love is to know me. | Includes index.
Identifiers: ISBN 9781586381332 (v.1 ; hardcover) | ISBN 9781586381356
(v.2 ; hardcover) | ISBN 9781586381370 (v.3 ; hardcover) | ISBN
9781586381325 (v.1 ; paper) | ISBN 9781586381349 (v.2 ; paper) | ISBN
9781586381363 (v.3 ; paper) | ISBN 9781586381455 (ebook set)
Subjects: LCSH: Bhagavadgītā. | Bhagavadgītā--Criticism, interpretation,
etc. | Bhagavadgītā--Commentaries. | Spiritual life--Hinduism. |
Meditation.
Classification: LCC BL1138.66 .E17 2020 (print) | LCC BL1138.66 (ebook) |
DDC 294.5/924--dc23

Nilgiri Press is the publishing division of:
The Blue Mountain Center of Meditation
Box 256, Tomales, California 94971
Telephone: +1 707 878 2369 | 800 475 2369

www.bmcm.org | info@bmcm.org

Printed on FSC® certified paper

MIX
Paper from
responsible sources
FSC
www.fsc.org FSC® C103567

Table of Contents

A Higher Image

One of the first lessons I learned in geography was that the earth is round. Our little village in South India had been left out of the march of modern civilization, and most of us hadn't heard this terrible news. Even my teacher was a little diffident in presenting it to us. "You may not believe this," he began, "and if you don't, I sympathize completely. But this is what they gave me to understand when I did my teacher's training in Madras."

When I went home that afternoon, my granny was waiting for me as always by the front gate, ready with her usual greeting: "Well, Little Lamp, what did you learn in school today?" Somehow this was never an automatic question; each time it was fresh and her interest genuine.

"Brace yourself, Granny," I said. "You may not believe this, and if you don't, I sympathize completely. But today my teacher told us that the earth is really round." Shattering the illusions of a granny's lifetime.

Not a hair fell out of place. "What does it matter?" she asked. "You can be selfless whether the earth is round or square or triangular."

That took some wind out of my sails. But there was still my mother; she was much easier to surprise. I marched over and said, "Guess what we learned today."

"I can't," she said. "You tell me."

"The earth is round!"

She fell into a paroxysm of laughter which still rings in my ears. She never let me forget that moment, and I don't think she ever believed me either. Now and then, when I would leave in the morning for school, she would send me off with "Goodbye – and don't slip off!" Even after I became a university professor, which is a very prestigious position in India, she used to introduce me to a new friend by saying proudly, "This is my son, who is Chairman of the Department of English. He writes for the *Times of India* and delivers talks over All India Radio." Then she would add, "But he still thinks the earth is round!"

I used to try to reason with her. "This isn't just some theory, Mother," I'd say. "It has been proved over and over again." Her point was inarguable: for her, a flat earth worked. "When I go to the temple," she'd say, "I don't roll off. When you go to school, you don't slide down the sides. It looks flat; why should I change my mind?"

Once I saw the practicality of this point of view, I ceased trying to convince her. In fact, when I reached this country I was impressed to learn that there is a Flat Earth Society with many members who probably function in life quite adequately. As long as you keep within a certain sphere of activity, believing that the earth is flat is a harmless piece of ignorance which interferes very little with daily living.

Virtually all of us, however, are subject to a much more pervasive kind of ignorance which affects every detail of our lives: we believe that we are wholly physical creatures, who can be satisfied in wholly physical ways. This belief has profound practical implications. On the individual level, it means we believe that if we can give a person the capacity to satisfy physical needs and desires, he or she will be happy. Technology will be able to solve our health problems and provide material comfort for everyone. It will also be able to solve our mental problems, since personality and behavior are determined by our chemistry. Progress is measured in terms of material growth, value in terms of material assets. Even a person's work is evaluated as a commodity. Finally, there is nothing like a moral order, only the principles of natural selection; so our only rational guide for action is self-interest.

The great religions of the world have always taught that there is more to the human being than the body: an essential core of personality that is not physical but spirit, divine. Yet at the very deepest levels of thinking, almost all of us identify with the physical body: "When my body dies," we say, "*I* die." All our responses to life are conditioned by this belief. In a sense, of course, this is simply the human condition. But today, I think, the physical approach to life has become a kind of epidemic in modern industrial civilization, East as well as West. Never in history, to my knowledge, has a civilization reflected a lower image of the human being: a physical, chemical organism with no motivation higher than self-interest, no aspirations that cannot be fulfilled on the physical level.

Sometimes I hear the same argument that my mother used to give to support her belief that the earth is flat: "Well, whatever you may say, this physical image *works*. It's true that I think of myself as just a physical creature, but I've done all right. I haven't fulfilled all my desires, but I've gained some of what I wanted out of life. With just a little more, I'd call myself happy. And in terms of human progress, it seems to me that the more we've concentrated on the physical level of life, the better things have been for everyone: more prosperity, more comforts, more leisure time, better health, more variety of things to do and have and enjoy."

I never try to argue with this at all. In small situations where there is no great challenge, you *can* squeak by in life with such a limited self-image, just as you can get to the store and back without believing that the earth is round. Unfortunately, however, "small situations" are becoming fewer and fewer: in today's troubled world, it is a major challenge simply to raise a family or to keep personal relationships intact. Individually and globally, I would say, this business of looking on the human being as no more than physical is leading us into disaster.

Let me give two or three examples; there are many more in the chapters which follow.

For one, I have just finished reading a well-written article in a popular magazine on brain research. Neuroscientists now have the technology to study brain activity at the molecular level, and they feel they are on the threshold of the human personality, the "last frontier." "Can you believe," the writer asks, "that the seat of the human personality is a three-pound glob of matter with the consistency of Jello?" I replied frankly, "No, I can't." To me, looking for personality in the brain is like taking apart a light bulb to learn about electricity. The brain is a physical organ; personality is a force – or, more precisely, a complex of forces, as the Gita will explain in the next chapter. The brain is necessary for the expression of these forces in a human being, and this has certain chemical consequences. But to confuse the consequences with the cause is not only superficial, it leads to dangerous conclusions as well.

I was quite interested in the details of this research. The brain, researchers now estimate, consists of perhaps a hundred billion neurons, each as complex as a little computer. During recent decades, with dedicated study and the help of sophisticated technology, they have isolated and identified more than a dozen neurotransmitters – chemicals produced in the brain which transmit electric signals, and therefore information, from neuron to neuron. Recently they have learned to map the myriad folds of this three-pound glob without invasive surgery. On this map researchers hope to locate the seat of various human characteristics, so they can locate, for example, the area of the brain that lights up when we feel jealous. If they can then synthesize a chemical block for the neurotransmitter involved, they say, and get it to the proper site in the brain, no one need be plagued by jealousy again.

Now, I am not saying this won't work. In fact, I suspect it will prove possible to control many human emotions in this way, at least for a short period of time. But in the long run, when the audit takes place, the price to be paid will be terrible. Jealousy, to continue the same example, arises from insecurity. The more insecure your mind is, the more jealous you are likely to be of anything and anyone. Jealousy is a terrible state; it can gnaw at your mind day and night, distort your judgment, wither your love. If a chemical solution to this becomes available, there will be many, many insecure people to provide a ready market.

Now I would like you to imagine the results. One of your co-workers draws a lot of praise and you get jealous: you want to be praised for a good job too, and after all you deserve it more than he did. When you can't shake all these thoughts off, you take a couple of pills. Then you can go up to your colleague, smile at him, talk to him cheerfully, and not care whether he has done well or not – or, probably, whether you can improve your own performance either. The next time this happens, you know what to do: take a couple more pills right away, so those gnawing self-doubts don't even start. I am not saying this is impossible chemically, but over a period of time you will become so insecure that you will not be able to function anywhere. You will not be able to face any challenge; you will doubt yourself in everything you do. This kind of result is the inescapable consequence of applying physical solutions to problems of the mind.

For another example on the individual level, look at personal relationships, particularly those between man and woman. Very often I hear today, "We're in love! Our chemistry is just right." I want to say, "How tragic!" That is not love; it is physical attraction. Love is a relationship; sex is a sensation, and sensations are terribly short-lived. If a relationship is based on physical attraction, it cannot last: not because of any moral judgment against it, but because that is the nature of physical phenomena. Just as in the war this country turned out "ninety-day wonders," our modern civilization is full of ninety-day relationships. We have come to accept this as the nature of love, simply because our image of the human being reduces everything to sensations and biological urges.

Third – on a much larger scale now – with this image, it is almost axiomatic that progress consists in multiplying material possessions and increasing physical comforts. We are physical creatures, so we can be satisfied with physical things. It follows that the more we can have, the happier we will be; the more a nation can produce, the better a place it will be in which to live. Today, I believe, we stand at a crisis in one of the greatest experiments in history. Believing that the human being is physical, we have by some three centuries of concentrated effort developed the technology to do what we like in the physical world. We have an unprecedented capacity to pursue material goals and produce material goods to satisfy every desire. If the physical image of the human being is accurate, we in the United States must be living in the Golden Age. Never have we had it so good. To begin with, we have so many things we can buy. The average man or woman can go into a supermarket or department store and find a variety of things to eat and own that a monarch of earlier times would envy. And we have such a wealth of ways to entertain ourselves. Whatever our means, almost all of us can watch TV as much as we like, go to movies, play video games, or listen to concert-quality music in our bedroom. Almost everyone who wants to own a car can do so, though admittedly it is more and more costly to drive anywhere. We have more leisure time than ever, and more sophisticated health care; we have a vast array of products available for easing the aches, pains, effort, tedium, and depression of daily living.

I won't ask you to look at the evidence of today's paper, from the front-page news through the entertainment section to the want ads and personals at the end. Just ask yourself, "*Is* this the Golden Age? Am *I*, Jonathan Doe, as happy as a human being can be?" As far as I can remember, I have never heard anyone claim that we have reached the pinnacle of progress. If you ask your neighbor, he is likely to object, "Are you kidding? Sure, I've got a good job and a car and a nice house with decent plumbing. But every year my paycheck buys us less. Every year my government spends billions of dollars it hasn't got to pile up weapons it can't use because they're too terrible – and then it keeps talking about ways to use them, even if it means the rest of us might be destroyed. I can't walk at night in my own neighborhood without wishing I had a police escort. My children are afraid to go to school, and so are their teachers: they're not even trying to teach any more; they're just trying to stay alive until they can retire. But we're luckier than most. Our family is still together. Most of our friends have given up on marriage now; their kids come home every day to an empty house. Seems like everybody is out for number one, angry with the world."

If we were merely physical creatures, all our material benefits should add up to happiness. If getting were the highest human motivation, all of us should be in seventh heaven. It is precisely because we are *not* merely physical creatures that these things are not enough to satisfy us: that, in fact, they only seem to make us hungrier for a life of lasting value. In the Bible's phrase, we are "sick unto death" of living on the physical level alone. In this country particularly, where we have had ample opportunity to evaluate the benefits of modern civilization, I think many, many people now feel in their hearts a deep desire for a more meaningful way of life.

From the spiritual perspective, this acute dissatisfaction with physical living is a very positive sign. If we have been measuring human existence by its shallowest measure, the Gita would say, it is good to feel "sick unto death." It would be terrible if we felt satisfied. The fact that we do not, that we are suffering with the consequences of our present values, gives hope that we can change direction and reclaim our spiritual dimension.

Here we encounter one of the dominant themes in this volume of the Gita: the law of karma. Put briefly, *karma* means consequences: all the effects that follow from our actions, words, and ways of thinking. Consequences, the Gita would say, are contained in an action the way a tree is implicit in a seed. If you plant an apple seed with the intent of getting apples, you don't simply get apples; you get the whole tree. Our modern civilization, in its desire for certain material fruits, has got the whole tree: a few good apples, many that are sour, and a lot of unexpected branches, all the effects that follow from the values of a wholly physical view of the human being and the world.

When you eat sour apples, you get a stomachache. As my grandmother used to tell me, this is proof that the Lord loves us. If your stomach didn't complain, you might eat half a dozen sour apples and never know what damage was being done inside. That is the purpose of karma too: when we violate spiritual laws, the consequences are painful, and that very pain serves as a reminder that something is wrong with our way of living. The longer we go on making the same mistakes, the more consequences accumulate and the more painful the suffering.

Karma is sometimes looked upon as a punitive force: if you do something wrong, you will be punished for it, as if by some cosmic Lawgiver out beyond Uranus. I do not share this view at all. Karma is consequences that we bring upon ourselves; and to me the law of karma is very much a corrective, guiding force, the "healing hand of God." Pain is not always an enemy; it can be an invaluable friend. When we are acting foolishly, thinking selfishly, making decisions that are at the expense of other people or other creatures, straying into illness, alienation, loneliness, or despair, it is good to feel anguished. In this sense, many of the problems that threaten us on a global level today – poverty, war, the arms race, our poisoned environment, the breakdown of the family, violence in our streets and homes, even the failure of the industrial economic order to provide for human needs – all these can be seen as the healing hand of life, telling us like the warning sign on the freeways: "Go back. You're going the wrong way."

The Gita, I like to repeat, is not a book of commandments but a book of choices. In this volume it tells us that we have two paths in life: one takes the highest view of the human being, as an essentially spiritual being; the other takes the lowest, as a physical creature governed by the biological drives of survival and self-gratification. Each of us, as individuals, has the choice between these two paths every day – the Gita would say many times each day, and it will illustrate how and when. But on a much greater scale, it is no exaggeration to say that we face this choice as a race today, at a particularly critical period in history. It is time to evaluate this immense gamble on physical living, on which we have staked so much of our material and human resources for the last three hundred years. And if we do not feel satisfied with what we have gained, we must choose a higher image of the human being to aspire to; the lower image will be proven worse than useless.

Like all the other great scriptures of the world, the Gita gives us such a higher image. It tells us unequivocally that we are not merely physical creatures; our innermost Self is divine. More than that, it tells clearly and in detail what we need to do to realize this divine image in our everyday lives – in our work, our relationships, our motivation, our health, our economic and social values, even our recreation. This has profound implications. It means that the Gita can be treated as a manual not only for the spiritual life but for what philosophers call the good life: life as it is worth living, in fulfillment, health, vitality, joy, and the abiding awareness that every day you live you have made the world a little better. This does not require that we become saints, but merely that we begin trying to live in accord with the highest image of ourselves. In the same way, on a much larger scale, the Gita shows how all the grave problems of our globe can be solved by basing our scientific, political, and economic decisions on this higher image of humanity. This is not impossible or impractical, as I hope to illustrate in this volume. All it requires is the same dedication we have given to physical achievements in this age of material progress, which is coming to a close.

Many years ago, when I first began teaching meditation in this country, I had many beatniks in my classes in San Francisco. They were a very earnest lot. I knew they were interested in Buddhism, particularly in Zen, so in my first talk I used the Buddha's word to refer to the goal of life: nirvāna. I didn't realize that the word was even more misunderstood than *karma*. After my talk, two or three fellows came up and said, "You know, we don't *want* nirvāna. We don't want extinction. We *like* to live."

I said, "Well, do you want real health? Not just to be free from disease, but to be full of vitality and resilience?"

"Sure," they said.

"Do you want your relationships to be deep and lasting? When something goes wrong in a relationship, would you like the quiet assurance of knowing you have the knowledge and the skill to set it right?"

"That sounds very good."

"Would you like the springs of creativity to flow continuously, instead of having to wait weeks or months for inspiration to decide to strike?" Some of them were artists or writers; they liked that idea very much.

"Wouldn't you like to know that you are equal to any challenge life can deal you? To enjoy life every moment, its downs and ups alike, knowing you have something to offer in every situation? Wouldn't you like to be whole in body, mind, and spirit?"

"Of course!"

"Well," I said, "nirvāna is all those things."

"In that case," they replied, "we *do* want nirvāna." For nirvāna is not the extinction of personality, as is often thought; it is Self-realization: the fulfillment of all that is highest in our nature.

Everyone, the Gita would say, is seeking this in some measure. Even if we do not want to dedicate ourselves to the spiritual life, all of us want the benefits of a life based on spiritual values. We want health, vitality, wisdom, courage, clear-headedness, the capacity to love and to draw love; we want a world at peace, free from fear, where everyone can earn an honest living with work of dignity and value. In other words, because the human being *is* more than physical, every human problem has a spiritual solution.

It follows that the Gita is not just for spiritual aspirants. It is a handbook for anybody in politics or education or medicine or the home or any other field who is dissatisfied with the kind of life that is offered to us today and wants to make it a little better. I have tried to address this volume of the Gita to all such people. They may come to it with no interest whatever in meditation or spiritual living; that is quite all right. They can see from these pages how great is our need for a higher image of the human being, and how practical are the Gita's suggestions for realizing it. If they then go on to try to translate these suggestions into their lives and work and thought, they will discover for themselves how essential meditation and its allied disciplines are.

For the transformation to a higher image cannot be accomplished easily. It goes against the full current of contemporary conditioning, and to swim against that current requires tremendous effort, endurance, faith, and a clear, constant vision of the goal – in a word, access to deep inner resources. So far as I know, this access can be gained only through the practice of meditation.

Since *meditation* can refer to so many practices today, I think it will be helpful to summarize the eight-point program for spiritual living which I have found effective in my own life. These steps are elaborated more fully in my book *Passage Meditation*.

THE EIGHT-POINT PROGRAM

1. *Meditation on a Passage.* The heart of this program is meditation: half an hour every morning, as early as is convenient. Do not increase this period; if you want to meditate more, have half an hour in the evening also, preferably at the very end of the day.

Set aside a room in your home to be used only for meditation and spiritual reading. After a while that room will become associated with meditation in your mind, so that simply entering it will have a calming effect. If you cannot spare a room, have a particular corner. Whichever you choose, keep your meditation place clean, well ventilated, and reasonably austere.

Sit in a straight-backed chair or on the floor and gently close your eyes. If you sit on the floor, you may need to support your back lightly against a wall. You should be comfortable enough to forget your body, but not so comfortable that you become drowsy.

Whatever position you choose, be sure to keep your head, neck, and spinal column erect in a straight line. As concentration deepens, the nervous system relaxes and you may begin to fall asleep. It is important to resist this tendency right from the beginning, by drawing yourself up and away from your back support until the wave of sleep has passed.

Once you have closed your eyes, begin to go *slowly,* in your mind, through one of the passages from the scriptures or the great mystics which I recommend for use in meditation. I usually recommend learning first the Prayer of St. Francis of Assisi:

Lord, make me an instrument of thy peace.
Where there is hatred, let me sow love;
Where there is injury, pardon;
Where there is doubt, faith;
Where there is despair, hope;
Where there is darkness, light;
Where there is sadness, joy.

O Divine Master, grant that I may not so much seek
To be consoled as to console,
To be understood as to understand,
To be loved as to love;
For it is in giving that we receive,
It is in pardoning that we are pardoned,
It is in dying [to self] that we are born to eternal life.

Do not follow any association of ideas or try to think about the passage. If you are giving your attention to each word, the meaning cannot help sinking in. When distractions come, do not resist them, but give more attention to the words of the passage. If your mind strays from the passage entirely, bring it back gently to the beginning and start again.

When you reach the end of the passage, you may use it again as necessary to complete your period of meditation until you have memorized others. It is helpful to have a wide variety of passages for meditation, drawn from the world's major traditions. Each passage should be positive and practical, drawn from a major scripture or from a mystic of the highest stature. Passages from the Gita which are perfect for meditation will be found at the end of each volume of this commentary. In addition, I heartily recommend the Lord's Prayer, the Twenty-third Psalm, the Beatitudes, St. Paul's *Epistle on Love* (1 Corinthians 13), and the first and last chapters of the Dhammapada of the Buddha. These and many other beautiful passages can be found in my collection *God Makes the Rivers to Flow.*

The secret of meditation is simple: we become what we meditate on. When you use the Prayer of St. Francis every day in meditation, you are driving the words deep into your consciousness. Eventually they become an integral part of your personality, which means they will find constant expression in what you do, what you say, and what you think.

2. *Repetition of a Mantram.* A mantram is a powerful spiritual formula which, when repeated silently in the mind, has the capacity to transform consciousness. There is nothing magical about this. It is simply a matter of practice, as all of us can verify for ourselves.

Every religious tradition has a mantram, often more than one. For Christians the name of Jesus itself is a powerful mantram; Catholics also use *Hail Mary* or *Ave Maria.* Jews may use *Barukh attah Adonai,* 'Blessed art thou, O Lord,' or the Hasidic formula *Ribono shel olam,* 'Lord of the universe.' Muslims repeat the name of Allah or *Allahu akbar,* 'God is great.' Probably the oldest Buddhist mantram is *Om mani padme hum,* referring to the 'jewel in the lotus of the heart.' In Hinduism, among many choices, I recommend *Rāma, Rāma, Rāma,* which was Mahatma Gandhi's mantram, or the longer mantram I received from my own spiritual teacher, my grandmother:

> *Hare Rāma Hare Rāma*
> *Rāma Rāma Hare Hare*
> *Hare Krishna Hare Krishna*
> *Krishna Krishna Hare Hare*

Select a mantram that appeals to you deeply. In many traditions, it is customary to take the mantram used by your spiritual teacher. Then, once you have chosen, do not change your mantram. Otherwise, as Sri Ramakrishna puts it, you will be like a person digging shallow holes in many places; you will never go deep enough to find water.

Repeat your mantram silently whenever you get the chance: while walking, while waiting, while doing mechanical chores like washing dishes, and especially when you are falling asleep. You will find that this is not mindless repetition; the mantram will help to keep you relaxed and alert. Whenever you are angry or afraid, nervous or worried or resentful, repeat the mantram until the agitation subsides. The mantram works to steady the mind, and all these emotions are power running against you which the mantram can harness and put to work.

3. *Slowing Down.* Hurry makes for tension, insecurity, inefficiency, and superficial living. To guard against hurrying through the day, start the day early and simplify your life so that you do not try to fill your time

with more than you can do. When you find yourself beginning to speed up, repeat your mantram to help you slow down.

It is important here not to confuse slowness with sloth, which breeds carelessness, procrastination, and general inefficiency. In slowing down we should attend meticulously to details, giving our very best even to the smallest undertaking.

4. *One-Pointed Attention.* Doing more than one thing at a time divides attention and fragments consciousness. When we read and eat at the same time, for example, part of our mind is on what we are reading and part on what we are eating; we are not getting the most from either activity. Similarly, when talking with someone, give him or her your full attention. These are little things, but all together they help to unify consciousness and deepen concentration.

Everything we do should be worthy of our full attention. When the mind is one-pointed it will be secure, free from tension, and capable of the concentration that is the mark of genius in any field.

5. *Training the Senses.* In the food we eat, the books and magazines we read, the movies we see, all of us are subject to the dictatorship of rigid likes and dislikes. To free ourselves from this conditioning, we need to learn to change our likes and dislikes freely when it is in the best interests of those around us or ourselves. We should choose what we eat by what our body needs, for example, rather than by what the taste buds demand. Similarly, the mind eats too, through the senses. In this age of mass media, we need to be very discriminating in what we read and what we go to see for entertainment; for we become in part what our senses take in.

6. *Putting Others First.* Dwelling on ourselves builds a wall between ourselves and others. Those who keep thinking about *their* needs, *their* wants, *their* plans, *their* ideas cannot help becoming lonely and insecure. The simple but effective technique I recommend is to learn to put other people first – beginning within the circle of your family and friends, where there is already a basis of love on which to build. When husband and wife try to put each other first, for example, they are not only moving closer to each other, they are also removing the barriers of their ego-prison, which deepens their relationships with everyone else as well.

7. *Spiritual Fellowship.* The Sanskrit word for this is *satsang*, 'association with those who are spiritually oriented.' When we are trying to change our life, we need the support of others with the same goal. If you have friends who are meditating along the lines suggested here, you can get together regularly to share a meal, meditate, and perhaps read and discuss this commentary on the Gita. Share your times of entertainment too; relaxation is an important part of spiritual living. Who has ever seen a mystic with a sour face?

8. *Spiritual Reading.* We are so immersed these days in what the mass media offer that it is very helpful to give half an hour or so each day to reading the scriptures and the writings of the great mystics of all religions. Just before bedtime, after evening meditation, is a particularly good time, because the thoughts you fall asleep in will be with you throughout the night.

By practicing this eight-point program sincerely and systematically, as I can testify from my own small personal experience, it is possible for every one of us to realize the supreme goal of life. Even a little such practice, the Gita says, begins to transform our personality, leading to profoundly beneficial changes in ourselves and in the world around us.

The Bhagavad Gita for Daily Living, Volume 3

CHAPTER THIRTEEN
The Field of Karma

श्रीभगवानुवाच ।
इदं शरीरं कौन्तेय क्षेत्रमित्यभिधीयते ।
एतद्यो वेत्ति तं प्राहुः क्षेत्रज्ञ इति तद्विदः ॥ १३-१ ॥

SRI KRISHNA

*1. The body is called a field, Arjuna. Only
those who know they are not this field
can be said to know the field truly.*

Many years ago I remember traveling north by train to Simla, once the summer seat of British government in India. We had not been long out of Delhi when suddenly I became aware of a chatter of conversation around me. The man beside me seemed particularly voluble. I asked him if something had happened. "Kurukshetra!" he replied. "The next stop is Kurukshetra!"

I could understand the excitement. Kurukshetra, "the field of the Kurus," is the setting for the climactic battle of the *Mahābhārata,* the vastest epic in any world literature, on which virtually every Hindu child in India is raised. Its characters, removed from us in time by perhaps three thousand years, are as familiar to us as our relatives. The temper of the story is utterly contemporary; I can imagine it unfolding in the nuclear age as easily as in the dawn of Indian history.

Everyone in our car got down from the train to wander for a few minutes on the now peaceful field. Thousands of years ago this was Armageddon. The air rang with the conch-horns and shouts of battle for eighteen days. Great phalanxes shaped like eagles and fish and the crescent moon surged back and forth in search of victory, until in the end almost every warrior in the land lay slain.

"Imagine!" my companion said to me in awe. "Bhīshma and Drona commanded their armies here. Arjuna rode here, with Sri Krishna himself as his charioteer. Where you're standing now – who knows? – Arjuna may have sat, his bow and arrows on the ground, while Krishna gave him the words of the Bhagavad Gita."

I agreed. But already I had begun to understand that the battle in which the Gita is set is not merely an historical event. The real battle-field the Gita talks about is this body and personality, where there rages an unceasing battle between the forces of selflessness and selfishness, of light and darkness, love and hatred, unity and separateness, harmony and violence. The ringing words with which the Gita opens – "Tell me what took place at Kurukshetra, the field of the Kurus, the field of dharma" – apply to us; the dialogue of the Gita takes place on this field within us, in every one of us, in every age.

In other words, when Sri Krishna compares the body to a field in this verse, he is talking about more than the physical frame. "Body" refers to the whole separate person with which we identify ourselves: in Western terms, not only body but personality. To call this a battlefield is vivid language indeed. It means that from the physical level – for example, in our health – down to the depths of the unconscious, we live in the cross fire of two opposing forces, what is selfish in us and what is selfless.

This is the war within, but it has spread increasingly to outer war all around us. There are enough nuclear weapons in national arsenals to destroy not just a battlefield in ancient India but life on earth, and not in eighteen days but in eighteen minutes. As many as a dozen countries are riven with cruel civil wars; yet Belfast even in the midst of conflict was less dangerous to live in than Detroit in times of so-called peace. Similarly, many families are private battlefields, whose conflicts spill over into our relationships, our work, our politics, and even our entertainment. All this is the net effect of the turmoil in our minds, the decisions and desires of millions of little people like you and me who together shape the world. That is why the Gita maintains that no matter how violent the times outside us, the real war is always the war within – the only war in which victory can bring real peace.

But we can also think of body and mind as a different kind of field, much less martial.

In India we have a story about a man who was asked his occupation. The man replied, "Farmer."

"You don't look like a farmer," he was told. "How much land do you have?"

"Five and a half feet."

There was a loud laugh. "How much can you raise in five and a half feet of land?"

"This is very special soil," the man replied. "This body is my field. My thoughts and actions are the seeds, and karma, good and bad, is the harvest."

The Gita is using the same image. Body and personality, it says, are very much like a farmer's field. In the soil of the mind we sow thoughts: desires, hopes, fears, resentments, and so on. There they take root and grow – into habits, attitudes, personality traits, patterns of responding to the world around us. And these finally bear fruit on the physical level, particularly in our health. That is the meaning of the much misunderstood word *karma*, which this whole volume will explore.

Sri Krishna begins by pointing out that we are not the field we till. Put that way, it sounds absurdly simple. Yet if someone asks us who we are, most of us point to our bodies. "This is me – five foot eight, one hundred thirty pounds, brown skin, not very luxuriant hair on the head." Sri Krishna would object, "That's not you. That's your field, your little garden. You are the gardener." To me this is a most comfortable way of looking on my body: a handkerchief kitchen garden, just the right size for my needs and abilities. I can appreciate other people's gardens, but I like mine as it is; what would I do with someone else's? So I take very good care of my body-garden: but I never believe that this is who I am.

I have a friend, Steve, with a talent for gardening. Every day after work in spring and summer he takes his children out to their large backyard to plant vegetables and flowers, and he lets them do a lot of the planning. The last time I visited, I saw none of the straight rows and tidy signs of a conventional grown up garden. Instead I found all kinds of twisted paths – Beet Boulevard, Carrot Corners, Artichoke Alley – making leafy, colorful designs through the yard. By August the garden was as lush and dense as the jungle in India near which I grew up. I was unable to locate anything there. But the children knew just where to find the reddest tomatoes and the sweetest snap peas, and just where to hide too. Their teepee of scarlet runner beans was so thick that all four could huddle inside without a grown-up ever seeing them.

Steve knows that garden too. With a taste he can tell if the soil lacks anything. He knows the nuances of sunlight, temperature, runoff, and mineral content from place to place, and how each plant affects the others around it. He and the children are able to bring me gifts of their finest produce all summer long.

But imagine what would happen if Steve believed he is his garden. I don't think he would know that plot of land at all. He wouldn't like being dug into and turned over with a spade; and as a result, the soil wouldn't get cultivated. He would object strenuously to people planting vegetables in him that he did not like. If somebody criticized his soil, he would take it personally and feel people were insulting *him*. And suppose he didn't enjoy children poking their fingers into him? All in all, that garden would do rather poorly. There would be no way for Steve to stand outside himself and see the garden objectively, no way to evaluate what it needed and what would do it harm.

Each of us goes through the day making a very similar mistake. We believe we are the body; we believe we are our mind. The consequences are disastrous. To the extent that we identify ourselves with the body, we are constrained to define happiness by what the body and senses find pleasant. It is a definition that excludes a good deal of life, especially as the body grows older. We might eat too much, or eat what is not healthful, simply for the sake of taste. We might smoke, drink, or take drugs because we find the sensations stimulating; we might fail to get enough exercise because inertia seems more pleasant than activity. Or we might spend all our time thinking about the body, trying to reform our complexion with queen bee preparations or to improve the definition of our biceps, as if who we are depended on how we look. All this can only make us more insecure. The body *has* to age and change and die. When we think that is all we are, the passage of time becomes a terrible burden.

In other words, unless you know that you are not this garden of body and mind, how can you cultivate it? You can have very little control. That is the essential message of this verse. But there is a deeper implication that should be spelled out too: that body and mind are not separate, but two aspects of the same field. The medical implications alone are far-reaching enough to shatter our conventional ideas of health and aging.

With all the progress of science over the last two centuries, modern civilization has reached a stage where almost all of us believe there is nothing more to life than the physical, biochemical level. Even thought is currently held to be reducible to electrophysiological events. This is the lowest possible view we can take of life, particularly of the human being. It is like thinking there is nothing to your garden except its harvests: no soil, no seeds, no nutrients, not even any roots. Plants simply adhere somehow to the surface of the earth, no one knows how, and we get good or bad harvests by chance. Our knowledge of the physical world amounts to the discovery that apple trees, to a statistically reliable degree, can be counted on to produce apples rather than pears or any other fruit; that is all.

Now, this is useful information, I agree. But a botanist would not be impressed. "If you think that's useful," she might say, "let me tell you about seeds and soil. Those little black things inside the apple are seeds. If you plant them in the right kind of soil and take care of them, you'll get more apples – every time." Imagine the significance of this kind of knowledge if you had never known about seeds! You would realize that you had never scratched the surface of gardening. It is the same with the garden of body and mind, which are as intimately connected as fruit and seed. When you see the way thoughts and desires grow into hard, physical conditions, and how surely a certain kind of thought leads to a certain kind of action, you will feel you have scarcely scratched the surface of life.

Our prehistoric ancestors, I imagine, might not know about anything but harvests. They like apples and know how to pick them, but they might not know there is any relationship between seeds and plants: after all, these look utterly different. And they might not know there is any relationship between the apple they eat and the soil, rain, sunlight, and so on by which it grew. They have all kinds of seeds lying around – apples, thistles, pigweed, pansies – but these are so tiny, so insignificant, that they don't pay any attention to them. If the apple seeds lie on clay and the thistle seeds in well-drained humus, what does it matter?

The person who thinks there is no more to a human being than the physical body is in a very similar situation. What does it matter to his body, his health, what thoughts he thinks? He thinks what he likes, waters his thoughts with a lot of attention, and after many years – for thoughts do grow slowly – he begins to suffer a few physical ailments, which look no more like a thought than an oak tree looks like an acorn.

"All that we are," the Buddha says, "is the result of what we have thought." He means even physically, as I can try to illustrate. Suppose a person is habitually resentful: that is, he frequently responds to unfavorable circumstances by thinking resentful thoughts about the people involved. Many unfavorable consequences follow from this, but here I want to look only at those that affect bodily health. Those thoughts are seeds; if he keeps on sowing them, and particularly if he keeps on watering and feeding them with his attention by brooding over them, they have to begin to germinate. All this takes place in the soil of the mind, out of sight. But after a while, if favorable conditions persist, those seeds of resentment sprout. In the language of medicine, the physiological correlates of resentment – stomach tension, elevated blood pressure, and so on – become a habitual conditioned response, which any adverse circumstance can trigger.

This response can be unlearned, just as it was learned; the garden of resentment can still be weeded and new seeds planted. But if it is not weeded, after many years there will be a harvest of ill health. Physiologically, the body will be living in a state of almost continual readiness for defense – a grossly exaggerated response, granted, but that is the only way the body knows how to respond. Its resources for dealing with stress will be mobilized day and night, like the National Guard in a state of emergency, as we can tell from the signs and symptoms that may come: high blood pressure, chronic stomach tension, digestive problems, migraines, irritability, perhaps a low resistance to common ailments like colds and flu. All this takes a severe toll on the body's resources for good health. For various reasons, including genetic factors, the final breakdown will differ from person to person. One might develop arthritis; another, a gastric disorder. But whatever the ailment, it is the fruit and harvest of a mental state, the seeds of resentful thinking.

Ironically, such people often respond even to these physical problems with resentment. Life, they say, has dealt them one more unfair blow. That is how entrenched the mental habit has become: resentment has taken over the whole field. And so, tragically, the harvest of ill health goes on reseeding the mind.

For a more cheerful picture, look at patience. Isn't there a flower called *impatiens,* which they say anyone can grow anywhere? Anyone can grow patience too, though it's not yet one of the twenty favorite houseplants of the mind. And it is a highly medicinal herb. Imagine the same people going through life with a garden full of patience instead of resentment. The same events that once provoked a stress response would be met with calmness, detachment, even a sympathetic respect. Those people are likely to live longer and feel better than if they lived in chronic resentment: good health is the body reaping the harvest of right thinking.

As long as we identify with the "field" – the physical, chemical organism that is the body – glands and hormones dictate our lives. Many people today believe in astrology, but almost everyone believes in hormonology. "I was born under the sign of Adrenaline," they say. "He was born under the Gonads, with Thymus rising." The lives of those who identify completely with the body *are* dictated by their chemistry; the Gita would not disagree. When life is reduced to biological functions, it says, what else can you expect? But those who break through this identification can undo this tyranny. They can rise above and eventually transform their chemistry; for the chemistry of our living follows rather than dictates the responses of our mind.

This breakthrough culminates a complete remaking of personality. Over and over again I hear talk about alternative lifestyles. Change your clothes, talk differently, grow a mustache or paint your eyelids mauve, and you have changed your life. This simply doesn't follow. But there is a way to change your life, and that is to change your ways of thinking.

When Michael down the street ceases to think of himself as his body, he is no longer Michael – at least, not the same Michael with whom you went to school. That was the old Michael, the pauper, as Meister Eckhart would say. This is the new man, a prince of peace.

This transformation is not all peaches and cream. There is a terrifying aspect to it. When mystics speak of the death of the old man, the pauper, the ego, this death is not at all symbolic. It is very real. The ego *is* done away with, or nearly so, and it does not appreciate the process either; it suffers. But even while it suffers we can experience the fierce joy of knowing that beneath the surface, a radiant new personality is being born.

क्षेत्रज्ञं चापि मां विद्धि सर्वक्षेत्रेषु भारत ।
क्षेत्रक्षेत्रज्ञयोर्ज्ञानं यत्तज्ज्ञानं मतं मम ॥ १३-२ ॥

2. I am the Knower of the field in everyone, Arjuna.
To know the field and its Knower is true knowledge.

If you think you are your field, there is no way to imagine a cultivator. Seeds, you say, come by chance; nobody plants them. Similarly, harvests are good or bad by chance. If you get a good crop – health, some happiness, a loving family, a few trustworthy friends – you say, "Well, fortune's been good to me." And if you get a few shrivelled ears of corn and a lot of weeds, that too has no connection with what you have done. You say what gardeners always say: "Fortune's been bad to me. Unseasonal frosts. Not enough rain. Too much rain. Right amount of rain, but at the wrong time." The Gita would correct this kind of talk gently but firmly: "*You* are responsible for what you grow and reap. Nobody else. If you let things go to seed, you can't expect a rose garden."

When you leave a field to itself, of course, it quickly reverts to weeds. Whatever grows best there takes over and crowds out everything else. The same thing happens to an untended personality: that is, to the ego. You can look on the ego as an abandoned lot of weedy samskāras. There are flowers there too, but they run a constant battle for survival against the thistles and dandelions and crabgrass.

Let's slip into Alice's Wonderland for a moment. We have been asking what it would be like if Steve believed he was his garden; now let me ask what would happen if the garden thought it was Steve.

Imagine that you have been visiting the children in their garden and have fallen asleep in the sun after a glass of Steve's dandelion wine. When you wake up you find that the garden has become a jungle, with immense stalks and flowers that tower over your head and make soft rustling sounds like whispers as they move. And after a while you become aware that you have grown much, much smaller, and those whispers actually are speech. The plants in the garden have learned to exchange "information," rather like neurons in the brain, and they have learned to function together like a biological unit. The cabbages and carrots come and go, but the Garden goes on forever. It is the Garden that is alive. It is the Garden that has intelligence, that can speak and reason and savor immortality – at least, to hear the Garden tell about it. "I'm the greatest," it says modestly. "Tell me frankly, do you know of anything more wonderful?"

"Be serious," you say. "You're nothing but a lot of stems and seeds!"

Science fiction readers will be aware that this is a dangerous way to talk to an intelligent garden, especially if you happen to be in the middle of it. For this garden obviously has plenty of ego: in fact, as you will have guessed, it is the ego itself. "Better watch yourself," it warns. "You're on *my* turf now. If you argue with me, I may just swallow you up."

"Who made you?" you demand.

"Nobody," says the Garden. "I 'just growed.' I make myself."

Yet there are the telltale paths, which now look to you as big as superhighways: Artichoke Alley, Beet Boulevard, Carrot Corners, Rutabaga Row. You get bolder. "Garden," you ask, "can you grow what you like?"

The Garden hems and haws: it cannot. "I grow what's right," it says defensively. "I like whatever comes up."

"And what happens when the big freeze comes?"

"I do die back," the Garden admits. "But after a while, I grow and flourish again. My plants come and go, but I'm immortal."

You shake your head. "Garden," you say, "by yourself, you amount to nothing at all. You have a gardener that makes you what you are – chooses your seeds, plants and waters and feeds them, and makes all these paths. You can't do anything yourself. You have taken all the qualities of your gardener and claimed them for yourself."

That is just what the ego does, and very cleverly too. Nevertheless, it is only a field, an assemblage of parts, a process; it has no intelligence of its own. Only the Self can be said to know.

Interestingly, the word used for 'field' in these verses – *kshetra* – also means 'temple' in many modern Indian languages. Mystics often speak of the body as a temple, for the Lord dwells in each of us. The altar of this temple does not have to be built. Each of us has a sanctum sanctorum in the depths of consciousness, where the Self is present always. He is the Knower, our real Self, the same in all.

Overeating desecrates this temple. So does smoking, which is just the opposite of burning incense. Merely remembering that the body is the house of the Lord should help us to refrain from addictions, get regular exercise, eat good food in moderate quantities, and in general do everything we can to keep the body at its best.

Even here, however, we cannot forget the mind. It too is part of the temple, and if it is not kept calm and kind, no amount of physical care will keep the body free from disease. Insecurity, for example, lowers everybody's resistance, no matter how sound the body may be. As I write this, the country is dwelling on another attack of some exotic flu. "It's coming!" the papers announce. "Are you prepared?" And everyone asks, "Is it coming *here*? Am *I* prepared? Am I going to get it – have I got it already?" When you dwell on flu, the Gita would say, you become flu. Take care of yourself, live for others, and then do not worry. Your security and resistance will be high, and if the flu does bite, you will probably throw it off easily.

The body *is* a temple, agrees the German mystic Johannes Tauler: but before it can serve as one, he adds, we have to drive out the money changers and pigeon-sellers and other squatters who have taken it over for their own purposes. This is a dig at the ego, who has ensconced himself in our inner chambers. If the Lord is to be revealed in this temple, the impostor ego has to go.

Christmas is approaching now, so I took my mother to a department store where they were setting up a full-size Nativity scene in the display window. Hindus respond easily to the Divine Mother in every tradition, and the display appealed to my mother deeply. But one thing was still missing; the window dressers hadn't finished their job. "Son," she said, "I see the cradle. But where is the baby Jesus?"

All of us, Tauler would say, have the cradle ready and waiting in our hearts. But when we look inside we don't see anything but the ego, so immense that his arms and legs are sticking out through the slats. Fortunately we don't have to hunt for a Christ Child to put inside. All we have to do is slowly get the ego out; once we do that, we find the divine child is already there.

This is what St. Paul means when he says, "I was dead, and yet I live: yet not I, but Christ liveth in me." Paul, as you know, was no spiritual aspirant in the early days. He was a violent tentmaker named Saul, who I imagine used to beat his competitors with his tent poles. Whenever a customer came to him and said, "I can't stand that Jesus of Nazareth," Saul would exclaim, "I'll give you a discount!" Yet all this time a force from the very depths of his consciousness must have been working up to the surface, to burst like a bomb while Saul was traveling to Damascus. Then the rough, violent, virulent ego of Saul was thrown out with the vigor formerly shown only to Jesus's followers, leaving the tent-maker of Tarsus blind and paralyzed for three days and nights. When he opens his eyes again he is a new man, with all that destructive capacity changed to tenderness, love, and tireless energy for carrying the words of Jesus throughout the world. You and I need not be so dramatic, but when we are able to extinguish our self-will, there will be celebration everywhere: "Glory be to the newborn king!"

I mention St. Paul to show that this can come to anyone. The most seemingly unregenerate person in the world can change his thinking if he desires. When I was teaching English literature, I sometimes illustrated this lightheartedly with Macbeth, who as you know was not exactly a gentle man in a gentle world. Even Macbeth could have learned to medi-tate. It might not have made much of a play, but no one wants to live a tragedy. Fierce, violent, tormented Macbeth could have become secure. He could have told those witches, "Why are you trying so hard to stir up greedy ambition? Here's a mantram, *Jesus, Jesus, Jesus*; why don't you take that and sing it around the caldron all night instead?" Those witches are not outside, you know. There is real valor in turning your back on a whispering witch inside your mind – valor and freedom and joy.

The Gita is presenting here two levels of knowing. Knowledge of the field – the world of change, whether within or without – is called in

Sanskrit *apara,* "lower knowledge." This is not deprecation; when wisely guided, science and technology can contribute immensely to human welfare. *Para,* "higher knowledge," is called higher simply because it enables us to make wise choices, based on a sure understanding of the unity of life.

When my friend Steve analyzes his soil and measures the density of his earthworm population, that is *apara,* invaluable for getting a good harvest. But as we have seen, it is important also for him to know who he is: that he is not his soil, seeds, and harvest. That is *para,* direct knowledge of the knower.

Unlike lower or intellectual knowledge, spiritual wisdom has a direct connection with the will. I can illustrate with the example of a young lady I met when I first came to this country as a Fulbright scholar. I was then at my first American campus, where this woman was a graduate student. She was intelligent, attractive, and quite strong-willed. With all this went a fiery temper, but fire can be an asset on the spiritual path if you can learn to harness it.

It hurt me deeply to see that she was a chain smoker. The medical evidence against smoking had not yet accumulated, but even so I had some idea of how harmful the habit was, not only to the lungs but to the will. I knew she trusted me, and I knew too that she had daring and will to draw on. So one day I asked point-blank, "May I take advantage of our friendship to ask you a personal question? If you don't want to answer, I'll never ask it again."

She was intrigued. "Please do."

"Why do you smoke like that? It hurts me to know what damage it must be causing."

She got defensive for a moment and gave all kinds of intellectual answers. I listened to them all. Then I asked simply, "Don't you know that there is much more satisfaction in defying a compulsive desire than there is in yielding to it?"

She just stared. Then she broke into a smile, and I saw that my words had gone in. So far as I know, she never smoked another cigarette. With that instant of insight had come an immediate connection with the will.

This connection is a sure sign of *para,* spiritual wisdom. By contrast, I have seen a highly qualified physician studying X-rays of a cancer-ridden lung with a lighted cigarette in his hand. That is *apara:* the man knows, but there is no connection between what he knows and what he does.

St. Francis used to say, "Your knowledge is only as deep as your action" – that is, no deeper than your will. Ironically, because of this, higher knowledge can actually be much more practical than lower knowledge when it comes to what matters most in daily living, as the contrast between that physician and my graduate friend illustrates.

Often someone objects to me that spiritual wisdom leads to passivity. They may even point to India's present condition as an illustration, ignoring the fact that when India was much more firmly established in its spiritual heritage, it was one of the most prosperous and culturally advanced nations in the world. I would go to the extent of saying that India's recovery from the devastating effects of foreign rule has more to do with rediscovering its spiritual roots than with adopting modern technology. That was the source of Gandhiji's strength, and his greatest contribution to India was to awaken its hundreds of millions of common people to the power and dignity of these timeless spiritual values. Even in India, I think most people do not realize how much of this work was begun in the tremendous spiritual reawakening sparked by Sri Ramakrishna. To anyone with a sense of history who has looked over these events, there is no more convincing evidence of the power of spiritual values. They can transform a culture; today, with global interrelationships inescapable, they can change the basis of our civilization.

Spiritual wisdom cannot lead to passivity. It deepens our sensitivities and magnifies our capacity to battle with destructive forces without and within. We live in a world of unity, where all peoples on earth share a single condominium. One room may have tables and chairs, another may have mats and polished floors, but all the rooms are under one roof. If there is poverty in one room, everyone in the place will suffer, not merely in some vague moral way but economically. Similarly, if we set fire to one room, the whole building may burn down; this is what we do when we wage war. And if there is plague at the other end of the house, we can't just sit back and think, "It's only those people at the back; there's nothing to get alarmed about." Plague is infectious. It is only a matter of time before we too fall ill, and who is left then to play the doctor?

With modern technology, we – *Homo sapiens* – have reached a point in history when we have the capacity to embrace the whole globe in health, peace, and welfare. As never before, we have the choice of two paths: one leading to unprecedented, unwarranted sorrow, the other to unprecedented prosperity and happiness. Without spiritual wisdom, "lower knowledge" can destroy – I would go so far as to say that it *will* destroy, for it has no capacity to choose where to go. But with spiritual wisdom as well, we have the capacity to make a heaven on earth.

तत्क्षेत्रं यच यादृक्क यद्विकारि यतश्च यत् ।
स च यो यत्प्रभावश्च तत्समासेन मे श्रृणु ॥ १३-३ ॥

3. Listen and I will explain the nature of the field and how change takes place within it. I will also describe the Knower of the field and his power.

Most of us, I imagine, think of ourselves as standing in the midst of the world looking out. We see trees, cars, animals, and people as separate objects; and we see ourselves as separate from all of them: the seer, the knower, looking out of the body at the world we know.

Yet a physicist would remind us that the things we see "out there" are not really separate from each other. We perceive them as separate because of the limitations of our senses. If our eyes were sensitive to a much finer spectrum, we might see the world as an atomic physicist describes it: a continuous field of matter and energy.

Once, I remember, it was considered a tremendous breakthrough when scientists agreed that matter consisted of molecules. The atom became the "building block" of the universe, and it was then believed to be a solid little entity of its own. Yet soon it was accepted that these supposedly solid atoms were actually made up of a few much subtler particles and were mostly empty space. Not only that, the "particles" were so elusive that they sometimes masqueraded as radiant energy instead of matter. Now scientists are probing so deeply into the nucleus of the atom that it too has become a shadow, with such a bewildering array of constituent particles that I have given up trying to keep count.

This adds up to a very intangible version of physical reality. Nothing in it resembles a solid object in our usual sense of the word; everything is elusive and nothing is at rest. "The external world of physics," wrote Sir Arthur Eddington, "has thus become a world of shadows. In removing our illusions we remove the substance, for indeed we have seen that substance is one of the greatest of our illusions." If we perceive solidity and separateness only because our senses are so limited, where does this leave our idea that we are separate, physical creatures?

I have been reading about a proposal for a new supermicroscope that would enable us to see the atomic structure of almost any solid material. Imagine what it would be like if this were the range of our ordinary vision. The boundaries of objects would be no more substantial than shadows; we would see life on a kind of threshold between separateness and continuity. It would be a wondrous world. You could watch air and water moving in and out of molecules that made up leaves, roots, rocks, and skin. Perhaps you could even watch sunlight becoming food in the tiny factories of plants, and watch food broken down again to be assimilated into the body of a growing organism. When that body died, you would see its shadowy boundaries fade as chemical elements and energy flowed back into the world around it. From the point of view of life as a whole, it would be clear that that organism is part of an indivisible unity.

Let me go back to Steve's garden. Behind all the vegetables is the fence that marks the boundary where Steve's place stops and his neighbor's dairy farm begins. He thinks of that fenced-off area as separate, and this makes sense on a practical level. I feel sure that the dairyman next door, for example, does not think his fences are arbitrary; he probably paid a surveyor to be sure they are not six inches too far south. But to an earthworm, those fences make no difference at all. The worm is sublimely indifferent. It sees nothing separate about Steve's garden. The soil goes right on, and so does the worm. And it is not wrong. There *is* only one field. If Steve's neighbor uses chemical fertilizers, to take just one example, they are going to leach into Steve's garden and be fed to Steve's two children. Our body is like that: separate in some important ways, yet continuous with the rest of the ecosystem in other, more basic ways.

In a larger sense, then, when Sri Krishna talks about the "field" he means more than simply the body. The whole of the environment is one field, in which we sow our actions and reap their consequences. It sounds simple, but the implications are vast. It means, in part, that the consequences of every action can extend the full reach of the field.

Let me illustrate on the physical level first. I have been reading about what I am afraid will become an all too familiar kind of tragedy: the fate of Times Beach, Missouri. Much more will undoubtedly have been added to the story by the time you read this, but today it is still unraveling; the outcome is uncertain. This much is known: many years ago a trucker sprayed the roads of Times Beach with oil to keep the dust down. Years later, by accident, it was discovered that the oil was contaminated with dioxin, one of the deadliest chemicals known. In laboratory animals, at the lowest levels tested, dioxin causes birth defects, nervous disorders, cancer and other diseases, and even death. Concentrations in some Times Beach streets measured one hundred times those levels, and floods have washed dioxin-contaminated mud all through the town. How many children have played in it? How deep has the poison penetrated? Has it entered the water supply, the food chain? How can the poison be tracked down and disposed of safely? All these are consequences of many little decisions a decade ago: by the hauler who had trucks spray this and many other sites with dioxin-laced oil, by officials who ignored early warnings of contamination, by scientists who advised that dioxin probably degrades faster than it actually does. And the consequences are still spreading: genetic damage, for example, can be passed on to later generations.

This is just one incident. I have read that the government estimates there are at least fourteen thousand hazardous waste dumps in the United States. You can see how vast this web of consequences can be, not only in space but in time too.

In another recent accident, much smaller, the consequences were actually tracked down. Feed contaminated with PCBs – polychlorinated biphenyls – from a damaged transformer in a single plant spread to ten states. Incorporated in various food products, the poisons were found in seventeen states. Some of these products had gone to national suppliers that might have spread the contamination all over the country, even overseas. This kind of tragedy often results from a simple error made by a single person – perhaps only a trucker confusing poorly labeled containers. Yet look how far the consequences can reach! That is the unity of this field of karma: a seed sown in one corner can spread harvests of sorrow everywhere.

This unity is the source of a grim justice about karma which will be amply illustrated in the rest of this volume. The point of karma is to drive home to us that we cannot live for ourselves alone. We ourselves are going to reap what we sow, even if we only intend to sell the karma-crop to others. Again, I can illustrate from agriculture. A number of pesticides and herbicides that have been banned or severely regulated in the United States because of their toxicity have been sold in the rest of the world, generally to Third World countries, without any warning or regulation. But the hazards, it turns out, do not stay confined to those countries. Expensive pesticides are not generally used on crops grown for local consumption, where the market value is not high. They are characteristically saved for export crops – and so the poisonous residues often come full circle and return to consumers in the United States.

These are all essentially illustrations of the law of karma, which is so crucial a concept in this volume – and so misunderstood – that it needs a detailed explanation right at the outset. Literally, the Sanskrit *karma* means something that is done. Often it can be translated as 'deed' or 'action.' The law of karma states simply that every event is both a cause and an effect. Every act has consequences, which in turn have further consequences and so on; and every act, every karma, is also the consequence of some previous karma.

This will turn out to have the vastest possible implications. But let me begin with karma on the individual level, where it is simplest: the karma we sow and reap in our own little agricultural field of body and mind.

To most people who are familiar with the word, in India as well as in the West, *karma* refers to physical action. In this sense, the law of karma says that whatever you do will come back to you. If Joe hits John, and later Jack hits Joe, that is Joe's karma coming back to him. It sounds mysterious, even occult, because we do not see all the connections. But the connections are there, and the law of karma is no more occult than the law of gravitation.

Let me illustrate. In the example I just gave, where Joe hits John, the law of karma states that that blow has to have consequences. It cannot end with John getting a black eye. It makes an impression on John's consciousness – predictably, he gets angry – and it makes an impression, probably subtler, on Joe's consciousness as well. Let us trace it first through John. He might take his anger out on Joe then and there, simply by hitting him back: that is what I call "cash karma," where you do something and are repaid immediately. But for many reasons, John might not act on his anger until later, quite possibly in unrelated ways: he might explode at his wife, for example, or throw out the cat unceremoniously when it tangles with his legs.

Now, karma is rarely so simple; this is only for illustration. But what is clear is that John's anger will have repercussions throughout his relationships. Those repercussions will have repercussions – say, John's wife gets angry at Jack's, and she takes it out on Jack, who works with Joe; and the next time Joe irritates Jack, Jack lets him have it. Poor Joe, rubbing his chin, can't have the slightest idea that he is being repaid for hitting John. All he feels is anger at Jack: and so the chain of consequences continues, and Joe's karmic comeuppance becomes the seed of a new harvest.

We do not realize how far our lives reach, how many people are affected by our behavior and example. Once you begin to see this, you get some idea of how complex the web of karma actually is. No one has the omniscience to see this picture fully. But I hope you can see that the idea of a network of such connections is plausible and natural – so plausible, in fact, that even though we cannot see the connections, we can be sure that everything that happens to us, good and bad, originated once in something we did to someone else.

The implications of this are terribly practical: we ourselves are responsible for what happens to us, whether or not we can understand how. Therefore – here is the wonderful part – we can change what happens to us by changing ourselves; we can take our destiny into our own hands.

As I said, all this is karma on the physical level, which is how most people think of it. The view is accurate, but it is not complete: in fact, the physical side of karma is only the tip of an iceberg. To get an inkling of how far karma reaches, you have to look at the mind.

Let me go back for a moment to Joe and John. I said that when Joe hits John, there are several effects: one on John's face, one in John's consciousness, and one in the consciousness of Joe himself. To put it simply, by acting on his anger, Joe has made it easier to act on his anger again. He may think he has relieved some pressure, but he has actually made himself a little more angry than before, a little less patient, a little more likely to respond to problems with violence.

Everything we do, in other words, produces karma in the mind. This is not at all theoretical; it has very tangible consequences. For one, look at how Joe is changed by his actions – not from without, from within. Over the years, if he keeps giving in to anger, he will become more belligerent. He may find himself swinging his fists more and more often; and by some quirk of human nature, he will find himself more and more frequently in situations that prompt his anger. Sooner or later he will get into a fight where he is more than repaid in kind; that is one way in which his karma with John can come back to him.

Even more intriguing to me is the karma of our health. Again, let me illustrate one or two kinds of connection.

For one, the Buddha says that we are not punished for our anger; we are punished *by* our anger. In other words, anger is its own karma. Joe may think he feels better for having hit John, but a detached physician would not say so. He would observe all that happens in Joe's vital organs and nervous system while Joe is getting heated up – watch his blood pressure soar and his heart race, measure the adrenaline and other hormones dumped into the body, and so on – and conclude, "You're putting yourself under severe physiological stress!" To my eyes, a bout of anger is one thousandth of a heart attack. You pay for it on the spot; and if you go on getting angry, you go on paying for it too.

Suppose Joe's anger does become chronic. Even if Jack never gets back to hit him, Joe is hitting himself from inside. He comes to live in a world of constant stress, with his "fight or flight" mechanisms on duty around the clock. There is good evidence that this kind of stress can lead to heart disease, to psychosomatic ailments like migraine and ulcer, and even to cancer; these too are routes by which the karma of anger can be reaped.

Further, Joe's aggressiveness and irritability make him harder to live with. His relationships deteriorate. Perhaps his friends start to avoid him; perhaps his co-workers respond to him with increasing irritation and anger, all of which provokes him even more. Life in these circumstances can be miserable. Joe may punish himself further by drinking heavily or smoking more. He may look for relief in high-risk activities like skydiving, rock climbing, or stock car racing. All these provide more ways in which karma can be reaped, and there are many more ways also, which I do not want to go into here.

One more fascinating point about karma: you can see that even if Joe does not actually strike anybody, the karma of anger is still generated in the mind and body. To the extent he gets angry, his blood pressure will still shoot up, his stomach get tense, his heart race, and so on. Of course, the consequences are much more serious if you hit someone than if you do not! But the point is that thoughts have consequences too. They shape the way we see life, which in turn affects our health, our behavior, our choice of work and friends – in short, everything we do.

I hope you can see how logical the law of karma is, and why I say that karma in the mind is the most potent kind of all. It *is* more subtle than physical karma, but it is also much more powerful and longer-lived. That is why I like so much this figure of speech that the body and mind are like a field. A thought is like a seed: very tiny, but it can grow into a huge, powerful, wide-spreading tree. I have seen places where a tiny seed in a crack in a pavement grew into a tree that tore up the sidewalk; its roots spread beneath a house and threatened the concrete foundation. It is terribly difficult to remove such a tree. Similarly, it is terribly difficult to undo the effects of a lifetime of negative thinking, which can extend into many other people's lives.

I never like to talk about this without presenting the brighter side, which is very reassuring. You may have seen from all these examples how much in our karma depends on us: what we think, how we respond. The real source of karma is the mind, which means that all our unfavorable karma can be undone by changing the way we think. If someone gets angry with us and we respond with patience and compassion and the "soft reply that turneth away wrath," that too is karma – good karma. Everybody benefits. The karma of the person who got angry is mitigated, even physiologically: his nervous system is calmed, so his anger subsides; he will not go on to spread it to other people and create still more bad karma. And our own mind and body benefit too. Even if we had to grit our teeth for a while to keep back angry words, afterwards we will feel good inside. All our vital organs can relax, put their feet up on the desk, and say, "Good job!" We know we have helped the other person, and we have the quiet thrill of self-mastery too. In St. Francis's words, which appeal to me very deeply, we know we have been an instrument of peace.

ऋषिभिर्बहुधा गीतं छन्दोभिर्विविधैः पृथक् ।
ब्रह्मसूत्रपदैश्चैव हेतुमद्भिर्विनिश्चितैः ॥ १३-४ ॥

4. These truths have been sung by great sages in a variety of ways, and expounded in precise arguments concerning Brahman.

"As ye sow," said Jesus, "so shall ye reap." Perfect words. Everyone who heard them in those times, on the Mount in Galilee, must have grasped the connections immediately. Push a seed into the ground, take care of it, and it will grow – but not into any old thing; you get the crops you planted. When Jesus added, "Your actions are those seeds, and so are your thoughts," the farmers in the crowd must have gasped with insight.

Most of us in twentieth-century America do not live close to the earth, and Jesus' words are so familiar that we probably seldom stop to think of them. Yet the truth of those words still holds. We cannot breathe a sigh of relief and think, "He must have meant that in some particular context, for a particular audience in Biblical times on the shores of Galilee." They are as valid today as they were in Palestine two thousand years ago, and they will be just as valid in the ages to come. Still, to make them fresh again, spiritual teachers interpret the truths of the scriptures anew for us from age to age, depending on our needs, our conditioning, our culture, and the times in which we live.

When the Buddha wanted to talk about mastering the mind, he used all sorts of images that would be familiar to his village audiences. One was a thatched hut. "If you live in a hut with a poorly thatched roof," he asked, "doesn't rain get in? You get wet, feel miserable, maybe catch pneumonia. It is the same with the mind: if you don't patch all its leaks through the practice of meditation, passions seep in." After a while, you may develop some serious psychosomatic ailments.

The Buddha's thatched hut is a perfect image. But in today's civilization, where psychologizing is the order of the day, the idea may benefit from more development. First, consider the body as a cottage, the dwelling in which you live. This is not really a metaphor; in a sense, that is all the body is. But it's a living house: the kind of place you read about in science fiction, where the walls grow and toasters talk back and the television watches *you*. I'll have more to say about this process-house later on, because it becomes particularly fascinating when you get inside, within the mind. But let me start with the building itself, the actual physical body.

The cottage I live in at our āshram is made of wood. My body-cottage, according to the Upanishads, is made of food: spinach from our garden, *desem* bread made by Laurel, soymilk made by Sandra, even some cheese from our cow, Shobha. It looks like a solid structure, but its tissues and cells are in a state of constant change and repair.

The other day, when I was visiting San Francisco with a teenage friend, we passed a store window displaying a remarkable cottage made out of chocolates and sugar candy, visited by Santa Claus and "eight tiny reindeer." "Julia," I asked, "what do you think of that?"

"I'd like to eat the whole thing," she confided candidly.

"Wouldn't you like to live in a house like that?"

"Oh, no!" she giggled. "It'd be icky. Besides, what would you do when it rains?"

If we eat enough chocolate, we *will* live in a house like that. We may not be what we eat, but our bodies are. The body is continuously remaking itself – brick by brick, so to speak. If I eat chocolate all day, whenever my body asks for a brick I am handing it a bonbon and saying, "Here, use this instead." If I end up living in extra adipose tissue, I cannot blame the landlord; no one but me has done the construction. We cannot afford to choose building materials on the basis of whether or not they titillate the taste buds; the foods we eat should be those that make for a strong, healthy body.

But there is much more to the house than this. It has an interior too, with many levels: senses, mind, intellect, and so on. A thatched hut is not complex enough for our times, for it cannot illustrate the fascinating workings of the mind. In this post-Freudian age, we live in highly elaborate mansions like the Victorian homes I saw the other day in a fashionable section of San Francisco. Most of us spend a good deal of time taking care of our exteriors, which does make for an attractive appearance. But I know many people who have never been inside their own houses. They may not even know they have a door. They camp in the patio, and when life sends a storm they just get wet. This distresses me deeply. Every one of us has a home in which to take shelter, and interior shelter is vitally necessary for our health, our security, and our relationships. Yet every message we get today says, "There is nothing inside. You're only the body. Getting wet and catching pneumonia is part of life."

The whole reason I like this simile of Victorian houses is that it allows for the endless complexities of the mind. Some years ago, when I was visiting in San Jose, I remember encountering a house with a fascinating story behind it: the so-called Winchester Mystery House. Mrs. Winchester, it seems, was a woman of occult leanings who has been told by someone else of occult leanings that she would not die until the renovation of her house was completed. Mrs. Winchester put two and two together and decided she would go on renovating forever.

I have to admit that I never went into the house; the privilege currently costs four or five dollars. But I have it on good authority that the interior is bewildering. A lot of the construction went on with no rationale except to keep on going. There are rooms that Mrs. Winchester probably never saw, doors that open onto walls, staircases that lead nowhere – she was, the guidebooks say, very fond of stairs. And probably there are the sliding bookcase panels and trapdoors and hidden chambers which a good mystery mansion ought to provide. You could easily get lost in a house like that and never find your way out. In a sense that is what happened to Mrs. Winchester, who became more and more absorbed in the idea that she was her house; when it ended, she was bound to end too. I don't know how it came about, but I suppose for some reason building had to cease: at any rate Mrs. Winchester did finally shed her body, though at a ripe old age.

That is how I would present the mind today. It has endless passageways and chambers, closets and vestibules, big bay windows that look out on scenes you never see from the street. It has several stories too – emotions, intellect, and so on – each of which literally recedes forever. You can never get to the back of any flat in the mind.

Just as there are people who never go inside, there are others who venture in and get caught in this fascinating labyrinth. They may lose all capacity to come out again and relate to other people. To function harmoniously in life, it is necessary to be able to come and go freely: that is, to turn outward in selfless action when necessary, and to turn inward regularly in meditation to restore our security, vitality, and will. And it is not enough merely to go inside. Many people who thirst for an interior life do manage to get into the vestibule; but once they get in, they do not know how to explore. They look around, see four walls and a velvet chair and the mailboxes where the senses drop their mail, and they conclude, "Well, this is all there is." There is much, much more, but you have to know where to look, what to look for, and how to open the doors and climb the stairs. All that is what you learn in meditation if you have the guidance of a good, experienced, loving teacher.

I once gave a talk on the house of the mind in which the ego lived in a penthouse suite, presiding over a private fantasy world and looking somewhat like Orson Welles in *Jane Eyre*. But instead of his mad wife being hidden in a locked garret, the prisoner is the Self, the rightful heir. All in all, I thought it would make a good radio drama.

Here, however, I want to look further into the other extreme of the house, the basement. Actually, the house of the mind has several basements, each of which would give psychologists material for a lifetime. Freud barely glimpsed two or three of these levels, and his discoveries literally revolutionized the way people conceive of themselves today. It gives a clue to how much might be changed if we knew how to get into these areas consciously and transform whatever we find.

As I write this there is a good deal of public interest in dungeons, mostly in computer games. You enter an abandoned house, find a trapdoor in the floor, and make your way down into the dark, there to find various treasures in endless chambers. The mind is somewhat like that. After some years of meditation you manage to get into the basement, just beneath the surface level of awareness. In this basement you make some important discoveries, the first of which is the light switch. It might sound trivial, but even to turn on the lights in this dark chamber is a tremendous achievement. Then you can look around and find some important clues to some of the problems that have been plaguing your daily behavior – sources of problems in personal relationships, for example, of which you might have been unaware.

Even on this level there is plenty to deal with. But the mystics say, "Look deeper! You've barely begun." Many passageways lead away from this basement to other rooms and levels, most of which do not need to be explored. As I said, there is a dark fascination about the unconscious that can lure away an aspirant who does not constantly keep his eyes on the supreme goal. For no other reason I can think of except my granny's grace, I passed straight through one level to the next without even looking to left or right. I was aware at crucial junctures that there were things to look at, but I had only one purpose in mind: how to reach the deepest level of the unconscious as quickly as possible, so that I could bring up to the surface treasures from which everyone around me could benefit.

The unconscious mind has many of these subterranean levels. Most remain unknown, though we may slip in unawares now and then – usually in dreams – and catch a glimpse of realms so unfamiliar that we shake our heads afterwards and wonder, "Now where did *that* come from?" As we go deeper, these levels are more and more alike from person to person. But of course we have no way of knowing this at first. We must not only learn to remain conscious in the unconscious, but to navigate these strange chambers as confidently as if we were in our own kitchen.

In many of these chambers we make some fascinating discoveries. If I remember accurately, I believe that archaeologists excavating some ancient cities once came across huge urns where seeds had been stored. Although they had been sealed away underground for thousands of years, once the seeds were exposed to the proper conditions they germinated and grew. Similarly, in the basements of consciousness we can find great urns of karma seeds, *karmabīja,* stored away waiting for the proper time and conditions for sprouting. We have been accumulating these seed treasuries for a rather awesome time: the whole of evolution.

At the upper levels, where they are readily accessible, are the seeds of individual karma – when John hit Joe, for example. But at deeper levels we find seeds from a common store: *yugakarma*, the collective karma of our times. Just our being in this same century together, the Hindu and Buddhist sages say, shows that we have some very basic karma in common – karma which our century provides the perfect climate for ripening. There is no hit-and-miss in karma. Our times, our country, our parents, our social situation all provide the conditions we need to grow, which we ourselves have selected from the seed catalogs of past thought and action.

At the deepest level of the unconscious, we find ourselves in a vast chamber which seems to have no walls anywhere. This is an extraordinary place, which literally seems to go on forever. The other basement levels have been individual, belonging to your house alone. But this chamber is universal. We could call it collective unconsciousness, for it belongs to everybody. But the Buddhist mystics have a more suggestive name: *karmabījālaya,* "storehouse consciousness." Everybody's basements open onto this one vast room, where the karma-seeds of universal samskāras are stored. Some are evolutionary heritages from our animal origins, like anger, greed, lust, and fear: millions on millions of seeds, stored there in huge containers. We get seed deliveries from this basement every day, and usually we carry the packages right out to the back yard for planting. We may think emotions like anger are provoked by someone or something in particular, but everybody gets these seeds.

When you can enter and move about consciously on these levels, you can draw daily on a limitless source of love, wisdom, strength, and inspiration. Words and actions from this depth have tremendous power to reach and help and inspire other people, for they come up from a level that is common to all.

There is much, much more to this subject than I can get into here. The unconscious alone would require volumes. But I hope I have said enough to show why I feel the mind warrants so much attention and illustration. The psychology of the Gita is profound, and a good deal of commentary based on personal experience is necessary to draw out its practical applications. That is why Sri Krishna says the scriptures keep drawing fresh commentaries. Yet at the same time, we should never forget that all great scriptures and mystics speak essentially the same language and deliver the same message. The experience of mysticism and the dynamics of sādhana are everywhere the same.

महाभूतान्यहंकारो बुद्धिरव्यक्तमेव च ।
इन्द्रियाणि दशैकं च पञ्च चेन्द्रियगोचराः ॥ १३-५ ॥

5. The field, Arjuna, is made up of the following: five essences of perception and their corresponding five elements; five sense organs and the five organs of action; the three components of the mind, manas, buddhi, and ahamkāra; and mahat, the undifferentiated stuff from which all these evolved.

I learned to drive in Berkeley about two decades ago: rather late by American standards, but then I learned to ride an elephant as a boy, which most Americans still haven't mastered. I finished the course, too, though I have to admit that out of respect for life I rarely drive. My driving teacher was excellent. He must have taught Berkeley professors before, for he was very good at explaining.

For a long time I had trouble changing gears. He began by trying to tell me just what was happening inside. "This stick is connected to a gear called a spider gear," he said, drawing deft, vague lines on the back of an envelope. "When the stick is here, so the gear's not touching any other gear, you're in neutral. But over here are four other gears –"

"Excuse me," I said. "Do I really need to know this in order to drive?"

"No," he admitted. "You can learn what to do with your hands without ever knowing what's going on beneath the surface. But some people learn more easily if they understand a little theory too."

"Please proceed," I said. "If what you say can be applied, I'll try to follow."

In verses like these, Sri Krishna too seems to be getting a little more technical than practical sense demands. We should bear with him, for these "twenty-four cosmic principles" are the components of a fascinating description of the universe with very practical applications. In

Hindu philosophy this theory is called *sānkhya,* which literally means counting or listing; *yoga,* or meditation, is its corresponding practice. Sānkhya and yoga are traditionally taught together, for they support each other: understanding helps your meditation, and meditation provides the experience that makes the theory real. Particularly after some years of sādhana, these ancient theories can throw a good deal of light on yoga or meditation and difficulties thrown up by the mind.

I know of no English words to use for most of these twenty-four constituents. It is misleading even to use approximations because they bring in all kinds of associations from Western philosophy, which has a wholly different orientation. Behind all the categories and philosophy of sānkhya lies a powerful, practical assumption: it is not trying to describe physical reality; it is trying to analyze the mind, for the sole purpose of unraveling our true identity. So sānkhya does not begin with the so-called material universe as something different and separate from the mind that perceives it. It does not talk about sense objects outside us and senses within and then try to get the two together. It says, This is one world of experience. Sense objects and senses are not separate; they are two aspects of the same event. Mind, energy, and matter are a continuum, and the material universe is not described as it might be in itself, but as it presents itself to the human mind.

Let me illustrate. This morning I had a fresh mango for breakfast: a large, beautiful, fragrant one which had been allowed to ripen until just the right moment, when the skin was luminous with reds and oranges. You can see that I like mangos. I must have eaten thousands of them when I was growing up, and I probably know most varieties intimately by their colors, shapes, flavors, fragrance, and feel.

Sānkhya would say that this mango I appreciated so much does not exist in the world outside – at least, not with the qualities I ascribed to it. The mango-in-itself, for example, is not red and orange; these are categories of an eye and nervous system that can deal only with a narrow range of radiant energy. Our dog Muka would not see a luscious red and orange mango. He would see some gray mass with no distinguishing features, much less interesting to him than a piece of buttered toast. But my mind takes in messages from five senses and fits them into a precise mango-form in consciousness, and that form – nothing outside – is what I experience. Not that there is no "real" mango! But what I experience, the objects of my sense perception and my "knowing," are in consciousness, nowhere else. A brilliant neuroscientist I was reading recently says something similar in contemporary language. We never really encounter the world, he says: because of the mediation of our senses, all we can experience is our own nervous system.

When the Gita says the physical world is made up of five "material elements," then, it is talking about the world *as we perceive it* through our senses. That is, the furniture of this world is not material; it is in the mind. In this sense, "physical objects" require a mental component also: five "essences" of perception, each corresponding to one of the five senses. From these five *tanmātras* derive, on the one hand, the five sense organs; on the other hand, the five material elements. You can see that the number five and the correspondences of sānkhya are not arbitrary, but reflect the ways we have of sorting information supplied to the brain in electrochemical code.

Four of these elements have names similar to those from ancient philosophy in the West – earth, air, fire, and water. It is not impossible, in fact, that the Greeks got this terminology from Indian philosophy. But if we remember that we are talking about principles of perception rather than "earth-stuff," "fire-stuff," and so on, it should become clear that this is not an antiquated theory left behind by the progress of physical science. It is quite sophisticated and accommodates contemporary physical thought rather well, for it assumes that in the act of knowing, the knower cannot be separated from what is known. *Tejas,* for example, is not really 'fire' but something more like 'brightness' or 'brilliance of light.' It is a quality of perception, dominant in the mind-form we make and call a fire.

The fifth gross element is *ākāsha,* which is sometimes translated as 'ether.' This word too has misleading associations from the history of science, where it referred to an elusive physical medium. Since nobody likes to talk about ether after Einstein, I prefer not to translate but to keep *ākāsha.* Physicists today tell us that matter and energy cannot be thought of outside a field of space and time – a kind of frame of reference which has no substance, yet is "shaped" by the objects and forces in it. Ākāsha is like that; it is the frame of reference needed to describe the physical universe.

Senses and sense objects, then, are intimately related. There is a causal connection, for example, between the things we see and the physical organ of seeing, the eye and its related branches of the nervous system: both depend on the underlying form in the mind that conditions how we perceive light. The objects we see are shaped, so to say, by the *way* we see. So senses and sense objects "make sense" only together. Yoga psychology explains that is why there is such a strong pull between senses and the sense objects that complement them – and why indulging the senses only makes this conditioned pull stronger.

On the other hand, the Gita says earlier, this pull has nothing to do with us – the Self, the knower. It is an interaction between elements of the field, very much like a magnetic pull between two objects. *We* are not involved. Unless we confuse ourselves with the field, we can sit back and observe these interactions without jumping in and getting all entangled. When I look at my Prince Alfonso mango, it is natural for my senses to respond; that is their nature. But I should be able to stand aside and watch this interaction with some detachment, the way people sometimes stand and watch while movers unload a van. In that way I can enjoy what my senses report, but I always have the freedom to tell my hand, "No more. We've eaten enough for one meal; let's save this one for tomorrow."

Sānkhya's twenty-four elements are parts of a vast saga: the evolution of unitary consciousness into the countless forms of sensory experience. This is analogous to the evolution of the physical universe from the Big Bang. Working backward, most cosmologists agree that the universe must have expanded from an incredibly hot, supercondensed "primeval atom" consisting almost entirely of energy. At the zero instant just before creation, we would have to conjecture a state in which all the matter and energy in the universe were condensed into a single point, a kind of universe-seed before time and space were born. That is applying words where they cannot go. Yet I cannot help feeling amused when I read such accounts, when science is led beyond the reach of language. When mystics talk this way, scientists pull out their hair or shrug it off as poetry.

In this model, the equilibrium of this pure, undifferentiated point of energy must have been disturbed, for the early universe exploded with an incredible release of radiation. Within four minutes, it had expanded and cooled enough for neutron clusters to survive, but it would be more than half a million years before these nuclei could begin to form the simplest of the elements we know today. Then, John Gribbin writes, "the entire universe resembled the surface of the sun. It was hot, opaque, and filled with a yellow light. As matter and energy decoupled, it suddenly became transparent," marking the ascendancy of matter over energy. Ever since, the cosmos has continued these trends, expanding and evolving toward increasing diversity in its forms.

The description of sānkhya runs parallel to this, but it begins not with energy but with consciousness. Its purpose is to show how the diverse forms we perceive in the physical universe evolved out of unitary consciousness. Following that thread, we can retrace this evolution and discover the unity that is the divine ground of existence.

I have six-year-old friends whose current hero is Johnny Appleseed. When they eat an apple now, they save the seeds: someday, they threaten, they will run away from home and plant them too. I looked at one little seed through their eyes. Who would believe a tree could come from something so tiny? Where could it come from? Yet plant it, water it, and watch: from the air, water, soil, and sunlight it somehow makes tree-stuff to do different jobs in different places, so that this becomes part of a root and that of a leaf; and it grows and becomes huge. How? How does something vast, complex, and alive grow from something tiny and inert? How does it know how to repair itself? Why doesn't it end up with some of its roots in the air? I know that biologists have good answers to these questions, but they remain good questions, no less wonderful if we understand enough to explain.

Here is an apple seed, tiny and inert yet full of potential, with an interior blueprint that can prompt it to sprout a root and a couple of leaves, diversify itself, and explode into a living tree. And here is a universe-seed without dimensions, yet with an implicit blueprint of laws by which energy evolves into stars, plankton, and human beings. Our cosmos too, sānkhya says, is a tree: the Tree of Life, "with its branches below, on earth" – on the sensory level of experience – "and its taproot above," in the undifferentiated consciousness called *mahat*. Like the conjectured seed-state of the cosmos, mahat is vast, for it contains in potential the entire universe. Yet it too is dimensionless and beyond time, for time and space, matter and energy, are still undifferentiated in this primal state.

And here too, it is said, equilibrium was disturbed and differentiation began. From mahat, step by step, the phenomenal world evolved in all its complex forms and forces, very much the way a huge tree emerges from a seed and bears fruit. First come *ahamkāra,* the principle of separateness, and *buddhi,* the faculty that separates, distinguishes, analyzes, and differentiates. From these evolve mind, senses, and the ingredients of the perceptual world.

This derivation can get terribly complicated, and the complications have no practical value. But the rough outlines of this process of evolution can be verified if you like in deeper meditation. The stages of this evolution, as I said, are levels of consciousness – from unity to diversity, from subtle to gross. In an individual, we might call them levels of personality. There is a level on which we are physical creatures; this is the level at which we are most separate. But it is only the surface. Beneath the physical universe are deeper and deeper strata of consciousness, until we reach a realm so deep that nothing individual can be found. The whole thrust of sense-oriented living is to keep us on the visible surface of life, with the rest of our personality in the dark. In meditation, however, we learn to turn inwards and retrace the steps that led to our identifying ourselves as a separate, physical creature. We get deeper and deeper into the mind until finally, in the very depths, we find our source in pure, unitary awareness.

"After a certain state of development," I read one biologist saying yesterday, "further progress in the life sciences requires breaking a system down to the molecular level." That is not the bottom floor of life. Even the atomic level is not the bottom floor. There is a level, as the Upanishads say, that is "subtler than the subtlest": consciousness itself. Only when you enter into the "dark waters" of pure, unitary consciousness, where there is neither name nor form, can you really understand how the mind and senses function, or even why the physical organism has evolved the way it has.

The end of evolution is to lead us back to the divinity that is our source. Meister Eckhart has a remarkable saying: "Whether you like it or not, whether you know it or not, secretly Nature seeks and hunts and tries to ferret out the track in which God may be found." The whole purpose of every experience, every human activity, every faculty, is to turn us inward and lead us back to our divine source. See the compassion of this view! Every person looking for something in the outside world, it says – pleasure, power, profit, prestige – is really looking for God. All the traits we develop, even those that seem negative, have a positive purpose: to enable us to fight this "war within" in the depths of the unconscious and discover who we are.

I don't know if I have managed to convey the vastness of this: it means that sādhana is really the culmination of evolution. When you undertake this battle, the negative forces that you are striving to transform are part of everybody's human heritage from our animal past, "red in tooth and claw." That is why the mystics say that everyone who takes to the spiritual life does so on behalf of all humanity. And every victory won is a victory for all; for it shows what is possible, what is our highest nature. Gandhi said, "I believe that if one man gains spiritually the whole world gains with him, and if one man falls, the whole world falls to that extent." And he added, "I do not help opponents without at the same time helping myself and my co-workers."

इच्छा द्वेषः सुखं दुःखं संघातश्चेतना धृतिः ।
एतत्क्षेत्रं समासेन सविकारमुदाहृतम् ॥ १३-६ ॥

*6. In this field arise desire and aversion, pleasure
and pain, the body, intelligence, and will.*

In the last verse, Sri Krishna gave the ingredients of the phenomenal world. Now he gives the recipe for blending these ingredients into a person. The body is part of this recipe, but you will notice that it is a relatively minor part. Most of what a person is belongs to the "world within": what we loosely call the mind. Yet within or without, the point is that all these ingredients are part of the same phenomenal world: that is, part of a continuously changing process, with which we have only a passing relationship.

Let me begin to illustrate with my body. It seems solid and warm and brown, yet my medical friends tell me it is constantly changing. In some sense, these are the same hands that I have always had; yet the skin is different, the muscles are different, even the bone tissue has changed. While I am sitting here, my hand is busily engaged in an immense kind of interior urban renewal project of which I am not aware. At the same time my hand remains a hand, and it remains *my* hand. The tissues do not decide to turn it into a flipper or something else instead, although each cell has that capability.

My whole body is like that. It is not the body I had twenty years ago, yet it also is not a different body; it is very much mine. In other words, the body is not so much a thing as a process. The realization subtracts considerably from personal vanity. You can be proud, I suppose, of having an aquiline nose, but who can feel proud of an aquiline process?

To add further insult, this process is mostly space. There is very little solid matter to it; most of the body is space. I read somewhere that if you could get rid of all the excess space somehow, you could fit your-self into a peanut shell. This is fascinating, if not exactly flattering. It makes us see that the space is as important as the material substance, which is why ākāsha is considered one of the elements. But how much self-importance can we feel about a thing that is mostly air?

If we could really absorb this idea, it would probably be quite unsettling. Romance might be difficult to maintain. What would Romeo think of a Juliet that was mostly not there? Would he fall in love with a process – something he could tuck into a peanut? Māyā cannot tolerate this kind of perception, so she draws a veil over it. One of the delightful contraries of human nature is that no matter how many times Romeo tells himself "just a peanut, just a peanut," his heart will still race and his blood pressure rise when he holds Juliet's hand; it will feel very solid indeed.

This is already dizzying, but we can take it further. Look at the mind. Every day you wake up the same person. Why? What makes you the same? You probably feel different: yesterday, perhaps, you felt on top of the world; this morning you have a chip on your shoulder. "Wait till after breakfast," you say. "I'm not myself till I get something in my stomach." And it is true that after a good meal, your personality may be different. All of us are like that: at different times and with different people, we are different too. At work we might be considered sweet; at home, a self-centered grouch – two separate personalities. Our moods shift and flicker, even in those who are emotionally stable. Similarly, our desires change. When you were two, you might have wanted to be a garbage collector and drive a big, noisy truck around at five in the morning; probably now you have something else in mind. And opinions change. I know a number of people who used to be radically liberal, but who today are bastions of conservative thought. Change is the nature of the mind.

Philosophers have observed this flux of thoughts and sensations in themselves and asked, "Then where am *I*?" The parts do not add up to who we are. They don't really add up to anything; they just flow by, "signifying nothing." The mind too is a process, and its contents so transient that if we reflect on it, we feel relieved to think there is enough of us to fit into a peanut after all.

Just as to the physicist, the physical world dissolves into a sea of subatomic particles and energy, the mind dissolves into a river of impressions and thoughts. Yet through all this change, there *is* something that is the same person from day to day, moment to moment. The mind-process is repetitive. It could think anything, but in fact it keeps throwing out the same old thoughts over and over. Just as the tissues in my hand keep remaking the same hand, though never *quite* the same, so the mind keeps remaking the same old mind – at least, until we learn to change it in meditation. Nothing in the stuff of the mind is solid, fixed, tangible in any way. All that we have to cling to as "real" is the patterns of remaking – the dominant traits, obsessions, and "hang-ups" of our personality, called in Sanskrit *samskāras*.

All this adds up to a very shaky self-image for the ego. It loves to take center stage, yet when the spotlights come on, we can scarcely see anyone there. Here is a haphazard bundle of desires, predilections, resentments, insecurities, tied together with some random associations. What can hold this bundle together? When you take it up in your hands, it all falls apart. It is no wonder that when we identify with it, we feel insecure down to our toes. Anything can threaten this shadow house of cards. As a result, much of the string with which the ego tries to hold itself together is made out of defenses.

Just as the mind's flow of thoughts makes sense only by reference to the ego, nothing holds the ego together except by reference to the Self. Only because there is an underlying Self can the ego usurp its place and put on all its qualities. This is a rather pathetic spectacle. The ego wants to be everything the Self is. It puts on the Self's evening jacket and Brooks Brothers tie and expects – demands – to be intelligent and creative and loved and even immortal, just like the Self. But some small part is never fooled. It goes to admire itself in the mirror and finds no reflection, nothing solid, nothing to last from moment to moment. All this fills the ego with insecurity and fear, which can only be erased from our consciousness by the discovery of who we really are.

In calling this whole process a field, Sri Krishna has hit on terminology that is remarkably apt for our modern way of thinking. We speak now of matter and energy as being grosser and subtler aspects of a physical field of forces – an idea which, though now presented on prime time television and taught in high schools, was considered preposterous and occult within my memory. It is good to remember this, because it reminds us how readily our ideas of reality can be enlarged. That is exactly what the Gita is implying. This concept of a field of forces, it says, needs to embrace a still subtler realm than nuclear energy: the forces of the mind.

This is not rhetoric. We cannot see a physical force like electricity; we can only know its effects. It is the same with the forces of personality too. When you look at a magnet, for example, you see only a simple bar of iron. But if you put the bar into a lot of iron filings, they jump into position along the magnetic lines of force. Then you can actually see the lines; you can see the shape of the field.

In the same way, you can learn to see what I might call the shape of personality by knowing how to observe its effects. The most obvious portrait is the physical body itself. On the atomic level, I read one biologist saying, the body could be described as a complex bundle of energy. What we ordinarily call our body is the "solid" part of this bundle, the aspect that is perceptible to the senses. In the same way, the Hindu and Buddhist scriptures go one step further: the physical body, they say, is the solid part of personality, shaped over many years by our ways of thinking. This is not as occult as it might sound. These scriptures are trying to remind us how much of our physical health, for example, has been determined by the decisions of lifestyle and behavior we have made from childhood on: what we have been eating (and how often), how we work, how we respond to life's give and take, how we spend our leisure time. All these make an immense impact on health status; and all, as this verse reminds us, are essentially a matter of our personal likes and dislikes, our will, and the deep, driving desires that motivate our lives. This does not deny the obvious importance of genetic factors. But in many cases, what our genetics contribute are *propensities*. A slow metabolism, for example, may mean we are liable to put on weight easily, but it does not condemn us to be overweight. It is our desires and behavior – the thousand and one little choices we make throughout each day – that actualize these tendencies and turn latent factors into real conditions.

But there is much more to the field of forces that is the mind, as we can see by its effects on others.

Once in a museum in San Francisco I saw a very powerful electromagnet. Two large poles as high as my waist were standing about a foot apart, bent towards each other at the top like two crooked fingers. When you passed your hand between them, you felt absolutely nothing. But it was a different story when the current was switched on. Then, when you tossed a handful of filings between the poles, the filings leaped into the lines of force and froze into a rigid bridge. You could push it and even rest your hand on it; though nothing seemed to be holding those tiny filings together, the bridge would remain intact. That is how real an invisible field can be; it literally molds and shapes the space around it.

A person can be like that too. Don't we say, "She has a strong personality"? Like a magnet, personality creates a field of forces around itself wherever it goes, for better or for worse. That is why a person may attract certain types and repel certain others. Interestingly enough, we do not necessarily attract those whom we would like to attract, or repel those we want to avoid. On the contrary. If I may mix metaphors somewhat, we often attract those with whom we can sow and reap our karma. A person who is always resentful may actually draw to him people and situations that provoke resentment.

Given fertile circumstances, the field of forces thrown up by such a person can reach far beyond the realm of personal contact. In the Invocation to the Gita, Duryodhana, the ruler who masses the powers of darkness in the *Mahābhārata*, is referred to vividly as a vicious whirlpool in the river of life. I don't know if you have seen a whirlpool; when

I was a boy we encountered them sometimes while swimming in the river, particularly during the monsoon rains. It was a terrifying sight to see those swift, dark, powerful swirls that could reach out across the river like an invisible arm beneath the surface of the water and draw a huge branch helplessly into its mouth. Duryodhana was just like that; his obsessive resentment and swollen ego drew the world around him into a vortex of destruction. I mention him not for any literary reason; to those who have read the life of Hitler and traced the resentments that came to dominate his life, the parallel is striking.

This image of a field of forces illustrates vividly the interconnectedness of our lives and the potential reach of our thought and actions. Just as you cannot separate an eddy from the rest of the river, the field of forces that is each of us cannot be considered limited to the physical body in which we live. The interplay of these eddies – the millions of little desires and actions of ordinary people like you and me – can create a whirlpool whose sweep reaches around the globe.

For illustration, I have been reflecting on some of the effects of one very common, innocent desire – the craving for high-beef living. I am not talking about meat-eating, either, but simply of the craving to eat a particular kind of meat out of all proportion to any physiological need or purpose – beef, beef, beef every day, often twice a day, so that it becomes not food but some kind of symbol. This has nothing to do with a normal diet, meat-based or not. It is an obsession, a desire fanned out of control; and whenever a desire gets fanned out of control in a society, there is a lot of money to be made. When these two, obsessive desire and greed, get together, you can expect a web of ill effects to spread.

As I understand it, the United States did not become a nation of what Russell Baker calls "beefaholics" until about World War II. But after the war, beef – particularly steak – came to stand for American affluence and a superior way of life. By the mid-fifties, the desire to share in this way of life had been fanned into a billion-dollar appetite. When I came to this country, the climate was saturated with beef ideals: Big Macs and Whoppers every day for lunch; steaks every evening, if possible, for dinner; barbecues in the patio when you wanted to entertain. I don't think many people could imagine an American Way of Life without steak and hamburger.

Since then, following the flow of prosperity, the hamburger habit has spread around the globe: to Western Europe, to Japan, to the wealthy elite of Latin America.

Now see how far the ramifications can spread, along chains of cause and effect that no one would suspect. This desire for beef, for example, is one of the biggest causes of deforestation in Latin America, which in turn has effects that threaten the future of our whole planet.

Let me focus on Brazil, where about half of the Amazon basin – one million acres, an area roughly the size of California – was opened to foreigners in the nineteen-seventies, with generous financial incentives for those who invested in the country's booming cattle business.

Because of the methods used for clearing land for grazing, however, cattle ranching is generally considered to be the most ecologically destructive of all tropical activities. "Ranchers" in the Amazon – often not individuals but corporations, including multinationals – carve their spreads out of virgin rain forest. Tractors shear vegetation off the thin layer of topsoil, and vast areas are cleared with herbicides like Agent Orange. The debris that remains, and the wildlife, are then burned. Three to five years later, soil fertility declines, grasses become less nutritious, poisonous weeds start poking up, and the range has to be abandoned; the cycle is repeated at a new forest site.

"So what?" investors argued. "There's still plenty of forest untouched. We can't afford to let millions of acres lie idle just because some bleeding hearts think wilderness is wonderful." The government of Brazil agreed; it liked the flood of finance capital.

But other floods came too. By December 1980, an article in Science had reported that "the height of the annual flood crest of the Amazon has increased markedly in the last decade" because of "rapid ravages of deforestation. . . . Perhaps a fifth or a fourth of the Amazon forest has already been cut, and the rate of forest destruction is accelerating." Higher floods meant a massive, irreversible loss of topsoil – and the loss of topsoil, together with the loss of transpired moisture from one-fifth less forest, pointed to a drop in rainfall that "might eventually convert much of now-forested Amazonia to near desert."

Reports of the repercussions kept coming in, pointing to an ever larger picture. Destruction of the forests threatened food sources throughout South America – even, it turned out, on the other side of the globe. Already enough forest had been destroyed to alter global weather patterns, causing monsoons to dump their rain at sea instead of on the parched fields of India, Burma, and Southeast Asia. Who would think cattle ranching in Brazil could contribute to drought, famine, and flooding twelve thousand miles away?

Within a few years, scientists were convening to discuss what threatened to become an unprecedented ecological disaster. "Rain forests are being destroyed faster than any other natural commodity," the Institute for Food and Development Policy observed in 1987. "If the present rate of destruction continues, in seventy-five years they will disappear entirely." Brazil, which contains nearly one third of the world's tropical forest, "has the dubious distinction of destroying more rain forest per year than any other country: over 3.6 million acres."

At stake, biologists realized, is a truly global resource. Although rain forests make up less than one twelfth of the earth's land surface, they are necessary for life as we know it. Besides their effects on food sources around the world, they have been called "the lungs of mother Earth" because they filter and cycle out pollutants like ozone and carbon dioxide, returning to the atmosphere vast quantities of oxygen and water. These processes, in turn, help temper the greenhouse effect: the overall warming of the globe, heightened by industrial pollution, which threatens to shift climate as drastically as the Ice Age. The Amazon forests, mysterious and misunderstood, have been helping all along to protect us from the effects of rampant industrialization.

Finally, rain forests are home to at least half of the earth's species. No one really knows the long-term consequences of destroying a gene pool like that, but at the very least we know we would lose an unimaginably rich source of new food crops and medicines. Only a fraction of these species has been studied, yet that fraction – barely tapped – includes four thousand species of edible fruits and vegetables, ninety-nine percent of which are still undeveloped, and at least one fourth of the ingredients for prescription drugs now on the market. The October 3, 1988, issue of *Science* put this kind of destruction in its proper perspective:

With the forests vanished or largely disrupted, up to half the

world's species of animals, plants, and insects would disappear too.
. . . According to David Raup, of the University of Chicago, a figure
of 50% extinction would be closely comparable with the mass
extinction of 65 million years ago, during which dinosaurs finally
disappeared together with 60 to 80% of the rest of the world's
species.

At this scale, one tragic consequence often goes unnoticed. I learned
about it years ago in a piece in the *New Yorker* about a remarkable
man named Robin Hanbury-Tenison and a small organization called
Survival International, which is trying to prevent the extinction of
whole tribes of human beings. Hanbury-Tenison got his start, it seems,
reading an article in the London *Times* Sunday Magazine entitled
"Genocide": not something about Nazi Germany, but about the Amazon
Indians. Perhaps six million Indians lived in Brazil in 1500, when Cabral
came. Today the count is just five percent of that figure, and declining to
extinction. During this century, an average of at least one tribe per year
has disappeared – cynically and systematically removed to make room
for the expanding demands of cattle ranchers, prospectors, road builders, real estate developers, and others at the leading edge of advancing
civilization. To me, it is an all too familiar example of the mental state
to which any kind of exploitation of the earth has to lead.

  I have been tracing the effects of one relatively innocent desire: let
us say, the simple desire to eat something we have been taught is good
for us and which shows that we have "arrived." In anybody, this is not
a strong desire; rather a small one. Yet it is widespread, it goes unquestioned, and therefore there is money to be made from it. Those who
can make that money fan the desire, particularly with very effective
advertising, playing on our natural aspirations: to nourish ourselves, to
give our children the best we can afford, to enjoy the fruits of our hard-
earned prosperity. Then with corporate growth come truly big ways to
make money, and the capital to finance immense, global efforts. Whole
countries, measuring economic progress by gross national product, get
involved at this stage, turning over precious resources to feed the habits
of the well-to-do rather than the needs of their own people. And so it
spreads. By this time the "desire" may be just a habit, well under the

advertiser's control. We need to be careful of every desire, even those that are small. Even a little desire puts a handle on us, which anybody can reach out and grasp and use.

अमानित्वमदम्भित्वमहिंसा क्षान्तिरार्जवम् ।
आचार्योपासनं शौचं स्थैर्यमात्मविनिग्रहः ॥ १३-७ ॥

7. Those with true knowledge are free from pride and the desire for ostentation. They are gentle, forgiving, upright, and pure, devoted to their spiritual teacher, filled with inner strength, and self-controlled.

This verse and the four which follow give a telling portrait of those who live in detachment, who have realized they are neither body nor mind.

There are portraits like this in every tradition. The words may differ, but the character portrayed is the same. I don't think you will ever find the Buddha saying that arrogance is the mark of wisdom. Nowhere will you hear Jesus say, "Blessed are those who are proud." The qualities mentioned in these five verses are signs of true spiritual wisdom. They shine forth wherever a man or woman attains Self-realization, independent of time, place, and culture.

But this is more than a catalog of inspiring virtues. We can think of it also as a seed catalog: each of the qualities mentioned is one we can cultivate to gain detachment. In other words, they are both fruit and seed. If we plant them and nurture them, they will thrive until they fill the field of the mind, yielding harvests that enrich us throughout our lives.

Such virtues are not unrelated. To my eyes this verse has a single theme beneath the surface, and that is forgiveness. The man or woman who knows how to forgive – not merely with the lips, but from the heart – can work in harmony everywhere without any fear. The secret is simple: a small ego. All the virtues of detachment come from that.

First comes humility, Sri Krishna says – literally, the absence of pride. For some reason I could never understand, pride is often taken as a sign of strength and humility as weakness. But anyone can see how pride weakens; for pride means rigidity. It is not different values or opinions that keep people from mending rifts in personal relationships; it is just plain pride. Neither party wants to take the first step. Those who are secure and strong can turn their backs on their pride and take not only the first step toward reconciliation but the second and third, and as many more as may be necessary.

There is a direct connection here with *ahimsā*, 'nonviolence.' Ahimsā means much more than refraining from harmful acts; it is essentially a mental state. You have made your mind free from anger – or, more practically, you have learned how to transform anger into kindness and compassion.

Ahimsā is our natural state, and it is very fertile soil. You don't have to plant kindness in it; kind words and actions come forth naturally. But the field is choked by self-will – all the selfish, self-centered behavior that comes when we think of ourselves as separate creatures. As self-will is weeded out, security and fulfillment grow – not as a reward from some external power, but as the natural fruit of your mental state of kindness. On the other hand, by the same law, if you sow the dragon's teeth of discord, you will reap a harvest of discord. Isn't it Jason who faced the consequences of this kind of gardening? Where each tooth fell into the soil, an army sprang up to fight. This may be fanciful, but it is not an inaccurate way of describing the violence we read about in the papers almost every day.

Violent attitudes spread like a chain reaction. The other day I was standing with a friend watching our dog Muka watch a neighbor's cat. The cat, in turn, was watching a flock of birds. For a moment the scene was tranquil. Then the cat, being a cat, suddenly leaped at the birds. Almost at the same moment Muka, being a dog, leaped after the cat. And my friend leaped after Muka. That is exactly what happens in human affairs too. If someone is rude at work, we take it out on our partner at home, and he or she spreads irritation to everyone the next day. It happens not only with individuals; you can see nations behaving to each other the same way.

Many years ago I remember a man on television demonstrating a chain reaction. He stood in a room filled with mouse traps, each of which would release two table tennis balls when sprung. At the blackboard he explained a little about uranium atoms being split by one neutron and releasing two. Then, without warning, he casually tossed a single table tennis ball into the traps. There was a *snap*, then a couple of other *snaps*, and in an instant, with a rattle like hail, the whole room was pelted with balls.

Without exaggeration, our globe is like that today. One person in a chronic state of anger spreads anger everywhere. When many people live in this state, continually on the edge of resentment, frustration, and hostility, the harvest is violence everywhere – in our hearts, our homes, our streets and cities, between estranged races, factions, and nations.

Detachment can break this chain reaction. A cat is conditioned to leap on birds; it has no choice. Muka, being a dog, is conditioned to chase cats. But you and I are human; we have the capacity to choose our response. We can snap the chain of stimulus and response behavior by meeting resentment with patience, hatred with kindness, and fear with trust, in a sustained, consistent endeavor to stanch the spread of violence that threatens us all.

Through meditation, as our minds become calmer and self-will fades, detachment comes and our vision clears. Only then can we see that most of the obstacles to forgiving others do not arise from ideological or philosophical differences. Put plainly, obstacles arise because we want to impose our way, our self-will, on others, and they want to impose their self-will on us. Seeing this clearly goes a long way toward releasing forgiveness; as Voltaire said, "To understand all is to forgive all." But something more than clear seeing is required, and that is the will. It takes a good deal of inner strength to remain calm and compassionate in the face of fierce opposition, never losing your balance or resorting to harsh language. But when you can do this, a kind of miracle takes place which all of us can verify. The other person becomes calmer, his eyes clear a little too; soon communication is established once again.

There is a cult of anger in our modern civilization, often propagated in the name of better communication. But anger only disrupts communication. It widens any gap between people, destroys relationships, says without needing any words, "You don't matter to me. You're not worthy of my respect." The only way to communicate is to be patient and sympathetic, even when it hurts. It *will* hurt; it will try your resources to the limit. That's why the spiritual life is so difficult. But the more you give, the more it will enlarge your capacity to go on giving. "To those that have," Jesus says, "more shall be given." Then he adds, somewhat mischievously, "And to those that lack, even the little they have shall be taken away." If a Philistine should complain, "Rabbi, that's not fair!" Jesus would probably smile and ask, "What's unfair? The choice is up to you."

There is only one way to learn this, and that is in the normal give-and-take of personal relationships. People who are close to us may sometimes provoke us, just as we may provoke them; that is the natural state of emotional relations in every country in the world. When two people – particularly man and woman – have gone to different schools, grown up in different backgrounds, developed different ways of working, playing, eating, speaking, and thinking, we should be deeply impressed if they do not quarrel sometimes. All these differences provide opportunities for practicing patience, forgiveness, and respect, which are not going to be learned in any other way.

Forgiveness is important in every relationship, but it is essential in love. When two people love each other deeply, if one makes a mistake, the other doesn't lose respect or say, "I'm going to do that too; then we'll be even." That is the time to stand by the person you love and offer support: not conniving at the mistake, but helping that person to overcome it and grow. This is a great art. It cannot be done in judgment or condescension, which means we have to get the ego very much out of the way. Most of us are not able to draw on a deeper will and a higher wisdom to do this; therefore our relations go wrong and we run away. There is no reason to bemoan this. I have made many mistakes in my ignorance, and so has everybody else I know. But from now onwards, by building our lives on meditation, we can learn to stand firm in situations where we used to crumble, stand loving and respectful when we used to get resentful, hostile, or vindictive.

We need not expect perfection. Robert Browning says in a magnificent simile that it is enough just to draw one small arc; the Lord will complete the circle. He will take into account the times in which we live – horrible times; just look at any paper to see: money and sex played up constantly, meaningless violence all over the globe. He will make allowances for our country, our culture, our physical and intellectual limitations, and then he will say, "Just do your best to forget yourself in the interests of those around you. Aim always for the welfare of the whole. If you can do that much, you will be a tremendous force for unity, harmony, and peace."

The Lord of Love is infinite compassion, infinitely forgiving. We receive this compassion to the extent that we show compassion to those around us. There is nothing otherworldly about this. When I forgive someone, the inner world of the mind is so real to me that I can almost see my tensions dissolving, which is a tonic to my nervous system and to every vital organ in the body. In orthodox language, that is the Lord forgiving me. Just as anger can cause severe physical problems, forgiveness can heal – not only emotional ailments, but even physical ones that have their origins in emotional disturbances.

The other day as we tried to leave a parking garage near the Berkeley campus I noticed a lot of spikes protruding from the asphalt, leveled at the car like lances in some medieval fortress. The sign warned, "Do Not Enter. Severe Tire Damage May Result." From the looks of those spikes, I would say that was putting it mildly; our tires would probably have come out looking like ravioli. There is a sign like this inside us too: "Don't Be Selfish. Severe Damage May Result – Spiritual, Emotional, Physical." When Jesus or Sri Krishna tells us not to retaliate or resort to unkind words, these are not copybook maxims intended only for Sunday pulpits. They are living laws. The more we indulge in unkind thinking, speaking, and behaving, the more damage we do ourselves. When you forgive, on the other hand – particularly when you forgive wrongs you have suffered in emotionally charged relationships – you are doing much more than repairing those relationships; you are discharging pent-up resentments and hostilities which are often responsible for severe physical problems. People used to ask me, "Does it help others if I pray for them?" I replied, "I don't know how much it helps others, but it certainly will help you."

This, Sri Krishna says, is right knowing: seeing the Lord in all, despite any differences that seem to separate us. The only way to know God is to try as hard as we can to become like him. To know Jesus, we have to try in all humility to be like Jesus, who forgave even from the cross. He gave us his life as a personal example of how to live – wisely, compassionately, for the benefit of all. Of all the ways to honor him, perhaps the most fitting is to give ourselves as gifts to him in return, so that in all our relationships we can show the spirit of utter forgiveness which made him say, "Father, forgive them, for they know not what they do."

इन्द्रियार्थेषु वैराग्यमनहंकार एव च ।
जन्ममृत्युजराव्याधिदुःखदोषानुदर्शनम् ॥ १३-८ ॥

8. Detached from sense objects and self-will, they have learned the painful lesson of separate birth and suffering, old age, disease, and death.

Sri Krishna is continuing his portrait of the man or woman who lives in detachment.

This verse emphasizes what I call the mechanical side of personality, for our body and mind are instruments which we use in life. The discovery that we are not our machinery frees this machinery to function smoothly, which is a state of optimum physical and mental health. Even more wonderfully, we learn that it is only this machinery that suffers, decays, grows ill, and dies. We, the operator, are immortal.

It is not too difficult intellectually to see the body as an instrument: a sophisticated, powerful vehicle which we use to get around with, just as we use a car or train or plane. When I want to go to San Francisco, I travel in our Volvo; the trip takes about an hour. In just the same way, if I had more time I could go in this subcompact car I call my body. That is very much the way I look on my physical frame: it is not I; it is the vehicle with which I get through life in time and space.

But here the confusion arises. We can point to our car and say, "That is the vehicle in which I came here." But we cannot point to the body and say, "This too is the vehicle in which I came here." If we could say this truly, we would have no difficulty in returning this vehicle to the rental agency after a hundred years. But we have identified ourselves with this particular car. Through a monstrous error called simply *avidyā*, 'ignorance,' in Sanskrit, we have come to believe that we are the body, subject to birth and therefore to death. In the Judeo-Christian tradition this is "the Fall" – the fall from the divine state in which we knew that we are not the body but a beneficial force, beyond division, beyond death. When we regain that state, we live again in paradise right here on earth.

I have a friend who is ardently devoted to Volkswagens. I point to my body and tell her, "You have a red VW bug; this is a brown one. It's a rent-a-car: get it here, leave it there." If I take good care of it – give it regular checkups, lubes, check the oil and tires – it should be good for a hundred years of service. And it is just the right size. Tibetan mystics say that between lives we line up in Bardo, the "in-between state," and wait for a car that is just right for our needs and personality. So this little brown car is perfect for me. I don't feel any jealousy over big luxury vehicles that take up so much parking space and drink a lot of gas. I have a car with minimum gasoline consumption and maximum maneuverability, and its engine is as powerful as a Ferrari's.

This kind of attitude brings detachment in how we regard the body we have. People without this detachment are highly body-conscious: in their clothes, their food, their pleasures, in everything physical. They have no choice where the clamor of the senses is concerned; if the senses want something, all they know is how to yield. Detachment from the body means the capacity to tell your taste buds, "That's not what my body needs! That's what Madison Avenue is telling you to buy. It may look good, but it's made for shelf life; it's not going to help *your* life at all." Only when we have the choice to say no if necessary to physical demands are we able to give the body the care it needs to make it healthy, resilient, and beautiful.

Athletes understand this. When a great gymnast has her eyes on an Olympic gold medal, she takes care of her body the way a race driver takes care of his car. Everyone understands the reason, too: after all, if you had a chance at an Olympic decoration, would you feel tempted by a pizza? What amazes me is that when it comes to a much longer lasting award – vibrant health and a long, full life – people object, "It's not worth it. Beer and pizza are what make life worth living." The Gita makes this distinction between the operator and the machine for one purpose: to show us that we do not have to obey the machine we operate; the machine should obey us.

To the extent we *do* take care of our car, most of us devote our time to the body – painting the chassis, fixing the windshield wipers, installing an eight-track sound system or a three-tone horn. These things *are* important; we certainly need a horn at times. But by spending our time and energy on the body, we have forgotten that there is an engine: the mind.

Many years ago, when I was still new to this country, a friend took me out to see his new car. "Look!" he said proudly. "I want to show you a mechanical miracle. They've finally developed a car that doesn't need an engine." He opened the hood with a flourish. Sure enough, I didn't see anything except some old rags and a little roll of tools. Only later did he confess that with this particular car, the engine was in the back.

That is how most of us think of ourselves. The body doesn't need an engine; it just goes. No wonder the engine is often in the worst condition possible! It has never been looked at; only by the mercy of the Lord does it function well enough to get us through the day without major mishaps. Therefore, the Gita tells us, work on your engine first: your ways of thinking, your emotional responses, your love, your will. If you have a powerful engine, it doesn't really matter if you don't have a horn. It doesn't even matter much if you don't have sides for your car: after all, jeeps don't have sides and people are able to drive them. Work on the engine; that's what you cannot do without. Work on your mind. After you have brought it up to specifications and tuned it to perfection, if you still have time, you can get a hula doll to hang in the rear window. Before that, Sri Krishna says drily, it's a little premature.

One of the greatest misunderstandings of modern science is that if we study the brain, we will understand the mind. "Despite massive research," a recent article reports, "neuroscientists say they still cannot answer the age-old question, 'Is the material body really the seat of consciousness?' Although there is a feeling of imminent breakthrough, such scientists have still to find the point in the brain where perception occurs – where nerve endings become music, or vision." And that is perception, which is only the tip of consciousness. "As a matter of fact," this writer adds, "the whole concept of consciousness has become even more uncertain." This is unavoidable, because of the way the question is asked. When you base all your study of something on the assumption that it is something else, "more uncertain" is all it can become.

"Looking at the human brain as some sort of intricate computer," says a specialist at Massachusetts Institute of Technology, "scientists confronted a system so vast and awe-inspiring that it makes all else simple to the point of triviality." That is how wonderfully complex the brain is; yet at the same time, it is nothing more than a computer, which is to say a machine. We can put it on the workbench and study it all we like; even if we succeed in duplicating some of its functions, we will learn nothing about the operator of the computer, who is seated beneath the bench waiting for us to get around to him.

Many years ago I went to a computer exhibition in Oakland. There were computers all around, their beady eyes blinking, going *beep, beep, beep*. After a few minutes a man came up to me. Seeing that I came from another country, he asked, "Do you know what these are?"

Out of politeness I said, "Please tell me."

"They are computers," he said with evident satisfaction. "Do you know what they can do?"

I said, "Please tell me."

"They can do *everything* you can do."

I just laughed. "Oh, no. They don't know how to meditate!"

The point may have been lost on him; I don't think he knew what meditation is, so probably he didn't feel any sense of loss. If he could have shown me a computer as sophisticated as the human brain, he would probably have felt very proud. But however complicated it may be, we can never make a computer that can do what every human being can, by virtue of being human: go beyond words, thought, and sensory experience into a higher realm of knowing, where awareness cannot be broken even by death. The reason is simple: the computer has no Ātman. It is just machinery; nothing can make it more than that. The terror some people feel of the machine, of computers and the like becoming a kind of Frankenstein, is a terror not fully warranted; machines will never be able to "take over" anything in the sense of coming alive. But on the other hand, the sublime confidence that machines will someday solve all our problems, elevate our consciousness, and enable us all to fulfill life's purpose is just as exaggerated and much more dangerous.

"This erring race of human beings," Sri Aurobindo writes, "dream always of perfecting their environment by the machinery of government and society. But it is only by the perfection of the soul within that the outer environment can be perfected. 'What thou art within, that outside thee thou shalt enjoy.' No machinery can rescue you from the law of your own being." And he concludes: "What then shall be our ideal? Unity for the human race by an inner oneness, . . . the pouring of the power of the spirit into the physical and mental instrument, so that we shall exceed our present state as much as this exceeds the animal state from which science tells us we have issued." Aurobindo is not talking from book knowledge, though he was a great scholar. Statements like these are stamped with the vision that comes from personal experience.

As detachment deepens, health improves. It is amazing to see how easily we can change physical habits: eat better food, get more exercise, sleep better. But more important, we get peace of mind, without which no amount of food and exercise can guarantee good health.

In most of the books on health that I see, the mind is hardly emphasized. Current research into heart disease or cancer, for example, emphasizes only external factors such as dietary fats, smoking, or high blood pressure. Very few are even asking about internal factors, the influence of the mind; and when they do ask, given the physical orientation of our times, they scarcely know what to look for. I am certainly not minimizing the importance of external factors. But I think the damage that anger can do to the circulatory system, to take just one example, may be much greater than the harm ascribed to cholesterol. Hostility, depression, fear, and greed – not just for money but for power or pleasure – all threaten our health as surely as junk food or sedentary living. I once read about someone who devoured a bag of potato chips with every meal. I doubt his body appreciated it. But if you can be kind all day, even with three bags of chips you may be better off than someone with an exemplary diet who seethes with resentment inside.

Coffee's adverse effects, for example, prompted me long ago to switch to a rare cup of decaf. But when people start telling me about the evils of caffeine, I sometimes try to restore a sense of proportion. "Mind you," I say, "I'm not disagreeing. But what you really ought to worry about is anger. If you can give that up, you can take a cup of coffee in your stride." The worst threats to health come from the Big Four: anger, fear, greed, and self-will. It is these we should focus on, for they sabotage our health, our security, and our capacity to love.

When you do not identify with your body, it is much less likely to be ravaged by disease. It doesn't even feel easily the ravages of time. Gandhi was an outstanding example of this. So was the Compassionate Buddha, who was magnificently fit into his seventies. The chronicles and art of southern Asia, where Buddhism is oldest, depict him as tall, strong, and vibrantly alive – clad only in an ochre robe, owning nothing but a begging bowl, but every inch the king that he was born.

After all is said and done, the passage of time is going to affect all of us physically. But it is the obsessive identification with the body that really leaves it prey to the ravages of time. Will Rogers, I think, used to say that when he saw a pretty girl, he had to remind himself that in twenty years she was going to look five years older. That can be true of spiritual aspirants too. When you are meditating, though twenty years pass, the body may show the effects of only five.

I am not speaking here about events after samādhi, which may well seem remote. Even before this, you enter a stage where you are not conscious of the body during meditation. In the later stages of sādhana you may slip into this state involuntarily while you are asleep at night. If this happens, don't jump out of bed; repeat your mantram for a few minutes and then get up slowly. The experience is exhilarating. After your first taste of it, you look on your body completely differently from the way you did before. You can develop a very affectionate relationship with it, as I have, but you no longer ascribe any personal significance to the body as the seat of satisfaction. And there is no more question of resisting temptations or cravings; the question no longer applies. Temptations and cravings belong in one world; you now live in another.

असक्तिरनभिष्वङ्गः पुत्रदारगृहादिषु ।
नित्यं च समचित्तत्वमिष्टानिष्टोपपत्तिषु ॥ १३-९ ॥

*9. Free from selfish attachment, they do not get
compulsively wrapped up even in home and family.
They are even-minded through good fortune and bad.*

Now we come explicitly to personal relationships: the perfect context for learning detachment, and for reaping its benefits too.

Once I went up to a three-year-old friend and said politely, "Good morning, Laurie. How are you today?"

"You'd better keep away from me," she said. "I haven't had my nap."

In fact, I was especially nice to her that day. I complimented her on her hair, her dress, even her appetite. No wise man wants to provoke a three-year-old, you know. But everything I said only got a nod.

With three-year-olds you can give a certain margin for this kind of behavior, especially if you are playing the role of uncle. But for grownups to act this way is quite another matter. I can't imagine an adult saying, "I only got four hours of sleep last night, so don't say anything I don't like," or "I'm hungry now, so I can't possibly see anybody's point of view except my own. Talk to me after I've eaten." Yet that is how many of us behave, at least at times, though we seldom put it into words. Just the other day I read about certain political negotiations being conducted after a fine meal, on the grounds that wining and dining "makes for communication."

When you know you are not your mind but the person who operates it, you get a good deal of detachment from your moods. If your mind is having trouble, the problem is mechanical; it can be solved. If someone contradicts you, even if you haven't slept very well or have a little headache, you may experience some irritation, but that will not affect your attitude of love and respect for others. You can imagine the beneficial effect on your relationships!

Getting detached from emotional states is one aspect of learning that you are not your mind. Another aspect is learning that you are not your opinions either. This is detachment from another mental instrument: the so-called higher mind, *buddhi* in Sanskrit, which corresponds roughly to the intellect.

We live in such a pseudo-intellectual climate today that this kind of detachment is hard to achieve. Most of us identify ourselves completely with our opinions. Even on university campuses – perhaps especially on university campuses – I have met very few intellectuals who could look at their opinions with cool detachment and say when necessary, "Oh, no, this isn't so good. Let me throw it away." Usually, instead of "This isn't good," we say "This is mine. Therefore, how can I throw it away?" Look at the logic! When we actually discover that we are not the intellect – not merely believe, but actually experience it at a deep level of awareness – we can listen to opposing opinions with great interest and a quiet sense of security. If we find that someone else's opinion is better than ours, even if we have held onto ours for twenty-five years, we can say cheerfully, "Where's the waste basket? I'll throw out my opinion and keep yours."

In the latter stages of meditation we come to look on the mind as an instrument not unlike a vacuum cleaner: it makes a lot of noise, but it can do a good job. I saw one of our little boys using a vacuum cleaner the other day; he had managed somehow to attach the hose to the wrong end, and it was blowing dust and paper all over the place. That is how we usually use the mind, to blow our likes and dislikes over everyone who comes by. But properly used, the mind can suck up all this litter and remove it. That is meditation: using the mind to clean up the mind; or, more precisely, using the higher mind to clean up the lower mind.

From my personal experience, I can give a very effective technique for learning detachment from moods and opinions: work on reducing your likes and dislikes, not only in personal relationships but in everything. They may be very well rationalized, but virtually every pet like or dislike is the ego indulging in what it likes to consider creative self-expression.

The sānkhya account of how the mind works can throw light on this kind of ego-art. In Sanskrit the stuff of consciousness is called *chitta*. We can think of it as amorphous mind-clay – unbroken, undifferentiated, without shape, contour, or size. By our thinking, we make this clay into anything we perceive, anything we dream, anything we imagine: trees, birds, dolls, people, even mental states like anger, sympathy, or regret. But through constant repetition of the same compulsive thoughts, we make our chitta into a Madame Tussaud's wax museum. Everybody in our personal world is represented there in some detail, depending on how close they are to us: parents, partner, children, Aunt Josie, the office staff, even our dog. Interestingly enough, the Aunt Josie in chitta may have little to do with anybody outside. This is a figure we have made ourselves, the Aunt Josie that *we* see. When we quarrel with her, we go back into our museum and add a fang. "I make 'em the way I see 'em," the mind explains. Sri Krishna would shake his head. "No, you see them the way you have made them." Everything we perceive, everything we experience, is through these chitta-models of consciousness. They condition how we see life; therefore they govern how we respond.

When anger, fear, or greed molds this clay into rigid shapes, it is very difficult to break the mold. "I know my faults," people sometimes say pathetically. "I know I'm not easy to live with. But I can't change." Everybody can change; that is the miracle of meditation. All the rigid pots and pans of chitta that we have been throwing at people in consciousness can be reduced to fresh, pliable clay again. Then chitta is plastic and responsive. We can make new things, beautiful things – forgiveness, patience, goodwill, fearlessness, anything we choose. The skill is the same. But formerly it was destructive forces that shaped consciousness; now creative forces make forms that are beneficial, not only for us but for others too.

Most mental turmoil, in fact, can be traced to trivial likes and dislikes that have been magnified by self-will: put bluntly, "I want this and I can't have it" or "I don't like this and I can't get rid of it." We don't have to put up with this; that is the whole point of having what Sri Krishna calls an "even mind." We can learn to hold our likes and dislikes lightly, and when we do, most of the difficulties in personal relationships evaporate.

Try this with jobs and responsibilities – the nagging little things you have to do but just don't want to. It's a rare spirit that can say, "I loathe this job – so let me at it!" For most of us, the voice of self-will has only to say, "Listen, count me out of this one. I can't stand licking stamps, and besides, I don't want to work next to Mabel." We say obligingly, "All right, you're excused." Self-will grows fatter and bolder. Next time it doesn't bother with formalities. It just says, "*Mabel*. Remember?" We say, "Excused." And finally it grows arrogant and tells us point-blank, "Forget it!"

If we give in to self-will like this in every little like and dislike, we get rigid. When we find ourselves in a situation where we have to yield to the needs of others, self-will complains up and down the nervous system. "I can't yield! I'm made of one bone; I can't bend." At the outset the protest may be only in the mind, but the mind has channels; as they get deeper, they dig into the body. Self-willed people are subject to all kinds of emotional and physical problems like allergy and migraine. When their self-will is thwarted and they cannot freely express their likes and dislikes, their breathing gets irregular, blood pressure climbs, the pulse races, the immune system is depressed. As Dr. Hans Selye observes, "Stress leads to distress" – first in the mind; then, if we don't reverse it, in chronic physical ailments that make us miserable while they shorten our lives.

Fortunately, the distress of self-will can be completely avoided by reducing likes and dislikes. Whenever somebody benefits from it, go against your likes and dislikes, especially in relationships. If you dislike Mabel so intensely that you go in the other direction when you see her, make yourself look her in the eye; make yourself smile. After two or three tries, it won't even be forced. You are stretching your compulsions, beginning to make them looser, more elastic. It is painful, it is difficult, but the benefits are tremendous. Your nervous system becomes sound and resilient, your vitality and resistance immense. If things don't turn out as you expected, you won't get depressed or irritable; if everything goes your way, you won't lose your equilibrium. Your castle in the air may be blown to bits; if others benefit, you will not care; you may not even notice.

मयि चानन्ययोगेन भक्तिरव्यभिचारिणी ।
विविक्तदेशसेविबमरतिर्जनसंसदि ॥ १३-१० ॥
अध्यात्मज्ञाननित्यबं तचज्ञानार्थदर्शनम् ।
एतज्ज्ञानमिति प्रोक्तमज्ञानं यदतो ऽन्यथा ॥ १३-११ ॥

*10. Their devotion to me is undivided. Enjoying solitude
and not following the crowd, they seek only me.
11. This is true knowledge, to seek the Self as the
true end of wisdom always. To seek anything else
is ignorance.*

Like the preceding verses, these two describe both a means to detachment and its end.

Once we have realized experientially that the Lord dwells in us as our real Self, we see clearly that everything else in life is transitory. We are here on earth to serve; nothing can attract us again into any kind of selfish attachment. People sometimes ask me, "Don't you ever feel tempted?" I reply, "By what?" When you know in every cell that you have the source of joy within you, where is the temptation in a chocolate truffle? It is not that I do not enjoy truffles, but compared with the joy of Self-realization, even the most sublime sensory satisfaction cannot be taken seriously.

Of course, this is the fruit of samādhi. The path of sādhana itself is full of temptations, and though they become fewer as we progress, they also grow immensely more compelling as our desires become unified. Right from the outset, therefore, it is important to do everything we can to make Self-realization our primary goal. The transformation of personality is so difficult that to accomplish it we cannot afford to dedicate ourselves to other objectives and try to practice sādhana on the side.

This does not mean we should have no other activities. In Sanskrit the earth is called karmabhūmi, which has a double-edged meaning: karma is work, but karma is also karma. This earth is the world of work, and the world of work is the world of karma. Harmonious work with other people is a vital part of spiritual living. It is indispensable. If we do not live and work with other human beings who differ from us, how can we undo the karma of our previous difficulties and mistakes? If we don't participate in life, particularly when it gets challenging, how are we going to learn to face challenges with courage, patience, courtesy, and unfailing respect? All this is part of what it means to see the Lord in all, which is the purpose of our being here on earth.

In the early days, however, this often means a change in some of our familiar activities. Several old acquaintances will gradually fade from our circle. Someone once asked Somerset Maugham, "Should auld acquaintance be forgot?" Maugham replied drily, "Sometimes." To rebuild our lives, we have to change our associations and our ways of living. This is painful at first. But afterwards, when we return to our old friends, it will not be a case of the blind leading the blind; we will be a beacon in their lives.

In many parts of India, horse-drawn carriages are still a common sight. Usually the owner puts blinders on his horses, so they won't be distracted by sights around them on the busy streets. Spiritual aspirants have blinders too. One is detachment, not identifying with the body, senses, and mind. The other is discrimination, constantly reminding yourself of the supreme goal in the midst of every activity. Without a goal, drawn here and there by the attachments of the senses, we become like horses without blinders on a busy street, willing to go in any direction, confused by what we see and hear.

In this connection we should remember to be on our guard against the influence of mass movements, which can sweep even the most sincere men and women off their feet. We need to be extremely vigilant too about the influence of the media, not only in the early days of sādhana but all along. I cannot emphasize this too strongly; it is one of the obstacles that spiritual aspirants in earlier times and less technological cultures did not have to face. Most of us have very little idea how easily the words and images of television, film, and popular music drop into the depths of the mind. On a seed catalog the other day I saw a confident guarantee: "Our seeds *grow!*" Let me assure you, media seeds grow too, as you will verify for yourselves in the later stages of meditation, when you get into the unconscious and look around. By that time every media-weed will have to be removed, which is a monumental task.

I can illustrate sādhana with different kinds of trains, based on my experience in India. Most of us begin meditation as passenger trains. We set out from Madras Central Station, say, bound for the Himālayas, over two thousand miles away. But a passenger train has to stop at every little station along the way. People have to get down or climb aboard, and every station has vendors with tasty wares to sample before the train moves on again. Similarly, there are aspirants who like to settle all their affairs before taking to meditation. Once they get started, they have to get down at every station and explore its possibilities before they move ahead again. When the sun goes down at the end of the day they are still in some rural station, hundreds of miles from their goal. Finally it has grown dark, and they have run out of time. ·

Like the passenger train, this kind of aspirant *will* reach his destination someday. But such an approach requires many lifetimes. Even if we are on the track and moving forward resolutely, all of us have a long way to go. The latter stages of the journey are a steep, arduous climb. Under such conditions, the human being simply does not have enough fuel in one lifetime to explore every byway that presents itself and still make it to the goal. If we had a thousand years to live, there might be no harm in this. We could play game after game in life, doing all the little things that appeal to us, and still have time left for realizing the goal of life. But a hundred years would not be too long, and most of us have but a fraction of that time before vitality and resolution begin to wane. We do not have time to dally with wayside distractions. "The affairs of the world will go on forever," says the Tibetan mystic Milarepa. "Do not delay the practice of meditation."

By contrast, there is the express. When I was teaching in India, the Grand Trunk Express used to leave Madras Central in the morning and go straight to Nagpur, at the heart of the Indian subcontinent, almost a thousand miles away. It did stop, but only at a few of the most important junctions. Even in those days the passenger bound for Simla, on the lower slopes of the Himālayas, could take express connections from Madras Central and reach his destination in two or three days. That is the second kind of spiritual aspirant, which all of us can become. Such a person may have made a lot of mistakes. His home town may still be talking about the trouble he caused. But when he takes to meditation and puts all his heart into practicing spiritual disciplines, he goes like an arrow to the goal.

ज़ेयं यत्तत्प्रवक्ष्यामि यज्ज्ञात्वामृतमश्रुते ।
अनादिमत्परं ब्रह्म न सत्तन्नासदुच्यते ॥ १३-१२ ॥

12. I will tell you of the wisdom that leads to immortality: the beginningless Brahman, which can be called neither being nor nonbeing.

The whole point of spiritual wisdom is to go beyond death. It *is* possible. It can be done, and it has been done, by cutting the nexus of identification with the body.

"When a person dies," Nachiketa asks the King of Death in the Katha

Upanishad, "there arises one question." All of us must have asked this question at some time or other, when we have seen someone dying or been robbed of someone we loved: *Where did he go? Where did she go?* Nachiketa continues, "Some say he still exists somewhere. Others say, 'Absurd. He's just disappeared; there's an end to it.' Teach me the truth, O Lord of Death; I want to know for certain."

I have friends, three fellows, who live in a geodesic dome, an apt symbol of the earth. They go out to work every day, and in the evening they come back to their dome. Imagine if one evening they came home and decided never to leave again. Someone brings them groceries and collects the garbage, but they never see who; they take it for granted. And after a while, their memory of the city grows dim. They forget their cars, for they never drive. They forget that there are roads leading to farther cities full of other people. Eventually they forget even the fields and pine trees beyond their windows, they become so preoccupied with the things inside: their books and records and old *National Geographics*, faded photographs and clippings from the newspaper, the patterns made by the stains from leaky plumbing, the drama of spiders on the ceiling. If you could ask them questions about San Francisco, they would shake their heads; the city would seem like something from a dream. "I don't know," they would answer. "I don't remember." After some years they would say in bemusement, "I doubt if it exists." Finally they would conclude, "It does *not* exist. San Francisco is unreal. What is the evidence that there is an outside world at all?"

How have we forgotten where we came from, "trailing clouds of glory"? How have we forgotten we are all one, come from the same divine source, to whom we shall return? We have simply become preoccupied. Over a long, long period of dwelling on ourselves, thinking only about our own private pursuits and basking in our separateness, we don't remember any of this; worse, we deny it. Those who subscribe to the biological school of thinking answer Nachiketa's question with, "It's over. When a person dies, that's the end." The King of Death says simply, "Not at all." When my friends ask what is the evidence for an outside world, I might reply, "Just open the door! Go outside, look around for yourselves, and tell me what you see." It is no answer for them to object,

"I don't want to open the door. Why should I? There's nothing there." If they do go out, they rediscover the world. If, through meditation, we step outside our egocentric personality, we rediscover who we are: part of the eternal, immortal Reality that we call God.

सर्वतः पाणिपादं तत्सर्वतोऽक्षिशिरोमुखम् ।
सर्वतःश्रुतिमल्लोके सर्वमावृत्य तिष्ठति ॥ १३-१३ ॥
सर्वेन्द्रियगुणाभासं सर्वेन्द्रियविवर्जितम् ।
असक्तं सर्वभृच्चैव निर्गुणं गुणभोक्तृ च ॥ १३-१४ ॥
बहिरन्तश्च भूतानामचरं चरमेव च ।
सूक्ष्मत्वात्तदविज्ञेयं दूरस्थं चान्तिके च तत् ॥ १३-१५ ॥

13. It dwells in all, in every hand and foot and head,
in every mouth and eye and ear in the universe.
14. Without senses itself, it shines through
the functioning of the senses. Completely
independent, it supports all things. Beyond
the gunas, it enjoys their play.
15. It is both near and far, both within and
without every creature; it moves and is unmoving.
In its subtlety it is beyond comprehension.

Our two dogs sit outside my door every morning, waiting to see me and to have their breakfast snack. When I come out after my morning meditation, I don't just see dogs; I see the Lord wearing two rather curious costumes. This is the best I can do to put the experience into words, but it is not metaphor; that is what I actually see. When I watch them playing with a stick, I see Sri Krishna playing – a small part of the eternal game that Sanskrit calls *līlā*, the play of life. The whole of creation is this divine game, in which the Lord plays all the roles: our dogs chasing sticks, the children who throw them; our neighbors, each with their different goals; the lilac outside my window that explodes in bloom every spring. "Look around," the mystics say. "The world is full of God."

In this vision you can see life struggling upward in evolution, like a plant reaching toward light. The field of the created world is full of these sunflower-creatures, all growing toward God. Our dog Muka, when he sees me after meditation, actually tries to talk to me in human sounds; one of them almost sounds like *Om*. To me he is saying, "I want so much to be human!" He wants to be like us, and if we meditate, he wants to learn to do so too. That is the force that drives evolution, reaching up through Muka for the goal. With that kind of unified desire, I like to think, he *will* manage to be born into an āshram as a human being the next time around. The whole of life is moving like this toward the source from which it sprang.

It is impossible to have this vision except through the grace of the Lord. As Sri Ramakrishna puts it, the Divine Mother must say, "Let Brian have this vision." She gives him a sidelong glance from those beautiful eyes and touches a desire deep, deep in his heart, deeper than all worldly desires. In the heart of every one of us this desire is lying latent, a seed of divinity waiting for its spring. After that, even if Brian tries to cling to selfish pursuits or to hold himself back in any way, her power will draw him forward – sometimes by deepening desire, sometimes by the heightened suffering that comes when you happen to forget your overriding goal. Every person who has attained the supreme vision will attest to the power of this grace, which will come to everyone who longs for it with an undivided heart and mind.

अविभक्तं च भूतेषु विभक्तमिव च स्थितम् ।
भूतभर्तृ च तज्ज्ञेयं ग्रसिष्णु प्रभविष्णु च ॥ १३-१६ ॥
ज्योतिषामपि तज्ज्योतिस्तमसः परमुच्यते ।
ज्ञानं ज्ञेयं ज्ञानगम्यं हृदि सर्वस्य विष्ठितम् ॥ १३-१७ ॥

16. *It is indivisible, yet appears divided in
separate creatures. It is to be known as the
creator, the preserver, and the destroyer.*
17. *Dwelling in every heart, it is beyond darkness.
It is called the light of lights, the object and
goal of knowledge, and knowledge itself.*

Again and again the Gita tells us that the Self is light, the very source of light. This is not merely metaphor, as can be experienced in the deeper stages of meditation. But until that experience, these words are very difficult to understand.

The Buddha might explain by saying that until we realize the Self, we *are* living in darkness, actually dreaming that we are the body. This is good scientific language. Even physiologically, there is much less difference than we like to think between the dream experience in sleep and the Māyā-dream we experience while we are awake. The Buddha would go so far as to say that most of us pass through life like sleepwalkers – coming and going on cue, reading our lines, yet no more aware of our actions than someone in a dream.

"Preposterous!" we want to say. "Don't I see? Don't I hear? The sun is shining, the birds are singing, the neighbors are quarreling downstairs; I'm not aware of any of these things while I'm asleep." But might not a sleeper say the same? After all, we see and hear not with our eyes and ears but with our mind. As long as we are asleep, the things we see and hear in dreams *are* real. Watch a dog dreaming: you can see its ears move and its nose twitch, and you know he is seeing and smelling – sensing a dream cat, made out of mind-stuff and memories, while his body slumbers. Our dog Muka runs on the beach in his sleep; you can see his paws trying to trot. Similarly, when you dream that something is attacking you, your heart races and adrenaline surges in your body just as if the attack were real.

"All right," we say, "but look at the sequence of events in dreams. One minute you're on a train in Canada at the age of five; the next minute you're paddling around in the Dead Sea wearing a fez. There's no logic in a dream world. You don't have any control over what happens."

But is our waking world so rational? One minute you're talking amiably with a friend; the next minute, for no reason you can follow, she says something unimportant and you explode. You find yourself being kind to people in the office and short-tempered with those you love. All of us are familiar with this kind of bewildering behavior in ourselves, and to someone who is truly awake – say, the Compassionate Buddha – it looks no more logical than a dream. In both waking and dreaming, we experience with the same mind through the same conditioning. Our waking responses are not always more rational than our dream responses; they are simply better disguised by the conscious mind.

To be able to say we are awake, the Buddha would say, we must be able to turn our attention freely, at will, wherever we choose. It is as simple as that; yet nothing in the world is more difficult to do.

Imagine that you are seated in your room, trying to concentrate on the report you have to present in tomorrow's meeting, when some word reminds you of college days. In a moment you have left your study. Your eyes do not see the pictures on the wall; your ears do not hear the noise on the street. You are back in Berkeley, wandering at midnight on Telegraph Avenue, recapturing dubious memories. This happens to all of us, much more often than we realize. Most of us can come back again with some effort, though usually only after the mind has finished exploring – in other words, when the mind gives us its permission. But some people actually lose the ability to come back. They keep wandering off to the same place in their mind so long that for practical purposes they actually live in the past. Their thoughts claim them; their memories oppress them. Such people *are* asleep, the Buddha would say. They are dreaming.

I have chosen an extreme example, but this is what a wandering mind means. When your mind is wandering from subject to subject, from memory to memory, from desire to desire, you say, "This is rational thinking. Continuous thought." "You are asleep," the Buddha would correct, "and you are having a series of dreams. The main difference with ordinary nighttime dreaming is that you can articulate some thoughts and make certain automatic responses." These are not trivial differences, but they are differences of degree, not of kind. To say you are awake – the literal meaning of the word *buddha* – you have to be able to put the car of your mind in one lane and drive it straight to where you want to go, without weaving in and out of anybody else's lane.

The consequences of this are enormous. If you are driving in only one lane, no anger can come to you. To get angry, your mind has to change lanes. To get greedy or jealous, your mind has to change lanes. This is a very compassionate view of human nature. If someone makes a mistake in a dream, who will hold it against him? It was a dream mistake, made with dream people: creations of the mind. Similarly, isn't it rather unfair to condemn people who do not have control over their thinking process? Isn't it rather unloving to condemn them? They have never learned to drive.

Quite a few people, though they admired and respected me, used to get terribly upset by the idea that we are living in our sleep once they saw the personal implications. "You sit laughing with the rest of us," one good friend told me, "and then suddenly you say something like this. It goes into my heart like an arrow and comes out on the other side."

Mostly this was in reference to sex, which is where many human beings naturally have their greatest vested interest in body-consciousness. "This is the highest summit of reality for me," this friend told me candidly. "If sexual experience isn't real, what is?"

I could tell from the way he was looking at me that he was expecting one of those arrows. So I just asked a simple question. "Do you have sexual dreams?"

"Of course."

"Do you experience pleasure in them?"

"Of course."

"Do you remember the experience afterwards?"

I did not have to say anything more; the arrow had gone in. For a thoughtful person, this observation is enough to prompt reflection on the permanence and validity of sensory experience. Later I came across a quotation from Havelock Ellis, the psychologist who spent so much of his life studying human sexuality. "Dreams are real as long as they last," he said. "Can we say more of life?"

Even when the body is sleeping, all of us experience dreams that are very similar to the experiences of waking life, complete with sensory content and even physiological reactions. This has profound significance. Even if physical consciousness is absent, mental activity continues and our identity remains intact, showing that body-consciousness is not a necessary criterion of life.

The Gita is not saying that life on the physical level is unreal. It says simply that the waking state is not the highest level of reality. Just because you are making a bit of money and have had a couple of meals, you cannot say you are awake. All too often this is a kind of automatic activity on a relative level of reality, very much like dreams.

At this level, all sense experience has a kind of magnetic attraction.

The moment the senses pull, we follow. In dreams, we know, we have very little say in what happens; we speak and act out of some kind of hidden compulsion. More often than not, we do the same during the day, with one important difference: in the waking state, if we can but exercise it, we do have a choice. Once we begin to exercise this choice by resisting the compulsive pull of the senses, we begin to wake up. I wish I could convey the joy that comes about then! You will be awake every moment, able to yield to a sensory desire when you approve of it and to say no to it effortlessly when you do not.

In the early days of meditation this is not at all effortless; often you will have to draw on the will to say no, and the mind will scarcely let you hear the end of it. But in the end this becomes as natural as walking or breathing. "My hand obeys me instantly," St. Augustine complained. "Why doesn't my mind?" Just as we train our hands to reach and hold through a million acts of self-control, usually when we are toddlers, we can train the mind to obey us gracefully and agreeably. This freedom defines the waking state. All that we lose by waking up is bondage.

इति क्षेत्रं तथा ज्ञानं ज्ञेयं चोक्तं समासतः ।
मद्भक्त एतद्विज्ञाय मद्भावायोपपद्यते ॥ १३-१८॥
प्रकृतिं पुरुषं चैव विद्ध्यनादी उभावपि ।
विकारांश्च गुणांश्चैव विद्धि प्रकृतिसंभवान् ॥ १३-१९॥

18. I have revealed to you the nature of the field and the meaning and object of true knowledge. Those who are devoted to me, realizing these, are united with me.
19. Know that prakriti and Purusha are both without beginning, and that from prakriti come the gunas and all that changes.

Three terms are introduced here that are basic in sānkhya philosophy. *Prakriti* is the field in its largest sense: energy, matter, and mind. The physical universe can be derived from energy, though strictly speaking we never encounter this energy as such. Similarly, sānkhya derives not only matter but the components of the mind from a kind of primordial energy-stuff, which is not knowable by the senses but is the substance of all the objects and events we experience. In my earlier account of the twenty-four "cosmic principles" of the field, prakriti is the first principle, the original undifferentiated stuff from which the perceptible universe evolved.

Purusha, which literally means 'person,' is the Knower of the field. Everything that can be an object of knowledge is prakriti; Purusha is the only knower. It is the Ātman, the Self.

Guna, the third term, has a very important place in this volume. According to sānkhya, the evolution of consciousness begins when prakriti differentiates itself into three basic states or qualities of energy. These are the gunas. Every state of matter and mind is a combination of these three: *tamas,* inertia, *rajas,* activity, and *sattva,* harmony or equilibrium. These are only rough translations, for the gunas have no equivalent in any other philosophy I know.

In high school we learned about three states of matter: solid, liquid, and gas. The gunas can be presented similarly. Tamas is frozen energy, the resistance of inertia. A block of ice has a good deal of energy in the chemical bonds that hold it together, but the energy is locked up, bound up, rigid. When the ice melts, some of that energy is released as the water flows; rajas, activity, predominates. We know what power a swollen river has; that is an expression of rajas. And sattva can be compared with steam when its power is harnessed.

Alternatively, in terms of the mind, we can think of the gunas as different levels of consciousness – say, from basement to upper story. Tamas, the lowest, is the vast unconscious. Most basements I have seen are piled with belongings: furniture, boxes, appliances, old books and magazines, and an incredible variety of odds and ends. The unconscious is like that: chaos, a dumping ground for eons of accumulated mental states. There is great power in the unconscious, but it is covered up and inaccessible to the will.

Rajas is the ground floor, the ordinary mind that races along desiring, worrying, resenting, scheming, competing, frustrating and getting frustrated. Rajas is power released, but uncontrolled and egocentric.

Sattva, finally, is the so-called higher mind – detached, unruffled, self-controlled. This is not a state of repressive regulation, but the natural harmony that comes with unity of purpose, character, and desire. Negative states of mind do still come up, but you do not have to act on them.

This forms the basis of the most compassionate account of human nature I have come across in any philosophy or psychology, East or West. It not only describes differences in character; it tells what the forces of personality are, so we can reshape ourselves after a higher ideal.

The rest of this volume will develop this theory, beginning with the next chapter; but I can give a preview here. In its natural state, consciousness is a continuous flow of awareness. But through the distorting action of the gunas, we have fallen from this native state into fragmented, divided, sometimes stagnant awareness. In this sense we can think of the gunas as spectacles, trifocals, through which we look at life. They are fragmented, so we see things as separate wherever we look: separate selves, antagonistic interests, conflicts within ourselves.

Evolution, according to the Gita, is a painfully slow return to our native state: pure, unbroken awareness. First we have to transform tamas into rajas – apathy and insensitiveness into energetic, enthusiastic activity. But the energy of rajas is self-centered and dispersed. It must be transformed into sattva, so that all this passionate energy is channeled into selfless action. There is great happiness in this state, which is marked by a calm mind, abundant vitality, and the concentration of genius. But even this is not the end. As long as we are wearing these spectacles of the mind, we cannot help seeing ourselves and the rest of life as fragments. The goal of evolution and of meditation is to take these spectacles off in samādhi: that is, to still the mind. Then we rest in pure, unitary consciousness, which is a state of permanent joy. Those who go beyond the gunas see no separateness anywhere; they see themselves reflected in everybody, and everybody reflected in themselves. This is seeing life as it is, indivisible and whole.

I think it is Ruysbroeck who says that we behold what we are, and we are what we behold. We see through the glasses of the mind. When you are divided, you cannot help seeing everybody as separate. When you are whole, you see the same divinity in your heart and the heart of every other creature.

कार्यकारणकर्तृबे हेतुः प्रकृतिरुच्यते ।
पुरुषः सुखदुःखानां भोक्तृबे हेतुरुच्यते ॥१३-२०॥
पुरुषः प्रकृतिस्थो हि भुङ्क्ते प्रकृतिजान्गुणान् ।
कारणं गुणसङ्गो ऽस्य सदसद्योनिजन्मसु ॥१३-२१॥

20. Prakriti is said to be the agent, instrument,
and effect of every action, but it is Purusha
that experiences pleasure and pain.
21. Purusha, resting in prakriti, enjoys the play of
the gunas born of prakriti. But attachment to the
gunas leads Purusha to be born for good or evil.

These are very difficult concepts to understand, because we identify so thoroughly with the field of matter and the mind. The Gita reminds us over and over that actions occur only within the field; thoughts take place only in the field; they interact and have consequences only in the field. Yet the field itself is inert. There is no consciousness in this field of matter and mind, which means that the mind does not really enjoy anything of itself; the intellect cannot really analyze; the senses cannot experience. Only the Self, pure consciousness, the same in all, can be said to see, enjoy, and understand.

All this is just philosophy until you begin to see the practical consequences, which are really shattering; they can turn our world upside down. To take one illustration, a good friend gave us a can of maple syrup this Christmas and our children have been making good use of it. I was watching them enjoy it with pancakes the other morning and reflecting on this nearly universal appeal of sugar. How many people, I wondered, would understand if I said that sugar is not *pleasant*; it is simply *sweet*? The words are clear, but the meaning is so deep to grasp. Pleasure is not pleasant. It is "apleasant": neither pleasant nor unpleasant, simply a sensation.

You can see this in many everyday experiences, but even if you make the observation, it is terribly difficult to generalize it and draw practical conclusions. Many experiences in sports, for example, I would find terribly unpleasant; yet a participant may enjoy them. I can think of few things less pleasant than bouncing along on the back of a horse, yet if I were to say that in riding circles, people would scarcely know what I mean. The sensations are the same, but the interpretations are worlds apart. I say, "Horseback riding is unpleasant." They say, "Oh, no, it is very pleasant!" Neither is right; it is apleasant.

It is the same with food. I know people who enjoy strong, bitter coffee. Millions find beer pleasant; millions would say the same about whiskey, which is even more bitter and burns all the way down. Indian gourmets like spices so hot that if you are not used to them, you feel that your mouth is on fire. And so on; we are all familiar with such differences. But we do not draw the conclusion: that the liking or disliking lies entirely in the mind.

Now take it one step further: an emotional experience is neither pleasant nor unpleasant. It is just an emotional experience, simply a mental state. You can watch it take place and then shake it off; the memory will remain without any emotional surcharge, which means that nothing can trigger that memory later and cause it to explode into words or action. This is what detachment means.

Incidentally, my friends – particularly parents – sometimes ask me how children get this kind of conditioning about food. Actually, a certain amount of this kind of experience seems to be necessary in life. That is why I don't object to children having sweets within reason now and then, so long as they get plenty of good-tasting, nutritious food at meals and so long as taste is not presented as an end in itself. As far as I can remember, I enjoyed my food as a child primarily because it was prepared by people I loved deeply. Tastes are learned, and there is no motivation like love.

In this connection, I don't think I have ever met anyone so free from the conditioning of the palate as my mother. Granny, you know, enjoyed good food. She never thought about it until it was time for her to eat, and while she was eating, it got her full attention. But to my mother, food really was apleasant. She was neither for it nor against it; eating was simply something one did, like washing dishes. This is a very rare capacity, which I am glad to say I did not inherit; I take after Granny. But my mother's detachment played a part in my spiritual education too.

She was an excellent cook. She used to prepare delicacies for me and then sit by my side in the Indian manner while I ate them, and I could never understand why she didn't feel any desire for them at all. What she enjoyed was my enjoyment. This, I am pleased to say, is a capacity I did acquire. Today, after long years of practice in detachment, I don't have any palate cravings, which means I can enjoy good food much more than any gourmet. Even when I take teenage friends out for ice cream or chocolate cake, I enjoy it more than they do; my enjoyment is multiplied by theirs, which I literally share.

उपद्रष्टानुमन्ता च भर्ता भोक्ता महेश्वरः ।
परमात्मेति चाप्युक्तो देहे ऽस्मिन्पुरुषः परः ॥ १३-२२ ॥
य एवं वेत्ति पुरुषं प्रकृतिं च गुणैः सह ।
सर्वथा वर्तमानो ऽपि न स भूयो ऽभिजायते ॥ १३-२३ ॥

22. Within the body the supreme Purusha
is called the witness, approver, supporter,
enjoyer, the supreme Lord, the highest Self.
23. Whoever realizes the true nature of Purusha,
prakriti, and the gunas, whatever path he or
she may follow, is not born separate again.

When I was on my way to this country via Europe over twenty years ago, I remember with what great interest I stood at the railing of our P&O vessel as it rounded the Arabian peninsula and entered the Gulf of Aden. I had many Muslim friends in India, several of whom were scholars and poets steeped in Arabic and Persian literature. From them I had intimate exposure to Muslim culture. All this made it a very personal experience for me to see the barren deserts of Arabia rise ahead of us and to reflect on their legacy to India and the world.

Most of all I remember the long passage through the Red Sea. I had never thought of it as being so large; I had thought we might pass through in a day and night at most, yet it took three. The air was warm and humid, and the waters unruffled by any breeze. The passengers were so wrung out by the heat and humidity that the ship soon seemed deserted above decks. I thought of myself as the Ancient Mariner, "alone on a painted sea." It was much too stuffy to sleep in our cramped, crowded cabin. When the purser wasn't looking, I took my bedding out on deck and watched for hours with quiet fascination while the mountains slipped by beneath the stars.

One night, I remember, I suddenly caught sight of pillars of fire rising against the dark shapes of the Arabian peninsula – an alarming, awesome sight, as if the land were licking the sky with tongues of flame. Was that the way the Prophet describes hell? Had Armageddon come?

A sailor laughed. "No," he said, "it's just the refineries."

When you know you are the Self, in a sense you pass through the turmoil of life with the same sense of detachment I remember from those nights on deck, watching deserts and refineries slip by without a sound. An unknown medieval German mystic wrote, "Nothing burns in hell except self-will." There is the desert of alienation, the flames of suffering and sorrow; yet you know you are not the refineries; you are not on fire yourself. You watch in peace. Life is not an empty illusion then, but full of meaning. Even when you pass through sorrow, you know that there is an eternal backdrop to all tragedy, an end to sorrow, and you get unending joy in knowing how to help and relieve the suffering of those who suffer around you. In the midst of activity, your heart and mind remain at peace.

Part of this peace comes because the vast burden of the past slips from your shoulders entirely, the way the mountains of the Arabian shore slipped by and disappeared: they were real, yet no more real to me than shadows. When we believe we are the body, separate from everybody else, all of us make mistakes. We can cause a lot of trouble to ourselves and others just because of the way we see. But when we see clearly who we are, all these mistakes no longer burden us. They belong to someone else, someone in the past, and the past is gone. People sometimes asked Mahatma Gandhi why he did a particular thing or said a particular thing when he was, say, twenty-two. Gandhi would reply simply, "That is how I saw life then. I see more clearly now."

Once you attain the Self, the scriptures say, you are not born again as a separate creature. This is not an easy statement to understand. In one school of Hindu and Buddhist thought, it is taken literally: you are not born again, full stop; you are out of the game. I am glad to say that I belong to the other school, in which I have good reason to believe. According to this view, though not born again as a separate personality entangled in the net of life, the man or woman who attains Self-realization may return to life again and again in order to help others and alleviate their sorrow.

Even having this perspective can help immensely in facing death, which is not an end but an open door. When I was a boy, I remember my granny once called me to the shed where one of our cows was dying. The cow raised her head a little to gaze at me, and I saw in her eyes the same fear, the same uncertainty, that I had seen in the eyes of relatives lying and waiting for death to come. They seemed to say, *What is happening? What comes next – or is everything over at last?* When you remove that uncertainty – not at a superficial level, but in the depths of the mind – the fear of death is gone. In every tradition the great mystics tell us quietly, "We are not afraid of death. We *know*."

When you go to sleep, you know that you will wake up. If you did not know, you would be terrified. That is the Buddha's approach. He would simply ask us, "Didn't you go to sleep last night? When you woke up, was it the same you? While you were asleep, wasn't there a period when you weren't aware of yourself as a separate individual?" It is the same with death, if we could only see. The body dies, being made of matter, but the Self can pass through this great change as quietly as my P&O vessel passed through the Red Sea.

I have had the privilege of being with many people at their hour of death, sitting by their side, holding their hand and repeating my mantram, helping them to understand that death is not the end but a chance to rest before a fresh beginning. One man several years ago responded as sweetly as a little girl. The others who were with him had gone out, but I remained for a few more minutes. "Is there any personal question you'd like to ask me?" I asked.

"Yes," he smiled. "Only one: after I shed this body, will I see you again?"

I just said, "That depends on you. If you deeply desire that we not be separated, sure, we *will* be together again."

When you love your teacher deeply, the scriptures say, that love becomes a bond that death cannot sever. And in the bodhisattva tradition, those who attain Self-realization love all of creation so deeply that they return to this life again and again to alleviate sorrow and help the rest of us realize the goal of life. "As long as a single creature is suffering," the Buddha said, "I shall not make the final crossing into nirvāna."

ध्यानेनात्मनि पश्यन्ति के चिदात्मानमात्मना ।
अन्ये सांख्येन योगेन कर्मयोगेन चापरे ॥ १३-२४ ॥
अन्ये वेवमजानन्तः श्रुबान्येभ्य उपासते ।
ते ऽपि चातितरन्त्येव मृत्युं श्रुतिपरायणाः ॥ १३-२५ ॥

24. Some realize the Self within them through
the practice of meditation, some by the path
of wisdom, and others by selfless service.
25. Others may not know these paths; but
hearing and following the instructions of an
illumined teacher, they too go beyond death.

In the Hindu tradition, there are four kinds of yoga or ways to God: *jnāna yoga,* the path of wisdom, *karma yoga,* the path of selfless service, *rāja yoga,* the path of meditation, and *bhakti yoga,* the way of love. If you look at the lives of those in India who have realized the Lord, you will generally find that they emphasize one of these aspects of sādhana over the others, according to their temperament and the needs of the times. But you will also see that none of these excludes the others, and that all have an important place in sādhana.

A luminous representative of jnāna yoga in recent times is Sri Ramana Maharshi, one of the most outstanding spiritual figures of any age, who lived in relative obscurity in South India until the nineteen-fifties. For karma yoga, the path of selfless service, you could not ask for a better example than Mahatma Gandhi. And for bhakti yoga, the way of love so well represented in the Christian tradition, I always draw on the life of Sri Ramakrishna, a perfect lover of God. But for those who consider these three yogas as watertight compartments, I like to point to a fourth shining example, my own spiritual teacher. Granny was not at all intellectual. If someone had tried to convince her that she could have her choice of wisdom, love, or selfless service, but not all three together, she would have found the idea absurd. Wisdom and service flow naturally from love, and all three are released through meditation and its allied disciplines. So where Gandhi says, for example, that the Gita is a manual for karma yoga, selfless action, I would add without contradiction that it is equally a manual for the way of love as embodied by my granny. As Sri Aurobindo says, all life is yoga. All the paths mentioned in the Gita are blended when we base our lives on meditation and work hard in loving, selfless activity during the day.

The word *yoga* itself contains the clue to this. Patanjali gives us the essence of it in a famous definition: "Yoga means stilling all waves of thought in the mind." By this definition, any set of disciplines that stills the mind is yoga, and this excludes some activities that are called yoga and includes spiritual disciplines from other, non-Indian traditions. What the Gita calls yoga is central to mystical experience everywhere.

यावत्संजायते किं चित्सचं स्थावरजङ्गमम् ।
क्षेत्रक्षेत्रज्ञसंयोगात्तद्विद्धि भरतर्षभ ॥ १३-२६ ॥

26. Whatever exists, Arjuna, animate or inanimate, is born through the union of the field and its Knower.

Hinduism represents the Godhead and its creative power as Shiva and Shakti. Shiva, the eternal masculine principle, is always united with Shakti, the eternal feminine. *Shakti* literally means power, strength, energy; in this unique tradition, strength is represented as a woman. Shiva is the changeless, Shakti the dynamic. Thus Shakti is prakriti – the whole field of creation, both mind and matter, and the forces by which it is shaped. Every woman embodies Shakti, which means that in spiritual terms the woman can make a much more important contribution to the world than can the man. One selfless woman can enable everyone around her to grow. On the other hand, an insecure and self-willed woman can impede everyone else's growth; so this is an awesome responsibility. Following my granny, I treat every woman with great love and respect because this is her potential; this tremendous power is what every woman represents.

For creation to take place, according to this tradition, Shiva and Shakti have to unite. From this union the world and all beings are born. Kālidasā, whom I would call one of the greatest poets and dramatists in the world, begins his epic *Raghuvamsha* with an invocation to Shiva and Shakti: "I meditate on the parents of the world, who are united like a word and its meaning." You cannot separate a word from its meaning; it would no longer be a word. Similarly, the world makes no sense apart from God, who is Mother and Father in one.

समं सर्वेषु भूतेषु तिष्ठन्तं परमेश्वरम् ।
विनश्यत्स्वविनश्यन्तं यः पश्यति स पश्यति ॥१३-२७॥
समं पश्यन्हि सर्वत्र समवस्थितमीश्वरम् ।
न हिनस्त्यात्मनात्मानं ततो याति परां गतिम् ॥१३-२८॥

27. He alone sees truly who sees the Lord
the same in every creature, who sees the
Deathless in the hearts of all that die.
28. Seeing the same Lord everywhere, he does not harm
himself or others. Thus he attains the supreme goal.

I remember a film in which there was a violent forest fire. Where it spread across the meadow, each blade of grass seemed to be made of flame; when the fire reached the woods, it leaped up to take the shape of trees. Each branch seemed to consist not of wood but of flame. While the trees stood, each tree of fire stood; when a tree fell, you saw a tree of fire lying on the ground, its branches glowing orange and gold.

Fire neither stands nor lies, of course; it takes the shape of the object it consumes. The Self does the same. The Katha Upanishad says,

As the same fire assumes different shapes
When it consumes objects differing in shape,
The one Self takes the shape of every creature
In whom it is present.
As the same air assumes different shapes
When it enters objects differing in shape,
The one Self takes the shape of every creature
In whom it is present.

This is not merely philosophy. I remember reading some comments by Jean Mayer, one of the world's foremost nutritionists, written after he attended the World Food Conference of 1974 in Rome. I respect his observations greatly, not merely because he knows his field but because his concern gives him wide, sympathetic vision. While the representative from Bangladesh was speaking to the conference about the imminent threat of starvation in his country, Dr. Mayer remarked, very few people were present in the hall. Most of the delegates were at a cocktail party, drinking alcohol made from grain – that is, from food. By his calculations, the quantity of grain converted to alcoholic beverages might have fed twenty million people. And he asked, Who at this conference on world hunger even saw the connection?

People sometimes object, "What does it matter? The alcohol has been made; why shouldn't we drink it?" The answer is that if we do not drink it, it will not be made. We have a choice, Dr. Mayer points out: there is a connection between a habit which benefits no one (except, of course, the industry) and the hunger of millions.

The intellect can see this, but it is the heart that enables the intellect to understand and empowers the will to act. A sensitive person, after grasping this connection, will not be able to lift a highball without seeing the eyes of a hungry child over the rim of the glass.

There is another common objection: "Even if I do give up drinking, so what? They're not going to give the grain I save to the poor. They'll make gasohol with it, or burn it to keep prices up, or fatten animals in feedlots with it." In the short run, there is truth to these objections; withdrawing our personal support of a particular industry is only the beginning. But withdrawing support is essential. The Gita is talking about a whole view. We have choices everywhere; one by one, we need to open them.

This is not a matter of the intellect, though a clear intellect can help. It comes from a change in consciousness, in which we gradually learn to see the Lord in all and to act and live accordingly.

Dr. Mayer observed that at that time the nations of the world, including many developing nations facing starvation, were spending almost a billion dollars every day on armaments. (In the 1990s the figure has been running almost two and a half billion dollars a day.) If a fraction of that money could be rechanneled into the development of local resources for self-sufficiency, the world food problem could be completely solved.

Look only at the arms industry; you will see what incredible things can be achieved in a few decades when some of the best talent in science and engineering and finance concentrates on a single area. If the same energy and imagination were brought to bear on getting food to those who need it, not only in the poorer countries but in countries like the United States too, starvation could be eradicated from the globe within a generation. It is not that the problems are so large, but that people's interests, self-interests, and attention are drawn to other things.

In an article contributed to the *Encyclopaedia Britannica Book of the Year for 1975*, Prime Minister of India Indira Gandhi wrote:

> No country can afford to take a narrow view of its own interests, since it has to live in a world that is closely interlinked. The richer regions cannot abdicate their concern. Prosperity for some cannot be enjoyed in the midst of poverty for most. It is not military confrontation alone that imperils world peace; disparity is an equal danger.

And she concludes: "The quest for an egalitarian society is not merely humanitarian. It is a practical necessity if the world order is to survive. . . . Unless the minds of people are remolded, infused with comprehension of and compassion for the suffering of the many, progress itself will be unreal."

Again, this is not rhetoric. The United States is the wealthiest nation the world has seen; yet programs and support for children, for the poor, and for social problems are being cut while weapons spending and the public debt soar. Literally millions of children and old people now live in such poverty that they do not get enough to eat. I wish I were exaggerating, but the reality is even more tragic than I care to paint it. All this is because we do not put people first, but greed. Not only the poor but the middle class too are beginning to pay the price of a material kind of "progress" that ignores the welfare of individuals.

A few months after that World Food Conference, a perceptive piece by James Reston appeared in the *New York Times*. He too was pointing out that times are changing fast for people in the developing countries, who are no longer likely to sit quiet and watch in resignation while developed countries maintain a standard of living that is excessive and wasteful, which exploits the raw materials and cheap labor of the poor. We have entered an era of international terrorism, Reston says, when even a small group can lay hands on nuclear materials and hold a nation to ransom or precipitate a war. By the end of this century, if trends continue, enough fissionable material will be in transport at any given time to make twenty thousand nuclear bombs. "The truth," as Fred C. Icklé said, "is that we are basically defenseless" – not only against this sensitive situation, but against an organized nuclear attack. All this massive expenditure on deterrents and detection systems has essentially come to nothing – except, of course, that it has left us more vulnerable to attack by enemies whom we should never have made our enemies in the first place. The law of compassion and unity cannot be violated without consequences.

There is only one basis on which we can live together, and that is to trust one another, considering the needs of the whole planet and subjecting ourselves cheerfully to small deprivations when necessary to serve those needs. This is not at all a negative note. Very little has been done along these lines. Very little has been done to make people understand that there is great joy in living like this, using all our personal resources in concerted, dedicated action to banish the threat of the suicide of the earth.

प्रकृत्यैव च कर्माणि क्रियमाणानि सर्वशः ।
यः पश्यति तथात्मानमकर्तारं स पश्यति ॥१३-२९॥
यदा भूतपृथग्भावमेकस्थमनुपश्यति ।
तत एव च विस्तारं ब्रह्म संपद्यते तदा ॥१३-३०॥

29. They alone see truly who see that all actions are
performed by prakriti, while the Self remains unmoved.
30. When they see the variety of creation rooted in
that unity and growing out of it, they attain
fulfillment in Brahman.

When I was a boy I remember being fascinated by the novels of Alexander Dumas the younger, particularly *The Man in the Iron Mask*. So far as I know, it has never been decided for certain who the real man in the iron mask was. History simply records a poor chap who was held as a state prisoner by Louis XIV for over forty years and finally died in the Bastille, his identity still a mystery. But Dumas' theory made a great story: the mysterious stranger is King Louis' twin brother, involved in a plot to impersonate and imprison the king himself.

This makes a good allegory too. Each of us, the Gita would say, goes through life in an iron mask, riveted on so securely that over the years – or, from the Hindu and Buddhist perspective, over many, many lives – we forget we have a face. We think the mask is who we are, and of course so does everybody else. But beneath this mask is the king, our real Self.

This mask is our separate personality, and what makes it interesting is that it is not material. To be more accurate, Hindu psychology might say we are wearing two masks, one inside the other and fitted to it perfectly. The outer mask is the physical body; the inner is called in Sanskrit *sūkshmasharīra*, the 'subtle body' – that is, the mind, intellect, and ego. Both are made of prakriti, created out of our obsessive identification with the body and mind. The wearer is Purusha, the Self.

Between these two masks there is a quiet correspondence, which has many ramifications for physical health. Put simply, the body can be said to mirror or materialize the more rigid conditions of personality. In many cases, disease processes in the body may be said to correspond to and develop out of compulsive ways of thinking.

This is not so occult as it might sound. For one thing, compulsive ways of thinking lead eventually to compulsive habits of behavior, which have consequences in the body. Chronically high blood pressure associated with some kinds of aggressive personality is a familiar example. But there is a deeper side too. The subtle body, as I said earlier, is a highly complex field of forces – anger, fear, desires, and so on – all consisting of prāna. The same prāna that is the vital energy for bodily organs and systems, including the brain, is the prāna that makes up the mind. If thought-patterns grow rigid and compulsive, parts of the body cannot help being deprived of prāna, of vital energy. Over the years this can lead to serious disabilities.

Of course, this is a highly simplified picture. Personality is complex, and each individual comprises many physical and mental factors that come together in the development of illness. Still, there is increasing evidence to indicate that especially the so-called degenerative diseases – cardiovascular disease, arthritis, even cancer – may have their origin in this kind of pattern. That is why I like the prescient advice Sir William Osier used to give other physicians: "Ask not what kind of disease a patient has, but what kind of patient has the disease."

Hindu and Buddhist mystics would say that we have been at work fashioning this subtle-body mask for many lives. Every thought, every feeling, every act, every choice, shapes the mask further. I find this a very fair, sensible exposition. Whenever we dwell on a selfish thought – or, for that matter, whenever we act on an unselfish one – we are shaping tremendous forces in consciousness into molds of selfishness or unselfishness.

At first we make just a temporary kind of mask: grease paint, putty, a false mustache. You can clean yourself up in a few minutes if you choose. This is the natural state of the subtle body: elastic, pliable, spontaneous, with no rigid shape of its own. But the mind's natural tendency, perversely, is not to stay in its natural state. It likes to think and think and think, to desire and desire and desire; and as it goes on thinking and desiring, it becomes more self-centered and more rigid. Finally we have a real iron mask, riveted on seemingly forever – so long that we believe it is part of us, our real personality. Fortunately, this mask can be taken off; that is the whole purpose of meditation and its allied disciplines. And when the mask is off, we see ourselves as we really are: pure, complete, inseparable from the rest of life.

अनादित्वान्निर्गुणत्वात्परमात्मायमव्ययः ।
शरीरस्थो ऽपि कौन्तेय न करोति न लिप्यते ॥ १३-३१ ॥
यथा सर्वगतं सौक्ष्म्यादाकाशं नोपलिप्यते ।
सर्वत्रावस्थितो देहे तथात्मा नोपलिप्यते ॥ १३-३२ ॥
यथा प्रकाशयत्येकः कृत्स्नं लोकमिमं रविः ।
क्षेत्रं क्षेत्री तथा कृत्स्नं प्रकाशयति भारत ॥ १३-३३ ॥
क्षेत्रक्षेत्रज्ञयोरेवमन्तरं ज्ञानचक्षुषा ।
भूतप्रकृतिमोक्षं च ये विदुर्यान्ति ते परम् ॥ १३-३४ ॥

*31. This supreme Self is without a beginning,
undifferentiated, deathless. Though it dwells in the
body, Arjuna, it neither acts nor is touched by action.
32. As ākāsha pervades the cosmos but remains
unstained, the Self can never be tainted though it
dwells in every creature.
33. As the sun lights up the world, the Self dwelling
in the field is the source of all light in the field.
34. Those who, with the eye of wisdom, distinguish the
field from its Knower and the way to freedom from
the bondage of prakriti, attain the supreme goal.*

Movies were rare while I was growing up in India. Our little village was
not much exposed to the routes of world trade, and we had no theaters
or auditoriums. But once in a while some enterprising individual would
come by with a truck, a projector, a gas-powered generator, and an
ancient print of a Hollywood film. We would set up the projector in a
tent, and almost everybody in the village would assemble at nightfall
to watch. It was all terribly new, and people in my village in those days
were quite unsophisticated. Many had never even gone as far away as
the neighboring town. So when we watched these films, most of us did
not have a clear idea of what it was we were seeing. On the one hand,
we knew it was not a live performance; nobody felt any reluctance about
translating out loud or offering an unsolicited explanation of the action
for the benefit of those who would listen. But the images had such

power that we forgot ourselves. It all seemed so real! The screen would show a thief sneaking up on his sleeping victim, and while we watched we would hold our breath like children. Then suddenly one of my uncles would shout to the sleeper, "Wake up! He's got a knife!"

It is interesting to look back on those days now, because we have become so accustomed to the illusions of film that we forget just how powerful they are. They hold us "spellbound in darkness," as Pauline Kael says, in a kind of willing suspension of the world in which we really live. Life – the world of separate existence – does the same. In fact, movies make a good illustration of how the illusion of separateness works.

The other day Christine and I went again to see *Gone With the Wind*. For an instant at the start the screen was still a screen, filled with dazzling white light. Then suddenly it became a window, losing all dimension of its own, as we lost ourselves in the Deep South of another century. Without counting the extras, we must have watched dozens of characters come and go at various times. For a while the screen would be full of Clark Gable, then of Vivien Leigh; then both would disappear and the window would fill with horses and soldiers and the noise of battle. But when it was over, all the images vanished and the screen was again a screen: flat, white, and unaffected.

My uncle in the village might have wondered. The pictures seemed so real, but nothing had been painted on the screen. The film never touched it. The passion, the warfare, the terrible flames as Dixie burned – none of this had left a trace. And all those characters that looked so different were made by the same light. Imagine, the light that brought Clark Gable to life also shone through Vivien Leigh! Similarly, we look at each other at work or in the supermarket and wonder, "They look so different. They act so different. I would never wear a dress like that, answer my boss that way, buy that brand of macaroni. How *can* we be the same underneath?" But just as the projector's light creates separate characters, the Gita says, the light of the Self shining through the field creates the illusion of separate individual selves.

We should not press this too far, for I do not want to give the impression that *we* are illusions. But our separateness is an illusion, and everything about us from body to personality depends for its reality on the Self shining through us. When a movie stops and the projector is turned off, even the most colorful character vanishes. There was nothing on the screen; it was the film that seemed to stain it with color and characters alike. Similarly, the Katha Upanishad asks, when the Self leaves the body, what remains? Nothing but inert matter. Life, light, intelligence, awareness, all come from the Self.

One theater in San Francisco, I notice, has been showing a highly popular disaster movie for the last several weeks. Now it is showing Richard Attenborough's splendid film *Gandhi*. The first, I would say, gave us the lowest possible image of the human being: violent, self-centered, motivated by fear and sexual desire. *Gandhi* shows us the highest possible image of the human being, an ordinary little man who transformed himself and uplifted us all by basing his life on love, truth, and nonviolence.

Of course, I was very pleased to see the theater make this change. I know the whole city benefited. Yet it made no difference to the screen which film was projected on it. You can show violence on it and it will not be harmed; you can show a fire and it will not be burned. Similarly, Sri Krishna reminds us, the Self remains untouched through all our thoughts and actions.

When we truly understand this, it can lift from our shoulders the whole weight of past mistakes. We are not our body; we are not our mind. The body is matter; of its very nature, it has made mistakes in the material world. The mind, of its very nature, has made mistakes. These are interactions in the field: the karma of the body, the karma of the mind. But *we*, the Self, are not stained or diminished by those mistakes. All human beings, no matter what we may have done, have this core of purity and perfection in the depths of personality. Therefore, whatever our drawbacks and past errors, every stain on our personality can be wiped clean, leaving no trace behind.

क्षेत्रक्षेत्रज्ञविभागयोगो नाम त्रयोदशोऽध्यायः ॥ १३ ॥

CHAPTER FOURTEEN

The Forces of Evolution

श्रीभगवानुवाच ।
परं भूयः प्रवक्ष्यामि ज्ञानानां ज्ञानमुत्तमम् ।
यज्ज्ञात्वा मुनयः सर्वे परां सिद्धिमितो गताः ॥ १४-१ ॥
इदं ज्ञानमुपाश्रित्य मम साधर्म्यमागताः ।
सर्गे ऽपि नोपजायन्ते प्रलये न व्यथन्ति च ॥ १४-२ ॥

SRI KRISHNA:

*1. Let me tell you more about the wisdom that
transcends all knowledge, through which the
saints and sages have attained perfection.
2. Those who rely on this wisdom will be united with
me. For them there is neither rebirth nor fear of death.*

The distinction here is between what the Upanishads call *para* and
apara: intellectual knowledge on the one hand, spiritual wisdom on the
other. The purpose of intellectual knowledge is simply to know more,
which can be useful. But the supreme purpose of spiritual wisdom is
to take us beyond death.

The more we identify with the body, the more terrible death is. I can
explain this in two ways. First, when we identify people in physical
terms – when we love them, for example, because of certain physical
characteristics they may have – we feel we are losing them when our
physical awareness begins to dim at the time of death. The anguish of
separation can be unbearable. Knowing that we are about to be deprived
of those physical personifications, we may go to pieces.

Second, death wrenches your own body away. If you believe you are the body, this is fraught with fear. You cling to your body with all you have, at the very moments when it is failing and full of pain. Physically oriented people suffer dreadfully at death, not only on the conscious level but even after their awareness has been withdrawn into the unconscious in the final phase of dying, simply because of this agonizing inability to let go. Even when the body lies motionless, a sensitive eye can sometimes see this dreadful struggle, sure to be lost, still going on in consciousness.

I mention these aspects of death for one reason only: to inspire you to break through this wrong identification with the body and to build your relationships with other people more and more on the spiritual level. It may take years, but as relationships become more spiritual and less physical, especially between man and woman, you cannot help discovering the unity between you and those you love. After that, there is no parting. It is not possible to understand this on the physical plane, but two people who do not want to be separated under any circumstances can be so completely united that death cannot part them at all.

मम योनिर्महद्ब्रह्म तस्मिन्गर्भं दधाम्यहम् ।
संभवः सर्वभूतानां ततो भवति भारत ॥ १४-३॥
सर्वयोनिषु कौन्तेय मूर्तयः संभवन्ति याः ।
तासां ब्रह्म महद्योनिरहं बीजप्रदः पिता ॥ १४-४॥

*3. My womb is prakriti; in that I place the
seed. Thus all created things are born.
4. Everything born, Arjuna, comes from the womb
of prakriti, and I am the seed-giving father.*

Last night I watched a documentary on the Pacific salmon, done so beautifully that I found myself identifying with these valiant creatures as they made their way through the cycles of their lives. Spawned high in the mountains, they grow to about six inches in the bright, clear, secluded headwaters of a river. But then something prompts them to follow the current down to the sea, a wholly different environment. The water is dark and briny instead of clear. In place of seclusion, they find a realm that teems with other creatures which they have to learn to eat, ignore, or fear – a realm that must seem almost unlimited in its breadth and depth. Waves roil its surface, and below the surface great currents sweep the length of continents. As I watched, I remembered the Gita's term for life as we know it: *samsāra-sāgara,* the sea of birth and death.

Here the salmon spends its days, adapting to its new environment completely. It even changes its appearance, much the way I used to see students do when they got away from home and came to the university at Berkeley. To all appearances it is a saltwater creature forever. But abruptly, for no apparent reason, a kind of alarm goes off inside. *It is time,* the alarm says, *time to return,* time to retrace its course.

The rest of the story is thrilling to see. Following that inaudible call, the salmon finds the mouth of a river – often the same river down which it came – and begins to fight its way against the current, back to the quiet waters where it was spawned. There seems nothing natural about this, certainly nothing easy. The little creature has to fight for every foot of the way. Somehow it almost seems to gain energy as it struggles along, so that by the time it reaches the fierce currents of the mountain heights it is leaping like a flame of prāna. As I watched, there seemed to be nothing in it but pure energy, no desire except the overwhelming, over-riding, exhilarating determination to reach its goal. "That *is* the battle," I said to myself. The words of the Gita's invocation came to my mind: this was *rananadī,* the river of battle, the river of life.

Then, finally, it was over. Somehow the little creature made it up the last waterfall, over the last rocky plunge of white water, into the quiet of a mountain lake. There it spent its remaining hours in the bright solitude of its birth, spawning the eggs of a new generation.

For some, I was pleased to learn, even this is not the end. Certain species spawn and then return to the sea, only to fight their way upstream again when the time comes, perhaps three or four times more. They come back again and again. Perhaps they remember the headwaters when they reach the sea again, and can assure the others that life has a source and the battle to return to it can be won.

In one hour, that show managed to capture the full lifespan of a Pacific salmon. If it could be spread out over five billion years or so, you would have the story of evolution from the Hindu and Buddhist perspective. Against the vast backdrop of reincarnation the individual creature, called *jīva* in Sanskrit, emanates from God, ascends the ladder of biological evolution, and finally enters the human context, where it begins the long struggle to return to its divine source.

सत्त्वं रजस्तम इति गुणाः प्रकृतिसंभवाः ।
निबध्नन्ति महाबाहो देहे देहिनमव्ययम् ॥ १४-५ ॥

5. It is the three gunas born of prakriti – sattva, rajas,
and tamas – that bind the immortal Self to the body.

From its divine source, according to the scriptures, life evolves through the differentiating power of three forces. This theory of the three *gunas*, as they are called, is one of the most important concepts in the Gita. The gunas are the very fabric of prakriti. All that exists in the realms of matter, energy, and the mind can be described in terms of these three principles, forces, or qualities, which unfortunately have no equivalent names in English. Roughly *sattva* stands for law, harmony, balance, *rajas* for energy, and *tamas* for inertia. In personal terms, sattva can be looked upon as the door into the kingdom of joy and security that is our source, our home. Rajas then is the force we can harness to take us there; unharnessed, however, it takes us everywhere else. And tamas is the obstacle that blocks our way.

Before the universe came into existence, the Hindu scriptures explain, there was undifferentiated consciousness, the indivisible unity called God. In mythology he is represented as Vishnu, 'he who is everywhere,' resting on the endless serpent Ananta in the midst of the cosmic sea. As long as consciousness remained unitary, any kind of separateness was impossible. But then, in the language of Genesis, "The Spirit of God moved upon the face of the waters." The Lord began to meditate on himself. Consciousness began to divide, so to speak, at the behest of the Lord, in accordance with three principles: inertia, force, and law. From these three, matter and energy were born. These are the gunas, the stuff of the phenomenal universe. In Hindu mysticism, strictly speaking, there is no creation; there is emanation. As a spider weaves a web out of herself, the Upanishads say, the Lord weaves the web of the universe out of himself; and the threads are the three gunas.

In human beings, after millions and millions of years of evolution, sattva, rajas, and tamas are found in differing proportions. One person is full of energy; another is the victim of inertia. A third, much rarer, is calm, resourceful, and secure. In each a particular guna predominates, representing different stages of personal growth.

Yet at the same time, all three gunas are present in each of us. Their interplay is the dynamics of personality. The same person will have times when he is bursting with energy – particularly when he has to do something he likes – and times when inertia descends and para-lyzes his will, usually when he is faced with something he does *not* like. The person is the same; he is simply experiencing the play of the gunas, though without his knowledge or control.

Sometimes this interplay is a function of time and energy. In the morning you may be full of life and vitality, able to get all kinds of things done "first things first." But by afternoon, particularly after lunch, you may drag around accomplishing nothing. A detached observer might almost say these are two different individuals, so differently does the personality respond. And there is a third individual in us at rarer moments too. In everyone, simply by virtue of our being human, sattva is present also: kindness, security, equability, self-restraint. These qual-ities may be latent, but their mere possibility means that to some extent we have evolved. We have used the force called rajas to overcome the obstacle called tamas, and then brought the energy of rajas under self-less control.

The concept of the gunas provides the most penetrating analysis of personality differences that I have found anywhere. But it does much more: it also tells us how our character can be changed. Its descriptions are not passive. The Gita tells us what the forces of personality are, so that we can reshape ourselves after a higher ideal.

None of us, in other words, is cast in a rigid mold that limits our capacity to grow. We can change ourselves completely if we really want to. But we must have a strong enough desire to change the direction of our lives, to swim against the current of our conditioning. First we have to transform tamas into rajas – apathy into energetic, enthusias-tic effort. This is the purpose of rajas: we have passions like anger, fear, and greed so that we can harness them all into the immense drive that is required to overcome the inertia of physical living. This is the power that will take us to the goal.

But that is far from enough. We then have to transform rajas into sattva, channel all that passionate energy into selfless action. And finally, if we want to cut ourselves free from all conditioning, we have to go beyond the gunas completely.

All three gunas evolve from the same source: prāna. Just as potential energy can be transformed into kinetic energy and harnessed for power, tamas can be changed into rajas and rajas into sattva. Tamas is frozen power. It has been kept in the refrigerator so long that it has become a block of ice. It just sits there, hoping someone will come along and pour ginger ale over its head. But a block of ice can be melted, and tamas melted is rajas, a powerful, flowing river. It can move things, overcome obstacles, get from one place to another. But it can also flood and rage, causing great destruction. And sattva is steam, harnessed to drive engines and turbines. The simile is apt. The energy of sattva and rajas *is* present in tamas, only it is locked up, potential. The more tamas is heated, the more power is released.

As tamas melts, a tremendous stream of energy pours into our lives. This gives a precise test of how meditation is going: if you find yourself postponing urgent projects, it means your meditation can be improved. When you are meditating it is extremely important to be active, both physically and intellectually, in ways that benefit family and society. Hard, active work harnesses the energy released when tamas is transformed into rajas.

Selfless action, says Teresa of Ávila, "is the end and aim of prayer. Works are the best proof that the favors we receive have come from God." Another simple, practical test: how *well* are we working – hard, with concentration, selflessly, for the welfare of all? Hard work by itself is not enough. That is rajas, whose signal danger lies in slowly inveigling us to do jobs just because we like them, even when they are neither necessary nor beneficial. I see a lot of rajas running amuck today, doing the most useless, futile, often harmful things on the face of the earth.

Yet restlessness is not at all a bad quality. Compared with stick-in-the-mudness, which is another name for tamas, it is a definite improvement.

Restlessness to me is a clear signal: "Learn to meditate. You are ready to turn inwards." People who feel restless usually misunderstand the signal and start running from state to state, country to country, job to job, deal to deal. This is just wasting the power that is rising. When you feel consumed by restlessness, you want to ship out on a tramp steamer, drive your van around the world, plunge into pleasure, turn the financial world upside down, perform all kinds of fantastic feats which appear adventurous to you but benefit nobody except your own ego. That is the time to take to meditation. When the energy of these activities is collected and harnessed in sattva, we are at the door to the kingdom of heaven within.

तत्र सत्त्वं निर्मलत्वात्प्रकाशकमनामयम् ।
सुखसङ्गेन बध्नाति ज्ञानसङ्गेन चानघ ॥ १४-६ ॥

6. Sattva – pure, luminous, and free from
sorrow – binds us to happiness and wisdom.

Sattva, rajas, and tamas can be looked on as three stages in individual evolution. Those who are easily overcome by inertia, who procrastinate, who feel they have very little energy and cannot bring themselves to do anything worthwhile in life, whose actions say, "I don't care; what does it matter?" – these are people in whom tamas is predominant. Those who have plenty of energy for compulsive activities, who are always "on the go" but with no particular direction, who have tempestuous passions but not the will to govern them, are people in whom rajas is predominant. And those who give their time and energy freely to help others, who are "slow to wrath" and quick to forgive, have attained sattva. They have released the energy latent in every human being and learned to harness it for the welfare of all.

Sattva and tamas may both appear quiet, even easygoing. But there is a world of difference between the two. Tamas is torpid; a really tamasic person can scarcely get up from his chair except to go to bed. The sattvic person is as full of energy as a Ferrari, but all his energy is conserved. He is not interested in being one of the ten most rajasic persons of the year; he knows when and how to spend his energy.

"So do I," Tamas objects. "When I think something needs to be done,

I do it. But usually," he adds candidly, "it doesn't need to be done. Wait and see; that's my motto. Things usually work out by themselves if you leave them alone."

Sattva does not get upset easily, and the result is a tremendous accumulation of energy. He has a normal prāna income and a modest amount in his checking account, but behind all that is an immense amount in liquid, leveraged investments. In an emergency, he can move thousands into checking at a moment's notice. Rajas, by comparison, keeps everything in checking. He has a big handful of credit cards which he uses freely; he enjoys living "close to the wire." His assets are large, but so are his expenditures. As he moves into the second half of life, he may find he is spending more than he has, paying more and more frequent charges for overdrafts. And Tamas just loses money. When the normal bills of life arrive, he puts them on his desk. He does mean to get to them, but each day there is too much else to think about; they pile up; they get lost. It isn't only outward activity that spends prāna; dwelling on yourself is a terribly extravagant expenditure. Tamas goes about from day to day worrying about himself, brooding on his problems and desires, and while he does so, the bills pile up. "Fantasizing about vacation, 20 pranadollars. Self-pity, 75. Rehashing what to say to boss, 100. Total June resentments, 477.95." No wonder he gets tired!

Our local utilities company has put up signs by the side of the road, reminding us how to save energy: "Don't do this. Turn off that." We can conserve prāna immensely through an equally simple process: by turning off attention from ourselves and switching it to the needs of others. Just turning attention away from ourselves – say, by repeating the mantram when you start to dwell on some personal problem – saves a good deal of expense. But switching attention to others actually builds up savings. That is the source of Sattva's fortune. St. Francis's line, "It is in giving that we receive," is literally true. If you give ten pranadollars to your partner, the Lord adds twenty to your account in savings. You can test it and see. You can also test the corollary: "It is in grabbing that we debilitate ourselves." Not only do we not get; we lose what little we have.

We can also compare in terms of the will. Tamas simply doesn't have any. It is a simple, accurate definition. He can't attend to the job at hand because he doesn't have the will. You can tell him over and over again the consequences of procrastination; he won't hear. Tamas keeps his ears open, but his mind is closed with the wax of inertia.

Rajas, of course, has much more drive, more passion. But his will is still rather small – unless, of course, it is compulsively harnessed by a compelling desire. This combination of strong desire and weak will gets Rajas into a lot of trouble. The one thing I can say in favor of Tamas is that he is immune to temptation, for the simple reason that there is no energy to be tempted with. If you take the world's finest chocolate cake and hold it in front of a pillar, the pillar will not feel tempted in the slightest. It is the same with Tamas. He loves to overeat, but he can't be tempted to exert himself even for the sake of self-indulgence. Tamasic people can pass themselves off as statues. Set them in some situation and come back a couple of years later; they will still be standing in the same old place, surveying the scene with blank hauteur. Similarly, tamasic people cannot get angry. It is not that they are forgiving; their desires are so feeble that if you thwart them, they shrug it off. What does it matter? And they cannot get greedy – not because they are detached, but because they have no capacity to feel or desire. They cannot love; they can't even have a passing fancy. Imagine how terrible it would be not even to have a passing fancy! If Tamas sees an ad for a three-week cruise to the Bahamas or a lavishly appointed new Mercedes, he can't even say, "Wouldn't I like to have that!" All he can respond with is, "Who cares?"

There is no sensitiveness in tamas, no awareness. Swami Vivekananda used to say that it is much better to be greedy than not to be capable of greed, better to feel angry than not to be able to feel angry, better to live a little than to sit there dead. This remark can help all of us in our moments of tamas. It is much better to move than to sit; even if you go in the wrong direction, at least you are going somewhere. When you're moving, you can always change direction.

Unlike those who are tamasic, rajasic people get angry easily; they don't have to take lessons. They find it natural to feel resentful, to crave things, to insist on their own way. It is no challenge for them to feel sustained hostility; they have a good memory, very well maintained. You may say, "What a negative state!" True, but at least rajas has possibilities. When you send a Christmas card to a resentful person, you can always write, "To a potentially ideal companion." Power is present; therefore, so is the capacity to change.

Tamas, by comparison, is a damp squib. Swami Vivekananda compares tamas with a sodden log: you can light match after match and never get a fire. All you do is waste the matches. Rajas is like Georgia fatwood; just show him the matchbox and he blazes. His volatility may be dangerous, but at least Rajas is active; he has power.

Rajas likes to be active. In fact, he can't be anything else. If he has to wait for a bus, he doesn't know what to do, so he lights a cigarette or practices cracking his knuckles. He can't simply sit and watch a movie; he has to keep his hands and mouth busy with a carton of popcorn and a soft drink. If the action is too slow, he gets up and walks out. When he's driving he plays the radio to relieve his restlessness, beating time with his fingers on the steering wheel and switching from station to station. At a stop light he pulls out the newspaper or dictates a letter. And at night, of course, his mind keeps on racing. His work and problems nag him into tossing and turning, follow him into his sleep. If he tries to count sheep, they *baa* derisively or turn into bulls and bears.

Tamas, on the other hand, would rather walk than run. Jogging around the block is his idea of torture. If you warn him about fatty arteries, he'll say, "I'll take my chances." The heart attack hasn't come yet, so he can't imagine it. Why exert any effort for something you can't imagine? Tamas would rather sit than walk, and the sticker on his car admits, "I'd rather be lying down." Unlike Rajas, he doesn't have any trouble sleeping. Unconsciousness is his specialty. But his mind keeps churning all the same. He may not do anything physically, but Tamas never really rests. In the dark recesses of his mind – which means, in most of it – the Midnight Rocky Horror Show is going around the clock.

Only Sattva knows how to rest. He works hard when work is to be done, but his mind is free from turmoil. It doesn't get worn down. And when the time comes to relax – to go to a movie with his family, to play tennis, to linger after dinner for good conversation with friends – he doesn't stuff unfinished business into a corner of his mind so he can peek at it when somebody else is talking. He leaves his work at the office, physically and mentally too. Wherever he goes he is all there, one hundred percent. He falls asleep easily, and his sleep rejuvenates. During the day he may get as much done as two or three of the rest of us. His secret is detachment: he doesn't get personally entangled in his work. He does his best, then doesn't worry; he leaves the results to the Lord.

I like to illustrate this with the example of a good actor. A few years ago I went to see Sir Michael Redgrave and others read some of my favorite pieces from English literature. They took first a scene from *Pickwick Papers* – that curious episode where Mr. Tupman succumbs to romance – and for a while, just for that scene, Sir Michael and his supporting actress actually became Tupman and Miss Wardle. Then they did a scene from Wilde's *The Importance of Being Earnest*, and everything changed. They spoke so differently, behaved so differently, that I thought they were different people altogether. For a poem of John Donne's they changed roles again; then again for Shakespeare, again for Shaw. Yet through all those roles, it was the same Sir Michael Redgrave. We never forgot that; therein lay half the artistry. More important, Sir Michael never forgot it either.

Sattva is like that. He knows who he is, so he doesn't confuse himself with the roles he plays. If he is a doctor, when he goes to his clinic in the morning he becomes a doctor – puts on a white coat and an expression of infallibility. This is part of his profession; it inspires confidence in his patients. But at the same time, he never forgets that this is Mr. Sattva playing the role of doctor. When he goes home, he leaves his infallibility at the clinic with his lab coat; it is not so welcome elsewhere. At home he has other roles: loving partner to his wife, loving father to his children.

Dr. Rajas forgets. He knows the textbooks backward and forward, but he is so caught up in himself that he gets emotionally entangled with his patients and their problems. When he goes home he is still the doctor, worrying about whether he will be able to do anything about Susie Smith's depressions and save Sam Bass from alcoholism. He scarcely sees his children or his wife. Interestingly enough, when he goes back to the clinic, the same preoccupation is going to keep him from giving his full attention to the next day's patients. He will still be carrying the burden of the past as if it were all his own. It doesn't help Susie Smith, and it doesn't help anybody else either.

This lack of detachment is the main source of professional burnout.

Recently I read a thick book on this subject, full of charts and case histories. I don't think it occurred to the author that a good professional need never burn out if he or she can learn to be detached.

It is the same for a teacher. Here I can speak from personal experience. The college professor is not really a professor; he is just a nice fellow, handy at home, normal, regular. But when he steps onto the campus, a pall of profundity descends on him. He goes into the library stacks and brings out the biggest books he can find. When he lectures, with his notes and diagrams and slides and prepared jokes, he speaks with an air of learned authority. But after he leaves campus, when he goes to look over the drugstore paperback collection, he is no longer the professor. He is Mr. Middle America, looking for something new in science fiction or the latest advice on inflationary investments.

Sattva plays each role with detachment. When she is a wife, she plays that role perfectly. With her children, she plays the perfect mother. At work she is the perfect doctor, teacher, accountant, programmer, clerk. After a lot of practice this becomes natural and spontaneous, as it must have been for Sir Michael Redgrave. You never forget you are really the Self, with many parts to play in life which require your best effort if those around you are to benefit.

Each guna has its characteristic problems. Tamas is full of fear. He doesn't necessarily run from his own shadow; he may never think of himself as fearful. But fear comes in countless disguises. Tamas worries, though it seldom leads to action. He is anxious about the economy and the latest strain of flu. He wonders what people think of him, whether they like him, whether they will respond the way he expects. Often too he responds only to fear, which is not the most elevating kind of motivation.

Rajas, on the other hand, has two ways of responding: anger and greed. He cannot choose, but at least there is some variety. Rajas has possibilities; he can learn to change.

And Rajas has some will: not much, it is true, but at least he has something to work on. The problems arise because his desires are compulsive. In rajas, will and desire are like a little boy with his daddy. Desire strides along, and little Will can't keep up. But Daddy Desire doesn't wait; he's too impatient. "Got to learn to keep up," he says. "Step along!" Usually Will does not step along. He lags farther and farther behind, and wherever the will lags behind desire, there is trouble. You become a victim of your desires. You have no freedom of choice; you are driven. You may even become obsessed. When you can't stop thinking about something, some thing or person you want, when you can't switch your mind off it or drop that desire at will, the will is lagging so far behind that it is helpless.

When a desire is that strong, it can split your consciousness until the desire is satisfied. On the job, over dinner, at the movies, behind the wheel, in your sleep, whatever else you may be trying to think about, some part of your mind will be on that desire. You can't concentrate, can't do a good job at work, can't keep your attention on those you love – all because the will is weak.

Fortunately, meditation can give the will walking lessons. I don't know how you go about this here, but in India mothers often use a simple kind of three-wheel walker when a child is ready to learn. The child holds on to the handles; when the device rolls forward a little, he takes a few faltering steps to keep his balance. He totters over to his mother in this way and gets an orange. Then one day the walker mysteriously disappears. "Never mind," his mother says. "Step over here and get your orange anyway." The child tries, falters, takes a step or two, then a third. "You're doing very well," she encourages. "Try another step!" When he finally reaches the orange, he falls over his mother in relief. But he has walked. Soon he will be running around and playing soccer; she won't be able to keep him home.

That is exactly how we teach the will too. We start with food – not eating between meals, turning down foods that are not good for the body, eating less sugar and fat and more fresh vegetables. This is not only good nutrition; you are teaching the will to walk.

You don't train the senses just for the sake of training the senses. The point is to get at the will, which is difficult to reach in any other way. I see ads in the magazines promising, "Make it a pleasure to quit smoking! Take our ten-day Caribbean cruise. When you come back, you'll think 'Lucky Strike' has something to do with bowling." Promises like these are fairy tales by which we shouldn't be fooled. Similarly, you don't strengthen the will just to get what you want or have your way. The purpose of a strong will is to free you from the compulsions of rajas, so that your passions can be harnessed for the welfare of all.

By training the senses, Rajas develops a stronger and stronger will. Gradually he is turning into Sattva, who has a will like Mr. America. The sattvic will has to spend a lot on clothing; he has so much muscle that he would burst the seams of an ordinary sports jacket. But he doesn't have much work to do. If a desire comes that Sattva doesn't approve of, the will just flexes his biceps; desire gulps and disappears. The only desire that can challenge the sattvic will is sex. Then the will meets a foeman worthy of his steel, and the real battle of sādhana begins. It goes on for a long, long time.

There is no need to feel embarrassed or despondent about this. Sex is the strongest desire we have, the highest physical satisfaction life offers. That is precisely why it contains such a tremendous amount of power. Strong sexual desires means a lot of gas in your tank. You don't want to throw the tank away; the choice we all face is simply, Shall I be victim of this desire or master? When sex is mastered, it leads to tremendous power and a magnetic personality. The power in that desire becomes *kundalini*, the energy we draw on to elevate our consciousness and go forward on the path of evolution. So much power is caught up in sexual desire that once it comes under control, it can lead even an ordinary person like you or me to great heights of spiritual wisdom and selfless action.

In sattva the will becomes so tremendous that even sex comes under its governance. Then, the Gita says, the heart becomes pure. As Jesus says, none but the pure in heart shall see God. It is to purify the heart of all selfish passions that we make the will immeasurably strong.

रजो रागात्मकं विद्धि तृष्णासङ्गसमुद्भवम् ।
तन्निबध्नाति कौन्तेय कर्मसङ्गेन देहिनम् ॥ १४-७ ॥

7. Rajas is passion, breeding selfish desire and attachment. These bind the Self to compulsive action.

Rajas binds us, ties us up, throws us into prison. Why? Because everything in this state is tainted with selfish attachment – "I, me, mine." This is Rajas's fatal flaw. He does represent a higher state than tamas; he has at least some sensitiveness with all that passion and energy. But everything is selfishly directed. "Sure, I'm sensitive," Rajas says. "I'm a very sensitive guy – sensitive to Number One. I'm really aware of what I want." Rajas knows what he wants, and he is going to get it come what may. If he hurts somebody in the process, it doesn't matter. If it means spoiling the landscape, "Well, we have to put up with it," say Rajas. "That's the price of progress." If it fuels an arms race, "Well, that's the risk we have to take."

Take smog. The curious thing to me about the smog issue is that antismog devices and so on are just tinkering with the problem. The cause of smog is not in the materials or the furnace or the engine; it is within you and me. In biology the human being is characterized as *Homo sapiens,* "the thinking member of the family." This is an unwarranted tribute. I think it was Bergson who said that a better name for the species would be *Homo faber,* "he who makes things." "I *have* to make things," Rajas says. "What else would I do with myself? I'm going to make products all over the place, as many as I can. Then I'm going to get everybody to want them, even if they don't know what to do with them." If something can be made, we have to make it – highways, cities, cars, games, toothbrushes, airplanes, bombs.

There is some satisfaction in making things; I do not deny it. But that very satisfaction is what binds us. While Rajas is making something, he gets caught in it. He climbs inside his product or project and seals himself in, and afterwards he is as deaf and blind as Tamas to the cries for help from the community outside.

Walk down Main Street, or through the malls of any shopping center. Look in the windows of the stores. How many of the things you see are necessary? How many are truly beneficial? If we rule out everything that is neither, things that were made because *Homo faber* fever has got us, the whole shopping center could probably be reduced to a single store.

As consumers, you and I have a close connection with this phenomenon. It is we who buy. When we go on acquiring new cars, new clothes, new appliances, when they are not really necessary, we are contributing to pollution. I am not pleading for poverty, merely for simplicity. The simple life is beautiful, artistic. A life that is cluttered with things we do not need, even if they are objects of art, is a life cluttered with attachments.

When my wife and I were living in Oakland, I remember looking out the window one morning to see a huge moving van pulling in down the block. "They're coming all the way from New Jersey!" our neighbors told me. Sure enough, World Movers announced on the side of the van that they would take you anywhere. I watched with great interest to see what kind of furniture and *objets d'art* were worth the cost and care of being transported three thousand miles.

The doors opened, and out came a stream of stuff you could have picked up at Goodwill – armchairs, bedsteads, lamps, chaise longues, gilt-framed paintings of seascapes and sunsets, and boxes on boxes of old *National Geographics,* stamp and button collections, figurines, coat hangers, and recipe cards. They could have left it all in Camden, picked up what they needed in Oakland, and never known the difference. But human beings get attached, and once attached we are bound. We carry everything around with us, without noticing the burden of our attachments to things and to the past.

Please don't rush out at this point, call Goodwill Industries, and say, "I've got a houseful. Come and take it all." The point is not to get attached to things. Even if you have the world's finest collection of Ming vases or Moghul miniatures, which are undeniably beautiful, please do not get attached to them. If you do, you cannot really even appreciate them.

We can get selfishly attached to people too. I always stress the word *selfish* here, because the words *attachment* and *detachment* are so easily misunderstood. Unselfish attachment is pure love. You have no thought of your own pleasure or gain; your only interest is the other person's welfare. But selfish attachment prevents love. Unselfish attachment deepens a relationship; selfish attachment disrupts it. As with things, once you get selfishly attached you are no longer free. You cannot see the other person's needs – in fact, you cannot see your own real needs either. To love completely, every taint of wanting to possess other people or to affix that stamp "Mine, Do Not Touch" has to go.

All of us have a certain desire to grab and to be grabbed; this is the human condition. So while we are young, the Lord gives us a margin for experimentation in order to learn that grabbing fulfills no one. At first everything seems perfect – that is one of the marks of selfish attachment. But then the sky begins to change. A little cloud "no larger than a man's hand" appears – some slight difference in how the toast should be served, or whether it should be whole wheat toast or rye. The two of you agree to disagree. But the cloud spreads to the coffee. Rajas wants dark roast, full of caffeine, to get him off to an unnecessarily fast start on an enterprising day. Mrs. Rajas wants decaf; she is speeded up already. The cloud no bigger than a man's hand is now the size of a man's head.

Then Mr. Rajas comes home for lunch. Mrs. Rajas embraces him warmly. "I've been waiting fifteen minutes for you, dear."

"Come on," says Rajas. "It's only five by my watch. Besides, do you remember how long I had to wait for you last month at the Dairy Queen?"

"Don't bring up the past, dear. Try to live in the present. Besides, that wasn't the Dairy Queen. You're thinking of Foster's Freeze."

Little by little. This is what happens in selfish attachment; it turns against itself. After a while comes one of the most painful ironies of what we call love today: the very thing that attracted you to the other person now becomes irritating. Her nose, as perfect as Cleopatra's, promised such delight; after a while, when the delight doesn't come regularly, you feel chafed just to look at it. He had the voice of your dreams; when those dreams don't materialize, the same voice starts to rasp at your nerves. This is what relationships are like in rajas, particularly today. But they do not have to deteriorate like this; and if they have deteriorated, they can be rebuilt by transforming rajas into sattva.

I was reading the other day about lichens, which shows how far afield my reading goes. I am always looking for ways to illustrate the changeless laws of life, and even lichens provide grist for my mill. My mind occasionally complains about this. "You're a man of letters," it tells me. "Why don't you dip into a good play once in a while, instead of reading about borderline organisms?" But I read to get material, and these lichens provided a very interesting illustration. They can thrive in environments where no other plant can, and scientists have always wondered why and how. The answer, it seems, is that a lichen is actually two organisms, an alga and a fungus, each supporting the other. Their metabolisms are different, their views are different, their temperaments are different. But one provides food and the other provides water and support, so that together they become a unity which can face great environmental stress and thrive.

This is what man and woman can do. They are made to complete each other, not only in marriage but in every relationship. If they support each other they can forge an unbreakable unity that no outside stress can tear asunder. In this atmosphere romance flourishes.

Where there is competition, on the other hand, there is neither romance nor love. Not even synthetic romance can subsist in that soil. Where competition rages, only death can flourish. One of the great tragedies of our modern life is the constant attempt, sometimes in the very name of romance, to play man and woman against each other in every field of life. I see it daily in books, in films, on television, on campuses, in homes; I hear it in popular songs. All of us can bend our will to prevent this tragedy by emphasizing the unity between man and woman in everything we do.

तमस्त्वज्ञानजं विद्धि मोहनं सर्वदेहिनाम् ।
प्रमादालस्यनिद्राभिस्तन्निबध्नाति भारत ॥ १४-८ ॥

8. Tamas, born of ignorance, deludes all creatures through heedlessness, indolence, and sleep.

Up until now Sri Krishna has only given what in India we call trailers about tamas – what you call previews. "Next verse, coming to this theater, one of the most interesting characters in the cosmos! With all his cohorts – heedlessness, indolence, vacillation, disloyalty, and stupor." A most motley crew. Everyone finds it entertaining to see a motley crew, so we may find Tamas dominating this volume the way Satan dominates *Paradise Lost*.

In this verse Sri Krishna lists some telltale signs of tamas. First is *pramāda,* 'lack of earnestness.' This is a fatal weakness. People who are not earnest do not go very far. They get diverted; their attention is drawn away by a few playthings of life. To those who *are* earnest, Patanjali says, success has to come. They have, keep, and continually deepen the capacity to follow one supreme goal without ever giving up or wandering. Spiritual teachers in India often wait a few years before accepting a student completely, watching closely to be sure he or she is capable of sustained effort. To do otherwise would not be a wise use of a teacher's time and energy, for this is the most precious gift any human being can give or receive.

Second is *ālasya*, for which the nearest English equivalent I know is 'indolence.' *Ālasya* means partly negative euphoria, partly positive inertia. You bask in your laziness. Even when you are simply walking along, you show you are not alert; your eyes are open, but nobody is home. Half your mind is thinking about what took place yesterday; the other half is on tomorrow. Naturally your body slows down. Your steps slow, your head droops; if you are sitting, you slump – which, incidentally, is hard not only on the will but on the spine, particularly for a meditator.

Last, Sri Krishna says, tamas ties us to *nidrā*, 'sleep.' This is not legitimate sleep, "that knits up the ravelled sleeve of care." It is a torpor in which we try to take refuge. When a problem comes knocking on the door, you go looking for your blanket. This is one of the commonest responses to problems. Suddenly you can scarcely keep your eyes open. You may be watching a movie, in a meeting, at the dinner table; it does not matter. Something reminds you of a problem left unsolved, a task left undone. You feel drowsy, you yawn, your attention wanders, and the next thing you know you are asleep.

This happens often in the classroom, of course. Hasn't someone defined a professor as a person who talks in other people's sleep? One fellow in my freshman class in India used to sit right in the front row, and while I was pouring out the wealth of my love of life and literature, his eyes would glaze over and slowly roll upward until nothing showed but unnerving white orbs. Then his chin would hit his chest. I once took the liberty of asking him to tell me exactly what he saw at a time like that. His answers were worthy of a Gothic novel. "For a while you look like a ghost," he said. "Then you become a kind of vapor. After that, you vanish into thin air."

When you have burdensome emotional problems, it is not really sleep that comes at times like this. Clouds of the unconscious rise and overpower you. Even if you try to wake yourself up, you cannot. It can happen at work, or in the company of particular people, or behind the steering wheel; it can happen anywhere. At such times, even if you try your level best to break out of that bout of unconsciousness, you will not be able to.

No amount of clenching your fists and sticking out your jaw is going to help. These are all physical attempts, and what is happening is not physical at all. That is where you need the mantram. You fight it out by clinging to the holy name, which St. Bernard called "the energizing Word."

Tamas's motto is "I Don't Care." He wears it on his coat of arms, beneath a rusty helmet and two turtles dormant. "I don't care what happens to other people," he says. "What does it matter? I don't even care what happens to me." Quite a lot of people today are victims of this what-does-it-matter attitude. The Gita would say these are people who are hardly alive. They might as well be made of stone. It is the nature of a stone to say, "I'm not going to move. Even if a fire comes, I'm just going to sit here. Let it burn all around me, even if it burns me up." In the same way, insensitivity is characteristic of tamas. I see it everywhere today. How many seem unaware of the dangers that confront us all! War, violence, hunger here as well as abroad, the breakdown of the family, a poisonous environment – insensitivity to others on a massive, staggering scale. These are fires that threaten to consume us all. It does not require much imagination to see the flames on the horizon; every newspaper brings reports.

Psychologists and sociologists say there is no motivation to do anything about these problems. That is another characteristic of Tamas; he just cannot get motivation. About the only thing he responds to is fear. Similarly, to be stuck in a groove is part of tamas. Many people like the safety of a groove, where nothing can happen to them. They don't have to do anything; they can just coast along, never seeing the world. Grooves, I would point out, do not usually touch. A man and woman may live in the same house, speak to each other at mealtimes morning and evening, raise children together, and never see each other. He is in his groove; she is in her own.

Change, therefore, is a particular fear of tamas. When we have to face a challenge or our life undergoes some alteration, many of us respond with tamas. Yet change is the texture of life. The Buddha reminds us that everything is change; nothing ever stays the same. We should be able to adapt effortlessly, yet still keep our center within ourselves. But Tamas, when change or challenge comes, simply says, "I can't. I can't change. I'm rigid; I can't bend or yield. I can only break."

The other day a friend's little boy showed me a Japanese doll weighted in a fascinating way. Push it and it yields without resistance; yet the minute you take your hand away, the doll jumps up again. That is how we should be. When circumstances overpower us, we may have to yield gracefully. But as soon as the burden of circumstance is off our backs, we should spring up again with even greater resilience.

Tamas, by contrast, lies down and stays down. Often you don't even have to push him; lying down is a state he finds natural and comfortable. "I give up" comes easily to his lips.

I used to see such people sometimes in my meditation classes. The first day they are full of enthusiasm. "I'm all set," they tell me. "I've got a new pillow to sit on and a special meditation robe. I know this is right for me. Everything *feels* so right." The next morning they sit down, close their eyes, and the monkey that is the mind goes berserk.

Isn't it an English author who says that the first time he sat down for meditation, a curtain went up on the theater of his mind? Books he had read poured into his consciousness. He started planning a novel with complicated subplots; the characters pushed and shoved themselves into his mind in a riot, all trying to capture his interest at once. Suddenly he realized his half hour of meditation must have been over long ago. He opened his eyes and looked at his watch: five minutes had gone by.

That is the pandemonium that erupts when we try to train the mind, and it is too much for Tamas. He takes his meditation pillow to the flea market. "Sell this on consignment," he tells the girl at the first booth, "and take anything you can get for it. I've had it; I'm giving up."

Tamas literally means darkness. Tamas can't see. He gropes in darkness throughout his life, stumbles around, bumps into things, falls down. He doesn't see war brewing, doesn't notice that he can't breathe the air, isn't aware when violence dominates his streets; his eyes are closed. The word "sleep" in this verse is especially interesting. Tamas may be able to walk about or get himself into a restaurant, but he is not really awake. He is walking in his sleep, which is a fascinating phenomenon. I remember reading about a whole family addicted to this nocturnal habit. They would get up in the middle of the night, go to the kitchen, and have a midnight snack together. Then the next morning everybody would say, "Who did all this?" It's not so different from what you and I do. Compared to the awareness we are capable of, most of us go through life having midnight snacks in our sleep.

Some years ago, when we took our nieces to the ice show, I saw a robot skating on the ice. A girl dressed in gauze and glitter was skating around beside him with some kind of electronic monitor in her hand, calling out commands as if to a little friend. "Turn, Robbie!" Robbie did a clumsy pirouette. "Run!" Robbie ran. "Open your mouth!" Robbie cranked open his jaws. This is what happens in tamas. The ego sits inside with a transistorized walkie-talkie through which he issues orders, and we obey. This is not living, the Buddha says, it's sleeping: being pushed and pulled about by selfish cravings which do no good to anybody, even us.

Sluggishness is one of the main characteristics of tamas. We find it difficult to think, to feel, to move, to get exercise, to get up from the TV to change the channel; naturally we find it difficult to resist evil and contribute something of value to the world. Tamasic people often put on weight easily. Their minds are heavy, so the body says, "Let me catch up!"

To strike a lighter note – which I always try to do with tamas, because its implications are so grim – I remember a piece of graffiti on a wall in Berkeley that makes a good epitaph for Tamas: "All I need is beer and weed." I wanted to add, "To go to seed." That is the song Tamas sings.

To release yourself from tamas, the first step is physical. You will be feeling listless, oppressed, weighted down by inertia; you won't want to do anything at all. You may feel persecuted: "Why shouldn't I be allowed to sit around if I feel like it?" You may feel you are not in the best condition physically, with aches and pains that nobody understands except yourself. But the worst thing you can do in tamas is rest. Rest is what you have been getting all along; what is required is the elimination of rest. Superficial physical symptoms may come by way of protest: a dull, throbbing headache, nerves on edge, no circulation in your legs, a head as heavy as your heart. Lying down and doing nothing only makes these conditions worse. Get up and go for a walk – and walk fast, repeating the mantram, even if you don't feel equal to it. Try to walk a little faster than you can. After ten minutes or so you will find yourself breaking through that physical lethargy. Don't stop then! Keep walking.

Or say you have a report to turn in – at your office, on your campus, wherever. And tamas strikes. You have managed to sharpen some pencils and bring them to the desk. You stack some supporting documents on the corner. But then all you can do is sit and stare. A fresh, blank pad of yellow paper stares up at you, waiting for the first words of inspiration. It has been waiting a long time. But the report is due tomorrow, and finally something has to be done.

You feel sure you haven't mastered the subject. Perhaps you are one of those people who will not write anything until they know all the facts that have been written about that subject in the world. Here "perfectionist" just means "procrastinator." There is nothing wrong with striving for perfection, but if you wait for perfection to come before you act, you are going to wait a long, long time.

Here I used to tell my students something I learned from personal experience: start writing with whatever knowledge you have. After all, you are not expected to make an original contribution. And do not worry about style. I know people who will not put a word onto paper, even if no one will see it except themselves, unless it is exactly the right word in exactly the right place. Sometimes you can sit for a couple of hours this way without writing a sentence. Style can wait; the important thing is to get started and keep moving. You can always polish and rewrite later.

That is the first step: physical activity. You just get the pencil moving; what you write doesn't matter. Gradually tamas will begin to melt, as rajas begins to get its teeth into the job. An idea creeps in, then another. They seem to contradict each other, but you write them down. And then you see a possible connection. You test it; you test again. After a while you realize that an hour has gone by. When somebody comes by to remind you of your coffee break, you say, "I'll take it later. Let me get this down first, while it's fresh."

By starting with physical measures – simply getting the pencil to move across the paper – you have begun to get tamas to melt, prāna to flow. Now you can work directly on your concentration. Try to give your attention completely to what you are doing. Tamas scatters attention everywhere, anywhere but on the job at hand. When it strikes, your mind will wander all over the map. This lack of attention is what makes a job dull – which, of course, means that it holds your attention even less. The worst thing to do in such circumstances is to drop that job; this only adds to the problem. Whenever you find a job uninteresting, the answer is to give it more attention. If you find your mind wandering, concentrate more. Bring your mind back just as you do in meditation; that is where this skill is learned. At first it will seem painful, but after a while it becomes natural and rewarding.

Meditation enables us to direct attention at will. I carry a powerful little penlight in my shirt pocket; in the evening I can take it out, push the button, and train the light where I like. That is how the will should work: it should be "ever ready." Most of us have a will that is never ready, for the simple reason that we leave it on in our pocket where it can't do any good. When we take it out and try to flash it on something, nothing happens.

When the will has been trained, we can give full attention to the job at hand. This is genius. Those who have trained their will from top to bottom can give their complete attention to any problem. They don't ask "Do I like this?" or "What's in it for me?" If it helps to solve a problem like pollution or violence, they can absorb themselves in it so completely that they are no longer aware of their private personality. In this kind of work, tension and frustration disappear.

सत्त्वं सुखे सञ्जयति रजः कर्मणि भारत ।
ज्ञानमावृत्य तु तमः प्रमादे सञ्जयत्युत ॥ १४-९ ॥

9. Sattva binds us to happiness; rajas
binds us to action. Tamas, distorting our
understanding, binds us to delusion.

Most of our responses are compulsive. They are not really responses; they are reactions. If money comes near, most of us immediately feel attracted, even without our knowledge. Pleasure is an even more universal magnet. It draws everybody, rich and poor alike. We may say, "I can take it or let it alone." But the magnet would have a different view.

When we start meditating, if pleasure starts to draw us and we feel ourselves slipping closer without meaning to, we find we can draw back.

The magnet naturally feels annoyed. "This isn't cricket," Pleasure says. "You *have* to respond to me. That's what life's all about, isn't it? Look around. Do you see anybody else running away? Everybody likes me; I'm everybody's friend." But someone like St. Francis would reply, "I'm not subject to the law of attraction and repulsion any longer. I go where I choose, not where you draw me."

It takes a long, long time in meditation to discover that what we call free decisions, made calmly and objectively without any trace of outside influence, are actually reactions that could not have turned out any other way. They are not decisions; they are deep desires. We get these independent decisions from a slot, like stamps from a stamp machine; we have no say in them at all. That is why one word for Self-realization in Hinduism is *moksha,* liberation, from the root *muc,* 'to release': meditation frees us from compulsions.

The tamasic person, overcome with inertia, wakes up and thinks, "I don't feel so good. I have decided to spend the day in bed." Old Tamas splits his sides laughing. "I just push this guy back with one finger," he says, "and he gives up. He might as well be tied to his bed with ropes." If you tell that person he has no freedom, he won't believe you. "What do you mean? Look, I can lift my arm. I can move my legs. I can roll over. Sure, I'm free."

We ask, "Then why don't you get up?"

"I could get up if I wanted to. I've *decided* to stay in bed."

Another person comes to work and announces, "I've decided to go to Las Vegas this weekend!" It is Rajas's turn to laugh. "This lady is so restless I can make her go anywhere," he says. "If there were a casino on the North Pole where she thought she could break the bank, she would go there." These are compulsive forces. They bind us to action because they bind us to a particular outlook, or *shraddhā* in Sanskrit: the firm, fixed, unquestioned belief that something *out there* will make us happy. This belief is not peculiar to modern times. Pleasure hunters have been around since the dawn of history. Virtually everybody hunts pleasure, at least for a while, yet no one manages to find it for very long.

Most of us go on thinking that sensory satisfaction *is* out there somewhere; we have just been missing it. Only a few have enough self-knowledge to conclude, "It's not here. I have to look inside." That is the transition to sattva, the state of maturity, where we gain some capacity to make real decisions.

The word "maturity" is bandied about so miserably that we often forget what it means. The song today is "Go After What You Like." In my ears this translates into "Be As Immature As You Can." Maturity demands detachment. Immature people are acutely attached to themselves – their desires, their opinions, their way of doing things, their view of others. Mature people can stand back from their own likes and dislikes and go against them easily, without resentment, when it benefits other people.

"Sattva," says Sri Krishna, "binds us to happiness." This is a subtle point: we can be bound to happiness too. It means that when you reach the state of sattva, you will not be content with any worldly satisfaction. A few minutes of pleasure, an hour or two of most refined aesthetic satisfaction, will not be enough. You will demand a state of fulfillment that lasts always. This is the immense desire that impels us beyond sattva, beyond all the gunas, into full freedom and joy.

I was perhaps ten or eleven, I remember, when I was introduced to the beauty of English literature. I couldn't believe there were such beautiful stories, such interesting people; here was a whole world I had never thought about. My high school library was just one big shelf behind the headmaster's desk. He loved literature, so he was quite selective about lending these books to those who could really get absorbed in them. English novels can be big, you know – particularly those of Charles Dickens, whom I liked very much – and English was a very difficult language for us. So my reading went slowly. The novels went on and on, and I was captivated with every page. As I got toward the end, I used to feel a little sad that the story would soon be over. I would close the book and keep it aside for a while, just to try to make it last. My young niece Meera used to do the same thing when Christine gave her a bar of Cadbury's chocolate: open it up, give it one lick, then hold it for a long time before licking it again. This is all right for children, but for you and me to lick at a bar of pleasure and then try to keep it around for another lick is not worthy of an adult.

When newcomers come to my talks on meditation, one of the simple ways I observe them is to see how easily they get dissatisfied with temporary satisfactions. Anybody quickly discontented with passing pleasure has good possibilities for spiritual awareness. Such a person has outgrown the toys of life. Many of the people I see around me today are like this. They may still be playing games with their clothes or hair style, but once they encounter the spiritual life as it should be presented – difficult, challenging, demanding a deep commitment to the goal – they can respond and go very far.

"Rajas," Sri Krishna continues, "binds us to action." When you are seething with rajas, you will be doing a hundred things and never concentrating on one of them. You will always be active, always restless.

Today on the way home I saw a big garbage truck with a sign at the back: "Frequent Stops." This is a good reminder for rajasic people. The garbage truck stops everywhere. It opens up with a loud noise, picks up a lot of stuff, and dumps it in; then it goes a few more feet and does the same thing all over again. Those who get caught in pleasure and reckless activities are like this. They go in some store and spend a while there, then into another store to do the same – from tavern to tavern, game to game, country to country. Life is lost like this, often in the name of change. "I need a change," we say. Change is the last thing we need; we have very little else. Our deep need is for something that abides.

Compulsive action is often responsible for tension and alienation. Those who are constantly trying to make more money, for example, will not have time to be aware of the needs at home. They will not be able to enjoy their family; they will not even be able to enjoy a vacation.

The slogan of rajas is "The end justifies the means." Actually it is not even a slogan; it is an axiom. Rajas thinks only about ends. The one criterion he applies to the means to an end is, Will it work? This is not only immoral, it is futile. One of the most fundamental spiritual laws is that only right means can produce right ends. War cannot produce peace; only peace can produce peace. War produces only more war. Greed cannot produce satisfaction; it can only produce more greed. Competition cannot lead to anybody's long-term welfare; it can only increase separateness.

Means and ends, Gandhi said, are one and the same. When you are using right means to bring understanding and unity to your home, you do not even have to ask, "Am I succeeding?" The question is not relevant. As Gandhi says, "Full effort is full victory." Similarly, all that you and

I have to do is give our very best to the solution of terrible problems like violence. We can use our time, energy, and resources to support causes like our own Blue Mountain Center of Meditation, which in the Buddha's words are doing the highest work by driving out anger, fear, and greed. All we have to ask is, "Am I doing my best – every day, every way I can?"

"Tamas," the verse concludes, "binds us to delusion." Literally, it smothers wisdom, wraps it up in a dense blanket of ignorance and sits on top to make sure no awareness escapes. The lowest kind of human being is the one who is overcome by tamas, who cannot and will not act because he or she does not care.

When we have to do something we don't like, Tamas overtakes us, ties us up, and throws us into the trunk of his car. We might as well be paralyzed. We can't act; we can't feel; we become utterly insensitive, utterly unaware of the suffering our attitude causes others. It is not that we want them to suffer; we are simply unaware of anything except ourselves. Many acts of infidelity or disloyalty are committed in bouts of tamas, when we don't understand what loyalty means and cannot imagine that acts have consequences.

In this state, if we see someone being exploited – some person, group, race, or nation – we feel neither sympathy nor anger. We cannot act to relieve distress; suffering and injustice scarcely make an impression on our consciousness. We are in the trunk, and there is no one behind the wheel to feel or act. It is a tragic situation. Many people today seem unaware of the suffering in which so much of the world lives, simply because they are insensitive to anything other than themselves.

Some time ago I opened the morning paper and learned that the mayor of San Francisco had been shot to death right in his office by a former city councilman. The assassin felt he had been treated unfairly, so he went and got a gun. I expected the city to be so shocked, so concerned, that everybody would demand stricter handgun laws to try to keep this kind of crime from going on and on. Instead there was mourning for a day, a statement or two, and then the tragedy was forgotten again – as it was for President and Senator Kennedy, for Dr. Martin Luther King, Jr., for over seven thousand others every year, men, women, and children, shot to death often by one of their own family or friends when anger raged out of control. The tragedy makes no impact. Life goes on as usual. That is tamas: business as usual. There is no capacity to understand that this is writing on the wall for all of us, demanding selfless, nonviolent action to set it right.

All of us, Sri Krishna says, are obliged to contribute to life. That is the sole purpose for our being here. Those who are so caught up in themselves that they do not care what happens to others, who cannot see consequences past their own nose, have pulled the covers of tamas over their heads and are trying to pretend to life that they are not there. Circumstances can treat such people very roughly. Yet even this kind of person can throw off the pall of tamas through the practice of meditation.

रजस्तमश्चाभिभूय सत्त्वं भवति भारत ।
रजः सत्त्वं तमश्चैव तमः सत्त्वं रजस्तथा ॥ १४-१० ॥

*10. Sattva predominates when rajas and tamas
are transformed. Rajas prevails when sattva
is weak and tamas overcome. Tamas prevails
when rajas and sattva are dormant.*

No one could want to live under the sway of rajas or tamas. But most human beings do. Why, in spite of good intentions, are we unable to remove the mental blocks that bar our way to selfless action? Why do we get caught so easily in self-centered activities, even some that are detrimental?

This is the human dilemma. Sometimes when we have a job to do, we feel paralyzed. We cannot bring ourselves to look at the job and if we do, we feel so inadequate that we say, "I can't do it! Better get somebody else." Yet when something we like comes, we can do it with energy and gusto. There may not even be any profit in it; it may actually bring us or others harm – the next day, some months later, or in the next generation. It does not matter. We get so absorbed that we never notice how time flies, and we neglect duties that have to be attended to even if they are unpleasant. Either way we fill our time but miss the point of life.

This simple verse gives a great secret: to live in sattva, get control over rajas and tamas. Keep rajas in rein and don't even let tamas out of the barn. When any two gunas languish the other will flourish, for these are the whole fabric of life.

You can watch this interplay yourself. You may read the Gita on Monday and feel inspired. The words touch you deeply; you immediately want to change your life and pursue its supreme goal. The next morning you get up early, have a good meditation, a sattvic breakfast, work with concentration at your job, speak kindly, return courtesy for unkindness. If you start feeling lethargic, you go for a fast walk repeating the mantram or turn to some job you have been putting off. If you start speeding up, you repeat the mantram and slow down. If you find yourself caught in some third-priority item because you enjoy it, you have the will and discrimination to drop it and turn to item number one. In all these ways you are withdrawing attention from rajas and tamas, and sattva flourishes – till the middle of the week.

By then, despite your intentions, the will is beginning to flag. Inspiration has lost its edge. And the pace of the week has quickened at work. Deadlines loom, people make demands; the old habit of speed starts to draw you in again, perhaps without your realizing it. You try to fit more things in, and begin snapping at people if they get in your way. Perhaps by Thursday you are taking work home, thinking about it at dinner, cancelling that date with your partner so you can finish the week's report by Friday. Sattva is neglected; rajas dominates the scene.

Saturday morning you crash. You can't get out of bed; it feels so cozy, and you're enjoying your dream. When you finally sit down for meditation, you fall asleep again. "Better relax this weekend," you say. "I've had a hard week." You treat yourself to a heavy breakfast and take your coffee cup out to the yard, where you can sit in the sun and plan a few improvements.

And Sunday morning you don't know what is wrong. You're not really in pain, but things just don't feel right. Your throat feels a little raspy and you're drained of energy. "Probably some virus," you say. "I'd better not inflict myself on others today. I'll meditate here in bed. Honey, will you call the church and tell them we can't make it to the work party this afternoon?" There is an old paperback on exorcism lying around. You start to leaf through it. A page catches your eye. . . .

Maintaining sattva in the teeth of rajas requires a fight that goes on for a long, long time. But most important, don't let yourself fall into tamas. When sattva is about to collapse, give it all your support. It will be excruciating, but you can develop your will only by exercising it; there is no other way.

सर्वद्वारेषु देहे ऽस्मिन्प्रकाश उपजायते ।
ज्ञानं यदा तदा विद्याद्विवृद्धं सत्त्वमित्युत ॥ १४-११ ॥

*11. When sattva predominates, the light of
wisdom shines through every gate of the body.*

This is the Upanishadic image of the body as the kind of city people had in ancient and medieval times, with a wall all around and gateways for traffic in and out. The body's gates, of course, are the senses. Sri Krishna is reminding us that there is a mayor inside, looking out through these gates. If the city is in order, the gatekeepers obey when the mayor says, "Let this fellow in; keep that one out." That is sattva. But in the city of Rajas the gatekeepers do their own thing, and in the city of Tamas they are fast asleep. In either case there is trouble.

To take a simple example, I still remember the time a particularly explicit horror movie came to our little city of Petaluma. Grown men and women stood in line to pay through the nose just to get sick in the stomach. That was the attraction. In one theater in San Francisco, I read, a lady went into convulsions right in the aisle.

I saw couples in that line, waiting to get in. I could imagine the scene at the box office window. "Here's my Juliet," Romeo says. "I love her so much I want to give her convulsions."

The eyes and ears are gateways to the mind. When we watch a movie like this, we are trucking everything we see and hear right inside, where the untrained mind can have a heyday with it.

The Self, the scriptures tell us, is light itself. We do not suspect this when we keep trucking in garbage, of course. Tamas is a blackout; rajas is a city riot. But in sattva, the city is peaceful. Your heart is full, rich, loving, and wise, so the splendor within shines forth freely.

लोभः प्रवृत्तिरारम्भः कर्मणामशमः स्पृहा ।
रजस्येतानि जायन्ते विवृद्धे भरतर्षभ ॥ १४-१२॥

*12. When rajas predominates, a person
runs about pursuing selfish and greedy
ends, driven by restlessness and desire.*

What prevents the light of the Self from shining through? What keeps us from having tender, lasting relationships? It is rajas, Sri Krishna explains, and the first sign of rajas is greed.

Rajas is full of passion, but passion that is unharnessed. It cannot help erupting in anger, fear, and greed. Wherever he goes, Rajas is always thinking, "What can I get out of this?" If he sees a beautiful landscape, he subdivides it and puts up tract houses. If he sees a dense forest, he wants to raze it and sell the lumber. If he sees a school of trout shimmering in a stream, his first thought is to get his fishing gear. This way of thinking is depleting our world today. Gandhi said, "There is enough on earth for every man's need, but not enough for every man's greed." In India, against the background of a poverty-stricken subcontinent, he went so far as to say that if you had one button more than necessary, you were a thief; that button was at somebody else's expense. In our affluent society, of course, it is not necessary to go so far. Everyone should be able to live at a reasonable level of comfort. But it is still good to simplify our lives and not spend time and energy acquiring things that add to pollution or deplete the resources of the world.

Greediness is a fierce, tenacious glue. It can stick a human being to anything on earth, without his even being aware that he is stuck.

Take the automobile. I have to be careful here, because misunderstanding comes so easily. I am not at all against automobiles; they perform a very useful function. But when we get greedy about what automobiles can do for us, we get glued to them. We cannot do without them. We change our way of living for them, rearrange our cities for them, do everything we can to accommodate more and more of them at higher and higher speeds. Nothing is without problems, and cars are naturally no exception. But when we get glued, we can no longer ask, "Is this still worth the cost? Do we have to have more cars every year? Do we have to keep building faster roads just because cars can go faster?" The cost includes pollution and suffering. Automobiles kill almost fifty thousand people in this country every year, and the long-term toll of pollution on our air, water, and food is incalculable.

Sometimes I see a country's progress toward civilization measured in terms of how many automobiles it has. Why not measure in terms of bananas? There is as much connection. We have become so attached to cars that we cannot imagine civilization without them. Automobiles *are* useful, but they have nothing to do with being civilized.

California, the papers say, is expecting to have its twenty millionth motor vehicle on the highways before long. We could observe that day as a day of mourning. When I drive to San Francisco I am always struck by how many cars cruise by with only one passenger; I would estimate at least seventy-five percent. By what standard do we "need" millions of cars to get the same number of people to work at the same hours in the same places?

On the positive side, I feel heartened to learn that car pools are slowly growing in popularity. People are increasingly willing to wait five or ten minutes for a neighbor in order to reduce pollution and congestion.

When rajas prevails, Sri Krishna says, *pravrittir ārambhah*: we take up all kinds of activities. Rajas makes big plans, then drains all his prāna in excitement. When he starts to act on those plans, he often runs out of steam. It is the nature of excitement that it cannot last. It has to die down, and when it does, the same project you began with such enthusiasm looks utterly boring. It is full of dull, drab details that you had not foreseen. And you give up. The project has not changed, but prāna is gone. When we say something is interesting, it is not that the project is full of some substance called "interestingness" that sticks us to it until it oozes away. We are full of prāna, the fuel of attention; that is what makes it interesting. Rajas takes the prāna and runs. Then Tamas comes in and says, "The place is mine!"

People who are prone to excitement, the Gita says, will find it difficult to achieve anything worthwhile in life. They do not have the sustained capacity to carry through. Sri Krishna takes a long view here. Many people – this country has an abundance of them – have enough prāna for decades of excited, enthusiastic activity. But activity, the Gita says, is not achievement. It is not enough to rush about beginning a lot of things or keeping busy. Even without reference to spiritual goals, a well-spent life is one that rounds out what it has begun. The life of a great artist or scientist is usually shaped by a single desire, carried through to the very end. Without this capacity to carry through, we scatter our lives. Like seeds broadcast on an uncultivated field, our activities do not bear fruit.

Restless activity is a hallmark of our age. It is not a wholly negative quality. I would say it is a signal bell, announcing readiness for the practice of meditation. When we feel restless, power is rising. We should never waste this power by running from place to place, flying from continent to continent, doing dangerous things just because they are dangerous or new things just because they are new.

With their immense energy and restlessness, young people sometimes get caught in daring activities – hang gliding, surfing, mountaineering, solo flying – simply because nothing else demands enough of them. They don't find much challenge in making money or getting ahead in the world, and they don't feel inclined to do what the rest of the world is doing. Sometimes they cause a lot of trouble to themselves and others, all because power is rising and they don't know what to do with it. They are ready for meditation.

The Meditation Aptitude Test has two questions: One, have you got a lot of energy? Two, are you so restless that nothing satisfies you? If the answer to both is yes, you are admitted to the class. This is a fertile combination. With immense restlessness and immense energy you can go very far, because this is the gas with which a human being travels.

I believe I am one of the few spiritual teachers who will come out and say that there is nothing wrong with desire. Desire is power, and power is neither good nor bad. What *is* good or bad is the use to which we put it.

All of us believe that a strong desire leaves us only two alternatives: yield to it or be repressed. Give in to it and be happy; repress it and suffer a host of horrible consequences we associate vaguely with Sigmund Freud. The Gita says there is a third alternative. When a fierce desire surges up until your mind feels as if it is going to burst, your heart is racing, your glands are working overtime, everything in you is clamoring for that desire to be fulfilled, Sri Krishna asks quietly, "Have you got daring?" You say, "Talk to me later." He says, "Anybody can give in to pleasure. Where's the challenge in that? If you're tough, defy it." This is power rising. Don't explode it all over the road; and don't just sit there in the lot and race your engine till you are out of gas, which is repression. Get behind the wheel and use that energy to take you fast and far to a selfless goal. That is what I mean by transforming a desire.

People with strong desires can go very far on the path of meditation. When I meet people with a passion for making money I say, "Come learn to meditate." All they have to do is get their hook out of money and get it into meditation. There is a technique for this. It is the same for sex or any other dominant passion; every desire can be harnessed to a spiritual goal.

अप्रकाशो ऽप्रवृत्तिश्च प्रमादो मोह एव च ।
तमस्येतानि जायन्ते विवृद्धे कुरुनन्दन ॥ १४-१३ ॥

13. When tamas is dominant a person lives in darkness – slothful, confused, and easily infatuated.

Now Tamas gets his turn again, which he always finds gratifying. Rajas, of course, he considers a bore. "Krishna," he says, "talk about *me*."

"First," Sri Krishna replies, "you're *aprakāsha*." *Prakāsha* is brightness: a glowing skin, luminous eyes, a vibrant voice, the whole body shining with pent-up selfless energy. Such a person is utterly alive, certain that he or she can face any emergency squarely. *Aprakāsha,* which describes Tamas, is just the opposite. His eyes are dull, almost glazed; he can scarcely keep them open. No amount of Lustre Tone or vitamin E can make glazed eyes glow. When the lamp of love is lit inside, on the other hand, even your skin has to show it.

Even physically, tamas makes us ugly. If we have a good bone structure and don't eat too much candy, we may be able to hide the worst physical effects of tamas while we are in our teens and twenties. After that, however, every body begins to wear, and I think every sensitive person is aware of the dullness that comes to the skin and eyes and mouth of someone who is aware of nothing but his own pleasure.

Second is *apravritti,* 'utterly inactive.' If you ask Tamas why he never contributes to anybody else's welfare, he replies candidly, "Why should

I? I don't do anything even for my own welfare." Tamas is a very impartial fellow: no work for anyone.

Interestingly enough, this is untenable. When Dr. Selye says that work is a biological necessity, that is another way of saying that no one can be one hundred percent tamasic. This is an encouraging comment. When his personal likes are roused, even the most tamasic person you can find will spend hours rearranging his record collection, playing cards, or clipping magazines. If he has something that appeals to his self-will, he may get so entangled that he forgets about dinner, which for Tamas is saying a good deal. All of us, in other words, have the capacity for working hard. All we need do is release that capacity and then harness it by gaining detachment from ourselves.

Third is *pramāda*, 'lacking in earnestness' without zeal or gusto. Everybody, I think, appreciates a person who is full of enthusiasm, intense both in attitude and in action. People like that are good material for spiritual living. Tamas, again, is the opposite. If he takes up art, he doesn't get past smearing large areas with color; he likes whatever goes onto the canvas. If he takes up gardening, he usually gets bogged down after the planting plan is finished, when the time comes to dig.

Fortunately, earnestness can be cultivated. Those who are not born earnest can become earnest. I admire a person who is earnest, but I have a special admiration for the lethargic person who has *made* himself earnest.

Last comes *moha*, 'infatuation.' Tamas gets easily infatuated, because he has very little discrimination. Any little thing can put its hook in him. He sees a teenager playing "Space Invaders" in a video parlor and immediately he gets fascinated; he will stay the rest of the afternoon putting in quarters and getting overcome by electronic extraterrestrials. When he sees his first electronic game watch, video recorder, food processor, or home computer, he has to have one.

Everybody knows how easy it is to get caught like this. The trend today is almost universal. A few years ago, I remember, San Francisco proudly hosted the First International Exhibition of Erotic Art. (I don't believe there was a second.) Cultured, well-educated men and women flocked to it, to show they had cast off the fetters of our Victorian past. Another show that lingers in my memory was an exhibition of coffins.

One was made in the shape of a Mercedes Benz; the entrance, so to say, was through the trunk. I have seen exhibitions of embroidered jeans, museum collections of corkscrews, beer cans, bread sculpture, candy wrappers, and buttons. These are not the work of unintelligent people; this is what happens to any human being when moha settles like a fog.

Moha is what advertisements exploit. Rajas is the ad agency and the client, but Tamas is the prime consumer. Label something "More" and he will buy it, even if it may kill him. Or don't promise anything at all. Show him a lissome blonde beside a babbling brook in a verdant field and say, "Wide-open flavor!" He won't even ask, "What's the connection?" As Emerson says, he loves to be deceived. Rajas asks, "Don't you want to be *alive* with pleasure?" Tamas says, "Sure. Do I have to do anything?" "Just buy this and put it in your mouth." Sattva would object, "The least you could do is show him the other side. 'Alive with pleasure', dying with pain."

Tamas gets caught in doing little things that benefit nobody. Then, as he dwells on them, these trivial activities begin to look *big*. He holds them closer than the nose on his face, so that they fill his field of vision. It sounds like a harmless case of myopia, but I think no state of mind is more tragic. When you get caught in doing your own pleasant little thing, even if it is not harmful in itself, a voice inside starts saying, "I don't care. I don't care what happens to anybody else, even to myself. What does it matter as long as I can keep on doing what I like?"

Sattva advises, "Move back a little." As we gain detachment, life falls into perspective. Games and hobbies appear trivial then against a world backdrop, where the lives of millions of people can be improved, even if only a little, by how we live and what we do.

यदा सत्त्वे प्रवृद्धे तु प्रलयं याति देहभृत् ।
तदोत्तमविदां लोकानमलान्प्रतिपद्यते ॥ १४-१४ ॥
रजसि प्रलयं गत्वा कर्मसङ्गिषु जायते ।
तथा प्रलीनस्तमसि मूढयोनिषु जायते ॥ १४-१५ ॥

14. *Those dying in the state of sattva*
attain the pure worlds of the wise.

> *15. Those dying in rajas are reborn among people*
> *driven by work. But those who die in tamas*
> *are conceived in the wombs of the ignorant.*

If the Lord lives in all of us, why are our lives so different? Why are many in such great misery and so few truly happy? Why do some succeed, find what they seek, yet die unfulfilled? Why do some attain fulfillment and others neither seek nor question?

Every sensitive human being asks these questions. I have never seen such a well-reasoned, sympathetic, or hopeful answer as in this chapter of the Gita, which lays the responsibility for our lives at our own doorstep, yet gives us full hope for changing ourselves completely.

Behind these two verses stands the immense backdrop of reincarnation. But the application of Sri Krishna's words is easiest to understand if we think in terms of this life only. Every day – the Buddha would say every instant – we are shaping our lives by how we think, speak, and act. If we lead a selfless life, we become secure and spread security to others. If we lead selfish lives, caring only about ourselves, we make ourselves insecure, rigid, self-willed, and alienated. We cannot blame God for this, nor Providence, Nature, society, or the times. The first act of adult growth is to say, "I did this to myself. Nothing brought me to this unpleasant situation except my own foolish choices. Therefore I can also get myself out, by making my own wise choices."

Scrooge, in *A Christmas Carol,* goes to bed an utterly selfish man. That night the ghost of old Marley, his former business partner, comes to visit him, rattling his chains. "Made every link myself," says Marley, "with every loan, every deal, every greedy thought. You have made a chain like this too, Ebenezer." Scrooge is terrified. The very next day he changes all his responses from selfish to selfless; he becomes a different man.

Why can't *we* change ourselves overnight? We get up in the morning and decide to do everything right – to be kind, detached, patient, and sattvic. But then the momentum of the day picks us up, and before we know it we have blown up at our partner or snapped at the children. By the end of the day we are all too clearly the same old person. What happens?

Samskāras are forces. When we go to sleep, the Upanishads say, these forces do not simply disappear. The dreaming state, in fact, is a Free Play Day. Unhampered by time or space, our samskāras get to run around and do whatever they like, acting out our favorite fantasies and fears. In dreamless sleep, however, they go backstage and sleep it off. Then it is that we truly rest. In this state, the Upanishads say, a king is not a king nor a pauper poor; there is neither old nor young, male nor female, sensation, sickness, nor sorrow. If we could wake up in that state, we could make choices free from any past conditioning. But we are unconscious in that state. After a while the samskāras start to wake up again, dragging us back to the waking state to take up all our desires and fears and aspirations just where we left off the day before – the same person, yet a little different too.

Similarly, the Upanishads say, samskāras do not vanish when we die. I know of no explanation more sensible, more down-to-earth. Just as we enter dreamless sleep every night, yet pick up every morning where we left off, so we pick up at birth where we left off the previous life, to continue working out the same samskāras.

That is why Hindu and Buddhist mystics lay so much importance on the state of consciousness we are in at the moment of death. Against this background, your life and mine this time around are entirely the result of the innumerable good and bad choices we made in previous lives. There is no such thing as an accident, the Hindu and Buddhist sages say. As Jesus puts it, "Not a sparrow shall fall without thy Father."

When I first came to this country, I was introduced to the "layaway plan." I don't believe I had even heard the phrase before. I was waiting in a big department store, looking at something expensive and useless which I could use as an example in my meditation classes, when the saleslady came up. "Wouldn't you like to buy this?" she asked. "It's marked down to sixty dollars."

I laughed. "I have only six dollars," I said, to be polite.

"That's all right," she said cheerfully. "That's enough for the first payment. We'll lay it away for you while you come and pay six dollars every month. Before the year is over, it's yours!"

I was impressed. "May I take it with me?"

"Oh, no! This is layaway. We keep it here on the shelf until you've paid for it."

I told the lady I would keep my six dollars too.

Karma is layaway on a cosmic scale. In every life we have done certain selfless things, helped a few people, served a few worthy causes; so we have a small packet of good karma, kept carefully in a pigeonhole with our name on it. When we die, according to the Tibetan mystics, we get a waiting period for rest and recuperation in which we are expected to look over our previous life to see what mistakes we have committed, so we can avoid committing them again – a little like our friend Scrooge. Then we claim our packets of karma, good and bad, and look for a suitable context – country, race, parents, environment – in which to try again.

When I explained this to a friend, she objected, "I don't know if I agree with that. If I had had a choice, I wouldn't have chosen to be born in Queens. Why wouldn't everybody pick rich parents and be born with a silver spoon?"

"That is the rub," I said. "You don't get a choice that way. You have already made your choice, by all the things you said and thought and did in the life before." After we die, all this information is fed into a cosmic computer which would be a hobbyist's dream. It has unlimited memory, and it never crashes or loses any of its data. It takes in all the particulars, looks over the available openings, and matches your karma with the karma of parents, cousins, neighbors, city, nation, and epoch. You are born to a family with similar or complementary samskāras so that you can work out your own samskāras; and you are born into times that will allow those samskāras to come to fruition. Your samskāras will lead you to behave a certain way in school, to go out with particular kinds of friends, to choose the right kind of partner for getting the kind of children you need in order for you to grow. If you were difficult as a child, you have to have a difficult child the next time around; how else could you learn? If you have been a good husband, you may get a context in which you have a good husband, so you can learn to be a good wife.

When this is understood, reincarnation ceases to be a mysterious product of the Eastern imagination and becomes a cogent, compassionate explanation of our lives and times. It offers meaning, and it offers hope. It means that we have selected everything ourselves, not so much consciously as by our desires. The appeal is simple. Life is an educational process, a kind of school, with all the responsibility of making progress left to us. Whatever situation we are in is the perfect context for us to learn to face a problem in ourselves. When we learn to face a problem squarely, the Hindu mystics say, that particular situation will not recur. There is no need to learn the lesson again.

But here let me again sound a note of caution. In India we seldom talk about reincarnation because everybody believes in it. In the West, however, the topic seems exotic, so people sometimes get caught up in it. I still receive invitations to attend workshops on reincarnation or to give a talk on who I was in some previous life. I want to reply, "I am much more concerned with who I am in this life." If the theory of reincarnation helps you to understand how to face difficult situations with patience and compassion, well and good. Beyond that, I would not advise getting intellectually caught up in it. All kinds of fruitless speculation can result.

Against this background, these esoteric-seeming verses make good common sense. Let me take up the second one first, because I like to end with the silver lining.

When a person dies in a mood of tamas, Sri Krishna says, he is born in a family full of tamas. I find this very reasonable. He has to learn to transform tamas; until he does so on his own, he cannot graduate to the next grade. So this hypothetical fellow is born into a family where everybody is inert. The father has no job, the mother overeats; every member of the family has the brakes on. They don't have much will, can't bring themselves to act, like to postpone everything. He will fit that family perfectly, because he is coming in with his brakes on too.

In India we have an official on the public roads called the brake inspector. He has only one job – to stop any car, any bus, any truck he chooses and say, "Let me see your brakes." He is not interested in any other aspect of the car; he just wants to see if the brakes work.

Tamas's brakes work fine; that is the problem. In those who do not have much will, who cannot bring themselves to act, who like to postpone everything, the brakes are permanently set. There is nothing wrong with the car. It is still in decent shape, and there is plenty of gas in the tank. The tamasic person cannot come into this life and complain, "I've got a lemon. Take it back and give me a better vehicle." All that has happened is that the hand brake is on. I don't have to tell you what kind of wear and tear results from this; that is what happens with tamas too. But there is no irremediable problem; we just have to release the brake and move our foot over onto the accelerator. Then the tamasic person can shoot forward like a Ferrari.

To continue this automobile language – which used to be as difficult for me as Sanskrit – one difficulty in tamas may be that the battery is dead. The car is in good condition, you have enough gas, but there is no power for getting the car started. I asked Christine what you do in such a situation. She said, "You call the auto club." The person comes, jump-starts your car, and then drives off with a cheery smile. That is what a spiritual teacher can do. There are certain situations in which the will is paralyzed; we feel unable to move a muscle. Then the teacher can connect the cables, tell you to stay behind the wheel, and start you off his own battery with his support, love, and continuing inspiration.

I am assured that this kind of thing is a free service of the auto club, but as you say in this country, there is no such thing as a free lunch. The same is true in sādhana. If we get a start from our teacher, he expects us to make the best of it – to keep on driving, recharge the battery, and head straight for our destination. If we pull off to the side of the road again, switch off the engine, and put our feet up, the battery will go dead again, and the dispatcher may not consider the second call as urgent an emergency.

If we find ourselves in a family which is ignorant of the unity of life, lacking both energy and initiative, that is all the more reason why we should release the brakes in our own lives. When others in our family see this, they may be motivated to learn to do it too. In many families I have seen, after watching John or Josie meditate for a few years, somebody thoughtful will ask casually, "How do you do this Indian thing?"

Similarly, when a person full of rajas dies, he or she is born in a car that has no brakes. Tamas keeps his foot on the brake and leaves the hand brake on too; Rajas doesn't have either. His transmission is automatic, and the only pedal on his floor is an accelerator.

When he was ten or so, my friend Josh had a kind of car he had made himself. It consisted of a platform with an uncomfortable seat, on which he had mounted four undersize wheels. Everything about that vehicle was primitive except those wheels. "Josh," I said, "How do you steer?"

"Simple," he said. "If you want to turn, you pull on this rope." It was fastened to the front axle at both ends; he hauled on it as he would reins on an ox.

"And where are the brakes?"

"It doesn't have any," Josh said cheerfully.

"What do you do if you have to stop?"

"You drag your feet."

Rajasic people are born into a car like Josh's. They have to keep going from morning to night, often doing things that help nobody including themselves. They can get caught in anything. Whatever they take up becomes an obsession; a casual hobby becomes a full-time occupation. I saw this many times when I was a professor, though it is by no means confined to campuses. Somebody writes a paper and gets praised for his understanding of punctuation; after a while he is working on his dissertation, "The History of the Comma Down the Ages." He *does* care about what happens in the rest of the world, at least to some extent. He feels regret when he reads that there is famine in the Sahel, or that one out of four in his generation will probably die of cancer from environmental causes. But these are vague issues to him, beyond anything he can do. The size of his universe is measured by just one question: "Comma or semicolon?"

The person who dies full of rajas, Krishna says, is born in a home where everybody is busy from morning till evening. Everybody in the family is making something, whether it is money or mischief; nobody has enough time to sit still and cultivate the garden inside, or observe himself or others. This kind of stillness can be healing. It makes us more sensitive, gives us an opportunity to see life whole. But the rajasic family has no time for reflection, and the rajasic child born into such a family rubs his hands together and says, "Perfect! This is the place for me." It is: perfect for getting more rajasic, but also perfect for suffering the consequences of rajas and learning to transform it, which is a service to the whole family.

Finally we reach the silver lining of these verses: the man or woman who has cultivated selflessness and learned to live for others becomes full of sattva. When they die, Sri Krishna says, such people are born into a selfless family. The father forgets himself easily in the welfare of his wife and children; the mother is a shining example of strength and tenderness, who can hold her family together when all the storms of life are blowing. The child born into such a family grows up strong, secure, and selfless. That is the climate in which he is born; that is the air she breathes. There is no contradiction between this and modern psychology. Such people take easily to the practice of meditation, sometimes very early in life. When they are earnest, they find a guide who will love them, cherish them, and show them how to overcome the conditioning of all the gunas and set their course for the supreme goal of life.

This is how I would account for someone like Thérèse of Lisieux, who when she was still a child could say with utter honesty, "There is only one desire in all my heart, and that is to become a great saint." She swept toward her goal so swiftly, with such single-minded purpose, that in the language of Hinduism we would have to say that she merely picked up in this life where she left off in the last. By the time of her death, barely twenty-four years later, she had attained such stature that Pope Pius X called her "the greatest saint of modern times."

The "other Teresa," Teresa of Ávila, tells us that she took twenty years to unify her desires. I would say that is one reason she became such an excellent teacher; she understood deeply the conflicts most of us face, and she knew from her own experience exactly how to deal with them. To me she is one of the most magnificent examples of womanhood in the world, as beautiful as she was spiritual. She had an unerring gift for selecting young girls of great spiritual promise, some even in their teens, to follow her way of life. According to the Hindu and Buddhist tradition, these are girls who have come into this life ready to take to spiritual disciplines. They responded to Teresa enormously. The Gita would say they must have been born into sixteenth-century Spain just to come into the orbit of this great saint, the perfect spiritual teacher for their needs.

कर्मणः सुकृतस्याहुः साचिकं निर्मलं फलम् ।
रजसस्तु फलं दुःखमज्ञानं तमसः फलम् ॥ १४-१६ ॥

*16. The fruit of sattva is a pure heart.
The fruit of rajas is suffering. The fruit of
tamas is ignorance and insensitivity.*

Sattva breeds kind actions, and the fruit of kindness is a pure heart: no malice, no hatred, no ill feeling, no compulsive desire to cling to or manipulate anybody else. The sattvic person is kind to everybody, regardless of how he or she is treated in return. This kind of attitude purifies consciousness, because it is the same in all circumstances; there is no room in it for resentment, hostility, or fear. We can purify our hearts like this by moving closer when there are differences between us and others. Moving away from difficult people serves no purpose at all; it neither heals the breach nor helps either party.

Understanding, insight, wisdom, proceed from sattva and sattva alone. Rajas can pursue a subject as long as it likes; it may ferret out a great deal of detail, but it cannot penetrate the inner whole in which the details cohere. If you are full of rajas, you can study religion for twenty years and still not understand those simple statements of Jesus or the Buddha, which men and women of no scholarly standing have grasped with the heart for hundreds of years after they were spoken.

Sattva sees into the core of life, into its unity; its understanding leads to deeper understanding. Rajas, intent on finding more and more, only succeeds in becoming more and more confused by what it finds. Every mental state, Sri Krishna explains, bears fruit of the same kind.

Rajasas tu phalam duhkham: wherever actions are restless or greedy, motivated by one's own self-interest, the immediate results may be pleasant, but the long-term result is suffering and sorrow. Sales people in the tobacco industry may make a good deal of money, enough to buy a lot of things for themselves and their families. They may never even question where the money comes from, never make the connection between the product they sell and the hundreds of thousands who die of lung cancer, heart attack, stroke, and emphysema every year in the United States alone. But whether they notice or not, the fruit of their work is sorrow: sorrow for others, sorrow eventually for themselves. Every state of mind has consequences, not only in behavior but in the mind itself. Just as the kindness of sattva is its own reward, the restless, burning desire of rajas is its own punishment. It is a painful truth, but most of us need this kind of suffering to teach us the consequences of living for ourselves alone. If we do not learn this lesson, as the preceding verse points out, we have to go back to the same classroom the next time around, to reap the fruit of our present state of mind.

Ajnānam tamasah phalam: those who are full of tamas, who are content to do as little as possible in a halfhearted sort of way, also reap the fruit of their own state of mind: they do not grow. Unable to settle their debt of karma, they manage only to add to it. Insensitive to anything outside themselves, they move from darkness into greater darkness.

Unhappiness, as someone has observed, is not the worst thing in life. The worst that can befall us is insensitivity. In our pleasure-oriented world, unhappiness is looked upon as something frightful. In my opinion it is much better to be unhappy and grow up than never to grow up at all. If we are sincere about leading the spiritual life, we should not be afraid to be unhappy if it enables us to become more sensitive to the needs of others. But the tamasic person, easily contented with what life has to offer, cannot take anything but pleasure. He or she is at the mercy of whatever life sends.

सत्त्वात्संजायते ज्ञानं रजसो लोभ एव च ।
प्रमादमोहौ तमसो भवतो ऽज्ञानमेव च ॥ १४-१७ ॥

17. From sattva comes understanding; from rajas, greed. But the outcome of tamas is confusion, infatuation, and ignorance.

Once again, let me start with tamas. *Pramādamohau* is a potent combination: Confusion and Infatuation, Inc. They have combined their fortunes, and Tamas owns most of the stock. In an utter lack of proportion, he gives his energy to little things, to foolish, trifling activities, for one compelling reason: he likes them. They give him pleasure, enhance his sense of self-importance, and generally swell his ego. Tamas may be no intellectual, but he reads a lot of books, billions of dollars worth every year. Yet even publishers admit that most of these works need never have seen the light of day. I am not thinking merely of mass-market "escape literature" either. Many of these books are written by gifted writers, whose praises are sung in reviewers' columns and the halls of great universities. But the authors are so caught in "doing their own thing" that they do not have the freedom to ask themselves what the effect of their books will be.

A few years ago, to take just one example, you could find a particular sex manual stacked in high piles in bookstore windows everywhere. It sold millions of copies; I believe it was even recommended reading for some college courses. The author is an honest professional with sound credentials. I feel sure he wrote his book with good intentions. But he is so entangled in his subject that he cannot see the results. He cannot see what that book will do to the millions of people who read it avidly and put its advice into practice, whose lives are so drab that they will jump at any avenue that promises some pleasure.

The theme of that book was simple: Put yourself first and every-body else last. Anybody who takes such advice seriously is going to become more lonely, more estranged, and more frustrated with every year. When we get caught in the sensory game, there *is* some satisfac-tion at the outset; no one would deny that. But gradually we get sucked in and entangled. Then we are in a compulsion. It is no longer a matter of choosing to go after a particular sensation; we are being driven to it.

This book calls itself something like a "gourmet guide to loving." It sounds tantalizing. How easy, how pleasant, to love! I can understand anybody in these sensation-saturated times being attracted by these words and experimenting for themselves. But in a short, short time it is no longer experimentation; we have no choice. Anybody with some detachment can see how soon this kind of advice breaks up relation-ships. You find yourself going from one partner to another, then to another, for shorter and shorter periods of satisfaction. If I wrote the blurb for that book it would be, "A gourmet guide to disrupted rela-tions." Instead of joy, I would talk about "the sorrow of separateness." That is what it leads to. One side of the coin is the promise of joy; the other is the fact of loneliness and despair. The Gita says simply, "Make your choice." Choose which you prefer. But if you find yourself living in increasing dissatisfaction, don't blame it on God or society or the times we live in. Sex has a beautiful place in a completely loyal, loving relationship between two people, but where there is neither loyalty nor faith nor honor nor tenderness, sex is a terrible, disruptive force.

Ignorance is the hallmark of Tamas, just as wisdom is the hallmark of Sattva. If Tamas's eye falls on a book that says, "Do this; you'll like it," he immediately takes it up. He doesn't even ask about the logic or the consequences.

Greed has subtler forms too. Going after "our own thing" is usually just being greedy: "I don't care if this benefits anybody, even myself. I'm going to do it because I want to!" I have seen people standing in line all day because they wanted to hear the Rolling Stones in concert – in a theater in one of the most depressed areas of San Francisco. If a little of that day, that endurance, that desire, went into improving the neighborhood, what could not be done?

Every negative quality, Sri Ramakrishna says, can be turned into positive. "You say you're greedy?" he asks. "Why not be *really* greedy? Instead of wanting things just for yourself, want them for everybody. Don't settle for anything less." We should not be content with getting the best just for ourselves. Why not go after the best for everybody? If we give it the same time and energy we give to our personal interests, we can make a real difference in people's lives. So if you meet a greedy person, congratulate him. If he can turn his greed to human welfare, it will be a tremendous motivating force. The greed will still be there, but harnessed and mastered. The same is true of anger and fear; they are power that can be transformed. When Mahatma Gandhi's secretary, Mahadev Desai, was asked where Gandhi got all his power, Desai replied in effect, "He has forged all human passions – fear, anger, lust, greed – into one selfless, irresistible passion for the welfare of all."

A theater in Berkeley recently offered an intriguing bill: *Tarzan and Jane* and *Planet of the Apes*. The marquee said, "Go ape!" I saw quite a few students standing in the queue, waiting to pay three dollars for this privilege. I don't know exactly what it means to "go ape," but I wanted to protest, "This is backwards! Go human; don't go ape." Being resentful, hostile, or vindictive is going backwards in evolution. Two tigers fighting is all right; that is their nature. It may be natural for animals to be red in tooth and claw, but you and I have forfeited that. If we wanted to be hostile, the Hindu mystics say, we should have told the Lord, "I still have a few violent hang-ups to work out. If you don't mind, I prefer to stay in the jungle a couple of centuries more."

ऊर्ध्वं गच्छन्ति सत्त्वस्था मध्ये तिष्ठन्ति राजसाः ।
जघन्यगुणवृत्तस्था अधो गच्छन्ति तामसाः ॥ १४-१८ ॥

18. Those who live in sattva go upwards; those in rajas remain where they are. But those immersed in tamas sink downwards through their own inertia.

Near my village when I was growing up was a *sadhu* or holy man with an unusual way of teaching. In the morning Mad Nārāyana, as he was called, would go to the foot of a hill nearby and start rolling a huge rock up the slope. It was terribly hard work, especially in the heat of the Indian sun. People came to stand around and watch while he struggled.

Finally, toward the end of the day, he had the rock at the top. Then he motioned his audience to move away a safe distance, and with one hand he gave the rock a push. It rumbled down the slope, bouncing from spot to spot as it gathered speed, until it reached the bottom and crashed against a tree. All the while Mad Nārāyana watched and laughed. "It's so hard to go uphill," he explained. "But to go downhill you don't have to do anything at all!"

It took a long time before I understood the profundity of this simple teaching. It *is* hard to go uphill in life. You have to struggle for every inch, and you can't afford to stop and rest; if you do, the weight of your load will begin to slide you back again. But anybody can go downhill. It takes no effort. You don't have to make any decisions, resist any impulses, deny yourself any desires. You just do whatever you like, and it is automatic: down you go.

This is the dynamics of will and desire. Tamas, the abyss of unconsciousness, is like the trunk of our car, where Will and Desire have been locked up trussed and chloroformed. Tamasic people have neither will nor desire, which is a deceptive state. They may look serene, tranquil, established in peace of mind. Worse, they may think of themselves in just such terms: relaxed, easygoing, easy to deal with, "just an ordinary man." As

Gandhi said, this is the tranquility of the graveyard, where nobody moves, nobody talks, nobody lives – in other words, just the opposite of sattva.

But gradually desire and will begin to help each other untie the ropes. They are still in the trunk, but once an arm gets free here and a leg there, a feeble desire begins to stir. You tell yourself, "I think I wouldn't mind a little coffee." It's not much, but that is all you can muster; most of your capacity for desire is still tied up. With effort you manage to reach the stove, put the water on, and get some instant coffee powder into a paper cup. The result is nothing a connoisseur would recognize, but it is stimulating. As you drink it, desire wakes up a little more. Your mind has made a subtle connection: "Physical effort can lead to satisfaction." The development of rajas has begun.

Now, Desire is a smart chap. Once he and Will are out of the trunk of the car, he wants to keep control. So he tells Will, "Now that I got us out, why don't we go for a ride? You don't have to do anything. Sit in the back seat; there is a blanket you can curl up in if you like, and safety belts to keep you from getting up. I'll get behind the wheel."

Will has just been rescued from utter immobility; he scarcely has enough power to move. "Good idea," he tells himself. "Desire certainly is an obliging friend. Those are wise words of help." "All right," he says aloud. "You do the driving. I'll sit back here, make myself comfortable, and offer a few suggestions from time to time" – to which, in the tradition of back seat driving, nobody is expected to pay attention.

Now Will and Desire enter a kind of Laurel and Hardy phase. Desire is Oliver Hardy; Will is Stan Laurel. Everything is "Stan, do this" and "Of course, Ollie; you're so right." For Desire is now behind the wheel, and the first thing he does is start making the rounds of those restaurants that offer drab food at exorbitant rates. "Where are we going?" Will wants to know. "I don't have much money, Des, and I know who's going to get the bill. I don't like paying through the nose to put that kind of stuff into my mouth." But Desire is getting stronger and stronger. The greed for food, for the stimulating titillation of the taste buds, has grown fiercer. "Hey, Will, keep quiet!" he says. "I know what's good for you." He looks so convincing – you remember Oliver Hardy, with those big, strong shoulders and that little hat? – that Will says meekly, "You must be right."

At this stage Will is a harmless, accommodating fellow. But as the calories and cholesterol go on and on, he finally has to protest. "Des," he complains, "I'm sick of all these restaurants!"

"You make me tired," says Desire. He has grown loud and aggressive through self-indulgence. "I do all this driving for you, and what do you do? Nothing but sleep on the back seat and complain." He shoves Will down and drives on.

When they stop for gas, there is a sale on cigarettes. "Try this," says Desire. "It'll make you feel *cool*. Alive with pleasure. You've come a long way, Baby. Don't you owe it to yourself?" Poor Will believes all this; he still hasn't grown.

Soon the trunk in which they used to be tied up is full of discount cigarettes and throwaway cans of wine. Desire is no fool. He knows that nothing strikes at the will like a compulsive habit. As long as he can keep Will incapacitated in the back seat, Desire can stay behind the wheel to do as he likes. .

Unfortunately, Desire doesn't really know what he likes. He is bursting with energy; he clamors for challenges, the bigger the better; but he has no idea of where he wants to go. He drives to Hollywood, then Disneyland, then Las Vegas; finally they manage to cross the Mexican border. By the time they come back, there is heroin in the hubcaps and hashish under the hood. Desire swells with pride. "Got past everybody!" he says. "What an achievement!" There is always satisfaction in a job well done, even if the energy is wasted in a wrong direction.

Actually, this is a state of tremendous potential. Rajasic people are full of energy; when they take to meditation, all that restless energy and the desire for challenges gradually come under control. After a while they clean out the trunk; those articles are not being used any longer. They ask themselves, "Why did I put this there, anyway? Why did I put all that stuff in the hubcaps and under the hood? Let it all go." That is sattva; you are in control.

In sattva, Will and Desire are driving in a dual-control car, like the kind in which I took my driving lessons. Desire is still behind the wheel, but Will is the driving instructor, behind the other set of controls. As long as we are motivated by right desires – for the welfare of the whole family, the whole community, the whole of life – Will sits back and enjoys the ride. But the moment Desire starts to take a selfish turn, Will grabs the master control wheel, touches his foot to the brake, and says sharply, "That's no way to drive!"

In the early days of this, of course, Desire will thump on the steering wheel and cry. "I'm going to call the Highway Patrol!" Will just says, "I *am* the Highway Patrol. You haven't got anyone else to call. I'm the instructor, the police, everything." After a while Desire realizes that Will is his friend and protector, who has kept him from disaster again and again.

You do not lose your desires in sattva; not at all. All your right desires become immense. But the will is always in control. Those in rajas are content just to drive around, always trying to see what is on the other side of the mountain. When night falls they are still driving aimlessly. The gas tank is almost empty, the tires are worn to the cords, yet they haven't got anywhere. And tamas, of course, can't even find his keys. He has an engine, but he can't use it; all he can do is roll downhill. "But those in sattva go upward," Sri Krishna says simply: upward toward the summit of consciousness, against the pull of gravity. You're not in an old Morris Minor any more. You're in a Ferrari, surging with power, taking the hairpin bends effortlessly.

नान्यं गुणेभ्यः कर्तारं यदा द्रष्टानुपश्यति ।
गुणेभ्यश्च परं वेत्ति मद्भावं सो ऽधिगच्छति ॥ १४-१९ ॥
गुणानेतानतीत्य त्रीन्देही देहसमुद्भवान् ।
जन्ममृत्युजरादुःखैर्विमुक्तो ऽमृतमश्नुते ॥ १४-२० ॥

19. The wise see clearly that all action is a product
of the gunas. Knowing that which is above
the gunas, they enter into union with me.
20. Going beyond the three gunas which form the
body, they leave behind the cycle of birth and death,
decrepitude and sorrow, and attain to immortality.

Everything with which we are familiar – things, thoughts, actions, personality – is woven from the gunas. When Sri Krishna talks about going beyond all this, it almost sounds like going beyond the human condition altogether. I would say rather that it is going beyond human *conditioning* – the obsessive belief that we are the body and mind.

When we rise above this conditioning completely, we are no longer just a person. We become a permanent, beneficial force released into the stream of life forever. The Buddha is such a force; he can never die. As long as even one creature is bound, as he himself said, he cannot die. When we learn to live as the Buddha lived – "for the welfare of all, for the joy of all" – this force is released in our own lives. Then the Buddha, the Christ, comes to life in us.

When I came back from India to Berkeley in the early sixties, I found an amazing number of people who believed this force could be released by chemical means. Leading figures spoke persuasively about "chemical grace," and millions of people who wanted access to some higher level of reality were exploring the whole smorgasbord of psychoactive drugs. This is the sort of thing that happens when you believe you are physical; it is just another side of the belief that you can solve a personal problem with a pill.

I have been watching with fascination a new doctrine: electronic grace. (It is very much the same.) We are fascinated by computer technology and laser magic, and we believe there is nothing more to personality than chemistry and physics; why not produce spiritual awareness, love, insight, imagination, through cerebral engineering?

Perhaps – who knows? – technology will find some way to analyze brain waves so accurately that we will be able to identify waves of patience and impatience, sympathy and resentment, and so on. Engineers may be able to invent electronic controls to carry in your pocket, so that when your partner is making you lose your temper you can set the indicator on Patience, sit back, and listen with a calm mind. They may even find a transformer for likes and dislikes, so that when you sit down for dinner and see something you detest, you can switch over your brain waves and enjoy it. I am not saying this sort of thing cannot be done. But at what expense? The human being would cease to be a human being. We would lose our sensitiveness, our originality, our tenderness, our creativity, all because we never developed the capacity to use our will. Without the will we have no freedom, and without freedom of choice we become machines. That is the theme of Huxley's *Brave*

New World, and I think it tells us why the increase of impersonality we see today has been accompanied by an increasing loss of sensitiveness.

I have seen claims, for example, that "illumination tanks" can bring about the integration of consciousness. You sit inside with light and sound and so on all cut off, and you stay there till you are illumined. This is picking up the stick by the wrong end. It is true that to enter a higher level of consciousness, you have to be able to leave the world of sensory awareness behind. The crucial difference is that in sensory deprivation, some external agent deprives the senses of their stimuli. In such cases, consciousness is not withdrawn from the senses. They are still full of prāna, which means that the eye is still clamoring to see, the ear to hear, and so on. As a result, they may see and hear what is not there. In meditation, however, consciousness is withdrawn from all the senses by the will. All desires to see, hear, taste, touch, and smell are withdrawn into an immense desire to turn inward toward the Self. The power of these desires is harnessed by the will, which grows huge and strong like Jack's beanstalk. When the will is that strong, the power of your desires is at your disposal.

When you can withdraw power from your senses at will, you go through life with such economy of personal energy that you scarcely feel stress at all. The Gita calls this "action in inaction." There is no tension, no friction, no effort. You have gone beyond the gunas, beyond all human conditioning.

अर्जुन उवाच ।
कैर्लिङ्गैस्त्रीन्गुणानेतानतीतो भवति प्रभो ।
किमाचारः कथं चैतांस्त्रीन्गुणानतिवर्तते ॥ १४-२१ ॥

ARJUNA:

*21. What are the characteristics of those who have
gone beyond the gunas, O Lord? How do they act?
How have they passed beyond the gunas' hold?*

When a man or woman is completely evolved, what happens? What does it mean to be completely integrated in character, conduct, and consciousness?

It is those who attain this state who show us what life really means. It is a mistake to think of Sri Ramakrishna, St. Teresa, St. Francis, or Mahatma Gandhi as consisting of body and mind. Their lives reveal the transformation from a separate personality into a universal beneficial force. These are not petty individual personalities from a particular period. St. Francis is much more alive today than most of the population of the world. We should not think of him in terms of a limited period of time – sixty or seventy years – or a circumscribed place. When a person is obsessively identified with a particular body and mental state, his influence is extremely limited; it cannot last long. But when we go beyond the gunas, we are no longer limited by time, place, and circumstance. We become a lasting beneficial force, as the immense power of the Self is released through us into the stream of life.

This force is called *kundalinī* or evolutionary energy in Sanskrit, and it is present in every one of us. No one should say "*I* can't make myself a beneficial force!" The force is already there. But we are spellbound by what Hindu mystics call Māyā, the potent hypnotism of the senses and self-will. We cannot suspect even for an instant that in this fragile, limited frame of body, mind, and intellect a virtually limitless spiritual power is compressed a million times, waiting to be released.

In my early days in this country people used to ask me, "Isn't meditation simply self-hypnosis?" It is just the opposite: meditation is self-*de*hypnosis. I saw an ad recently that said, "Learn to hypnotize your friends!" This is carrying coals to Newcastle. Continual, constant hypnosis is the human condition; we live in a hypnotized world. Sri Ramakrishna, I believe, compares it to a puppet show. If we could interview Punch of "Punch and Judy," he would tell us, "Sure, we're free! I can hit Judy; she can throw a pot at me. Isn't that what free choice means?" But those of us outside the puppet theater can see a fellow with red hair standing in the back and pulling the strings.

In our case, Sri Ramakrishna says, *we* are Punch or Judy. The puppeteer is the ego, pulling strings from inside. A little tug and we flare up. Afterwards we say, "I *chose* to get angry." I have actually heard people say this. Or perhaps the strings go slack and we fall into tamas. We say, "This is a personal choice I have made. I want to be lethargic. I like to feel dull." The Buddha would smile gently at this kind of talk. "When someone is angry with you," he would say, "if you can remain calm, compassionate, and respectful, *then* you can call yourself free." You will have broken loose from the puppeteer's strings. After that the ego can tug at them as long as he likes; it will not govern your responses.

श्रीभगवानुवाच ।
प्रकाशं च प्रवृत्तिं च मोहमेव च पाण्डव ।
न द्वेष्टि संप्रवृत्तानि न निवृत्तानि काङ्क्षति ॥ १४-२२ ॥
उदासीनवदासीनो गुणैर्यो न विचाल्यते ।
गुणा वर्तन्त इत्येव यो ऽवतिष्ठति नेङ्गते ॥ १४-२३ ॥

SRI KRISHNA:

22. *They are unmoved by the harmony of sattva,*
the activity of rajas, or the delusion of tamas. They
feel no aversion when these forces are active, nor
do they crave for them when these forces subside.
23. *They remain detached, undisturbed by the actions*
of the gunas. Knowing that it is the gunas which act,
they abide within themselves and do not vacillate.

In practical language, those who transcend the gunas go beyond likes and dislikes.

This may sound like a trivial, even undesirable achievement. "Do you want me not to like or dislike *any*thing?" people sometimes ask. "I might as well not be living!" In fact, life as we usually live it does mean mostly liking this and disliking that, liking him, disliking her. But this is what makes us the puppets of our circumstances. When you are subject to likes and dislikes, you are standing on the street with an old tin can and begging of life, "Please treat me kindly. I can't walk; I can scarcely stand. Look at my tin can and drop in a few crumbs of pleasure as you pass." Most of us, I feel sure, would much prefer my granny's attitude. "Little Lamp," she used to tell me, "you just tell life, 'I don't care what you bring me; I'll make the best of it. I'm prepared for anything.'"

It *is* pleasant when life gives us something we like. That is what the mind lives for. When things go our way, the mind gets all excited. It calls its friends, talks incessantly, and runs around trying to do twelve things at once. "If only things could be like this always!" it says. "Wouldn't that be heaven?" But of course, things are not like that always. After a while, life perversely goes against us. Things happen that we do *not* like, often without warning. And the mind has run out of steam. For the time being, its vitality and vivacity have been spent. All it can do is lie down with a couple of aspirin and a cold washcloth over its eyes and wonder, "Why does this have to happen to me?"

Most of us, I think, believe this is all life has to offer: some precious periods of excitement and ebullience, when we are full of *joie de vivre*; some stretches of depression; and in between, our normal state – not bad, not good, a little irritable, but civil enough as long as nobody crosses us.

"It does not have to happen to you," Sri Krishna explains. "You don't ever have to feel depressed again. But you have to stop tying your moods to circumstances. Stop getting excited over what you like; then you won't get depressed by what you don't like."

Virtually all of us get excited easily. Nobody can escape this pressure today. The mass media promise us excitement from everything on the face of the earth: movies, news programs, holidays, hair sprays, investments, toothpaste, towels. Is it any wonder that when these promises go unfulfilled, we live on the edge of frustration and depression? Millions of men and women in this country suffer from serious depression every year. In addition, since negative states inhibit the immune system, I would say depression is a hidden causal factor in billions of cases of colds, flu, migraine, dyspepsia, herpes, allergies, and asthma. And then there is the dull, minimal, just-able-to-cope state that the vast majority of us have come to regard as normal, which I would classify as subclinical depression. All in all, perhaps one quarter of the people in this country walk about in a chronic state of resentment or depression because life is not giving them what they think it promises – blaming the mango tree, my grandmother would say, because it can't give coconuts.

If you don't want to get depressed, Sri Krishna says, the first thing is not to get into situations where you know you get excited. This requires some self-knowledge, and a good deal of vigilance. If, in spite of doing your best to avoid such situations, you find yourself caught and your mind beginning to race out of control, start repeating the mantram.

The mantram is a stabilizer, the kind that enables ships to steer through rough seas and keep on an even keel. On my way to this country from India I traveled as far as Marseilles on an old P&O vessel that had no such device. When the monsoon burst on the way to Aden, one moment we would see only sky, the next moment only water. The ship pitched and rolled like that for two or three days, and virtually everybody got seasick, including most of the crew. It was a British vessel out of Australia, with some real empire builders on it. That is when I discovered that empire builders are human too. After a while they were asking for a brown bag and rushing to the rail with the rest. It brought home to me the unity of life.

The first day of this I managed to avoid asking for a paper bag. On the second morning, however, I woke up with my mind thinking, "Boss, this is it! I've gone as far as I can go." My stomach felt terribly sick. Although I am not easily subject to nausea, my first thought was to get a bag like everybody else and spend the rest of the day at the rail looking down at the water.

Instead, without my even thinking about it, the mantram came to my rescue. I was determined to let nothing come in the way of my meditation. I went to a corner, sat down for meditation, and in a few minutes I had gone so deep that I had left my body behind. A couple of hours later I got up feeling terribly hungry. The ship was still pitching about. I walked into the breakfast room and sat down in solitary dignity, the monarch of all I surveyed. The purser couldn't believe his eyes. He was a hard-boiled type, but he was so intrigued that he came over and asked, "What kind of tablets do you use?"

That is the power of the mind. When it is calm, the body stays calm; when it gets excited, the body too is thrown into turmoil. So whenever your mind starts surging up and down like that P&O liner, repeat the mantram. Then the mind becomes more like the majestic *Queen Elizabeth,* on which I crossed the Atlantic a week or two later. We slid through rough seas with quiet, steady grace. When I asked the captain why, he replied, "This ship has stabilizers. She's not afraid of any storm."

समदुःखसुखः स्वस्थः समलोष्टाश्मकाञ्चनः ।
तुल्यप्रियाप्रियो धीरस्तुल्यनिन्दात्मसंस्तुतिः ॥ १४-२४ ॥

*24. Established within themselves, they
are equal in pleasure and pain, praise and
blame, kindness and unkindness. Clay or
a rock are the same to them as gold.*

Many years ago, a little fellow about four or five years old who was stay-ing in our household came up and tried to sit on Christine's lap. She said, "I'm sorry; I'm typing an article for the *Little Lamp.* Can you find somebody else for now?" He came to me, but I said, "I'm writing an article for the *Little Lamp.* Can you find somebody else?" He went to sit on Mary's lap, but Mary was busy folding the current *Little Lamp.* Finally he said in exasperation, "Then I'm going to sit on my own lap!"

That was a profound remark. *Svasthah,* which I have translated as 'established within themselves,' means literally something like 'self-standing' or 'self-seated' The only lap on which you can sit comfortably is your own. If you try to sit on somebody else's, you can feel secure only as long as that person remains seated; if he or she stands up, you get dumped onto the floor. If you learn to sit on your own lap, you rest there always. You are not dependent on anything external – the prime rate, the praise of your employer, the moods of your partner, the perfor-mance of your car.

Yesterday Christine and I went downtown to get a library card. She had a card in her name which she had lost, though I hinted that if it had been entrusted to me, I would have taken good care of it. When she said she had lost it, I was almost tempted to say, "What did I tell you?" But like a gentleman, I refrained.

We walked up together to the librarian, who explained that due to some technical difficulty a new card could not be issued to her just then. "But," she said brightly, "your husband could take out one in his own name."

I stood before her and gave the usual information: name, address, and so forth. Then she wanted a telephone number. "I don't have a tele-phone," I said.

"That's all right," she said. "Can you establish your identity?"

"I can," I said confidently. "That is my profession."

She waited, but I failed to produce anything tangible. Finally she asked, "Do you have a driver's license?"

"No," I said.

"Don't you drive?"

"I do. I mean, I know how to drive. But I have too much respect for the public interest."

She stared. "Do you have any credit cards?"

"As a matter of fact," I said, "we did get a credit card in the mail some months ago. We had great difficulty destroying it. We couldn't tear it, we couldn't cut it, we couldn't burn it. I think we may have buried it. You see," I added, seeing her expression, "I like to pay cash for things. I don't like being in debt."

"That's very admirable," she said. "But I need something that tells me who you are. You must have some letter sent to you by somebody? Some card?"

That made a connection. "Yes," I said, "I do have a card." I owned the only membership card that the Blue Mountain Center of Meditation ever issued, and it was right in my wallet. "I happen to be the first member," I explained with a touch of pride. I opened my wallet, and out fell Christine's library card.

Sri Krishna is trying to tell us, "You already have your card. You don't have to get another one. If you can get into your wallet, deep in that inside pocket you have forgotten, you will find the source of security and joy."

मानावमानयोस्तुल्यस्तुल्यो मित्रारिपक्षयोः ।
सर्वारम्भपरित्यागी गुणातीतः स उच्यते ॥ १४-२५ ॥

25. Alike in honor and dishonor, alike to friend
and foe, they have given up every selfish pursuit.
Such are those who have gone beyond the gunas.

These are astonishing statements, which deserve careful reading and reflection. *Gunātīta* means literally someone who has gone beyond human limitations. He or she has transcended the barriers of separateness and self-will, which are the greatest scourge of this century. Only by rising above these states do we enter our true nature, which is to love, to forgive, to heal.

"Alike to friend and foe" has nothing to do with being indifferent. Sri Krishna is talking about good will, patience, forgiveness, understanding – not only to those we like or when it is convenient, but to everyone always. These are not moral maxims. When St. Francis says "It is in pardoning that we are pardoned," he is giving us a truth on which our very survival may depend.

For example, although most people buy handguns to make themselves feel safer, merely having a gun often heightens the sense of insecurity and suspicion. You start looking on everyone not as a friend but as a potential threat. Your guard is up everywhere. You are prepared to defend yourself against anyone, and you know that "the best defense is a good first strike." Someone seems to be following you, he does something suspicious, and you shoot. If you get in a quarrel, your gun is handy. It has been estimated that 65 percent of all homicides are committed in a spasm of anger, jealousy, or fear, with handguns purchased for "self-defense." Ironically, the same guns place the owners in greater danger too. It makes them aggressive, even cocksure, so that they are almost looking for trouble. Rather than deter assault and robbery, it seems to invite assailants to use a gun themselves. But guns are only the instrument. Suspicion and separateness pull the trigger.

The situation is the same between nations. Historians look back at the beginning of this century and see how clearly the seeds of World War II were sown in the fear, hatred, suspicion, resentment, and retaliation that accompanied World War I. Similarly, well before World War II was over, the Allied powers had begun among themselves a suicidal race for military supremacy that might well have ended in World War III. And in the last analysis, the atomic bombs dropped on Hiroshima and Nagasaki seem to have been significantly motivated by a desire to "get even" for Pearl Harbor, as well as to impress on the Russians the kind of power we had and were willing to use. Violence breeds violence, resentment breeds retaliation, hostility perpetuates hostility – on a vaster and vaster scale, for higher and higher stakes. With nuclear weapons now in the hands of at least nine nations, each with its own alliances and desired spheres of influence, war between two countries might precipitate not only world war but worldwide disaster. Even scientists who worked on the first atomic bombs say today that they were not aware of what these weapons can do. They are not alluding merely to the deaths of twenty or a hundred million people in one or two nations. They are speaking of the effects of a nuclear exchange on the air, water, soil, vegetation, radiation levels, and species survival all over the globe. Now more than ever it should be clear that we live in "one world or none." When two countries fight, even if they are not superpowers, the war involves much more than those two countries. The whole unity of life is violated.

मां च यो ऽव्यभिचारेण भक्तियोगेन सेवते ।
स गुणान्समतीत्यैतान्ब्रह्मभूयाय कल्पते ॥ १४-२६ ॥

*26. By serving me with steadfast love, a
man or woman goes beyond the gunas.
Such a one is fit to know Brahman.*

Sri Krishna uses a strong word here, *avyabhicāra*, for which "steadfast" is a pallid translation. The opposite is *vyabhicārinī* – a prostitute, who tries to please many people. Those who give away their love and loyalty in many directions, the Gita says, can never reach life's goal. This is not a penalty enacted by an outside power. When we scatter our love, consciousness is dispersed; how can we expect it to be whole?

For many years, sādhana means learning the skills by which we can unify desires. Gradually we subordinate everything else to the attainment of life's supreme goal. Personal activities, attitudes, conditioning, prejudices, predilections, everything has to take second place. There is pain in this and a tremendous amount of self-denial from the flouting of self-will. The supreme quality here is endurance – the capacity to go on whatever the odds, to grow in determination as the challenges grow greater.

This requires tremendous discipline. Excellence in anything requires discipline; even to play marbles you have to practice, and here we are talking about the highest state of evolution. I was reading an interview with Nureyev, one of the greatest male ballet dancers in history.

Ask him if he found it easy to scale the pinnacle of his art! All you and I see on the stage is spectacular, graceful, apparently effortless movement. Backstage, Nureyev says, it is a bloodbath. Margot Fonteyn uses equally strong language: if we only knew the torture a dancer imposes on herself to achieve that effortless grace, she says, we would feel we were watching a bullfight.

The Gita talks the same way. Sri Krishna reminds us, "This is a battle." If you want to live at the summit of life, free from conditioning from the surface of consciousness clear to the basement, you have to fight for every inch of progress. It is not enough merely to transform rajas into sattva, which is a tremendous achievement in itself. Even in sattva thinking is conditioned, although your motives are pure. To be free you have to go beyond the gunas completely – beyond time, space, and circumstance, where the mind is completely stilled and the ego disappears.

To understand what this means, we need the personal testimony of men and women who have succeeded in this immense endeavor. Recently I have been reading the life of St. Teresa of Ávila, a remarkably modern woman of great spiritual genius who sanctified medieval Europe. She grew up with every possible advantage a girl in that age and place could have: she was cultured, talented, attractive, and high-spirited, with a bright intellect and a strong will that in those days did not always work to her advantage. Yet she was so highly evolved that nothing fleeting could satisfy her. Even as a girl she could say passionately, "I want something that lasts forever!" This is the mark of mystical genius: not to be satisfied with something you can get today and lose tomorrow, but to demand a legacy that will be yours always.

This woman who was to become one of the world's greatest mystics went through twenty years of doubt and struggle, torn between the pull of the world and the pull of God. When someone talks about attaining illumination overnight, I always want to reply, "Teresa took twenty years. Do you really think people like you and me should be able to do it in less?" Her words can inspire all of us, for everyone begins with doubts and conflicts and is likely to feel disheartened:

On the one hand I felt the call of God; on the other, I continued to follow the world. All the things of God gave me great pleasure, but I was held captive by those of the world. I might have been said to be trying to reconcile these two extremes, to bring contraries together: the spiritual life on the one hand and worldly satisfactions, pleasures, and pastimes on the other.

When you have doubts about your capacity for spiritual progress, which is only natural, it is good not to feel despondent, dispirited, or defeatist. That is the prerogative of tamas. Instead please remember St. Teresa and act as if you had no doubts at all. Keep on striving, keep on trying, and if you fall, pick yourself up. But never give up the struggle. This is all we are expected to do. Little people like us are likely to be haunted by doubts and conflicts for a long, long time.

Teresa was about forty-five when she became established in God. In Hindu mysticism this supreme state is called *sahaja samādhi*, 'samādhi that never leaves you.' Waking or sleeping, your awareness of the unity of life is not broken even for an instant. Then you have gone beyond the gunas once and for all.

ब्रह्मणो हि प्रतिष्ठाहममृतस्याव्ययस्य च ।
शाश्वतस्य च धर्मस्य सुखस्यैकान्तिकस्य च ॥ १४-२७॥

27. For I am the support of Brahman, the eternal, the unchanging, the deathless, the everlasting dharma, the source of all joy.

In this final verse, Sri Krishna is reminding us gently of the close connection between the gunas, time, and death. One of the pathetic characteristics of modern civilization is to try to cling to time as it rushes past, almost begging time to stop. We want to continue to be what we are now. We don't want to be subjected to the ruthless physical changes that are an inescapable part of life. The deep-seated insecurity that results is what comes from a physical approach to life. As we grow older it leads to all kinds of problems, physical, emotional, and psychosomatic. None of our affluence or technology has been able to guard us against this nagging fear of inadequacy in the face of time's advance, which haunts millions of lives today.

Nothing we do can prevent the body from growing older from the day that we were born. In the grim language of mysticism, our death began the moment we were conceived. When my mother dips her finger in ashes every morning to put a white mark on her forehead, it is to remind her and those around her that the nature of the body is to change, up to the last change we call death. Anybody who tries to stand on what is changing, who tries to cling to things that are slipping away, cannot help getting more desperate and insecure.

"When you live for the whole of life," Sri Krishna says, "your state of consciousness will be mine" – that is, unfathomable love, which brings the unshakable security of knowing that every moment your life counts. In this state you are much more than a single, separate person. You become a permanent force that is released wherever you go, to ameliorate the terrible conditions which threaten the world today. Your life is an investment for every creature. No bear market can threaten this investment. It increases through good fortune and bad, and nobody has to buy shares to get the dividends; they are distributed to all. You are *avyaya*, inexhaustible: the more you give, the more you receive in patience, endurance, security, resilience, and love.

गुणत्रयविभागयोगो नाम चतुर्दशोऽध्यायः ॥ १४ ॥

CHAPTER FIFTEEN
The Supreme Self

श्रीभगवानुवाच ।
ऊर्ध्वमूलमधःशाखमश्वत्थं प्राहुरव्ययम् ।
छन्दांसि यस्य पर्णानि यस्तं वेद स वेदवित् ॥ १५-१ ॥

SRI KRISHNA:

1. Sages speak of the immutable ashvattha tree,
the Tree of Life, with its taproot above and its
branches below. On this tree grow the scriptures;
seeing their source, one knows their essence.

This image of the Tree of Life is one of the most magnificent in the Gita. Most of this tree is not physical. The whole phenomenal universe – matter, energy, and mind – is only its canopy of leaves. This is all we can see. But each leaf grows from a twig, which grows from a branch, which in turn grows from a vast trunk. And supporting the trunk and all its leaves and twigs and branches, completely hidden, is the taproot, extending deep into pure being. Farthest from the root is the world of multiplicity and change: countless little leaves. But the taproot of this tree is the Lord, the eternal, changeless Self.

The application of this tremendous image is personal and practical. As long as we live on the surface of life, we believe we are separate, individual leaves. We lead private lives that bear no relation to the rest of the tree, even though when we are cut off from that tree we have no life. Look at the problems that face the world today because of this crude superstition that we are separate. We have violence in our streets and homes because individuals value no one's welfare but their own. We have poverty and war around the globe because nations and corporations pursue private ends without regard to the cost to others. Most poignantly of all, we see men, women, and even children cutting themselves off from others around them so they can pursue what they want without hindrance. When we are driven by self-will like this, we cannot imagine we are forfeiting the whole of life for the little leaf we call our individual personality. So when you get up in the morning, while you are at work, before going to bed, or whenever you feel ruled by private passions, remind yourself of this magnificent simile, which asks us to claim the whole Tree of Life and not be content with being one passing leaf.

अधश्चोर्ध्वं प्रसृतास्तस्य शाखा
गुणप्रवृद्धा विषयप्रवालाः ।
अधश्च मूलान्यनुसंततानि
कर्मानुबन्धीनि मनुष्यलोके ॥ १५-२ ॥

*2. Nourished by the gunas, the limbs of this
tree spread above and below. Sense objects
grow on the limbs as buds; the roots hanging
down bind us to action in this world.*

The Tree of Life, called *ashvattha* in the Hindu scriptures, is traditionally considered to be one of the giant fig trees found in southern Asia. A great deal has been written on the question of proper botanical classification: is this *Ficus bengalensis,* the banyan tree, or *Ficus religiosa,* the sacred pipal or bo tree, under which the Buddha attained illumination?

Shankara, who often drives Western scholars to exasperated footnotes, does not seem to care about this question. Instead he goes to the heart of the matter with a touch of imaginative etymology. *Ashvattha,* he says, can be derived from three little words: *a* 'without,' *shva* 'tomorrow,' and *stha* 'standing.' This is the tree of what will not be here tomorrow: in other words, of all created things. The universe today is not what it will be tomorrow; it changes even from instant to instant. Your body today is not what it was yesterday, and tomorrow it will not be what it is today. Every tissue is changing, even the bones. After some decades, the body will not be around at all.

Trees like the pipal and banyan are extremely long-lived. In an ancient temple compound, where you can see one still growing and spreading while the stones around it are cracked and worn with age, you feel that its roots must reach into the beginning of time. These species of *Ficus* also have another characteristic alluded to in this verse: what botanists call aerial roots. In some cases the seeds germinate not in the earth but high in some other tree (such as a palm) where they have been deposited by birds and monkeys. From there they send out long shoots that twine around the trunk of the mother tree until they reach the ground. Then they burrow in and become true roots.

The senses, Sri Krishna says, are like these aerial roots. When we yield to the clamor of the senses we are pushing consciousness out into sensory offshoots, making them longer and longer. Finally they reach the ground and burrow in, rooting us in the world of change. This is what the media promise us: the senses will supply everything we desire of life. "Indulge your senses," they say. "Don't be afraid to build your life on pleasure. If it feels good, do it!" By the time a person in this country reaches the age of twenty, he or she may have received this message a million times – from television and the movies, from magazines, newspapers, and books, and of course from the daily example of other people. With this kind of brainwashing, is it any wonder that our lives are as shaky as leaves?

The more we try to put our senses out to enjoy the world, the more we are sticking out our necks. I may be mixing metaphors, but this is an apt expression. People who are highly taste-oriented, for example, are extruding their palate farther and farther and farther. Obsessed with food, always thinking about what to eat and when and where and how often, they squeeze all their consciousness into their taste buds; they are feeling the world through the palate.

You will find such people very physically oriented – which means, among other things, that they get easily upset. Since they do not have much security within themselves, they try to correct their upsets by getting something from the pharmacy or the refrigerator and putting it into their mouths. Overeating is one of the most familiar illustrations of how consciousness can be concentrated on a particular sense organ, which really leaves it out on a limb. That is why Gandhi said the control of the palate is such a valuable aid to controlling the mind. If you can withdraw consciousness at will from the sense of taste, your mind will be much less upsettable.

The same can happen with any other sense. Children who grow up watching TV four, five, or six hours a day are squeezing much of their consciousness into their eyes. Those who listen for hours on end to quadraphonic sound are putting consciousness in their ears. In this way, consciousness is a little like toothpaste: it is easy to squeeze it out, but excruciatingly difficult to get it back into the tube again. When consciousness has been extruded into the senses, not much is available where it is needed – for concentration, security, sensitiveness, self-reliance, and imagination.

We should be able to withdraw consciousness from the senses at will, the Gita says, as easily as a tortoise withdraws its limbs into its shell. When we see a lot of goodies displayed in a bakery window and the palate is clamoring for us to move closer and glue our eyes to the glass, we should be able to say "Withdraw!" and recall consciousness back from the palate into the core of our being. The sense organs – taste buds, nerves, and so on – will be physically the same, but consciousness will not be present to activate them. Later, when we approve – say, when faced with a nutritious, tasty meal – we can send consciousness back out to the senses and enjoy our food.

All the senses can be trained this way. You are not forcing them inside or putting them in jail to punish them for their excesses. You are telling them, "When the sun is shining and it's good to play, come on out; make hay. But when the weather gets cloudy, come in and take shelter."

This means a tremendous consolidation of energy. Prāna ebbs out through the senses; that is why people who overindulge their senses often feel tired and inadequate. Their resistance is low, the will is weak, and judgment gets clouded just when it is needed most. When you can regulate your senses, you can enjoy everything beneficial and still protect your mind and body against the ravages of undue indulgence.

I see advertisements for vacation cruises that proclaim, "Our dining room is always open!" After breakfast you're not locked out until noon;

you can come for a snack, come again for lunch, and still return for high tea before dinner. The variety of dishes is endless. And when you're not dining, you can float in the pool with a cocktail: the drinks are free, so you can drink as much as you like. Then at night there are parties, movies, and gaming tables going until dawn; you never have to sleep. Now and then you get a day in a duty-free port, where you can pick up a few expensive items you don't need. When the cruise is over, I imagine, they even have a fleet of ambulances waiting to take you to intensive care. This kind of indulgence leaves us vulnerable to every wind that blows.

When the senses come under control, prāna is consolidated in the will. I like to repeat that what matters in life is not so much IQ as WQ, "will quotient." There is no harm in having a high IQ, but it is not of much value in helping you deal with anger or fear. I have known gifted people with high IQs who were utterly unable to tackle their fears and conflicts. No amount of talking or reasoning could help; they had to deepen their will by digging through stratum after stratum of consciousness. When the will gets deep enough you can reach down into your unconscious, pick up a fear, and throw it out. After that, if you encounter a big fear again in your digging operation, you know you will be able to deal with it. Then that fear can no longer make you afraid.

It is the same with anger. Angry people are usually quite self-willed. They don't have the strength to be patient or turn back harsh words because self-will eats away the will. If you want to transform anger and harness it, you have to strengthen the will.

When you have some detachment, the will becomes a kind of emotional barometer. You can use it to tell when storms are coming, probably more accurately than your local weatherman can predict rain. You go to your willometer in the morning, tap it a couple of times, and ask, "What's the weather going to be like today?" If you did your best yesterday to control your senses and reduce self-will, your will *has* to be stronger. Then it doesn't much matter what external events come your way; the day is going to be clear for you.

Trying to talk out anger and fear has become so commonplace today that I never mind repeating the Gita's very practical advice. Instead of

analyzing your fears and resentments – putting them under a micro-
scope, scrutinizing them from different angles, classifying them, talking
about them, reading books about them – work on strengthening your
will. Brooding over these problems only makes them more obsessive.
But as the will gets taller, emotional problems like fear, anger, and greed
get smaller. When you have a strong will, if you feel lethargic, you can
flex its muscles and watch your lethargy disappear. If you feel diffident,
flexing the will brings self-confidence. A strong will can transform fear
into fearlessness, anger into sympathy, resentment into compassion,
hatred into love.

The intimate relationship between senses and sense objects is a recur-
ring theme in the Gita. Just as aerial roots reach out for the ground to
dig themselves in, the senses reach out to root themselves in objects of
sensory experience. There is nothing wrong with this. It is the nature of
senses to grasp, and there is nothing immoral about the force of their
attraction, any more than there is about physical forces like magnetism
or nuclear binding energy. Forces are not wrong; it is the use to which
we put them that can be wrong.

In meditation, we learn to withdraw and consolidate prāna from the
senses back to its source. This takes years to learn. At first, though we
are trying to give our attention completely to the passage on which we
are meditating, we hear everything that goes on outside us. The reason
is that consciousness is still in the ear, waiting to catch sounds. But as
you learn to sink deep into yourself, you withdraw consciousness slowly
from the ear. The organ still functions, but no hearing takes place. It is
the same with the other senses too. St. Teresa of Ávila relates that she
was so absorbed in prayer one evening that the candle she was holding burned down to her fingers without her being aware of the pain.

When we are pleasure-oriented, on the other hand – as our
whole modern civilization is – consciousness is always looking for
sense-stimulation. Some part of the mind is constantly watching for
pleasant experiences on the surface level of life. Consciousness is out on
the patio with binoculars, searching for sensations like a bird-watcher.
The patio is the skin: most sensory stimulation is only skin deep. When
we live in a world of skin-deep pleasures, they seem to be fabulously

sweet, incredibly intense. Only when we leave the patio to retire deep into what Teresa calls the "interior castle" do we get a real standard of comparison. Once we discover the riches of this inner realm, we laugh at ourselves for sitting in the patio and gloating over some third-class mail from the senses.

न रूपमस्येह तथोपलभ्यते
नान्तो न चादिर्न च संप्रतिष्ठा ।
अश्वत्थमेनं सुविरूढमूलम्
असङ्गशस्त्रेण दृढेन छित्त्वा ॥ १५-३ ॥
ततः पदं तत्परिमार्गितव्यं
यस्मिन्गता न निवर्तन्ति भूयः ।
तमेव चाद्यं पुरुषं प्रपद्ये
यतः प्रवृत्तिः प्रसृता पुराणी ॥ १५-४ ॥

3–4. The true form of this tree – its essence, beginning, and end – is not perceived on this earth. Cut down this strong-rooted tree with the sharp axe of detachment; then find the path which does not come back again. Seek That, the First Cause, from which the universe came long ago.

Most of the Tree of Life, we should remember, lies in the world within. Sri Krishna is telling us to get beneath the surface and trace our way back to our source.

One school of thought speaks of this Tree as an illusion, because separateness is an illusion. But I would say each leaf is precious. Each individual creature deserves our respect, love, and protection. So instead of talking about cutting down trees, I would rather talk about digging to the root, deep in the soil of consciousness.

Meditation is the tool for digging. I don't know if you have ever had to dig up an old, established tree; when the surface of the ground is knotted with thick, hardened roots, it can be painfully difficult to break through. Similarly, for many years in meditation we have to dig hard to break through the crusted strata of samskāras we have accumulated over the years – or, from the Hindu and Buddhist perspective, over many lives. To do this, we have to keep a sharp edge on our meditation. Like any tool, it must be kept in good condition. If it is not used for a week, even for a day, it will get rusty.

Sometimes the surface level of consciousness is soft loam, easy digging for the first twelve inches or so. You are still on the surface, but because the blade of your shovel is turning over soil you say, "This is easy! Isn't meditation great?" Then you strike something hard and impenetrable. Your hands sting from the shock, and your arms ache. That is the first stratum of bedrock – a dense, rock-hard layer of tamas, sheer resistance.

One of the most common signs of hitting this layer is that you find yourself overcome by waves of sleep in meditation. It is very much like your shovel striking a rock. You are saying, in effect, "My shovel is getting blunted, and my arms are tired. Why not stop digging and have a snooze?" It is extremely important not to yield to this inclination, right from the first days of meditation. These are problems that continue for years. We have a lot of strata to dig through, and those who do not learn to deal with sleep in the early stages have a terribly difficult time later on.

When you have learned to dig effectively, you strike through this bedrock of resistance and change your level of consciousness. This has to be done under the skilled, personal guidance of your teacher. You can no longer afford to be self-willed or to be a victim of your senses. If you haven't reduced your self-will and trained your senses and passions well, on a deeper level of awareness you will encounter serious difficulties in daily living. That is why I always tell those around me not to increase their period of meditation without meeting the basic requirements. They should be getting enough exercise, nourishing food, and adequate sleep, and they should be careful not to isolate themselves from the give-and-take of life, which is essential for reducing self-will.

The signs that you have changed a level of consciousness are utterly practical: better health, more energy, better control over your cravings, less self-will, and more of the joy that comes from drawing nearer to the unity of life. Unless these tests are satisfied, I say over and over again, please don't go by anything you see or hear in meditation, any sensation you experience, any "vision" or dream. All these have very little relevance to daily living. Do you have more patience and security? Do you find it easier to get along with difficult people? Can you turn your back on your own likes and dislikes when necessary, to contribute to the welfare of those around you? If you can, you have changed your level of consciousness. If you cannot, the chances are that you are not yet ready to change.

Sri Ramakrishna, I believe, describes the role the gunas play in this. Sattva, rajas, and tamas all have to come on stage; otherwise life's drama cannot be enacted. Tamas, he says, is the rock of resistance. This is a reassuring description: without a rock, how can you develop your digging arm? Rajas, of course, is hard, energetic, sustained digging. And sattva is the mastery that comes when you have overcome tamas deep in consciousness and are making steady progress.

निर्मानमोहा जितसङ्गदोषा
अध्यात्मनित्या विनिवृत्तकामाः ।
द्वंद्वैर्विमुक्ताः सुखदुःखसंज्ञैर्
गच्छन्त्यमूढाः पदमव्ययं तत् ॥ १५-५ ॥

5. Not deluded by pride, free from selfish
attachment and selfish desire, beyond the duality
of pleasure and pain, ever aware of the Self,
the wise go forward to that eternal goal.

Self-will is responsible for most of our spiritual problems, many of our emotional problems, and even some of our physical problems too. Broken relationships, disloyalties, and disruptions in spiritual progress can generally be traced to self-will. Everyone who wants to attain the supreme state, Sri Krishna says, must fight self-will until victory is won. It is a long, hard, uphill battle.

One very helpful strategy is to remember the needs of the whole always. Don't ever go just by what appeals to you or what you find pleasing; that is the way to separateness. Go against your likes and dislikes whenever it is in the interests of all, and then continue to go against them resolutely until victory is won.

This can't be done just from ten to twelve on Sundays. We have to go on fighting all the time, everywhere. Most of us have two personalities, the public and the private, which makes for tension, conflict, and vacillation. When you learn to fight self-will continuously, this deep division heals. Public and private personalities merge, until you are the same in all circumstances and all roles.

Selfish desires need a lot of attention. They are not very hardy; unless their needs are met precisely, they cannot last long. If we do not water and fertilize them regularly – thinking about them, dreaming about them, planning, wishing, fantasizing over them – they will wither and die. To get plants to thrive, I understand, it is considered helpful to talk to them in soothing, friendly tones. Selfish desires thrive on talk too; the more we talk about them, the stronger they get. So whenever you feel driven by a compulsive, selfish desire, throw yourself into work for others. It can starve the desire away, at least for the time being.

In the way we work, the way we eat, even the way we play, we can always do what is in the interests of the whole. For a long time, of course, this cuts across our likes and dislikes. But even then we reap benefits. The more likes and dislikes we have, the more physical and psychosomatic problems we are likely to develop; worst of all, the more turmoil we will feel inside. People with strong likes and dislikes go about with a little sign that says, "Upset me." Everywhere they go, they meet a lot of other people wearing the same sign who are only too happy to oblige. Those who are free from likes and dislikes, on the other hand, are full of security. They function in freedom wherever they go. Once you reach this state, Sri Krishna says, you will live there always. You will never fall back into insecurity, turmoil, or disloyalty.

न तद्भासयते सूर्यो न शशाङ्को न पावकः ।
यद्गत्वा न निवर्तन्ते तद्धाम परमं मम ॥ १५-६ ॥

6. Neither the sun nor the moon nor fire can add to that light. This is my supreme abode, and those who enter there do not return to separate, selfish existence.

The Self is the source of light. When you attain it, as Sri Ramakrishna says, you feel like a fish swimming in a sea of light. Everything separate disappears, everything that is dark with ignorance.

We are so used to this darkness that we mistake it for reality. We cannot recognize light because we believe the darkness *is* light. This makes for a very upside-down world. People who exploit separateness are called successful; those who make war are immortalized in bronze or marble. This is living in pitch darkness, Sri Krishna says, and calling the darkness day. Those who really see are those who forget themselves completely in living for the welfare of all.

St. Teresa of Ávila refers to the various levels of consciousness as different mansions in the interior castle of the soul. When you go from one floor to the next, there are sudden experiences of blinding light. This seems to be a characteristic phenomenon in the deeper stages of meditation. You are so completely absorbed in going through the words of the inspirational passage that your mind is completely one-pointed; not a single ray of your mental energy is flickering. As the Gita says, your mind is as steady as the flame of a lamp that is kept in a windless place. Then you are ready for the tremendous experience of dazzling, radiant light that St. Augustine describes so vividly:

> I entered into the secret closet of my soul, led by Thee,... and beheld with the mysterious eye of my soul the Light that never changes, above the eye of my soul, above my intelligence. It was not the common light which all embodied creatures can see; nor was it the same kind but greater, as if the light of day were to grow brighter and brighter and flood all space. This light was none of that, but something other, altogether different. ... He who knoweth truth knoweth that light: and who knoweth it, knoweth eternity. Love knoweth it.

Not only dazzling light but limitless love floods your heart, the infinite compassion that Buddhism calls *mahākarunā,* which embraces all life. The Franciscan mystic Jacapone da Todi says,

> Love above all language,
> Goodness unimagined,
> Light without measure
> Shines in my heart!

"Love above all language": your heart is flooded with love; it bursts its barriers. The dam of separateness breaks, and a great sea of love surges up from inside – "goodness unimagined," love for all creatures, all individuals, all countries, even those who may have offended or wronged you. And "light without measure": even the sun blazing in the sky, the source of all physical radiance, borrows the effulgent light from your heart and mine. To understand this is to realize the immense glory of being human.

ममैवांशो जीवलोके जीवभूतः सनातनः ।
मनःषष्ठानीन्द्रियाणि प्रकृतिस्थानि कर्षति ॥ १५-७ ॥
शरीरं यदवाप्नोति यच्चाप्युत्क्रामतीश्वरः ।
गृह्णीतैतानि संयाति वायुर्गन्धानिवाशयात् ॥ १५-८ ॥

7. An eternal part of me enters into the world at birth, assuming a body and mind made of prakriti.
8. When the divine Self enters and leaves a body, it takes along its samskāras as the wind carries a scent from place to place.

In the long drawn-out drama that is sādhana there are three actors. One is the Self, the changeless Ātman, pure Being. This shining Self is within all, yet it cannot shine forth because of the mask of negative qualities and self-will that we call personality. This is the second actor, called *jīva* in Sanskrit – the separate, individual ego with which we identify ourselves. And third is Māyā, the compulsive sense of separateness: as Evelyn Underhill puts it, the "web of illusion, here thick, here thin, [which] hems in, confuses, and allures" us in our evolution toward Self-realization.

Part of Māyā's power comes from the fierce clamor of the senses. This is an inheritance we have received from the animals, a natural part of our evolutionary heritage. Its power is especially poignant in personal relationships; for as everyone who has been through the experience knows, any relationship based on physical attraction *has* to end in heartbreak. It is not merely that the relationship comes to an end so soon; physical desire sets up such fierce expectations, and the disillusion that follows can last so long that some people never recover from

·it. All this is the work and delusion of Māyā. Even today, when I see a movie depicting scenes of entanglement and sorrow, I breathe a fervent prayer from the bottom of my heart to Krishna, the same prayer that Sri Ramakrishna used to repeat over and over: "May I never fall under the spell of Māyā again!"

In the terms of classical mysticism, only one of these three actors, the Self, can be called real. Yet to the extent that we identify ourselves with the jīva, our ever-changing personality, we live as well in the "unreal" world of change, bound to it by self-will and the fierce, compulsive play of the senses. The farther we progress spiritually, the more we become aware of the gulf that yawns between these two worlds: the one of sheer physical existence, the other of pure spiritual being. Yet eventually – this is the marvel of samādhi – a bridge is built between the two. Then, as Sri Aurobindo says, the divine invades the physical world; even in physical things we see the radiance of the Lord.

"In every creature," Sri Krishna says, "a little part of me is present." Those are very personal words that go right into my heart. Not only human beings but even the lowest creature has a spark of divinity within, infinitesimal but inalienable. It is this tiny part, he tells Arjuna, that travels through time in the process of reincarnation. The life-line of the jīva runs back five billion years or more; in five billion years, I could say, the amoeba has become me. This is perfectly compatible with biological evolution. But spiritual evolution does not consider this blind growth; it would not even call it arbitrary. We play a part in our own evolution; that is the vital difference. The other influencing factors – time, circumstance, and so on – are still present, but we hold the key in every life. "All that we are," the Buddha says, "is the result of what we have thought." And not merely the result: the word he uses is *manomāya*. This jīva is actually 'made of the mind' that we have used for many, many lives. There is no reference here to any external or supernatural power. My growth is entirely in my hands; your growth is entirely in yours. The continuous improvement we are able to make in the quality of our thinking is what decides our lives.

Not only that, this is what decides even the kind of body we have. According to the Gita, I have worked on my body for many lives. There is a quiet correspondence between the kind of body I have and the kind of mind I have. Just in the course of one life it is not difficult to see how the way we think shapes the way we eat, work, sleep, and exercise; how it determines the risks we take, the occupations we enter, the places we live in, the people we live with, and the way we respond to stress. All of these have an obvious bearing on our physical well-being. Now, says the Gita, extend the same influence over many lives: just as in this life we develop the health and physical condition that our thinking warrants, we enter the next life with the right kind of body to pick up where we left off.

There are many, many factors in this, as I shall attempt to illustrate. Personality is not at all a simple picture. So I would not recommend that anyone try to analyze why he or she has a particular kind of body or wonder how some physical liability can be traced to a past life. It is enough to understand that there is a connection, and that whatever our physical condition, we can rest assured it is the right one for working out our samskāras and going forward on the spiritual path.

In the same way that each jīva shapes the body by its thinking, each of us lives in a personal world very much of his or her own making. We experience the world as we are; we respond to it as we are; we are continuously reshaping it according to how we are. That is what the Christian mystics mean when they say, "My sin is stamped upon my universe." But the Hindu mystic would say, "My goodness is stamped upon my universe." Both statements are true: one simply takes the perspective of the jīva, while the other looks at the world through the shining Self.

The divine fragment called the Ātman is the same in all people, all races, all creatures. This is not theory; that is how you actually see life after the Self is realized. The other day a kid was born prematurely to one of our angora goats, and a friend took a picture of me holding the tiny, fragile creature in my arms. When I saw the photograph I said, "That's not just a guy and a goat." I was not looking at myself; I saw the Ātman, realized in me through billions of years of evolution and still latent in little Gautami, the goat, to be revealed in her after perhaps millions of years of evolution more. In that picture Gautami and I are gazing into each other's eyes. She is marveling, "I'm going to look like you someday!" And I am smiling back: "Well, millions of years ago I looked like you." That awareness fills my heart with joy and releases an immense desire to save the lives of all these creatures, knowing they are not merely my kith and kin but the same spark as you and I.

This divine fragment travels through time from stage to stage in evolution, revealing a little more of its divinity at every stage. Our dog Muka, for example, shows more of the spark than a tiger does; our cow Shobha shows more than a panther. Even in the human context this development continues. People who are terribly violent may look like human beings, but they still live largely in the animal world. Similarly, though someone who has extinguished self-will may look like the rest of us, he or she is no longer in the animal world at all. Such a person, Sri Krishna says, "lives in me" – in the state of Krishna-consciousness, Christ-consciousness, from which there is no fall.

As the jīva travels through time, it picks up a samskāra in every stage of evolution. Our dog Muka is adding a samskāra to his jīva-nature, and so are his canine friends Hebbles and Ganesha – three very different dogs. The black cat who lives in our greenhouse, whom the children call Luther Purrbank, is developing a samskāra of his own: he still claws the hand that feeds, and I have very little doubt that he will continue to do so when he becomes a human being. Every creature adds a samskāra of its own, a tiny seed of a samskāra in every life. And, these verses explain in thrilling poetry, the jīva blows through time like a wind, starting five billion years ago as a little breeze and growing stronger and stronger, blowing through the phenomenal world to its end. When a spring breeze blows through a garden, it picks up fragrances from the roses and nasturtiums and sweet peas so that though the flowers remain, their essences are carried on. In much the same way, this jīva-wind picks up samskāras in every life. That is how the immaterial karmic legacy of each of us is carried on: not in the body, not physically or chemically, but by this wind of prāna.

And from life to life the samskāras become heavier, more complicated. Good and bad, kind and unkind, selfish and selfless, mingle into a complex perfume that we call personality. Against the background of millions of lives, this makes for highly elaborate combinations. One person's greed, another's anger, may be a million years old. But no one is all greed or anger. Each of us has redeeming qualities too: a bit of love, a little forgiveness, a touch of sympathy to offset our jealousy. That is what makes the human personality such an elaborate, complicated affair.

This verse adds a subtle but very interesting touch: it is not only the samskāras of the mind that are carried along like this, but also those of the senses. The mind is called the "sixth sense" here because there is such a close relationship between it and the other five members of the sense family. Each sense can have its own samskāras, carried on from life to life, and these sense-samskāras have a telling effect on health.

Modern medicine, for all its triumphs, has one serious limitation: it looks for a cause of illness in something outside us. This approach is valid on the physical level, but it is incomplete; therefore it is inadequate. Of course external circumstances or agents can cause sickness. But there is also a mental factor, not only in so-called psychosomatic ailments but in every case of illness, because of the effect the mind and senses have on the immune system. So when the Buddha says, "All that we are is the result of what we have thought," it includes our illnesses; it includes our general health.

The Gita, I would say, goes a step further than the world of medicine today. It takes in not only the physical body but also what spiritual psychology calls the mental or subtle body, which is closely linked to the physical organism by a very quiet correspondence. In this view, for an illness to develop, bacteria or bacilli are not enough; you must also have developed a susceptibility to that illness. How is it that of ten people who are exposed to the same bacillus, nine may succumb and one escape? Some say chance, others luck. Most physicians would offer the explanation that there are innumerable differences in individual physiology and genetic makeup, including resistance to disease, but this is still on the physical level and only begs the question. The explanation I would give in the light of verses like these is that the immune system is not just a physiological or biochemical network; there is a corresponding mental network also. Resistance is not merely physical, and among all the myriad factors it involves, I would give the mind primary importance.

There is scope for a whole volume on this subject, and someday I hope to write one; the ramifications for the healing professions are tremendous. Here let me just touch on a few aspects, to give some idea of the depth of application these verses offer.

First and foremost, I would say that if you want the highest resistance to illness of any kind, then a deep desire to live for others is a tremendous immunological force. The same is true for resistance to the ravages of time. From my own experience, as well as from the towering example of my grandmother, I can testify that the vast majority of problems associated with old age – problems with vitality, memory, attention, endurance, resilience – need never arise at all.

Every older person, even those who do not meditate, can draw inspiration from my small example. I have probably ten times the vitality I had when I was thirty, and perhaps a hundred times the capacity to contribute to life. I may not be able to run the way I did then, but my judgment is sounder, my understanding is deeper, and my endurance is greater; I can work long hours without tension or fatigue.

If you lead the kind of life many older people do, of course, the problems of senility are inevitable. Living for oneself, indulging the senses, having no overriding goal, all make tremendous demands on prāna, and in the latter part of life we do not have prāna to lose. But if you have an overwhelming desire to contribute to the welfare of others, if your heart is full of love for all, Sri Krishna promises that he will magnify all your faculties – your memory, your creativity, your energy, your resources, your capacity to draw people and win their love and respect and help them to change their lives. All this happens naturally when prāna is conserved.

This desire to live for all can extend to the roots of your being. Psychologists talk about the importance of the will to live, but that generally means no more than the will to live for oneself. It can go no deeper than the ego, beneath which lie vast worlds of consciousness. Because we see only the surface of personality, we cannot understand how shallow the ego's will to live often is. But the will to live for the whole of life, because it goes so deep, preserves and strengthens us down to the core of our being.

Second, and closely related, is what happens to the immune system when your heart is flooded with love. I am not thinking of love for one person here and another there, no matter how deep or genuine. I mean love universal, continuous, "love without an object." It expresses itself in countless little choices you make throughout the day, all of which have a direct bearing on physical health.

I can give my own example again. When you haven't been able to
sleep for two or three nights, as everyone knows, the adverse effects can
be terribly debilitating – not only physically, but mentally and intellectually as well. It is only natural at such times, especially for those who are
older, to want to sleep on until the sun is high in the sky and then go and
sit in the patio over a cup of tea. This is the body's legitimate response,
dictated by certain physical principles. But the body also responds to
spiritual principles – because, among other things, they dictate the flow
of prāna, on which the body draws for energy. Depression, for example,
inhibits the immune system because it drains prāna. In the same way,
I would say, the capacity to love others more than yourself floods the
immune system with prāna, strengthening it immeasurably.

I get very little sleep, often only three to four hours a night; I have
not had more for many years. This is one of the developments that
can take place after samādhi: once you wake up in the depths of the
unconscious, you feel a very deep-seated reluctance to abandon, even
for a few moments, the continuous awareness of God. I have actually
had to teach myself to fall asleep again, and I feel rather pleased with
myself when I manage to drift off in the mantram in the early hours
of the morning. This kind of pattern produces a good deal of physiological stress, and once I do fall asleep, my body's natural need is to go
on sleeping late into the morning. Instead I get up early for meditation
and then go to the beach for a long, fast walk. Ask yourself if this is the
natural response to a sleepless night! Northern California beaches are
cold and foggy in the morning; I do not go for pleasure. I go for exercise,
so that my body will stay healthy and strong for many years more – not
to enjoy life longer but to continue the work of our meditation center,
which stands to benefit millions. That is the motivation. I come back
from the beach with a ravenous appetite and have a really good breakfast to see me through another long day of work.

All this is to illustrate how even physical faculties can be invigorated
and physical limits extended by the immense desire to live for others.
This is not at all like driving oneself for personal gain, which takes a
terrible toll on the body. Though I have maintained this pattern for years,
day in and day out, I do not feel fatigued by it; I thrive on it. So I have no

hesitation in saying that none of the problems associated with advancing age are necessary. Not only that, you can look forward to doing much better in the second half of your life than you did during the first.

Sickness, I said earlier, is caused by an external agent with the cooperation of an internal agent, the mind. The link is the immune system, through which resistance to disease is lowered or enhanced. To connect this with this verse I have to bring in the law of karma to some extent; for Sri Krishna says that from one life to another, it is not only the samskāras of the mind that are carried along but also the samskāras of the individual senses. This is a subtle distinction, but it means that samskāras which begin in the mind gradually become more physical, until they begin to invade the body through the senses. This is the first stage of disordered health.

A samskāra of pleasure, for example, can become particularized through constant overindulgence in eating – and not only eating, but reading about food, talking about food, cooking, observing, thinking, tasting, imagining; in short, through dwelling constantly on the pleasures of the palate. Over years, over lifetimes, what began as a mental habit takes over the sense of taste and becomes a physiological compulsion with very real physical problems. I don't like to sound occult, but when you know this is a person's mental state you can actually anticipate the kind of problems he will have in the next life. You can list them for him, *a, b, c.*

The implication is acutely practical: because such problems are not caused only by something outside us, they cannot be cured only by something from outside us. I wonder how much drugs can cure an illness, however much they may help with symptoms. To solve even a physical problem you have to get inside the mind, which is the purpose of meditation and the mantram.

Take the most pronounced characteristic of our contemporary society, rage. You can take a person who is full of rage and almost predict the kind of physical and emotional problems he will have the next time around. There is nothing particularly occult about this. When a person comes into life with certain pronounced proclivities, he will find himself drawn into situations that provoke those proclivities. Without realizing it, an angry person will seek out circumstances that enrage him; he will get into situations that make him more hostile or resentful. These are the natural consequences of an anger samskāra, and their purpose, if I may so call it, is to teach us to change our way of thinking.

If we do not learn, however, the samskāra gradually invades the body. This can happen in many ways, depending on the individual. We have to remember that each of us comprises countless samskāras, which can reinforce or counter each other in patterns as complex as those of the ripples that dapple a lake. One angry person, for example, may develop peptic ulcer; another, some pulmonary disorder: anger changes the breathing rhythm, and chronic anger can lead to chronically disordered breathing. This process continues over many lives, but you can see it develop even in the span of a single lifetime. In any case, once the condition is established, that person comes into life with a tendency to serious breathing problems. As soon as he finds himself in contexts that provoke him – an angry home, an angry teacher, angry classmates, an angry partner – the physical problem erupts.

The positive side is this: Meditation, as I can testify from helping thousands of people, can help you use the same situations, formerly detrimental, to *improve* your health and state of mind. The same circumstances that once would have wrecked your health can actually be used to rescue it. That is why I say when someone is angry with you, put up with it cheerfully; return good will and do not withdraw your support. It will help that person, but it will help you even more, by helping to solve your physical and emotional problems too.

This is tough, I agree. But isn't surgery tough? That is the way the Buddha talked; he always called a spade a spade. Surgery is a frightful procedure. It amazes me to see how willingly people in this country submit to it. Instead of getting myself into an untenable health problem and then paying through the nose to go through the trauma and indignities of surgery, I much prefer to take my health into my own hands.

You do not have to attain samādhi to do this, but you do have to change not only your lifestyle but your thoughtstyle. Then, as meditation deepens and you can repeat your mantram from a deeper level of awareness, prāna is gradually withdrawn from sense-samskāras and consolidated as vitality, resilience, and resistance to stress and disease.

श्रोत्रं चक्षुः स्पर्शनं च रसनं घ्राणमेव च ।
अधिष्ठाय मनश्चायं विषयानुपसेवते ॥ १५-९ ॥

*9. Using the mind, ears, eyes, nose, and the senses
of taste and touch, the Self enjoys sense objects.*

In Sanskrit the stuff of the mind is called *chitta,* which you can think of as a peculiarly elastic modeling clay. Chitta is pure, shapeless consciousness, which takes the form of individual containers like you and me. It flows out through the senses, following desire; it goes where our attention goes. When you are listening to your favorite rock group in quadraphonic sound, chitta runs out of the mind and into the ear. Then it is difficult to get it back in again. This is prāna that is flowing out, vital energy that is lost. That is why people who get conditioned to loud, agitating music usually find their security falling and their restlessness swelling past endurance.

The other day I went into a record store in Berkeley while Christine was shopping across the street. Loud rock music was playing as I went in, and everybody in the store – customers and staff alike – was doing a kind of St. Vitus's dance in time to the beat. I just stood and watched; I couldn't believe my eyes. Imagine doing this every day! When you subject yourself to this kind of music regularly for a couple of years, this is how you are going to be inside. Not only your limbs but your nervous system will jerk and bob about everywhere you go, even during your sleep. Your body may not be bobbing, but the movement has got into the mind. When the mind is dancing to St. Vitus's tune, it is in a constant state of excitement or depression, a condition that has become endemic today.

As the mind travels further and further from the center like this, the lines of communication with the Self become overextended. We need fresh supplies of security, energy, judgment, willpower, but the supply lines are broken; we cannot get in touch with the center of our being. Depression or despair may set in; discrimination, sound judgment, is exhausted. We may set off in pursuit of anything that promises satisfaction, whatever the cost, though our vital capacity for enjoying anything has already been drained. Like a ship that has lost its anchor, we are at the mercy of any storm that comes.

In reaching out through the senses, we travel far away from the indivisible unity of life at the center of our being. To get back, we have to rise above everything that is separate in us: our physical urges, our emotional cravings for aggrandizement, our compulsive imposition of self-will on all around us. These are powerful forces that fling consciousness away from its center. If we are to turn and travel inward, each of these forces has to be harnessed.

To do this, it helps a good deal to look on everybody else as an extension of ourselves and on ourselves as an extension of everyone else. When we are physically oriented, we think we stop with the outermost layer of our skin. Inside that boundary is home territory. There I have to consider my comforts and conveniences, my pleasure and profit, because this is home. After all, if you don't take care of your own home, who will? But beyond that, we don't care what happens. "That's not my problem," we say. "It's Bob's. That's *his* home, not mine."

Those who live for physical satisfaction are driven by this sense of otherness, which cannot help leading to alienation. They become estranged from others because they are estranged from themselves. But if you can break through the surface stratum of consciousness, you will find the gap of separateness becoming narrower and narrower. You get a sense of nearness to people. Where formerly you saw a chasm between you and your partner, now you see only a little creek; with practice, you can jump right over.

How close can you move to your partner, your boyfriend or girlfriend, when some disagreement is pushing you apart? How easily can you yield your own opinions for the sake of the relationship? How gracefully can you go against your own self-will? When someone you love is going off in a wrong direction, can you correct that person with respect and sympathy, even if it means some temporary agitation? If you can do these things, you are making excellent progress. These are the arts of love, which have been completely forgotten in the modern world.

As long as you are self-willed, you will find a long distance between you and those around you, even your boyfriend or girlfriend. No matter how much you try to be together, you will not be able to lessen this distance until you raise the banner of revolt against your own ego. If you want to assess your meditation, take your tape measure out every

New Year's Day and measure the distance between you and your family. Our natural tendency is to think of ourselves as the center and others on the circumference. Instead, think of yourself as the circumference; the rest of life is the center. Every year we should be able to move closer to the center. The marks are more patience, deeper understanding, greater security when things do not go our way.

To draw closer to others, you have to rebel against yourself. Often you will have to hurt your own private feelings so that others can benefit. "Thy will be done," Jesus says, not "my will be done." Thy will is unity; my will is separateness. It is so terribly difficult to practice this that most people do not try; those who do try often do not persist. But if you have the inner toughness this fierce fight requires, you will find you need less and less tape to measure the gap between you and others. Finally you discover you are at the center, no longer separate from the whole. Then you can throw the tape away.

उत्क्रामन्तं स्थितं वापि भुञ्जानं वा गुणान्वितम् ।
विमूढा नानुपश्यन्ति पश्यन्ति ज्ञानचक्षुषः ॥ १५-१० ॥

10. The deluded do not see the Self when it leaves the body or when it dwells within it. They do not see the Self enjoying sense objects or acting through the gunas. But they who have the eye of wisdom see.

Until the mind is stilled it is not possible for any human being, however gifted, to see the unity underlying life. The mind is not equipped to see unity. It is meant to register change on the surface of life, and to that which does not change, which has no parts, it is simply blind.

In the Buddha's presentation, the mind is not a thing or a state; it is a process. James Joyce and Virginia Woolf might have been interested to learn that the idea of a stream of consciousness was well worked out in Buddhist circles twenty-five hundred years ago. According to the theory of *kshanikavāda*, each thought is born and dies every moment. There is no connection between one thought and the next and the next; each is separate from the others, like frames on a movie film. And just as in a movie, what makes things look connected is the speed at which these separate thought-frames move by.

Some time ago a filmmaker friend brought home a print of an old Humphrey Bogart movie. For almost two hours we watched a lot of fast, furious action. Afterwards, before it was rewound, I went to look at the film. Terry obligingly unrolled a few yards at the end and brought out his little magnifying glass. There was no action at all. We saw a lot of shots of someone standing with his hand up, then out; then some other chap is leaning precariously backward. But no blow takes place. You see this, then you see that, and you put two and two together and say, "Ah! He hit him. Hit him again, Bogie!"

This is what happens in the mind. A fast mind means a lot of thoughts crowding through, trying to get by at once. Each is separate, but they are all crowded so close that they are like a row of dominoes. You knock over the first thought – "She is looking at me with the corner of her mouth turned up" – and all the rest fall over in an instant, until the last thought topples off the edge of the table and you conclude that she is smirking because of that one stupid remark you made at Henry's two weeks ago. "What a small mind she must have," you say, "to go on acting amused because of something that happened two weeks ago! What about all those stupid things *she* said?"

This absurd process is the ego – *ahamkāra* in Sanskrit, that which makes us feel separate. This is the film that is always going on in the theater of consciousness, even while we sleep. When we slow it down through meditation, the day comes when we can see for ourselves that every thought is separate. Where formerly thoughts were crowding and jostling each other like rush-hour commuters on the downtown subway, you begin to separate them. I remember a cartoon in an English magazine showing a team of American football players bent over in a huddle. A goat on the sidelines, taking this as a personal invitation, was lowering its head to charge. This is what you do in meditation; you start butting clinging thoughts apart. Finally you slow the thinking process to such an extent that each thought comes freely, without dragging any others along with it. Then your responses are free; conditioned thinking becomes a thing of the past.

When thoughts are crowded close together, it is very difficult to get free from the tyranny of thinking. We are helpless, particularly in the peculiar instance of circular thinking, in which the same old thought goes round and round: "I hate her, I hate her, I hate her, I hate her." That is all anger is, the same compulsive thought over and over. Most of us do not know what to do with this. If it gets particularly oppressive – usually as we are tossing and turning in bed – we may exclaim to ourselves, "If only I could stop thinking!" But we do not know how.

This kind of obsession is like a scratched record. The needle has got stuck, and all the mind can do is repeat the same thought over and over. Yesterday a friend was playing a Beatles song that made no sense to me at all. John Lennon, I believe, was singing, "I am the egg man, I am the walrus . . ." "Very good," I said to myself, "this is a song about the unity of life." Then he went on, "I am the walrus, the walrus, the walrus, the walrus."

"Julia," I said, "why does he go on like this? Can't he think of anything else?"

Julia just laughed. "The needle's stuck," she explained. "Doesn't it sound funny?"

When the mind gets stuck, it makes very little sense to wail to yourself, "Why does it do this to me? Can't it think of anything better?" Once you can elbow your thoughts apart, you can lift the needle when it is between two thoughts and place it a groove or two ahead, where the whole thinking process can pick up as if nothing had happened. This is a truly amazing accomplishment. Most of us know that when we get angry, resentful, afraid, or agitated, although we may have honorary degrees or be the union's toughest negotiator, we cannot do this one little thing: put out a finger, lift the needle, and make the song move on. That is what meditation can do.

The more self-willed we are, the closer thoughts get to each other. Self-willed thoughts are a gregarious, pushy lot; they like to put their arms around their buddies, climb on each other's shoulders, and generally make themselves at home. But as self-will subsides, thoughts become as orderly as if they were on parade. In a marching band, aren't you supposed to keep a precise distance from the person in front? Your thoughts will become like that; they keep a certain distance. If someone offends you, it will not provoke a resentful response. You may feel a little displeased, but you can drop your displeasure immediately.

यतन्तो योगिनश्चैनं पश्यन्त्यात्मन्यवस्थितम् ।
यतन्तो ऽप्यकृतात्मानो नैनं पश्यन्त्यचेतसः ॥ १५-११ ॥

*11. Those who strive resolutely on the path
of yoga see the Self within. The thoughtless,
who strive intermittently, do not.*

One of the reasons Sri Krishna gives for people being self-willed, separate, and selfish is laziness. It's a simple but penetrating diagnosis. They
are not prepared to make the effort of reducing self-will, even if they
would like to be secure. They are not willing to work on their consciousness to try to remove what is negative. They follow the path of least
resistance; wherever self-will flows, they follow. As a result they often
end up becoming automata, without any life to their credit.

People like this remind me of the trucks I see sometimes taking a big
mobile home along the freeway. They have red warning flags sticking
out on both sides, front and back, and big signs that warn, "Wide Load."
Everybody on the road moves over as far as possible, because they know
there is no arguing with this fellow; he will just get into your lane.

Self-willed people are very much like this. You may not have meant
any offense, but their nerves are so raw that they will take offense. You
may have meant only a slight joke; all you expected was a laugh. But
they go home, dwell on it, and come back the next day with that remark
inflated into a big problem.

This is what happens when you dwell on yourself: you take a limp
little balloon of a problem, keep on blowing it up, and make it huge. It
is helpful to remember that the personal problems we talk over with
confidants, write up in our journals, brood over, and dream about are
not as big as they seem. We have inflated them by thinking about them
for hours, until they become huge. We may not be able to see the red
flags or read those warning words, "Wide Load"; but others know, and
avoid us when they see us coming.

Many, many people today who are intellectually gifted, materially
prosperous, personally attractive, culturally advanced, have been hypnotized by separateness and inflated by their own importance. Whatever

their gifts, Sri Krishna says, they cannot see unity. Therefore, their opinion or contribution cannot be of permanent benefit to humanity.

यदादित्यगतं तेजो जगद्भासयतेऽखिलम् ।
यच्चन्द्रमसि यच्चाग्नौ तत्तेजो विद्धि मामकम् ॥ १५-१२॥

12. The brightness of the sun, which lights up the world, the brightness of the moon and of fire – these are mine.

Yesterday Christine and I went to the Hyatt Regency hotel in San Francisco, which has achieved notoriety for its unusual architecture. I always appreciate a good view, and I wanted to visit the revolving penthouse restaurant from which you can look out over the whole city.

We entered the Regency's portals and went straight to the top, the Equinox. I felt like a wide-eyed boy set down on another planet. A nice server came and showed us to a plush corner with huge windows and mirrors on all sides, where she promised we would be able to get a good view.

Then the usual restaurant topic of vegetarian food came up. This can lead to highly philosophical discussions about what comes with what and how it is prepared, whether fish and birds can count as vegetables, and other botanical and ontological topics. At the end of all this the server said, "I'll bring you a special chef's salad." That suited me perfectly. "There's no need to hurry on," I assured Christine. "Why don't we sit here until we've seen the whole city pass by?"

Out of the window we could see the ships coming and going in San Francisco Bay. While we worked our way through the salad, the Bay slipped out of sight and more and more of the city swung into view. "Look at that!" I said to Christine after a while. "You can see Coit Tower."

Christine laughed. "That's not really Coit Tower," she said.

"Of course it is," I said. Everybody in the Bay Area knows Coit Tower; it looks like a giant fire hose nozzle.

"You're looking at its reflection," said Christine.

She was right. I realized suddenly that I had been looking in the wrong direction, gazing into one of the full-height mirrors with which our booth was paneled. How much of what I had been watching had been real? I couldn't tell what was window and what was mirror.

"There," I said, pointing in another direction. "Isn't that the Equitable Insurance building?" Another landmark; I recognized the parking lot.

Christine looked closely. "That's not a window either," she decided. "In fact, I think it's not just a reflection; it's a reflection of a reflection."

I lost all confidence in my vision. Only when we escaped from the Equinox and got back to Union Square did I feel I knew where I was and what I was seeing.

Shankara compares the whole phenomenal world to a city seen in a mirror. This is not a poetic fancy. When we look at people as physical entities, talk to them and deal with them and try to possess or manipulate them as if they were physical entities, we are dealing with reflections of our own mind-making. Just like Coit Tower, they *do* seem real. Until Christine pointed out that I was looking in a mirror, I would have sworn that I was looking at the real Coit Tower. Even then, in order to understand that this was only a reflection, I needed to be able to compare it with something real. In the Equinox I could do that simply by looking in a different direction. But in life, if you want to see what is real, you have to get below the surface level of consciousness.

This illusion can lead to painful comments on relationships, particularly the romantic. "Making love," for example, has no necessary connection with love. I would say this is "making physical relationships" – making reflections of reflections of love. Love means affirming the unity between two people; indulging in physical relationships for physical satisfaction is denying that unity. Anyone who has tried to build a relationship on sexual attraction knows how fleeting it is, how soon satiation and irritation come.

We have a story in India about a courtesan who was notoriously fond of money. One evening a rich man came to her salon and happened to see her standing before a mirror. The image was so voluptuously beautiful that he went and gallantly kissed the reflection. Immediately she said, "That will be one hundred rupees."

This was a resourceful chap. He took out a hundred rupees, held it up, and gestured toward its reflection in the mirror. "You may collect that," he said.

It is tragic, but in personal relationships we are often dealing with a reflection. Trying to possess somebody is trying to possess a reflection; it cannot be done. Imagine Romeo seeing Juliet's reflection and carrying away the mirror! That is just what physically oriented people do when they try to possess, manipulate, and enjoy. Sooner or later this is accompanied by negative reflections of reflections: doubt, jealousy, insecurity, alienation, frustration, anger, depression. Love never asks "What can I get from this person?" It asks only, "What can I give?" That is the way to go beyond reflections to the real person.

After we finished our salad at the Equinox and paid the bill, we didn't know how to get out. We wandered around the periphery looking for one of those glowing exit signs, but all we could see in that eerie half-darkness was windows, mirrors, and red plush. Finally we asked our server for help. "You just walk out," she said. We had been looking for some special exit, but right in front of us was a gap through which we could pass from the Equinox back to the everyday reality of San Francisco.

"Don't wait for signs," Jesus says. Right where we are standing we can find the exit from the world of separateness and enter into the world of unity. All we have to do is turn our backs, to the best of our ability, on our private needs, demands, and self-indulgences.

Otherwise, the Gita says, the world we live in will become darker and darker. Living in separateness means being dominated by private urges, trying to have our own way and do only what we like, unable to see what cries out to be done for the welfare of the world around us. When this darkness becomes deep enough, we can't see which direction to go; we will always be losing our way, never coming out at all. When we decide to say no to private, personal urges, we start to enter a world of light where the path is clear. We know where we are going, and we can travel safely and surely.

गामाविश्य च भूतानि धारयाम्यहमोजसा ।
पुष्णामि चौषधीः सर्वाः सोमो भूबा रसात्मकः ॥ १५-१३ ॥
अहं वैश्वानरो भूबा प्राणिनां देहमाश्रितः ।
प्राणापानसमायुक्तः पचाम्यन्नं चतुर्विधम् ॥ १५-१४ ॥

13. *With a drop of my energy I enter the earth*
and support all creatures. Through the moon, the
vessel of life-giving fluid, I nourish all plants.
14. *I enter each living creature and dwell*
within as the life-giving breath. I am the fire
in the stomach which digests all food.

These verses again refer to prāna, the primordial energy underlying all the forms of matter and energy with which we are familiar. The universe hums with prāna, and its forces and processes can be described as the flow of prāna. The Upanishads say that prāna streams from the sun and flows into plants to be stored, to be released later in human beings and animals when the plants are eaten, to power the work of the body, senses, and mind. No biologist would find this inaccurate; it is a poetic description of what the life sciences would call "energy flows in an ecosystem." I have seen textbooks refer to the oxidation of food as "the fire of digestion," which echoes the Gita almost word for word.

We can also think of prāna as flowing through time, powering the growth of the Tree of Life since the universe began. It is the energy of evolution, pushing its way through root, trunk, and branch to feed each individual leaf. And when a man or woman nears the end of the evolutionary journey and takes to meditation, this immense power bursts into new levels of activity.

I can illustrate this with an incident that occurred yesterday evening while we drove across the Richmond Bridge. Suddenly the roadway began vibrating wildly. I thought to myself, "Well, the earthquake has finally arrived." Every few years, you know, papers and magazines in California start carrying fresh predictions that this is the year in which the San Andreas Fault is finally going to allow half the state to slide into the sea. But as it turned out, this was no quake. A huge ship was passing beneath the bridge, unseen in the gathering darkness and the fog. Its horn went off just as we reached the central pier, shaking the car with its blast.

That is how it feels when a long-standing samskāra comes to the surface from the depths of the unconscious. You have to face it and do battle with it, which brings upheavals on every level of personality, physical, emotional, intellectual, and spiritual. We have to be prepared to change with these impacts and develop new ways of living – more aware of the unity of life, less and less aware of the fragmented personality we once were.

This tremendous adjustment is accomplished through the energy these verses call *ojas*. The word has several implications. Partly *ojas* means the will, running all through the conscious mind to the very depths of the unconscious. Partly it means the prompt obedience of the senses, body, mind, and intellect to the slightest signal of the Ātman. Few of us have ever experienced this. Our usual state of personality is a free-for-all, where senses, feelings, judgment, and so on behave like those electric bumper cars at county fairs, skittering about colliding with each other. When this erratic activity subsides, there is a great consolidation of vital energy that flows into your life like a steady stream.

Ojas is prāna in the intense, superconcentrated form called *kundalinī*. All of us have a vast reservoir of this vital energy, which is the power that impels the individual creature through higher and higher states of evolution. In those who are selfish, kundalinī is hardly used. They do not need it; they are living just for themselves. To get along on the surface level of life, we need just one candlepower of kundalinī. But we have much vaster capabilities, merely by virtue of being human. As we begin to economize our extravagant expenditure or sense-energy, kundalinī gradually rises. Every time we defy a strong sensory urge, a little more of its power is available to us.

On the other hand, indulging a powerful desire like sex for the purpose of sensory satisfaction prevents kundalinī from rising. There is a vitally close connection between kundalinī and sex, and though we are not asked to become ascetics on the spiritual path, it is essential to get hold of this vast source of power and bring it under our control. I always have to repeat that this does not mean the faculty of sex is lost. It means simply that you have a choice in when and how it is expressed – which very few of us ordinary human beings can honestly say we have.

When sexual passions are fanned into flame, how difficult it is to understand that we are not our desires! Once we are caught in the fire, we have no freedom. The push is so fierce that we feel we have to succumb. At such times we are not using our desires; our desires are using us. All the Gita is saying is that we should not serve them; they should serve us. When sexual desire is mastered, it floods the body with the invigorating energy of kundalini and strengthens the will until it cannot be broken by any tragedy, calamity, or danger.

सर्वस्य चाहं हृदि संनिविष्टो
    मत्तः स्मृतिर्ज्ञानमपोहनं च ।
वेदैश्च सर्वैरहमेव वेद्यो
    वेदान्तकृद्वेदविदेव चाहम् ॥ १५-१५॥

15. *Entering into every heart, I give the power*
to remember and understand; it is I again who
take that power away. All the scriptures lead to
me; I am their author and their wisdom.

Sri Krishna is continuing the same theme: that everywhere in the universe he is prāna.

When Einstein discovered that matter and energy are interchangeable and began looking for a unified field theory, he may have had a concept like prāna in mind. But prāna not only underlies matter and energy on the physical level; it is also the power supplying the world within. If there is potential energy in a body at rest, imagine the energy in a strong desire or in compulsive anger! One fixed desire can launch a man or woman through thirty years or more of sustained, energetic action; it can overpower a continent, free a nation, transform a technology, eradicate a disease. All that power is prāna. We have ample evidence of the immense energy in the nucleus of an atom, but when I say that there is as much energy in a thought, people think I am being poetic. As an acorn gathers prāna and explodes into an oak tree, thoughts explode into action. If the thought is big enough it can work on for decades, draw in thousands of lives, change the course of history.

Dr. Hans Selye discovered that a laboratory rat can adapt to cold and other kinds of physiologic stress until it can not only survive but thrive under conditions where an unadjusted rat will perish. If the rat gets enough food to meet its body's energy needs, it should be able to continue in this state indefinitely. Yet, curiously, there comes a point at which something "gives out." After that, this well-fed rat will die if it is exposed to even moderate stress. Selye asks properly, What is lacking? Some other kind of energy, he concludes: some inner reservoir of vitality that stress has finally drained. He calls it "adaptation energy." I would call it prāna.

Dr. Barbara Brown, a physiologist in biofeedback research, made some related observations. She came to the conclusion that vital energy – she calls it "nervous energy" – is leaking out from us into the environment all the time. I differ with some of her conclusions, but I admire her originality of mind, and I found this an amazingly perceptive observation. This energy too I would call prāna. Dr. Brown says she does not know how prāna leaks out, of course; the loss is not physical, though it has physical effects. And she does not know how to stop it. But the Gita and the Upanishads would explain that whenever we desire something through the senses for their satisfaction, prāna ebbs out. Not only the physical act of satisfying a desire, but the desire itself depletes our vital energy.

This leakage means loss of vitality, of will, of the capacity to adapt to and thrive under the normal stress of life. To prevent this, it is absolutely essential to be able to close and open the sluice gates of the senses at will. This means developing the inner equipment and the skill to release prāna whenever you have a giant job to undertake for the welfare of all – as did, say, Mahatma Gandhi, St. Francis of Assisi, St. Teresa of Ávila – and to withhold prāna when some private, personal yearning is clamoring to be fulfilled. This magnificent capacity can strengthen the will immeasurably and make the body healthy, strong, beautiful, and vital.

Ultimately it is in the depths of meditation that prāna is dammed until our reservoir of vitality is full. For prāna is not lost only through the senses. It is drained whenever the mind is scattered and divided, pulled in all directions by different thoughts – which, for most of us, is most of the time.

Conflict, for example, is a prime drain on prāna. Most conflicts arise because a selfless thought and a selfish thought want to occupy the same place in the mind. Often the selfish thought comes in first; when the right thought opens the door, there is Mr. Wrong with his feet up on the table. "This is *my* mind," he says. "Nobody was at the door, and I got here first." He doesn't want to go, so naturally a tussle ensues.

Much of our prāna is wasted not in making decisions but in the conflict we go through before we make decisions. We put ourselves on both sides, as Augustine says, and then we fight it out. Whichever side wins, we lose the prāna. We enter a dark arena to fight with the wrong thought, and after a while we discover we are pummeling Mr. Right by mistake. "Excuse *me!*" says Right. "I thought you were on my side." "Right you are," we confess. "Where's Wrong?" We go back to hitting the wrong thought for a while, and then somehow we switch sides again; and so it goes, back and forth, through the day and into the night. The next morning we are exhausted, and the problem is no closer to being resolved. "Arjuna," Sri Krishna asks, "where is the need for all this? Why not just post someone at the door? If the right thought knocks, let it in. If the wrong thought knocks, tell it to leave." When conflicts disappear, we get a tremendous accumulation of energy.

The next great consumer of prāna is worry. Worry means that prāna is leaking out through a thousand little wormholes. Most worms I have seen are small. Worries, similarly, may not be big thoughts, but a thousand of them means a lot of prāna lost. When a person generally feels unequal to challenges or tries to avoid personal problems, the reason is often this constant leakage of vitality through worry.

Some people cannot help worrying. You give them a job like opening an umbrella and they immediately start thinking, "Suppose it doesn't open? Suppose I get wet and catch a cold?" It is better to try to do a job, even if it turns out wrong, than to keep worrying about it and putting it off. "If I do this, there's going to be this trouble; if I do that, there will be that trouble." Do it and get into trouble if necessary; then you will at least know how to do it better the next time.

The cure here is "The early mantram gets the worry." Worry only enervates; it serves no purpose. If you can learn to peck up worry-worms with the mantram, you will have so much energy that you will never feel unequal no matter how big the challenge. You will have energy and time to offer even after your regular duties are done: time to do more, to give more, to live more.

A third waster of prāna, perhaps the biggest, is depression. Your doctor will tell you that most people today accept depression as a condition of life, largely because they think it is biologically unavoidable. We live; therefore we get depressed. Most of us have even lost the capacity to question this. We say, "Well, we just have to learn to live with it."

Again, this is because no one is watching the door of the mind. When excitement arrives, blowing its trumpet and trying to knock the door down, we say, "Whoopee! Somebody's brought me some joy; bring it right in!" We get so excited that we can't sleep, we can't stop talking; the mind is in overdrive twenty-four hours a day. In short, we fling the door of the mind open wide, all because we're so anxious to be pleased. And while we're entertaining Pleasure, her twin, Depression, slips in. You can't keep her out, because you're holding the door open to every thought you can get in. But you don't notice Depression till a few days later, when you come home and find, instead of your dream date, a little note taped onto the door: "Thanks for a lovely time – someday we'll have to do it again. Last night's lasagna is in the fridge. I asked my sister to keep you company." There is Depression, looking up at you with sunken eyes; she hasn't even got enough prāna for a smile.

Sri Krishna always gives Arjuna free choice. "You can go after pleasure if you like," he says. "But if you do, you have to accept depression too." Arjuna doesn't say anything, but his eyes ask, "What's the alternative?" So Sri Krishna adds, "Control your mind." When Excitement knocks and wants to move in, just say, "Why don't you try next door?" Then you can entertain angels. For when excitement and depression vanish, the state of mind that remains is joy. You have freed yourself from conflict, anxiety, anger, and fear; sorrow will come no more.

द्वाविमौ पुरुषौ लोके क्षरश्चाक्षर एव च ।
क्षरः सर्वाणि भूतानि कूटस्थोऽक्षर उच्यते ॥ १५-१६ ॥

*16. In this world there are two orders of being, the
perishable, separate creature and the changeless spirit.*

I have been reading a thoughtful book, *Mankind and Mother Earth,* in
which Arnold Toynbee refers to the human being as a "psychosomatic
organism" – part *psyche,* spiritual; part *soma,* physical – who lives necessarily in two realms. "In the biosphere," he says, we act "within a world
that is material and finite." That is precisely the language of this verse.
Kshara means limited, exhaustible, perishable, finite. The term has
become particularly poignant. Until recently, most of us believed that
the biosphere was inexhaustible; we could do what we liked with its
resources. Today we know that everything in our physical environment
is limited: food, trees, minerals, soil, even water and air.

"On this plane of human activity," Toynbee continues,

> Man's objective, ever since he became conscious, has been
> to make himself master of his nonhuman environment,
> and in our own day he has come within sight of success
> in this endeavor – possibly to his own undoing.

This is a simple point, but it is often ignored. No matter what technological miracles we achieve, Toynbee says, we can never separate
ourselves from the rest of the biosphere. We are a part of this "nature"
that we want to master.

But our "other home, the spiritual world, is also an integral part of
total reality," says Toynbee:

> it differs from the biosphere in being both nonmaterial and
> infinite; and in his life in the spiritual world, Man finds that his
> mission is to seek, not for material mastery over his nonhuman
> environment, but for a spiritual mastery over himself.

Our nature is infinite. Therefore, the Upanishads say, nothing less
than infinitude can ever satisfy us. If we forget that our real home is the

world of the spirit, imperishable and changeless, we will go on trying to mine, refine, extract, harvest, and manufacture an infinite number and variety of things out of an acutely limited world.

The very air we breathe is exhaustible. Berkeley used to scorn Los Angeles for its smog, yet already clean air in the Bay Area is the exception rather than the rule. Last week children in San Francisco were asked not to run and play outside because the air was so thick with smog – smog caused by greed. If we loved our children as we profess to, we should remember that the air is limited, exhaustible, a perishable member of the family of life. Treat it gently, the Gita says; treat it with care. Don't blow fumes into the air or dump poisons into the rivers and oceans just to make more money; and don't fan overconsumption by buying more and more things you do not need. It is not only manufacturers who carry the responsibility for pollution. Insofar as we tell them, "Produce all you want! We'll buy whatever you make," the rest of us are responsible too.

In economics it is considered imprudent to live off your capital; in fact, in times of inflation it is imprudent even to live off your interest. We have been spending the stuff of the world wantonly, as if it were profligate interest on some eternal trust. Instead it is apparent that this is irreplaceable capital.

This is the first point made by the perceptive economist E. F. Schumacher in his brilliant little classic, *Small Is Beautiful.* I like the subtitle very much: *Economics As If People Mattered.* Schumacher, who has absorbed a great deal from Gandhi and the Buddha, questions all the assumptions of modern economics, and he does so in language that is simple, persuasive, practical, and profound. Other economists probably find this exasperating, but he is not writing for other economists. He is writing for people like you and me, who he feels can make a difference. "A businessman," Schumacher says,

> would not consider a firm to have solved its problems of production and to have achieved viability if he saw that it was rapidly consuming its capital. How, then, could we overlook this vital fact when it comes to that very big firm, the economy of Spaceship Earth and, in particular, the economies of its rich passengers? . . .

Look at the figures that are being put forward under the heading 'World Fuel Requirements in the Year 2000.' If we are now using something like 7000 million tons of coal equivalent, the need in twenty-eight years' time will be three times as large – around 20,000 million tons! . . .

What is so special about the year 2000? What about the year 2028, when little children running about today will be planning for their retirement? Another trebling by then? All these questions and answers are seen to be absurd the moment we realize that we are dealing with capital and not with income: fossil fuels are not made by men; they cannot be recycled. Once they are gone, they are gone forever.

Then he comes to the essential conflict:

An attitude to life which seeks fulfillment in the single-minded pursuit of wealth – in short, materialism – does not fit into this world, because it contains within itself no limiting principle, while the environment in which it is placed is strictly limited.

Thus even a great economist is led to the theme of this chapter: our isolation from the Tree of Life. We do not think of ourselves as part of nature, Schumacher says, "but as an outside force destined to dominate and conquer it. [Man] even talks of a battle with nature, forgetting that if he won the battle he would find himself on the losing side." That is what separateness does, and in this "outside force" we can recognize our old friend rajas. As Barry Commoner reminds us, technology has become such a terrible threat not because it has failed but because it has been so successful. It has succeeded so tremendously that since 1945 we have witnessed more technological progress, if that is the term I want, than in all the preceding years of human history; and the consequences of this progress threaten to close the pages of human history.

"Man," Toynbee points out, "is the first species of living being in our biosphere that has acquired the power to wreck the biosphere and, in wrecking it, to liquidate himself . . . . [He] is an integral part of the biosphere, and if the biosphere were to be made uninhabitable, Man, as

well as all other species, would become extinct." It is good to remember
that this is not rhetoric but a literal possibility, fraught with suffering
drawn out over generations on a scale this tormented world has never
seen before.

उत्तमः पुरुषस्त्वन्यः परमात्मेत्युदाहृतः ।
यो लोकत्रयमाविश्य बिभर्त्यव्यय ईश्वरः ॥ १५-१७॥
यस्मात्क्षरमतीतो ऽहमक्षरादपि चोत्तमः ।
अतो ऽस्मि लोके वेदे च प्रथितः पुरुषोत्तमः ॥ १५-१८॥
यो मामेवमसंमूढो जानाति पुरुषोत्तमम् ।
स सर्वविद्भजति मां सर्वभावेन भारत ॥ १५-१९॥

17. *But beyond these there is another, the supreme
Self, the eternal Lord, who enters into the
entire cosmos and supports it from within.*
18. *I am that supreme Self, praised by the scriptures
as beyond the changing and the changeless.*
19. *Those who see in me that supreme Self see
truly. They have found the source of all wisdom,
Arjuna, and they worship me with all their heart.*

"Supreme Self" here is *Purushottama,* after which the chapter is
named – the highest ideal we can have.

Even without talking about spiritual values, it can be said that most
of the meaninglessness in modern life comes from our having no ultimate purpose, no overriding goal. The strongest argument I can offer
against personal pleasure and profit is that they cannot function as a
goal. And without a comprehensive purpose, events cannot make sense
to us; incidents cannot be related to a whole. We don't have a framework
for making wise choices. That is why every one of us has a crying need
for the highest ideal, on which we can keep our eyes always. Whenever
we wander, we can still find our way back. All of us, being human, are
likely to make mistakes in life. But when we have a great purpose that
transcends passing, personal satisfactions, a goal that rises high above
the horizon like the polestar, we need not get lost and wander in the

maze of our mistakes. By keeping our eyes on this shining ideal, we can retrace our steps, correct our error, and continue to pursue our journey until we reach the goal.

The pursuit of wealth is often placed before us as a goal. Most of us know people who launched some enterprise with the best of intentions and then slowly got possessed by the profit motive, losing all vision of life. There is nothing wrong with a fair profit on a beneficial product or service. But without a higher goal, there is no point of reference to warn you when the profit motive begins to lead you into activities and ways of living that can wreck your life or the lives of others.

Every country today has examples of how the compulsive desire for profit has driven people to make things that ruin human health. Many of the handguns used in violent crimes in this country are assembled here from parts made in Germany, so that manufacturers in both countries can realize their profits without actually violating the law. Drugs prohibited in the United States because they may cause cancer or birth defects are pushed shamelessly in Third World countries where regulations are lax or nonexistent. And there is probably no growth industry so bullish this century as that of munitions, where companies from a handful of countries – led, I am sorry to say, by the United States and a few other developed countries – thrive on the business of pumping lethal hardware into any nation that will buy, washing their hands of any consequences. The list could be multiplied dozens of times without effort, so commonplace has "business as usual" become today. Once you see this, you rule out the giants of business and finance as ideals to be followed.

Similarly, in almost every country, personalities from sports and entertainment are held up as ideals. People want to look like them, talk like them, live like them, though they may be far from happy. Sports, movies, and the like do have a place; all of us need some time for exercise and relaxation. But if you do not have any higher purpose, you can end up setting your goal in life on perfecting your tennis strokes or cutting down your time on the mile. We must have an ideal. If we do not have anything big enough, we clutch at whatever is available: football players, race drivers, rock singers, movie stars.

All the great religions give us a supreme goal that brings out what is best in us from the very depths of consciousness. Jesus or Sri Krishna or the Compassionate Buddha is placed before us as an ideal for one reason: so that insofar as is in our capacity, we may gradually become like these luminous figures in our lives and hearts.

Toward the end of his life, St. Francis of Assisi asked his companions to stay behind while he went up into the wild, secluded heights of La Verna for solitary prayer. After some thirty days and nights, just before sunrise, he entered a state of deep ecstasy – what the Hindu mystics would call samādhi, union with the Christ within. In that supreme state he prayed fervently for two favors: "The first, that I may, as far as it is possible, feel in my soul and in my body the suffering which thou, O gentle Jesus, sustained in thy bitter passion; and the second, that as far as it is possible I may receive in my heart the overflowing love that moved thee to suffer so much for us." So complete was his identification with the Christ, the chronicles say, that he experienced both: the unutterable joy of complete love and the other side of that love, the cruelty of the wounds which Jesus suffered on the cross.

This complete identification is the meaning of samādhi. Those who attain it feel the joys and sorrows of others exactly as they would their own. They suffer and rejoice with all. The rest of us – less evolved, more self-centered, more separate – are scarcely aware of the full extent of suffering around us. The more separate we feel, the easier it is to forget about others' troubles, ignore the tragedies that surround us all, and bury ourselves in the pursuit of personal satisfactions.

The more you grow in selflessness, the more deeply you will feel the sorrow that throbs at the heart of life. But this is not a paralyzing sentimentality. Wherever you see suffering, you will have to do something to relieve it. You will never throw up your hands at the magnitude of a problem and say, "There's nothing I can do. The world is going to pieces; let it go." Your deep identification with all of life will release the resources to go to the causes of sorrow and devote your life to alleviating it.

इति गुह्यतमं शास्त्रमिदमुक्तं मयानघ ।
एतद्बुद्ध्वा बुद्धिमान्स्यात्कृतकृत्यश्च भारत ॥ १५-२० ॥

20. I have shared this profound truth with you,
Arjuna. Those who understand it will attain wisdom;
they will have done that which has to be done.

This simple phrase was a favorite of the Buddha's too: "That which was to be done has been done." No grand poetry, no trumpets, no philosophy; just a quiet statement that life's supreme purpose, the goal of millions of years of evolution, has been attained.

The implication is sobering: until we reach this state, nothing has been done. If you come and tell Sri Krishna that you have won the Irish Sweepstakes, climbed Annapurna without a sherpa, become the first woman to venture beyond Mars, he would say, "That isn't what has to be done. You haven't accomplished what you are here for."

Once you have done what has to be done, you have no interest in making money; therefore you do not exploit others or pollute the environment. Greed has left you, and so have anger and fear. You are no longer interested in your personal pleasure, so you are not capable of selfish attachment. You see life clearly, and you will not do things simply because they please you. There is nothing more you can want from life, nothing more that life can offer you except the opportunity to give.

पुरुषोत्तमयोगो नाम पञ्चदशोऽध्यायः ॥ १५ ॥

CHAPTER SIXTEEN

Two Paths

श्रीभगवानुवाच ।
अभयं सत्त्वसंशुद्धिर्ज्ञानयोगव्यवस्थितिः ।
दानं दमश्च यज्ञश्च स्वाध्यायस्तप आर्जवम् ॥१६-१॥
अहिंसा सत्यमक्रोधस्त्यागः शान्तिरपैशुनम् ।
दया भूतेष्वलोलुत्वं मार्दवं ह्रीरचापलम् ॥१६-२॥
तेजः क्षमा धृतिः शौचमद्रोहो नातिमानिता ।
भवन्ति संपदं दैवीमभिजातस्य भारत ॥१६-३॥

SRI KRISHNA:

*1–3. Be fearless and pure; never waver in your
determination or your dedication to the spiritual
life. Give of yourself freely. Be self-controlled, sincere,
truthful, loving, and full of the desire to serve. Realize
the truth of the scriptures; learn to be detached from
material things and to take joy in renunciation.
Do not get angry or harm any living creature, but
be compassionate and gentle; show good will to all.
Put others first and yourself last. All these, Arjuna,
will reveal your real nature, which is divine.*

Some time ago I was reminded of this chapter when I picked up the
morning paper and exclaimed to Christine, "This layout artist must
have been reading the Gita!" There, facing each other on inside pages,
were stories illustrating the two paths between which the Gita says each
of us has to choose continually: an upward path that leads to abiding
joy, a downward path that leads to increasing sorrow.

The left-hand page was an interview with a man offering advice on how to come out "on top" in the economic, social, and ecological disaster that he says is sure to come. Without reading more than the opening sentence, I knew which path he represented and where it had to lead. Because of its very premise – how to grab, not how to give – the advice he offers cannot lead anywhere but down.

He started with some grim forecasts: an economic collapse, acute food and energy shortages, rioting and pillage in the cities until production could be restored. Against the backdrop of ecological hazards and the likelihood of nuclear war, it did not make an attractive picture of the future – particularly, I thought, if you went on to follow his advice about how to face all these calamities. By the time I finished, I felt I was back in the Stone Age, defending myself with rocks against neighbors who wanted to steal my spark plugs and cans of tomato soup.

It was a great relief to look on to the next page and find it entirely devoted to the upward path, the way of love. The layout was dominated by photographs and eyewitness accounts of the arrival in Oslo of Mother Teresa of Calcutta, come to receive the Nobel Prize for peace. To me this was one of the most promising events of the year. As you know, the prize doesn't often go to a real peacemaker, and here it was being presented to someone who had never addressed herself to war directly but had simply gone about trying to help the poor. There was a charming photo of her with the children of Oslo, presenting her with a gift that must have meant more to her than the one she had come to collect: a "Poor People's Nobel Prize" of money collected from grassroots supporters. And there were stories about her childhood, her work, and her reception in Oslo, where she won my heart by asking the Nobel Committee to forgo the usual banquet in her honor and give the money to the poor instead.

Mother Teresa is one of those beacon figures who represent what the Gita calls here "the path that leads to the divine." Her life provides a very personal illustration of how the qualities in these verses gradually purify personality, allowing the divinity within us to shine through.

Mother Teresa was not born in India but in Yugoslavia. She went to India at the age of eighteen as a missionary, and took her vows as Sister Agnes to become a teacher in a girls' school in Calcutta. She must have been an excellent teacher; even now she confesses, "I love teaching most of all." If she had continued in that profession, doing what she loved, the world would rightly have considered her a success.

Instead something happened to change her life completely. At the age of about thirty-five, I believe – well into her vocation – she was travel-ing northward to Darjeeling, seven thousand feet above sea level in the Himālayas. The route passes through some of the most spectacular scen-ery in the world, vistas of such beauty that the cities and problems of humanity seem as distant as a dream. But for Sister Agnes, a bomb burst in consciousness that must have been ticking away for more than a decade. "In that train," she recalls simply, "I heard the call to give up all and follow Him into the slums to serve Him among the poorest of the poor."

Calcutta in those days was "the second city of the British Empire," an enclave of British power and a center of Indian culture. St. Mary's School for Girls was a tranquil, well-kept, secluded place, with beautiful gardens and bright, responsive students from the aristocratic families of Bengal. Leaving her school, Mother Teresa has said, was harder even than leaving her home. St. Mary's must have held for her the fulfillment of most human desires: beauty, companionship, comfort, security, the rewarding awareness of success in a selfless profession. She left it all without hesitation to join the homeless who lived in the streets and slums outside the school walls – with one rough, white cotton habit draped like a sari, a few rupees, and no plan but to follow her call. It was not an impulsive act; she was careful first to get some training in medical care. For the rest, however, she proceeded just as St. Francis had at a similar stage in his life: step by step, by helping the first person she encountered, then the next, then the next.

Today, like Francis, Mother Teresa has an order of spiritual descendents that ministers to the poor and dispossessed around the globe. Millions, I feel sure, revere her as a saint. Yet to me, what is most memorable in her story is that like the rest of us, she was not born a saint. Step by step, over decades, by making selfless choices that any man or woman can make, she ascended what the Gita calls the bright path that leads toward divin-ity. We do not start life with virtues perfected; no one does. We simply do our best to practice them, and as we practice they get stronger.

There were portrait photos on each of these two pages: one of the doomsday counselor, the other of Mother Teresa. The first showed a solid, honest man in his forties, confident, energetic, and self-reliant. You could see from the look in his eyes and the set of his jaw that he was sure of his ability to take care of himself and his family come what may. I guessed that he set high standards for himself, and expected others to measure up to them too. It was difficult to imagine him defending spark plugs against marauding neighbors. Yet if I were a gambler, I would bet any odds that at least in the physical sense, this man and his family would survive the future whatever it brought. He would pay the cost without even being aware of how high a price this kind of survival exacts.

How different to look at Mother Teresa's face, shining from the opposite page! Small, frail-looking, but suffused with vitality, she wore her body as casually as she wore that white cotton sari; like Gandhi, she scarcely seemed aware of it. And in every photograph – with children in Oslo, with dignitaries, with the poor again in Calcutta – you could see how her smile and her deep, dancing eyes lit the faces of those around her. She would not survive whatever the future might bring; she would thrive. The more life tried to take, the more she would give. No one seeing her would ever question if she were happy. From their faces you could see where each path leads.

दम्भो दर्पोऽतिमानश्च क्रोधः पारुष्यमेव च ।
अज्ञानं चाभिजातस्य पार्थ संपदमासुरीम् ॥ १६-४ ॥

4. Other qualities, Arjuna, make a person more and more inhuman: hypocrisy, arrogance, conceit, anger, cruelty, ignorance of the unity of life.

I wish I could go on about Mother Teresa, but it is Sri Krishna's unpleasant duty in this chapter to show Arjuna the dark alternative. It is a grim picture, but sooner or later every spiritual teacher finds it necessary to say clearly what will happen if the teachings of the scriptures are not followed. It puts life in proper perspective for us and gives us motivation.

In Sanskrit the two paths of this chapter are named after the states of consciousness to which they lead. *Daivī*, 'divine,' comes from the word *deva*, which literally means a god. The root sense implies something shining, effulgent, full of light. And *āsurī* comes from *asura*, which means a demon. In Hindu mythology the devas are the forces of light; the asuras, their perpetual enemies, are the forces of darkness. These forces interplay throughout history, and from time to time, when the powers of darkness become so strong that they threaten to overwhelm the earth with suffering, the Lord is born as a savior to rally the powers of goodness and restore dharma, the unity of life. In the *Mahābhārata* he has come as Sri Krishna, and we should picture him now speaking these words to Arjuna as they stand by their chariot between the vast armies of light and darkness, waiting for the outbreak of war on the Armageddon of their world.

This is history from a spiritual perspective, and it is not at all inaccurate. Yet at the same time, we should keep reminding ourselves that these are essentially forces within each of us. Self-will does wreak havoc on a global scale, but every disaster we face today – war, violence, starvation, cruelty, terrorism, ecological suicide – has not only been "born in the minds of men" but fostered there, nurtured, and unleashed in the world.

By folk etymology the devas are also called *suras*, as if *asura* meant 'not sura' the way *ahimsā* means 'nonviolence'. Scholars may not agree with the derivation, but it makes a practical point: without what is *sura*, divine, what is left is demonic. If you want to make yourself into a demon, you don't have to take a correspondence course or buy expensive paraphernalia. All you have to do is never do what a deva does. You won't achieve success overnight, of course. To become a real king of demons, you have to allow your personality to deteriorate for a long period of time. It happens so slowly, so naturally, that you may not notice the change from day to day. But as old Mad Nārāyana used to show us, it's as easy as rolling downhill. Before you know it, you're at the bottom.

In the previous verse Sri Krishna listed many qualities that make personality more divine. Imagine that you had a roommate who never practiced any of these: not somebody evil, but simply a person who always took the course of least resistance. He would have no control over his thoughts, words, acts, or passions, but would be vacillating and self-centered twenty-four hours a day. He would never tell the truth, and he would have an awful capacity to hold a grudge. He would be anxious, arrogant, lazy, greedy, and bad-tempered. You would say, "Not exactly heaven!" That is what "demonic" means.

No one, I would venture to say, is born an out-and-out, incorrigible demon. Because the Ātman is present in each of us, each has the innate capacity to make choices that benefit others instead of only ourselves. Personality is a process: we make ourselves more and more demonic, or more and more divine, with our own thoughts, words, and actions. Very simply, the qualities Sri Krishna lists here are moods and attitudes that worsen us. Almost everybody suffers from them at some time or other. But if we indulge them and go on indulging them, we deteriorate – physically, emotionally, and spiritually.

Self-will is the proper name of this affliction, and it is worse than any of the killing and crippling diseases we know of today because it brings distress not only to us but to everybody around us. The main reason we cannot see it as a disease is that there is such a lapse in time between cause and effect. The course the Black Plague took was clear enough; a person might cough two or three times in the morning and be dead by the next day. But in the case of self-will, you cough and think it's just pollen in the air. The adverse effects are too subtle to be recognized, too apparently unrelated, too far down the line of cause and effect.

Even physical ailments can be like this: a person exposed to radiation may not show signs of cancer for twenty or thirty years. Similarly, we may notice that our relationships are growing rocky, or that we can't find a job we like, or that our allergies are worse or our blood pressure dangerously high, without ever suspecting that all these can be traced to inflated self-will. We watch our neighbors arm themselves in fear, read in the papers about the breakdown of the family, suffer through erratic cycles of inflation and recession, bleed the economy bankrupt amassing weapons we can never afford to use, and send our children into war without ever reflecting that all these happen because of self-will raging on a national, even global scale. It spreads like the most virulent disease. Unless it is fought, selfishness deepens in us, spreads, reinforces selfishness in others. We support it with the votes we cast (or do not cast), the purchases and investments we make, the silent consent we give to the operations of our governments and businesses and institutions.

Let's look again at the doomsday advisor I mentioned. How could the path he had chosen lead anywhere but down? Once we accept the idea that what is most important is to look out for ourselves, the rest follows so naturally that we scarcely notice where it leads.

He began very reasonably. Since food shortages are almost certain, he advised, "stock up as much food as you can. If your cellar or attic will hold it, a twelve-month supply is not too much." This made sense enough from his perspective. But I couldn't help thinking how different my own response would be, drawing on the examples of my granny and Mahatma Gandhi. If I were told that food was going to be in short supply, my first thought would be, "What can I do without that I don't need? Is there anything that I would actually benefit from giving up?" Most of us, according to nutritionists, would thrive if we ate less. Not only that, in terms of our national health, millions of dollars could be saved in medical bills. It amazed me to see this man talking about stockpiling cigarettes, beer, wine, or your favorite candy bars – let alone, if worst came to worst, actually sitting around and enjoying such things while hungry neighbors roamed in search of food.

My second thought would be, "How much food can I grow myself?" You can see my granny's emphasis: always on self-reliance and turning obstacles into opportunities. Why go to the supermarket and spend your remaining currency on cans and packages of the same old stuff, just because it has a shelf life of twenty-four months? You can grow your own vegetables and even a number of fruits in many interesting places besides back yards and front lawns. Containers can go anywhere there is some sun: in patios, on doorsteps and rooftops, in windowsills and window boxes, suspended from eaves. Community vegetable gardens are blooming now in formerly vacant city lots. These are appealing, strengthening, sattvic solutions. Instead of subtracting from the food supply, they add to it. Instead of aggravating adversity, they actually improve the quality of life.

The next suggestion for survival follows from the first. Start hoarding other physical necessities: automobile parts, soap, razor blades, deodorant, paper towels, anything you do not want to do without. If you believe that life is not worth living without paper towels or that you can't be happy without a car, this too is reasonable advice. Once you have achieved a lifestyle you like, perhaps anything is worse than changing it. On the other hand, we should look at the price. The consequences *may* be worse after all; and as far as answers to deprivation go, our lives might benefit from simplification.

Third, this expert advises, buy gold. Buy silver. No matter what happens to the economy, he reasons, you should always be able to get enough canned vegetables and spark plugs for a Krugerrand. A good part of your savings should be in bullion, perhaps even in a foreign bank; but you should also keep a bag or so of silver dollars and a number of small gold coins for emergency spending, preferably hidden somewhere that no one else in your family knows about. It is not that you should mistrust your partner, but the less everyone knows, the safer your treasure is – and, he adds, the better everybody else will sleep.

Of course, it would not be prudent to invest everything you own in precious metals. So this chap advises diversifying somewhat. For one, he says, you should "own real wealth": that is, material goods. Even gold and silver are substitutes, he points out. "Wealth" is *things,* items that you can either use yourself or barter. The idea is simple: as much as possible, convert all your paper assets to material ones. So when you go out to purchase a year's supply of paper towels, you can add to your shopping list an imaginative selection of products you think you and your neighbors are likely to value most in an emergency. His suggestions were revealing: lumber, tools, candy bars, soft drinks, toilet paper . . . "Why," he demands, "should you be forced to abandon your chosen lifestyle just because your government can't pay its bills?"

The other alternative took me completely by surprise. "A reasonable portion of your assets," he said, "should be in things of lasting value – in the timeless treasures that have held their worth through decades, even centuries, of boom and bust, war and peace, depression and prosperity." "Ah," I thought to myself; "he is finally getting to spiritual values." I read on in increasing disbelief: "For example, great masters. Antiques. Collector's coins. Stamps. Comic books. Things that only go up in price because enough people always want them."

Then came the inevitable last step. Doesn't Jesus say, "Where your treasure is, there your heart is also"? It is not enough to stock up on the material "necessities" of your chosen lifestyle and all the things required to support it. You should be prepared to defend it – yourself, your family, your food, your gold, your auto parts – against anyone who might come seeking help or shelter. Without any wrong intentions, without any desire for animosity, that is where the path has to lead. "I don't want war," Bismarck is said to have remarked. "I just want victory." We say, "I just want to get what I want."

Sri Krishna will show all this to Arjuna – all the consequences, from individual to global, of a life based on self-seeking. "If that is the kind of life you want to lead," he will say, "no one can stop you. But don't talk about love; this way leads to hatred. Don't talk about peace; this way only leads to violence and war." And Arjuna will shake his head and say simply, "I don't want it."

दैवी संपद्विमोक्षाय निबन्धायासुरी मता ।
मा शुचः संपदं दैवीमभिजातो ऽसि पाण्डव ॥ १६-५ ॥

*5. The divine qualities lead to freedom; the
demonic, to bondage. But do not grieve, Arjuna;
you were born with divine attributes.*

My doomsday expert liked to think of himself as a self-reliant, self-made man. Among personal values, one of his highest was freedom. How surprised he would be, I thought, if he could hear the Gita's evaluation. Sri Krishna would not call such a person free at all. "You're a slave to your desires," he would explain. "You can't change when circumstances demand it; all you can do is hang on tighter." After all, what could be less free than feeling compelled to shoot another human being because you think he is after your canned goods and gold coins?

In fairness, Sri Krishna would add, very few of us can call ourselves free. Our responses are conditioned; we don't really have that much say in what we do. By contrast, it is easy to see how Mother Teresa radiates freedom. Whatever life brings her, she is always free to give.

What is important here is the mental state, for that is what colors our actions. It is very likely, for example, that our financial friend will never shoot anyone. He says sincerely that he never wants to. Yet the fact that he is willing to recommend it tells us something about the mental state behind everything else he does and recommends. The mental state is the seed; the fruit, Sri Krishna says, is bondage – bondage to the consequences of our values.

In the mid-seventies, after acute famine had flared up in many parts of the world, a prominent California biologist showed us the global version of this protect-your-gold-and-spark-plugs mentality. The term he used, *triage,* originated in the trenches of World War I, when medical personnel had to sort the wounded into categories so that they could decide whom to help first. One category was those who did not require immediate attention. They could hold on until the medics had taken care of soldiers in the second category: those who would probably live if given immediate care, but who otherwise would die. And the last was those who would probably die anyway, though perhaps later, even if they received first aid. The medics had to decide, "These people are going to die, and nothing can be done about it. All we can do is not listen to their cries, turn our eyes away, and hope that they die quickly."

Triage is still a part of military and emergency vocabulary; you see it in articles on "surviving" a nuclear war. But in the seventies it became fashionable in some circles to use the term in a new context: as a way of allocating food in times of famine. The argument was that there are certain countries facing famine which may be able to "pull out of it" and be of service to us later for political, economic, or military reasons. To those countries it makes sense to give food aid. But there are also countries that we decide are hopeless, not capable of solving their own problems; these we should allow to starve.

Perhaps because he is a biologist, this man takes a singularly biological view of the poor. Often, he says, they show so little self-restraint that they overreach the capacity of the land to sustain them. Then they run out of food. Countries with many such people, he says, are "basket cases" – another terrible term from war. For such countries we need an "adjusted ethics of survival dominated by unsqueamish self-interest" – a very interesting assemblage of words, for which I think you could find a good, blunt Anglo-Saxon translation. The term he coined is "lifeboat ethics." The rich nations, he says, are like lifeboats. Prosperous peoples in the developed countries look around from these lifeboats and see people from poorer nations drowning, calling out for help. If we keep taking all these people in, he says, our boat will sink. Therefore it is best for us as well as for them if they drown as quickly as they can; otherwise everybody will die.

A good student of logic should have no trouble in reducing this argument to pieces, beginning with the central metaphor. But it is not really a logical argument. It expresses an attitude, a mental state of fear and possessiveness very much like that of our survivalist friend: "I've got what I want, I deserve it, and nobody's going to take it away from me." The only way to dissuade people from this point of view is to allay their fears on the one hand and to open their sensitivity on the other. For the first, some facts and observations can help.

In their excellent and hopeful book *Food First*, Frances Moore Lappé and Joseph Collins quote from *Road to Survival*, in which one William Vogt wrote about a populous Asian country that it "quite literally cannot feed more people." He predicted, "Millions are going to die. There can be no way out. These men and women, boys and girls, must starve as tragic sacrifices, on the twin altars of uncontrolled reproduction and uncontrolled abuse of the land and resources." Most of us have heard similar words about many countries in Asia, Africa, and Latin America. They must be true, we feel. The graphs show population soaring, and we know food supply is limited by the amount of land.

Yet Mr. Vogt's words, so obviously true, were written about China in 1948. I am not at all advocating that any nation follow the Chinese example, but it does show how misleading it can be to pronounce a country hopeless and then turn away to allow its people to die.

In Mr. Vogt's day, when someone wanted to talk about basket case nations, nine times out of ten it was China and India that came up first. Today it is often Bangladesh, one of the areas of South Asia that was longest under colonial rule. Yet a report to Congress stated that Bangladesh is rich enough in agricultural resources "not only to be self-sufficient in food, but a food exporter, even with its rapidly increasing population size." Lappé and Collins go so far as to say that no country they investigated is a basket case; every country has the capacity to feed itself.

Agricultural experts say this planet can produce enough food without any kind of agricultural miracle. Put simply, the problems are not physical or geographic but economic. Food raised by the poor in poor countries is predominantly raised for and sold to rich countries, which can pay much higher prices for it. But the profits go to landowners and middlemen. The poor stay poor, and they have to buy their food at prices bid up beyond their reach by the demand of the world's well-to-do. This is a profitable arrangement for middlemen, but it guarantees poverty for the poor around the world. Those who can buy, eat; those who cannot buy, starve.

The main reason why there is starvation in parts of Asia, Africa, and South America is that these places have been reduced to poverty by centuries of exploitation. The material resources and labor of these continents produced a good deal of the prosperity that "developed" many of the developed nations, as any close student of history can testify. It is largely because of this kind of exploitation that one-sixth of the world lives in affluence while five-sixths are poor. If the United States has a lot of food at its end of the lifeboat, we should remember that much of it was raised by those we see appealing for help in the sea around us.

"Lifeboat ethics" has been called "deathboat ethics." Perhaps more to the point, someone has remarked that instead of a lifeboat, this biologist is talking about a luxury liner. In any case, the whole earth is a kind of lifeboat: "Spaceship Earth."

Here, I think, the metaphor becomes a little embarrassing to the developed nations. If, to simplify the picture, we say there are a hundred people on this lifeboat – representing all the peoples of the earth – then twenty seated at the stern have five-sixths of the provisions. To make the picture worse, a good deal of this has been taken from the eighty men, women, and children who remain. The "haves" complain that there are too many poor to feed; and by continuing to take what they want from the stores, they are ensuring that anyone "extra" is pushed out into the sea. The world's poor haven't jumped out of the boat. They have been conquered, colonized, and bled of their mineral wealth and their labor, and in many ways they are still being so treated today. The least we in the developed nations can do is help them back into the boat.

I am not saying that food aid will solve these problems, or that it is a solution for the developed nations to feed the rest of the world. In fact, I believe it is essential – and quite possible – for every nation to develop the capacity to feed itself. But I *am* saying that when people are starving, you share what you have; that is a simple matter of love.

Some months ago I saw a very moving performance of *The Diary of Anne Frank*, done by the Berkeley Repertory Theater. Towards the end, Anne and her family, her father's friend's family, and an utter stranger have been hiding together in a garret for well over a year, in constant fear of being discovered by the Nazis. Food has become terribly diffi-cult to get, and the refugees in the garret are dependent on what can be smuggled in. After months of getting by like this, they discover that it is not rats that have been gnawing at their meagre stores; Mr. Frank's friend has been stealing food for himself while the others sleep. No one is more shocked and repelled than Mrs. Frank. "You've been steal-ing from the *children*," she cries, "while you could hear your own son crying in his sleep from hunger!" When the children are our own, or in our own house, most of us find it easy to identify with them. Would we ignore them if we could not see their faces or hear their cries?

By contrast, I read a story the other day from Mother Teresa that moved me deeply – partly because it comes from Calcutta, where the differences between Hindus and Muslims have been exploited to the point of terrible violence. "Some weeks back," Mother Teresa says,

> I heard there was a family who had not eaten for some days – a Hindu family – so I took some rice and I went to the family. Before I knew where I was, the mother of the family had divided the rice into two, and she took the other half to the next-door neighbors, who happened to be a Muslim family. Then I asked her: "How much will all of you have to share? There are ten of you with that bit of rice." The mother replied: "They have not eaten either."

I began by talking about freedom. Who shall we say is free, the woman who gives like this or the man who feels so terribly compelled to take? Behind all the sophisticated language of "lifeboat ethics" are the same primitive feelings that make for bondage: insecurity, possessiveness, fear.

You can see the same lack of freedom on an international scale in the web of dependencies that bind the rich and powerful nations to the small. The rich and powerful find it humiliating to discover this, and sometimes they resort to violence to "show who is boss." But the fact remains. United States foreign policy, for example, is not made in freedom. It could be debated how much freedom the most powerful nation on earth actually has. Our policy decisions are usually reflexes, determined by what some other country does. Because of our dependence on certain minerals and the strategic balance of power, we have felt compelled to prop up illegitimate, repressive regimes, sometimes to the cost of billions of dollars and thousands of lives in war. Presidents and other leaders have repeatedly declared their willingness to go to war with some vastly weaker nation on the other side of the world to ensure that we keep getting "our" oil. And it is not only oil: many strategic minerals are supplied primarily by small, undemocratically governed nations whose leaders can dictate their terms to the industrialized giants. Our national response is the same as for doomsday: buy and hoard, and be prepared to go to war if necessary to keep the stockpiles from being used.

This is the kind of world that self-interest leads to – the only kind of world self-interest *can* lead to. The virus, Sri Krishna warns, is in all of us. Unless it is resisted, self-will can so invade the personality that an apparently good person – or nation – becomes an instrument of suffering for many others.

द्वौ भूतसर्गौ लोके ऽस्मिन्दैव आसुर एव च ।
दैवो विस्तरशः प्रोक्त आसुरं पार्थ मे शृणु ॥ १६-६ ॥

*6. Some people have divine tendencies, others
demonic. I have described the divine at length,
Arjuna; now listen while I describe the demonic.*

Almost every day, a physician friend tells me, she sees a patient who smokes. "I have to tell them they're bucking the odds," she says. "The scientific consensus is that smoking kills more than a third of a million Americans every year. But people can't identify with statistics. They just say, 'I know that, doc. But I've tried to quit and I can't.'"

"What do you say then?" I asked.

"It depends on the person. I never try to scare anybody. But if they have some imagination, and especially if they are still young, I try to bridge the gap in time that they can't bridge. I want them to look thirty years down the road and give the future a fair chance.

"When I see them, they're in their twenties or thirties. They're still active, nothing but a little cough; they think they'll feel like that forever. I try to help them feel what it's like to wheeze with every breath. I describe the panic that comes when you just can't get enough oxygen. I show them what happens inside their lungs and blood vessels. I try to turn the statistics into something real. Then I say, 'At the roulette table, you at least get to see what you stand to win or lose. Don't you want to see what you're gambling against here? If you lose, you get emphysema, lung disease, or stroke. If you win, you get a pack of cigarettes a day. Now you choose.'"

When we persist in a wrong course of action, a good physician has to tell us the consequences. She knows the laws of physiology, and she has seen perhaps hundreds of cases like ours. She may not be able to predict with total accuracy – there are many imponderables – but she knows vividly the sequence of cause and effect in the human body. To us it is only a vague possibility. But to her it is so real that if she sees a disease in its early stages, she already sees its end.

In the same way Sri Krishna, noting the signs and symptoms of our times, has to describe what will be the outcome if we do not change our ways. It is not too late to turn back. But the mental states of fatal illness – greed, separateness, and anger – are present in our times, and unless they are eradicated, their consequences are inexorable. Here the theme of karma that runs through this volume finds its most explicit statement. We need not dwell on it, but at the same time we need to know what selfish thinking has to lead to if it goes unchecked, no matter how pleasant or harmless it may seem at first.

प्रवृत्तिं च निवृत्तिं च जना न विदुरासुराः ।
न शौचं नापि चाचारो न सत्यं तेषु विद्यते ॥ १६-७॥
असत्यमप्रतिष्ठं ते जगदाहुरनीश्वरम् ।
अपरस्परसंभूतं किमन्यत्कामहैतुकम् ॥ १६-८॥
एतां दृष्टिमवष्टभ्य नष्टात्मानो ऽल्पबुद्धयः ।
प्रभवन्त्युग्रकर्माणः क्षयाय जगतो ऽहिताः ॥ १६-९॥

*7. The demonic do things they should avoid
and avoid the things they should do. They have
no sense of uprightness, purity, or truth.
8. "There is no God," they say, "no truth,
no spiritual law, no moral order. The basis
of life is sex; what else can it be?"
9. Holding such distorted views, possessing scant
discrimination, they become enemies of the
world, causing suffering and destruction.*

"There is no God, no truth, no moral order; the basis of life is sex." The words sound so contemporary that it is hard to believe these are opinions expressed thousands of years ago. You could go to the newsstand of any supermarket and find the same argument repeated over and over. It says simply that there is no unity in life, no underlying order, nothing but the events that we can apprehend through the five senses: in short, nothing to life but the physical level.

Once someone is said to have complained to G. K. Chesterton, "The trouble today is that people don't have anything to believe in."

"Not quite," Chesterton replied. "The trouble is that because they have nothing to believe in, they'll believe in anything."

That is a very penetrating remark. How many of the problems we face as a society are the result of people just believing in anything that comes along? This is one of the characteristics of Tamas. If someone on television or in the popular magazines tells him "Do this; you'll like it," he will go out and do it, so long as everybody else is doing it and it doesn't require too much effort.

When you don't have a reference point to refer to, Sri Krishna says here, you do what you should not do and you don't do what you should. This is a classic definition of confusion. The capacity to know what should be done and what should not be done is called *viveka*, discrimination, and it is one of life's most precious secrets. My granny used to be fond of a Sanskrit proverb, which unfortunately we gave her numerous opportunities to quote: *Avivekam param āpadām padam*, "Lack of discrimination is the source of the greatest danger." When discrimination goes, there is no reason *not* to do anything. If you look around, you will see intelligent, educated, cultured people throwing their energy and resources into enterprises that help nobody – enterprises, as this verse says, that even end in widespread harm.

Here we find ourselves in an age of unprecedented technological development, yet much of our mastery over nature has gone to find ways to hide or postpone the natural consequences of doing what we want. As a result, it becomes easier and easier to believe there *are* no consequences. You can do what you like and never pay for it.

This is not merely an individual weakness. We may deprecate people who go on buying and buying on credit cards without ever asking the price, but from the point of view of ecology, for example, modern industry and agriculture are continually mortgaging the future to pay for the profits of the present. "Buy now and pay later" has become "Buy now and refinance later," so you never have to pay at all.

Yet there are consequences, even if the asuric mind manages to hide them from its view. You may buy whatever you like with your credit cards in March, but in April or May the bills start rolling in. You have to start paying something – at first perhaps just the finance charge, but sooner or later the principal. We can always try to circumvent physical consequences by more technology, but what we really ought to worry about, the Gita says, are the consequences for the mind.

I would like to write a story in which science had come up with pills that could eliminate the physical consequences of our behavior entirely, so that every day you could indulge yourself however you liked without any ill effects. You could eat as much as you liked and not gain an ounce. You could drink as much as you liked and never get sick or face another "morning after." You could party all night and still be fresh the next day. And so on; each of us can supply our own favorite details. Doesn't it sound wonderful?

The Gita would object, "It sounds horrible!" Even if nothing untoward took place on the physical level, what would happen to the will? Not many people value the will these days; it's slightly out of fashion. But imagine going through life with a will like limp spaghetti: you couldn't say no to anything. If a foot-high challenge came out from behind a bush, you would lie down and say, "I've got a headache. I can't go on." And you would be so insecure that if someone said anything critical, you might go to pieces or carry a grudge against that person for years. We don't usually see the connection with the will in such situations, but that is what willpower means: a mind that does what you say.

Now we can trace the thread running through these verses. When you can't say no to anything, as this verse says, you end up "doing things that you ought to avoid and avoiding things that you ought to do" – eventually, though it pains me to say it, "without any sense of uprightness, purity, or truth."

Sex makes a good example here, not only because it is emphasized in the verses but because it is such a popular focus for our attention. "The basis of life is sex," the asuric mind proclaims. "What else can it be?" Most people might not agree so openly, but how do we live? What do we value most, to judge from our magazines, our movies, our books, our songs, our advertisements, our choice of words, our idea of a "good time"?

I dislike being a wet blanket, but the long-term consequences of this trend are ghastly. Rajas looks at sex and finds it grand. Naturally he proceeds to do with it what he tries to do with everything: maximize it. "If a little is the greatest thing on earth," he reasons, "more must be better."

But the corollary of "More is better" is "Anything goes." Once you accept the premise that life is physical, there is no basis for judgment. There is no one to explain that the real damage is done to the mind. Children who are continually exposed to sex in the media are particularly susceptible. By the time they reach adolescence, their minds and senses are going to be completely out of control; they will be at life's mercy before their adult lives have truly begun. Their minds will be full of anger and frustration, and putting themselves first will have become a constant, conditioned habit. What will support them during the fierce buffeting of the teenage years? What will they have to build a lasting relationship on? Even setting aside the questions of love and loyalty, they won't have the will to face any kind of challenge. Life treats such people mercilessly. No parents want this for their children; it is just the opposite of love.

I am not talking about right or wrong now; but simply in medical terms, look at where all this leads. What is at stake is prāna, which is life itself. In younger years we are allotted enough prāna to experiment with pleasure and discover what it can deliver; but we are expected to learn, not to go on performing the same old experiment over and over and over. For overindulgence drains prāna, and prāna is the very energy of life. Loss of sexual capacity in later years may be the body's compassionate way of saying, "Let's start to conserve! I'm running low on gas."

It grieves me deeply to read that patients recovering from serious ailments – especially those who are older – are sometimes given hormones or other drugs to whip an exhausted body into action to satisfy the mind's desires. That is just the opposite of therapy. The body needs rest so that all available prāna can be marshalled in the processes of healing. Instead, the pleasure centers open the prāna petcocks and drain the day's tank almost dry. From the body's point of view, it seems so unfair: the mind demands the pleasure, but the body pays all the bills.

The other day I saw some of our āshram children playing in the sandbox with their toys: a couple of dump trucks, some blocks and wooden animals, a few big spoons and cans for digging. "They can go on like that forever," one of the mothers told me happily. "From one fantasy to another to another." That is fine for toddlers – but even then, not forever. Imagine their parents playing there instead! Two computer experts, a professor, and a physician, pushing sand around with old tin cans and bursting into tears when one person's road construction project destroys another's farm. There is a time for toys, the mystics say, and a time to grow up. From this perspective, nothing is more tragic than to see men and women in the last stages of their lives doing everything they can to become like teenagers again.

In a sense even this is not an end; for though the body dies, the samskāras of desire carry over to our next life. I still remember vividly a friend in the twilight of his life recalling his teenage years and saying plaintively, "How I wish I could live through all those experiences again!" I don't think I have ever felt a deeper stab of sorrow; for these last deep desires sum up our lives. That wish was like getting through second grade and then saying at the end, "That was fun! I'm going to go back and do it all again."

"Life is not worth living without pleasure." The logic is relentless: when your very capacity for sensory pleasure runs out, why go on living? What does life hold? Some years ago I remember reading that a distinguished philosopher and his wife swallowed overdoses of sleeping pills in order to avoid the prospect of a "useless old age." The assumption is that life is physical; we are the body. Old age is "useless" only if you are living for yourself, in which case any age could be called useless. If you live for giving, you can go on making a vital contribution to the rest of life right up to your last day in this body. Even if you are confined to a wheelchair, you will be able to inspire, support, and strengthen many people who come in contact with you.

काममाश्रित्य दुष्पूरं दम्भमानमदान्विताः ।
मोहाद्गृहीबासद्ग्राहान्प्रवर्तन्ते ऽशुचिव्रताः ॥ १६-१० ॥

10. Hypocritical, proud, and arrogant,
living in delusion and clinging to deluded
ideas, insatiable in their desires, they pursue
unhesitatingly their own selfish ends.

The other day I saw a book on economics with an intriguing title: *Greed Is Not Enough*. This is true of most demonic activities also. Asuric Enterprises, as we might call it, is a joint venture of two partners. Rajas, "Mr. Greed," is the senior, but Tamas is almost as important. His role is generally to be insensitive, but he also knows how to vacillate, postpone, prevaricate, refuse to change his mind, and simply do nothing when necessary, all of which provides Rajas with the support he needs to do his work. Rajas doesn't understand this; he likes to think of himself as independent. But if he were capable of some self-knowledge, he would see that he is utterly dependent on Tamas for support.

Tamas clings to the status quo; he doesn't like to "make waves." But Rajas thrives on crisis. Where times are turbulent or technology is in flux, he knows there are markets to be cornered, power to consolidate, profits to be made. In fairness, this is not simply a matter of greed. Rajas just likes to keep busy. He can't possibly sit still when opportunity is knocking, even if he is already juggling more opportunities than he can handle. His style is to keep moving, even if he isn't sure where he is going, while Tamas sits in back and writes memos to cover his tracks.

Thoreau, I think, had a good remark to make on this subject. "It's not enough if you are busy," he said. "The question is, What are you busy about?" This is a terribly practical question. You may remember my quoting a Sanskrit proverb that was often on my granny's lips: "Lack of discrimination is the source of the greatest danger." I don't think this is exaggeration at all. If you look around, you will see that most of the dangers that threaten us today are not the result of wickedness. I would say they are the result of intelligent, educated, well-intentioned men and women running as fast as they can after what they want, never caring to slow down, look around, and ask where they are going.

Rajas has a good reason for this: if you stop to look around, he would say, you may not like what you see. Worse, you may try to reason, by which time the opportunity – whatever it is – will have passed. If problems arise, Asuric Enterprises has two ways of dealing with them: Rajas likes to push them aside and keep on going; Tamas prefers to ignore them and hope they will go away.

I can give you one example that is highly relevant today: the way we pursued nuclear power. This is what you might call a national obsession: a very large number of individuals compulsively caught in the same idea. It illustrates very well the power of a particular mental state – part rajasic, part tamasic – to acquire a life of its own, regardless of facts or circumstances.

In the forties and fifties, crowning a century of breakthroughs, nuclear technology must have looked like the grandest of them all. It offered two heady promises: unlimited energy and perpetual peace.

The very idea raised Rajas to poetic heights. "For the first time in history," he liked to say, "man has released power that did not come from the sun!" Perhaps – Rajas tends to get easily inebriated by break-throughs – perhaps soon we wouldn't even *need* the sun. We knew how to grow vegetables in water with the help of lights; we were making "food" out of chemical constituents and planning space colonies with their own water and air. Now that we could turn matter into energy, what could we not do? "In a decade or so," Rajas proclaimed proudly, "energy will be so cheap that you'll have to give it away."

The other promise was the Bomb. The irony was fascinating: here was the most terrible weapon ever discovered, and just because it was so terrible it could be the instrument of world peace! It was a military dream come true, the secret weapon that nobody else seemed likely to get. In our enemies' hands it could hold the world hostage; in ours, it could enforce peace and democratic principles around the globe.

This was a package too good to pass up, and as this verse suggests, we bought it without hesitating – that is, without ever asking about the consequences. We knew virtually nothing about atomic energy except that its potential for energy release – constructive or destructive – was staggering beyond imagination. Many nuclear scientists say they felt like the Sorcerer's Apprentice, letting loose unknown, supernormal forces without any hope of turning back. Sheer common sense would object, "Let's go slowly and be sure where we are going." Yet from the first, Asuric Enterprises scarcely questioned anything. It was obsessed by a Big Idea.

In my high school physics class, I remember our teacher explain-ing about inertia. "It doesn't just mean sitting and doing nothing," our teacher said. "A body at rest tends to remain at rest and a body in motion tends to remain in motion, unless acted on by some outside force." As an illustration he might have used the rock that Mad Nārāyana used to roll down the hill outside our village, which had tremendous iner-tia. You could deflect it only at great risk, and you could stop it only by absorbing all that energy, which usually meant a crash.

Ideas are similar. I like to say that thoughts are things – in fact, in some ways, they are more "thingy" than material things. A rolling idea can have tremendous inertia. It is hard to stop, hard to deflect; often it even goes unquestioned. That is the power of tamas.

"We've got a tiger by the tail," Rajas liked to say about nuclear power. "We've *got* to go forward, whatever it costs." Without going into details, I want to look at some of those costs. Two or three I find particularly moving, for the karma of this Big Idea has led to widespread sorrow.

Here we encounter one of the truly dark corners in the asuric mind. By the time the Bomb was developed, Tamas was already on the stage. Even in wartime, a certain measure of insensitivity is required to destroy a city of civilians, but I do not want to dwell on that; the decision-makers must have felt they were saving thousands of American lives. What I find more astonishing, because the callousness is so calculated, is what happened after the war. Tamas is not very discriminating; his job is to be insensitive. He begins by being insensitive to enemy lives, but he quickly goes on to show the same insensitivity to those he is supposed to protect.

The first to experience this were U.S. soldiers, from whom I have been reading some moving personal accounts. Just forty-five days after Nagasaki was bombed, Marines and Seabees were sent in to clean up without any word about radiation hazards. "We didn't want to worry anybody," Rajas explained. "We had every reason to believe that after the fallout subsided, there was no danger from radioactivity." (The scientists who visited these areas must not have been told this, for they wore protective suits.) For weeks these men were billeted near ground zero, around which the wind must have strewn radioactive dust and particles for miles. They drank the same water as the survivors, ate locally grown food, breathed the same dust-laden air. Today, thirty years later, they are dying of the same kinds of cancer.

"I don't hold a grudge against my government for sending us in like that," one man said in effect. "They had their reasons for not telling us, and anyway I was a soldier; it was my job to take risks for my country. What makes me so bitter is that now that we are sick or dying, our country won't acknowledge any responsibility." The official position is the same today as it was then: "There was no danger from radiation in Hiroshima and Nagasaki after the first five days."

There is an important reason for this kind of prevarication, which is part of the mental state involved. In the official view, we had the Bomb and therefore had to use it; and that had certain implications too. Like it or not, we had to develop a nuclear arsenal. We had to prepare citizens to accept and deal with the possibility of nuclear attack. And we had to develop nuclear energy. Therefore, in asuric reasoning, it was "counterproductive" to question the Bomb and its consequences, whatever facts might come to light. To worry people or to admit how little we knew was dangerous. It might mean we could not proceed, and that would be playing into enemy hands – for although we were at peace, all this was pursued as a continuation of war.

The Bomb aside, there remains the complete lack of caution in how we pursued nuclear energy for utilities. It looked so wonderful then! "Makes itself," Rajas liked to say. "Breeds its own fuel. What more can you ask? Power too cheap to meter." Surely it is fair to ask by now, too cheap for whom? It is not cheap in human health; it is terrifyingly expensive. According to articles I saw some months ago in the *Wall Street Journal,* it is not even cheap in money. Fortunes have been poured into nuclear plants, though no doubt it could have cost much less if we hadn't begun to require safe construction. But even from the earliest days, nuclear power was so fraught with unknowns and potential hazards that no one would invest in it unless the government agreed to underwrite it; no insurance company would touch it.

Much more significant are the human costs. Another example is the uranium miners. Uranium is expensive, but fortunately it was discovered in the United States – on the supposedly worthless lands that had been given (if I may use that word) to Native American tribes when the rest of their lands were engulfed by the spread of Western civilization. I don't know if anyone was embarrassed to discover that something valuable had been given away. In any case, the Bureau of Indian Affairs – created ostensibly to protect Native American interests – persuaded them not only to lease their lands for uranium mining but to do the actual mining themselves. Nobody warned them about radioactivity; they might not have wanted to proceed with the deal.

A Public Health Service director has since called those mines "radiation chambers," with "one hundred times the levels of radioactivity allowed today." Millions of tons of exposed radioactive waste –"tailings"– have been piled near people's homes. "Much of the land where our people have lived for thousands of years," one Native American spokesman says, "is now poisoned by radioactivity – and will remain poisoned for many thousands of years." This applies not only to the water and air, but even to many homes made from local building materials.

Finally, in spite of the incredible ingenuity that has gone into nuclear power development – and it has drawn some of the best scientific and engineering talent in several countries – we still don't have the slightest idea of what to do with nuclear waste. To me that is like admitting that on a proposed trip from San Francisco to New York, we haven't yet left the garage.

Some months ago we had a big holiday dinner at our āshram, which meant several people working in the kitchen at once to prepare a gracious quantity of food. Suppose you showed up to help and were told, "Sorry, we don't have a garbage can. Why don't you put the garbage in the back seat of your car and figure out what to do with it later?" You say, "At least you can give me a plastic bag!" "We haven't got plastic bags," Laurel says, "but maybe you can fit it into these grocery bags. If you line them with waxed paper, they won't start to leak for three or four hours." Pretty soon, of course, they will fall apart. But why talk about such things now? You've got to get dinner on the table. Lug the garbage out, stuff it in the car, and enjoy your feast. Maybe you'll pass a dump on the way home. If not, well, half of it will decompose every twenty years . . . .

That is exactly what we have done about nuclear waste – except, of course, that we are talking not about messy potato peelings but about substances like plutonium, which is fatally toxic in microscopic amounts and has a half-life of twenty-five thousand years. We haven't the slightest idea of what to do with the stuff, and it is one of the most poisonous substances known. Yet we are so greedy to proceed with our wonderful new discoveries that we just bury what we can't deal with and hope we won't be around when it starts to poison the rivers and soil where our children's food is grown – or, worse, the oceans that sustain the world.

"Just do it," says Rajas, "and then we'll see. Technology will improve. If we can't come up with anything better, we can always toss it into outer space. A few hundred garbage cans of radioactive waste hurtling around in a billion billion cubic miles of nothingness, what can they harm?" It is not only lack of love and logic, it is such a fatal paralysis of imagination. We had the same idea about the oceans and air just a few decades ago, and now we are surprised when a school is closed because of poisonous air, or when we read that lead from industrial emissions is accumulating in the trenches of the deep ocean floor.

"Well, what do you know?" Rajas muses. "Who could have predicted things like that?" Perhaps no one, but we could at least learn from such unexpected outcomes that we live in a complex world in which there is no such thing as "out of sight, out of mind." There is already more radioactive waste than we can hide; it is leaking from its containers, poisoning livestock and people, and altering our genetic material, not to mention providing enough weapons-grade plutonium to put a nuclear weapon in the hands of every terrorist group and small-time dictator in the world; yet still we want our energy so badly that we keep on producing more of this stuff and talk about sending our garbage to Alpha Centauri. It makes one wonder. Cross the seas, fly in the air, burrow into the ground, the Buddha says; you will not be able to hide from the law of karma.

चिन्तामपरिमेयां च प्रलयान्तामुपाश्रिताः ।
कामोपभोगपरमा एतावदिति निश्चिताः ॥ १६-११ ॥

*11. Although burdened with fears that end only with
death, they still maintain with complete assurance,
"Gratification of lust is the highest that life can offer."*

In Hindu psychology, the forces of self-will are often grouped under three big categories: lust, anger, and fear, all of which are closely related. These three are the source of most personal problems, for they are working away almost incessantly in the deeper regions of the mind.

I have written predominantly about lust and anger for what I might call first-aid reasons: these are the forces that cause the most direct damage to others, and they are rampant today. But here I would like to give due attention to fear, which this verse connects subtly to the lust for selfish satisfaction.

"Lust" here, I should point out, is not just sexual desire. It can be any kind of fierce craving for personal satisfaction. There is lust for money, of course, and lust for any kind of pleasure; sex is merely the most acute. Lust for power is one of the most furious of lusts. So here I will be talking about no particular passion, but simply lust in general.

I sometimes see recruitment posters that say, "The Marines are looking for a few good men." General Lust, by contrast, is not particular about who fills his army. Any obsessive, personal, self-centered desire can qualify. The recruitment application asks only one question: "Are you willing to let other people get in the way of your fulfillment?" If the answer is a resounding no, that desire is in.

General Lust is tough – at least, in his own eyes. He knows what he wants, and he gets what he goes after. He has tattoos on his arms, smokes cigarettes without filters, and wouldn't dream of letting some namby-pamby speed limit law keep him from driving the way he likes. I saw a book of jokes on the best-seller list the other day: *Real Men Don't Eat Quiche*. General Lust doesn't even want to know how "quiche" is pronounced. He would be furious if he understood what Sri Krishna is hinting in this verse: that in every selfish desire is hidden a corresponding fear. That is part of the karma of lust; and as usual with karma, it is not some separate punishment. If lust is one side of a coin, fear and anger are imprinted on the other side, inseparable.

Fear is a whole world of its own within the mind. Most of us never see this world with our conscious eye, though it prompts much of our waking thought and action. I think it is Carl Jung who says that in the depths of the unconscious of every human being lies the fear of death and dissolution – the fear that we may cease to exist as a separate, personal creature. This is the root of all other fears. In a sense, every human being lives in a world of fear of which we are not aware. That is our protection. If we were to become consciously aware of all the great fears that lurk in the unconscious, life would become impossible. It is a merciful amnesia that we do not remember these fears. We may not even suspect that they lurk within us, far below the threshold of consciousness. To an experienced eye, however, the signs are clear. Wherever people overreact in anger, or get agitated easily, or are excessively rigid when they cannot have their way, there is a good chance that fear is pulling the strings from deep within. Almost every kind of insecurity or anxiety fits the Gita's definition of fear.

In his *Century of Verses on Renunciation,* the great Indian poet Bhartrihari wrote a stanza of epigrams on fear. The first line sets the keynote: "In the pleasures of the senses lurks the fear of decay." The poet is playing off two rhyming words: *bhoga,* which means sensual enjoyment, and *roga,* one of the sights that impelled the Buddha to seek Self-realization: disease, decrepitude, dissolution, decay.

We need a good deal of detachment to understand the depth of Bhartrihari's statement. It can be taken at several levels, on each of which the consequences are subtler. The simplest is that of physical consequences, which the modern mind finds repellent and vaguely medieval: if you indulge in such and such a pleasure, you'll be punished for it. Today we do not believe in being punished, and many of the efforts of modern science have been to find ways to avoid the physical consequences of sensual indulgence.

Perhaps the most obvious example is overeating. All thinking people, though they may not put it into words, are aware that if they go on eating more than they need, they are going to put on weight. Today even corporation executives are mindful of this, for obesity is more than an aesthetic flaw; it is a health hazard. Too much body fat aggravates heart trouble, high blood pressure, diabetes, and other ailments, and in addition it adds to the risk of smoking – all of which doctors and the popular media are making widely known.

Wherever there is any understanding of this, overeating carries a slight but nagging fear. Even while you are eating your second helping of french fries or chocolate cake and thinking, "This is really good!" there is a little voice inside, barely audible, saying, "It's *not* so good. You're asking for trouble." We have learned to stifle this voice, even ignore it with a show of bravado. "Who cares? I'm not that fat, and I can still take it or leave it." Even so, the Gita says, we have planted another tiny seed of fear beneath the surface of consciousness: the fear that we have added a little more weight not only to the body, but to the unknown burdens of the future.

This is even more clear with addictive habits like smoking, drinking, and drugging. I have never deprecated people who are caught in these habits, because I know how easy it is to get caught. Today a boy or girl can be an alcoholic even before getting into high school. Many children smoke by then, and probably most have at least sampled drugs. There must be very few today who think these activities do not have danger-ous consequences. They just don't care. Often they feel they have very little to live for, which is a tragic state. In any case they are young; they like to "live dangerously." Consequences are far down the road, and words like *cancer* and *emphysema* convey only vague conditions. Yet as many smokers have confided in me, the fear *is* there. Even while they are inhaling, a little part of their consciousness is thinking about cancer.

This kind of fear has a useful function. It can act as a brake, keeping us from overindulging our senses or getting caught in addictive habits, both of which drain prāna terribly. When you cannot see the connec-tion between sensory pleasure and prāna, the Lord says, how can you be expected to act on it? So to try to keep us from wasting our prāna as fast as possible, life provides these fearful physical consequences, which anyone should be able to see.

In other words, if you are going to smoke, it is good not to be fear-less about it. You can use that fear; you can capitalize on it, by drawing from it more will and more resolution. To be fearless about the risk of cancer, the Buddha would say, is not a sign of a strong character but the sign of a thick head. The Buddha was not one to mince words; some chapters of his Dhammapada are just as fierce as this chapter of the Gita.

Most of us, however, do not regard adverse physical consequences as a blessing. Here we are, trying to enjoy ourselves, and once we cross a certain line the pleasures start coming hand in hand with problems. The universal human response, the gift of rajas, is straightforward: find some way to get around the problems, so we can go on doing what we like. *Homo sapiens* has probably been doing this since the dawn of civilization, but it is only in the age of rajas, the age of science, that we developed the amazing technological capacity to suppress any physical consequence we choose.

Vast industries are built on this idea, which can be called the Free Lunch promise. "Every pleasure," it maintains, "can be safely indulged indefinitely. Adverse consequences are incidental. Being physical, they can be physically prevented, just like the causes of a disease. All that is necessary is to find the chemical or mechanical means." This was widely held and hailed when I arrived in this country, and it opened my eyes to technological progress. Why not eat too much when you can avoid stomachache and heartburn by dropping a couple of fizzing tablets into a glass of water? Why not have a few extra "meaningful relationships" when there's the Pill? Why be afraid of burning yourself out in pursuit of pleasure when you can get a new face for the price of a new car? "For every fear we have a cure": that is the motto of Asuric Labs.

Of course, Asuric has had its problems. The fizzing tablets don't keep you from getting fat, and that new face may cost you your health. And there is good evidence now that the Pill, which is used by millions of women in the world today, is a causal factor in thromboembolic diseases and, in some, heart attacks. The Gita would ask, How do you expect to get rid of consequences? It has never been done; it can never be done. If you block one effect, another will occur; if you block them both, you will get a third. As the Buddha says, nowhere in the universe can you hide from karma, for the simple reason that action and consequences are one.

Nonetheless, the search goes on. There is money in it, and if someone invents a better diet pill or contraceptive, the world will happily beat a path to his front door. As long as we can even hope for such a breakthrough, fear is held at bay.

Trying to avoid consequences like this reminds me of a scene I once saw at the beach, when our children were trying to dam a little river that flows through the dunes into the sea. They managed to block the channel, but the water wouldn't obey. It forced its way through the dam, and when those holes were plugged, it flowed over the top. When the children made the dam higher, the water burst around at the end.

That is how the law of karma works too. If the effects of an action are blocked in one direction, they have to find expression somewhere else. This is not a moral principle; it is simply cause and effect.

Rajas pursues consequence-blockers like a beaver racing against time. If an unwanted consequence bursts through here, he patches it; when another erupts over there, he patches that too. Like the Corps of Engineers, he believes perfection is just a patch away. If you suggest to him that it may not be possible to create a dam without adverse consequences, he would find the suggestion foolish, irresponsible, and vaguely immoral, as if you were pleading a case for evil.

Adverse consequences include physical illness, because body and mind are part of a whole. In every human being, there is a deep-seated sense of disquiet provoked when we ignore this fabric of responsibilities and think and act just for ourselves. We *know*, deep down, that we are not separate from the rest of life, but the primordial urges of the unconscious – the pleasure principle, the sex drive, the instinct for self-aggrandizement – pull us in a different direction. Freud is not wrong when he says we have stuffed these dark forces into the basement of consciousness and slammed the door tight. But repressed urges don't lie around meekly. They hold mass meetings, pass resolutions, go on strike, hold demonstrations that have to be suppressed with the mental equivalent of tear gas. This round-the-clock control is a constant drain of prāna. And since prāna is the energy for every function of life, low prāna means less vitality, more frequent depression, less ability to cope with stress, lower resistance to disease.

This model may have important implications for health. Emotional factors may well inhibit the immune system: negative mental states like depression, for example, seem associated with susceptibility to illness. I suggest that not only negative emotional states, but any chronic drain on prāna – including excessive indulgence of the senses – weakens the immune system, leaving it more vulnerable to infection. If true, one promising corollary of this hypothesis is that activities which conserve prāna – training the mind, training the senses – should enhance our capacity to heal ourselves and resist disease.

Up to this point we have been looking only at physical consequences. Yet this is only the surface. There are more subtle consequences which take place in the mind, and the fear of these goes deeper even than the fear of disease.

This level is much more elusive and difficult to talk about, but we have some clues in everyday experience. I think it is Art Hoppe who remarked that someday they will invent a pill to take away every conse-quence of our actions except guilt. "Guilt" is not a word that I like to use, because there is nothing positive about it. But when we do something selfish, the Gita would say, even if no harmful physical consequences follow that we can see, there will always be a quiet witness inside to observe and comment, "Shabby, shabby, shabby." This is a good sign. The observer is the Self, who is sometimes referred to in yoga psychol-ogy as the Inner Witness of all action. The Self is never involved in our behavior, good or bad, or in its consequences, because the Self is not at all physical. But this dry comment of "shabby, shabby, shabby" is its way of reminding our "lower mind" – our emotions, feelings, and senses – that it has not been acting in harmony with the unity of life.

Most of us today never hear this verbalized, as people used to in simpler times. Instead we feel vaguely divided within ourselves – a little uncertain of ourselves, a little anxious, unself-confident, insecure. That is the beginning of fear. If I had to put it into words, I would say it is something like the fear that our behavior is moving us farther and farther from our real Self – in a word, the fear of alienation. The more we indulge a selfish desire, the deeper this fear becomes. In people who are compulsively self-indulgent, the results can be terribly debilitating. Such people can get caught in a vicious circle of behavior: they have a low self-image, expect very little of themselves; so they act the way they believe themselves to be – say, raid the refrigerator on a midnight binge – and plunge their self-esteem even lower.

Fear of being caught in these negative forces goes very deep in us, because without meditation most people feel they are being swept away by a power beyond their understanding or control. Meditation offers great hope to such people, for we can learn to transform these forces completely.

Subtlest of all is the deep, nagging fear that the pleasure in which we are indulging cannot last. Until we have made some progress in meditation, I think it is asking too much of even a good intellect to grasp this. The intellect will object, as my beatnik friends used to, "I don't buy that." And even when it does buy, the mind – our feelings – will balk. "You and your theories," it will say. "To say I suffer from anxiety when I enjoy some private pleasure is absurd." Yet deep down – "on the gut level," as my medical friends say – every one of us knows this fear. The evidence is simple: if we were not afraid, we would not have to clutch at pleasure and try to make it last.

Ultimately, this is the fear of the final deprivation. Death in Sanskrit is called *Antaka*, 'he who puts an end to everything.' This fear is lurking in the depths of the consciousness of every human being – written there, as the Hindu and Buddhist mystics would say, over and over and over through countless lives. Death in the West has been called "the great unknown." The Gita would not agree with this; you can't really fear what you don't know. Each of us does know in the depths of the unconscious what death is like, because each of us has experienced it many times. Even a tiny creature, when it dies, suffers the agony that a human being suffers. Because of this, yoga psychology maintains, every attempt to grasp at some outside support – pleasure, power, prestige, possessions – is prompted at the deepest level by the fear of death. On the downward path, this fear swells until it becomes obsessive. But it can be healed through meditation and the allied disciplines, and the relief from insecurity this brings is one of the great benefits of spiritual living.

आशापाशशतैर्बद्धाः कामक्रोधपरायणाः ।
ईहन्ते कामभोगार्थमन्यायेनार्थसंचयान् ॥ १६-१२ ॥

12. Bound on all sides by scheming and anxiety, driven by anger and greed, they amass by any means they can a hoard of money for the satisfaction of their cravings.

Some years ago I saw a very entertaining movie, *The Treasure of the Sierra Madre*. Humphrey Bogart plays the part of Fred C. Dodds, a man down on his luck in the Mexican port city of Tampico. He and a friend meet up with an old prospector, played by Walter Huston, who knows the gold country of Mexico like the back of his hand. Interestingly enough, though he has spent the greater part of his life prospecting, Walter Huston is rather detached about gold. Bogart feels detached too. "What's gold going to do to change a guy?" he asks. "A guy's a guy, whether money comes to him or not." Walter Huston smiles back knowingly. "You don't know gold," he says.

The three go prospecting together, and after a long while they discover a rich vein. They are hard workers, and they dig and carry for all they're worth. All three are equal partners. But slowly the consciousness of Bogart and his friends is changing, and presently, when a stranger is discovered following them, a very interesting discussion takes place: shall they kill him, or shall they not? Bogart, you know, is a "right guy," and right guys don't kill out of greed: if the man wants to dig too, there is plenty of gold to go around. But the question has been raised, and both men know now in their hearts that there are circumstances under which they would have gone ahead.

Gradually Bogart becomes more entangled. An idea takes hold of him: if the others were gone, the gold would all be his. He projects this idea onto his friend also – "he must be thinking the same thing" – and grows increasingly suspicious. Finally, convinced that the other man wants to kill him for his share, Bogart kills his partner, takes the gold, and runs away.

In the end nobody gets the gold. Poor Fred C. Dodds loses his life, and all the gold dust he and his partners had accumulated is caught up in a sandstorm and dispersed in every direction, hopelessly mixed with sand. Even Hollywood appreciates the law of karma.

"Money can't do anything to a guy," said Fred C. Dodds. "A guy's a guy, whether money comes to him or not." This same "right guy" becomes suspicious, starts to distrust his friends, and ends up murderous, without even realizing what has happened. In a smaller way, this can happen to almost anyone. You don't have to look to movies or history for examples; just look in the daily paper, talk to people around you. You will see how many relationships have been disrupted by the love of money: how many marriages it has broken up, how many friendships embittered, how many families torn in two. Beyond that, on a vaster scale, I can only suggest some of the costs the profit motive exacts from many millions of workers and consumers around the world. We have no idea, I think, of how powerful and how destructive a force the lust for money can be; it can soak up our capacity for sensitivity so insidiously that we do not even see it happening.

Many people would reject categorically the idea that they love money. "I like what it can buy," they might say. "I like to be able to buy whatever I want; who doesn't? But 'love'? Oh, no." This is sincere enough as far as the surface level of awareness goes. But the test of what we love is what we think about, what consumes our attention through most of the day. By this test, it must be admitted, money is one of the top two objects of devotion in the modern world.

When we give our love to money – think about it, read about it, worry over it, measure people and activities by it, give it our attention, our time, our energy – we are helping to spread an epidemic of misery. "Money" here means not only currency but any kind of wealth in the economic sense: the obsession with accumulating material possessions is the same bacillus.

This is not just a moral issue. I am trying to focus on the consequences of greed, not merely on how it deprives other people but on the corrosive effect it has on those it infects. Little by little, the desire to have what we play up everywhere as "the good things of life" – cars, clothes, jewelry, expensive vacations, home entertainment equipment, the million and one ridiculous, costly, useless insignia of excess wealth – can consume so much of consciousness that a father doesn't realize he has neglected to love his children, a wife her husband, a grown-up son his parents.

Let's start with the children. I was shocked to hear a friend say the other day that many young couples think of children as an economic liability. All they do is cost money! One recent magazine article estimated it takes almost one hundred and fifty thousand dollars to raise a child in an average family through the first eighteen years of life. I would question those figures; but in any case, these young couples see that children are going to take a lot of money out of their paychecks for a couple of decades, and they conclude, "Why not spend it on ourselves instead?"

The tragedy is that this realization often comes only after a child is born. Then the child grows up unwanted, a constant burden and irritation to one parent or to both. Many of the million of America's children who run away from home every year must be in this category. Often they say they would return if even a little love awaited them. The homes they leave are often literally empty, with the parents (or parent) away at work during the day and away for entertainment in the evening. Frequently they are escaping from serious abuse or criminal neglect. Frustration in such a family is high. A parent with an unwanted child and strong selfish desires is going to be frustrated often, as the child demands time, costs money, encumbers personal pursuits like recreation or a career, or simply gets in the way. I don't want to go into the details of the kind of treatment that results; it can be terrible and even fatal. Child abuse cases number in the millions, increasing every year, and that is only what is reported; many, many incidents never come to light. I vividly remember one journalist asking a runaway boy why he was living in the streets. "Mister," the boy said, "if you lived with my mother and father, you'd run away too."

Parents today are "putting their own needs ahead of those of their children," a university psychologist said recently. "My concern is that if they don't feel cared about, then they can't ever care about anybody else – or about themselves." They grow up angry, rigid, and unresponsive to those around them – including, of course, their own parents and their own children, if they have any. That is where the law of karma comes in.

It has been many months since Christine and I went to San Francisco. I still think of it as "Baghdad by the Bay," but much of the beauty is gone; it saddens me deeply to see how much this city of St. Francis has ceased to care about its people. Within a block or two of Union Square, I read, thousands of America's grandparents are living alone in poverty and fear. Some have a room in a tawdry hotel, where friends who have worked with these people say they may not have adequate clothing for the cold, or furniture, or sheets and towels, or even food and heat. Soup lines feed some eight to ten thousand people, most of them elderly; for many, it is said, that is the only meal they will get that day. Literally thousands of others do not even have a room; they carry their worldly belongings in a shopping bag and sleep in parks and lobbies and theaters, in constant fear of robbery and attack. Can so many be without families to take them in and help take care of them, even if it means some hardship? The city seems full now of runaway young people and abandoned aged, many of them living in literal starvation and despair; and I am told the same is true in almost every big city in the United States today.

I am glad to say that San Francisco is trying to provide housing for its homeless. I deeply hope other cities will do the same. But these are first-aid solutions. In a country like ours, where national wealth is so high, no one should have to spend the last years of life in such terrible poverty. It is our privilege to help care for those whose income is inadequate, and on a larger scale, the karma for putting desires and careers ahead of the welfare of others is a dog-eat-dog society in which no one should want to live.

Similarly, millions of elderly Americans live in nursing facilities. They may be physically cared for, in the sense of having food to eat and a bed under a roof in which to sleep, but often they have been virtually abandoned by those they love. Their children may send cards on Mother's Day and candy at Christmas, but by their actions they are sending a different message: "We're too busy. We have our own lives to lead. You had your chance to make money and enjoy life; now we're having ours." Tragically, they are probably teaching that attitude to their own children; they may go on to become the abandoned aged of tomorrow.

The reverse can happen too. Many people are entering retirement age with the values of the "me generation": they have money, their children are grown, and they are ready to put themselves first for the rest of their "golden years." Their watchword, I'm told, is "I've paid my dues." Whatever happens to the rest of society is no longer their concern. They are not interested in paying taxes for child-related programs, even schools; they don't want to be bothered with all the troubles that children and teenagers cause; they choose a carefree lifestyle with the intention of avoiding as much of life's difficulties and challenges as possible. An article in the *Saturday Review*, I think, pointed out the central irony: such people are behaving like children again. At a period in life when, with their experience and financial freedom, they could be doing great things to benefit the rest of life, they want to throw all this away and live only for fun. Most of them, I imagine, will tell you candidly that they are not living in fun; they are dying of boredom. As Dr. Selye says, work is a biological necessity. I would add, a spiritual necessity too. We *need* to work, need to give, need to love; otherwise, at any age, we wither and die.

Throughout these verses I am trying to emphasize that greed is a process, the slow corrosion of personality. It can take over our lives quietly, little by little, so that we never feel different from one day to the next; yet like Scrooge in *A Christmas Carol,* we may be appalled toward the end of our lives to see what we have become. But the positive side, as I keep emphasizing, is that because it is a process we can arrest it, turn around, and go the other way. These verses, though grim, are not intended to condemn anyone. They are meant to help us see what tangled jungles of selfishness can grow when common, ordinary self-will is allowed to flourish, so that we remember to weed out self-will every day.

इदमद्य मया लब्धमिदं प्राप्स्ये मनोरथम् ।
इदमस्तीदमपि मे भविष्यति पुनर्धनम् ॥ १६-१३ ॥

13. *"I got this today,"* they say; *"tomorrow I shall get that. This wealth is mine, and that will be mine too."*

On the highway between my home and Berkeley is a billboard advertising a particular variety of noxious weed. It makes no appeal to logic or taste or sensory satisfaction; it simply touts the brand name: "More."

Whenever I pass I think to myself, "That ad sums up our epoch." The civilization ushered in by the Industrial Revolution, in whose crises we are caught today, has been called the Age of Progress and the Age of Science; I would call it simply the Age of More. The word has two aspects here. The first is *There is always more of everything;* the second, *The more you have, the happier you will be.*

Several years ago I remember reading about a survey done over a wide base of salaries and occupations. One response caught my attention: almost everyone said they would be satisfied if they just had a hundred dollars a month more. The interesting thing was that it didn't seem to matter how much a person was getting; everyone wanted just a little bit more.

That is the human condition. The very nature of the mind is to desire, to desire, to desire; if desires could be satisfied once and for all, the mind would be out of a job. "Today I got this; tomorrow I'm going to get that": the words must have sounded contemporary even in the Stone Age, when the first caveman stepped out of his cave. But through most of history, the vast majority of human beings had narrow limits on what desires they could actually satisfy. The Industrial Revolution changed that, at least for some parts of the world, ushering in what the mystics might call the most potentially explosive epoch in history: an age when, to all appearances, any material desire can be satisfied. This is a terribly dangerous state of affairs; for as Schumacher points out, desires are infinite but material things are limited. There is only so much of everything to go around, and we have so cleverly magnified our means of getting and producing that it is now possible for human greed to despoil an entire planet and impoverish the lives of billions of people.

Recently I read an article celebrating the Great Exhibition of 1851 in London, the world's first industrial fair. The British Empire was at its zenith then, and the exhibit hall that journalists called the Crystal Palace was full of promise: the new engines and inventions of the Industrial Revolution; vast material wealth taken from places like India and China; the world's first display of consumer products. Science was conquering nature, medicine was conquering disease, Europe was conquering Asia and Africa. To those who visited the exhibition, two things must have seemed clear: that there was plenty of the earth's bounty for everyone, and that everything necessary for human happiness could be brought within reach through modern science, commerce, and industry.

There are still a good many people who believe this today, more than a century later. The difference is that it is no longer Great Britain which embodies the promise of prosperity. The ideal worshipped by most of the rest of the globe is the American Dream, which a European economic leader captured in four simple watchwords: "More, bigger, faster, richer."

How vast this promise must have looked in London in 1851! Every door was labeled "More": more lands to discover, more knowledge to acquire, more things to invent, more resources, more markets, more products. Wealth was everywhere, and you could not only pursue and get it but thereby be a benefactor of society. The history of those times is an epic story of Rajas Unbound, freed from every physical limitation – in a word, the story of greed. If you ask historians what made the miraculous progress of modern civilization possible, they will answer something like, "Coal. Iron. The concentration of capital. The rationalization of science." There is truth in all these, but I would answer on another level: "Desire." Behind all the seminal developments of the nineteenth century, you can trace the deep, driving desire for more, more, more. The Age of Progress made a science of greed. We have perfected that science, and now we are beginning to reap the karma.

Look at some examples, which I hope will provide a global perspective for these verses. Sri Krishna is trying to show what the result is when we allow the desire for profit to grow until it breaks out of every natural restraint, so that it is free to do what it likes. There are many sides to this, but here I want to look simply at greed on the largest scale.

It is an axiom of modern business that there is always more money to be made. The polite word for this is "growth." Not only should your bank account always be growing, the rate at which it grows should always be growing too. No matter how much you made last year, this year you should be able to make more.

Where is this growth to come from? The answer is one of the great discoveries of the Age of Rajas: unlimited growth comes from unlimited consumption – more energy, more materials, more capital, more labor. The more you consume, the faster you can grow.

"Progress," in this view, depends on resources being cheap and inexhaustible. Rajas's natural movement is expansive: use up what is cheapest and closest; then, when local resources run out – or get too expensive, which is the same in effect – you look farther afield. Today, of course, we can envision a time when "farther afield" no longer exists, though Asuric Enterprises still talks blithely of mining other planets. We know too that even before a resource runs out, it may simply become too expensive. But at the dawn of the Age of Rajas no one guessed this. Somewhere in the world there was always more to take. Who could consume all of the mineral wealth, the agricultural potential, the cheap labor of the vast continents that lay waiting, perhaps two thirds of the globe?

Thus in need of materials and markets, Asuric Enterprises rushed into the business of empire-building, which is the inevitable end of greed.

Last week I saw a movie version of one of my favorite plays by Bernard Shaw: *Caesar and Cleopatra,* starring Claude Rains and Vivien Leigh. The play was written around the turn of the century, when the British Empire seemed at the height of its power, and Shaw added a biting prologue about imperialism which the movie left out. The Egyptian god Ra comes out onto a dark stage, wearing his hawk's head, and scornfully tells his English audience how empires grow, whether British or Roman:

> Then the old Rome . . . robbed their own poor until they became
> great masters of that art, and knew by what laws it could be made
> to appear seemly and honest. And when they had squeezed their
> own poor dry, they robbed the poor of other lands, and added those
> lands to Rome until there came a new Rome, rich and huge. And I,
> Ra, laughed; for the minds of the Romans remained the same size,
> whilst their dominion spread over the earth.

As an Irishman, Shaw had reason to feel familiar with this process. The English, like the Romans, began at home. When I was in school in India, I remember reading about the terrible Irish potato famine as seen through English eyes. Our books had columns of figures that showed the Irish population shooting upwards, clearly out of control. They were too poor, we were taught, to raise anything except potatoes. But the land ran out – "too many people, too little land," a classic case of Malthusian overpopulation. (We Indians were to consider ourselves warned.) In 1845 the potato blight attacked and destroyed the one food crop of the Irish poor. Within five years at least a million Irish men, women, and children died of starvation; the actual number may be more than a million and a half. Another million or so others escaped to

North America in such terrible destitution that they died in the thousands on ship and shore.

What Shaw knew about this was something we were not taught in our English schools: that Ireland was as much a colony of England as India was. We never thought of this in India, you know. Ireland was part of the British Isles to us, and an Irishman was indistinguishable from an Englishman. So I was surprised to learn later that Ireland was colonized very much the way India was – in fact, the relationship was cemented through military force during the reign of Queen Elizabeth, at roughly the same time that the British East India Company was establishing itself in India.

The parallels continue, beginning with control of land. In Ireland, after a terrible attempt at simply liquidating the population, the Irish were driven off and disenfranchised and their land given to landlords and settlers supplied by England. The English landlords – who, understandably, found it safer as well as more pleasant to live in England and were therefore not in close touch with affairs on their estates – grew not what would feed Ireland but what could produce the greatest profit in England; those profits (and the high rents) were the reason they were in Ireland at all. Just as a gardener might set aside a particular plot for raising tomatoes, Ireland became an agricultural backyard for industrial England.

Over the same period, except for the manufacture of linen in what is now Northern Ireland, Irish industries were undermined and destroyed, creating a huge population of unemployed, landless poor. The English did not need industrial competition. They preferred to take out cheap raw materials and sell back finished goods, which was a highly effective way of making money. This remarkably profitable relationship is the essence of colonialism everywhere. It is the ultimate refinement of the profit motive.

One problem in Ireland was that Irish peasants, who numbered in the millions, did not constitute much of a market. They could not afford to buy back food they grew for others; the price was determined by what could be paid in England. Millions, in fact, could literally not afford anything; they lived in a subsistence economy. With no occupation open to them in Ireland except sharecropping, they had theoretically four alternatives: they could provide cheap labor for industries in England, join the English army, emigrate in destitution, or starve. Most were willing to pay almost anything to rent a piece of some absent landlord's land and till it for his profit. Demand kept rents exorbitant, and demand was forced higher by the fact that to keep surplus commodities from pushing prices down, a good deal of arable land – at least two and a half million acres, according to one English historian – was simply held idle. Nothing was grown on it; no herds were grazed.

The result was that Irish food, insofar as it came back to Ireland at all, fed those who were well-to-do. The poor ate potatoes, the best crop they could raise on a tiny plot of ground. The rest of the land, and all their labor, went to raise grain and other commodities to pay the rent.

In brief, there were not too many Irish for Irish land to support. There was plenty of land, and it supported English landlords bountifully. While perhaps two million Irish starved during the "Great Hunger," ample quantities of meat and grain went on being shipped across the channel for sale in English markets. One contemporary English observer wrote that every ship sailing in with relief grain was sure to meet six ships sailing out with food for England.

As Shaw suggested, the English no sooner began to work this system out at home than they exported it – notably (and most profitably) to India, the "brightest jewel in the British Imperial crown." What happened in Ireland happened in India too, and on a much vaster scale. I should add that the same exploitation took place all over what is now called the Third World, not only at the hands of England but of many other European powers. But India makes a very good example, and one I can write about from personal experience.

Westerners are often surprised when I remind them that ancient India was the United States of the world. It had tremendous wealth and thriving village industries, and in medicine, astronomy, mathematics, and technology India was teacher to the rest of the world. Precisely because of that wealth the country was invaded again and again, some twenty times in its recorded history.

Last to come were the British. Counting from the 1750s, when the

English East India Company began to establish a dominant military presence in Bengal, for almost two centuries India's material resources and labor were systematically drained for British profits, first for enterprising individuals, later for the Crown. And those profits were enormous. "Possibly since the world began," wrote the American historian Brooke Adams, "no investment has ever yielded the profit reaped from the Indian plunder."

This is a very important connection, and one of the great ironies of modern progress: the material development of the West was paid for largely by its colonies in the South and East. In particular, the explosive growth of Britain's industrialization – some fifty years ahead of her competitors – was directly financed by the wealth that poured in from India. One cartoon in an English magazine summed up the relationship very well: the Empire was portrayed as a huge cow with her udder in England, methodically eating up India.

The methods employed for this incredible venture were essentially the same as in Ireland, only more systematic, more sophisticated, and applied on a much vaster scale. Briefly, the English took control of the land and destroyed domestic industries, creating a landless, impoverished work force numbering eventually in hundreds of millions. The colonial government and its beneficiaries could pay minimally for materials and labor while charging impossibly high taxes and rents. On top of everything else, India paid the costs of being looted, up to the point of paying all the expenses of supplying Indian soldiers to die in British wars. This too became a standard feature of colonial rule everywhere.

"Well, so what?" says Rajas. "This is over and done with. Colonialism is dead, and no one mourns it. Why drag in the past?" Because it is not over and done with. I am bringing up the past to write about the present. The idea of systematically developing – or "underdeveloping" – poorer countries as a cheap source of resources and a huge market for finished goods is very much alive. So are the techniques of controlling land and its use, and the basic skill of draining capital. The ways in which global corporations control their land, labor, and sources of materials in the Third World are generally very similar to those developed by the English, French, Dutch, and other colonial powers in those same

countries. Huge businesses have taken the place of colonial governments, but the relationships remain the same.

So the colonial inheritance is very much alive. Just last week I was
reminded of the specter of bountiful harvests of wheat being shipped
out of a starving Ireland when I saw an article describing the tragic
famines in the Sahel area of Africa, on the edge of the Sahara. The
Sahel is one of the places you see photographed most often when
papers, magazines, and television want to show what they call "the
face of famine." For years the area experienced severe droughts in which
hundreds of thousands of people died. Yet while food aid was being
shipped in during the drought, record harvests of food from the same
region were being shipped out: peanuts, cotton, vegetables, and beef,
the cash commodities that have taken the best agricultural land since
the days when the Sahel became a colony of France. The main difference between now and colonial times seems to be that instead of the
French government, it is large corporations – mostly French – which
profit. Those who starve may not find the distinction of much interest.

In this sense, colonialism is not so much a relationship between two
countries as it is an attitude of exploitation. The essence of colonialism is the control of one country's resources – not necessarily its other
affairs – by and for some other power, rather than for its own people. It
is no longer fashionable for one nation to colonize another, but there are
more subtle and effective ways to make money than through outright
physical possession. So today we have economic and military colonies:
instead of the British Empire in India, for example, an Asuric Fruit
Empire in Central America. To me the differences do not seem particularly great. Peasants in Haiti, Mexico, or Bangladesh may not care
much who owns their crops. What matters is that they are not theirs,
and that they have no control over what they raise, how much they can
sell it for, or how they spend the little they can earn.

When Asuric Enterprises comes before the court of karma, it will
have some answering to do. We can expect it to ask for rewards rather
than punishment, for it claims nothing less than to have financed the
progress of modern civilization. Without the free pursuit of profit,
according to Rajas, we would still be living in mud huts and dependent

on the land. There is truth to this claim, and I do not want to indict the profit motive as such. But the wanton pursuit of excessive profit, without regard to anyone's real needs or to the consequences, has bought prosperity for less than a third of the world at the cost of keeping at least one half in poverty.

असौ मया हतः शत्रुर्हनिष्ये चापरानपि ।
ईश्वरो ऽहमहं भोगी सिद्धो ऽहं बलवान्सुखी ॥ १६-१४॥
आढ्यो ऽभिजनवानस्मि को ऽन्यो ऽस्ति सदृशो मया ।
यक्ष्ये दास्यामि मोदिष्य इत्यज्ञानविमोहिताः ॥ १६-१५॥

14. "I have destroyed my enemies. I shall destroy others too! Am I not like God? I enjoy what I want. I am successful. I am powerful. I am happy.
15. "I am rich and wellborn. Who is equal to me? I will perform lavish sacrifices and give away lavish gifts, and rejoice in my own generosity."
This is how they go on, deluded by ignorance.

It is easy enough to picture a demented individual saying this kind of thing. Emperors have made a litany of it; in the days of Caligula and Nero, in fact, you actually could proclaim yourself God and get away with it, though often not for long. In our own times, these lines could be spoken by a captain of industry or a king of organized crime like Marlon Brando's "Godfather." But in all these cases the picture is so extreme that we may find it difficult to relate it to ourselves. "Well," we say, "at least I'm no Nero. I may have my problems, but I'll never be like that!"

Yet the shrill voice that mouths these verses does not belong exclusively to tyrants. It is the ego's, and one of the most sobering experiences in meditation comes when we realize that this is what arrogance sounds like in any of us, even those who are likely to be forgotten by history. When we finally break into the greenroom of the unconscious, we find Mr. Ego there stripped of all the masks and makeup he wears for the outside world, parading before a mirror like some demented

Peter Sellers character and uttering lines like these. Very few, of course, ever verbalize such thoughts. But the more inflated self-will becomes, the easier it is to hear these verses beneath the conventions of civilized behavior – not only in individuals but in the arrogance of a race, a nation, even a corporation.

"I have destroyed my enemies," says the voice of Power. "I shall destroy others too, if they get in my way. Am I not like God? I do as I like." This is the essence of gangsterism. Not all gangsters come from Chicago and hide from the law. Some have held positions of distinction; some have even been accorded titles, such as "the Great." Entrepreneurs like Commodore Vanderbilt built empires by translating these verses into a ruthless but colorful way of business: take what you want and eliminate your opposition. Men like Leopold II and "Baker Pasha" did the same when carving out millions of square miles of Africa for Belgium and Great Britain. Their names are all honored now, as are those of other great empire-builders of history – Alexander the Great, Napoleon, Drake, Cortés, Clive – remembered not for what they took from life but by the "civilization" they spread in the wake of their conquests.

These are men of tremendous rajas, who felt themselves allied with destiny. In a world that measures success by competition, power, and physical might, they are considered immensely successful. The Gita would object. In the arrogance that comes with power they rolled across history like steamrollers, causing suffering to millions of innocent people who often did not even oppose them, but only happened to stand in the path of their desires.

The inheritors of the mantle of power today are often not single individuals but boards and committees. They may not literally believe themselves to be "like God," as this verse puts it; but it does quite enough damage simply to believe unquestioningly that you have God on your side. In practice it means, "I have unlimited power, and it is right to do what I want."

Alexander the Great, who actually did believe he was a god, was once unhorsed in man-to-man combat when he invaded India through the Khyber Pass. Alexander was rescued, but to punish the obscure Indian soldier who committed the sin, he destroyed the man's whole town – mostly women, children, and the aged, since the men were away fighting Alexander. The bloated ego takes this sort of thing very personally. Its response is officially known as "righteous wrath," and especially in war it can infect not just individuals but groups, communities, and nations. Dresden and other German cities were firebombed in World War II to "get even" for the arrogance of bombing England. Dresden was a city without military significance, and most of the population were civilians. The decision to reduce it to flame was made not by an enraged despot but by a presumably sober, sensible committee, carefully considering pros and cons. Hiroshima and Nagasaki – also cities of civilians, without military importance – were destroyed for the same kind of reason. The message to any future antagonists was as clear as the words of this verse: "We have destroyed our enemies. We can destroy you too!"

When I first came to this country, in 1959, I found many people for whom these verses might have expressed the American national sentiment. This is the natural euphoria of power and success, and if any nation ever had both, it is the United States after 1945. It had emerged triumphant from a terrible war, the protector of the "free world" from the forces of destruction. It was still protecting Western Europe and felt a moral and military obligation to enforce a Pax Americana over the rest of the world. It had the world's most powerful weapon and by far the strongest economy. It had destroyed its enemies and was supporting its friends with foreign aid, which is precisely what these verses mean on an international level. By the time I arrived, advertisements were proclaiming, "America's the greatest land on earth!"

But with so much prosperity and power came a measure of natural superiority. Most of the people I spoke with then were convinced that the United States had God on its side. "America" was synonymous with "freedom"; to oppose the United States was to stand aligned with the powers of darkness.

Just fifty years earlier, however, these verses would not have been the voice of America. Germany would gladly have spoken them, but more than to any other nation they belonged to Great Britain. Arnold Toynbee, the great English historian, recalls at the time of Queen Victoria's Diamond Jubilee in 1897 that the English "saw their sun standing at its zenith and assumed that it was there to stay." That is the world into which I was born. The Empire was colored red on the maps in our schools (patriots had some cynical remarks to make about the reason for the choice of color) and it made an effective display; a red chain of power seemed to throttle the globe. England's proud boast then was, "The sun never sets on the British Empire!" A cousin of mine used to add, "It's afraid to." England had everything then. She controlled the world's trade, the world's seas, the lion's share of the world's resources; she dominated world technology; her industrial capacity was unexcelled. Great Britain seemed poised on the edge of a great new epoch of world domination: a global peace, ensured by British military might, and a thriving global trade.

She also had something less tangible: an inherent moral superiority that destined her, at least in her own eyes, for world leadership. She tried to carry the mantle wisely. Everyone remembers Kipling's phrase: "the White Man's burden" of "new-caught, sullen peoples, / Half-devil and half-child." Often they had reason to feel sullen. This sort of extreme power easily becomes high-handed, ruling over matters of life and death like an instrument of divine judgment.

In brief, what the United States was after World War II, Britain was at the end of the nineteenth century. The parallel gives us a chance to look at the karma that comes from the arrogance of power, which I believe throws a good deal of light on contemporary superpowers whose military and industrial power has never been equalled.

Since I come from India, I would like to illustrate from the experience of my mother country what the arrogance of power does to both exploiter and exploited. I do not want to dwell on the abuses of military rule, which are always extreme. I would rather try to give some idea of the mental state that goes with the exploitation of any race or country by another. This attitude can infect even good people, and the indifference it breeds is the root of tremendous suffering, whether in British India or South Africa or the United States.

The vast majority of the British in India, when they came to our country to govern, were fair-minded people with some sense of fellow-feeling. But the world they stepped into was founded on inequality; it could not exist without callousness. Over and over we saw English men and women acclimatize themselves to injustice and exploitation that they never would have tolerated in their motherland. We watched them insulate themselves from the terrible poverty around them without ever asking if there might be some connection between their wealth and material progress and the poverty of the country whose resources they were there to take. Without such indifference, I think, exploitation cannot go on for long. But once we become insensitive to those around us, there seems to be no limit to what we can ignore.

These two verses of the Gita convey something very interesting about the arrogance of power: with one hand it glories in its capacity to destroy; with the other, in the lavishness of its own generosity. Like Rome in its days of empire, the British sincerely believed that despite a few excesses, they were doing good throughout the world by bringing the products and virtues of Western civilization to backward nations at the point of a gun. This was a common colonial attitude. Not only the British but the French, the Belgians, and the Dutch who carved up and converted most of Africa felt quite sure that they were bringing civilization while they carried away wealth, and that the first justified the second. It was a comforting combination of altruism, power, and profit.

I had a number of English friends in India in the days before independence, and even the most liberal of them often held this view. "You have to admit, old boy," they would say, "that on the whole, England has done India rather a lot of good. We've unified the country, and we're leaving you a first-class railroad system and all the administrative machinery of good government." They were shocked when I pointed out that the railroads were built to deploy troops swiftly all over India, and volunteered that if efficient trains meant that any of our cities could be occupied by armed garrisons on forty-eight hours' notice, most of us would have preferred to travel by bullock cart. And since by that time hundreds of thousands of Indians, not only men but women and children, had been imprisoned without charge or trial, beaten, and even killed for offering nonviolent resistance, we were also prepared to do without the machinery of British administration.

To be very clear, I want to repeat that no country is immune to the arrogance of power and the indifference it breeds. Most countries and races that have been in positions of superiority have succumbed to it, even the United States. If I have chosen to illustrate with Great Britain and India, it is because I can do so from personal experience and because I believe it throws light on the uses and abuses of power today. I am not inveighing against any country here. I am simply trying to illustrate the natural consequences of power: in the language of these verses, the unavoidable results of feeling "like God," rich, powerful, able to do what one likes. The very attitude that you have the right to control other people has certain seeds of karma. Arrogance is part of that attitude; it *has* to bear fruit. Exploitation is part of that desire. So is jealousy. And so, curiously, is fear: the fear success breeds, that someone who is stronger will come along and take away what you have.

It is from these seeds of fear and jealousy that war finally springs, the last of the fruits of power. To me it is impossible to look over Britain's "golden years" between 1850 and 1914 and fail to see the forces of international jealousy gathering. Great Britain had everything, and Germany wanted its share. By the end of the century, in their race for "defense," the nations of Europe had massed standing armies vaster than any ever seen before in times of peace. The war that erupted impoverished and devastated its participants, excepting the United States. It devoured the money, men, and materials of the British Empire, colonies and "motherland" together, and sowed the seeds of yet another war.

Modern history moves swiftly. The Roman Empire took centuries to collapse; from Queen Victoria's coronation to the cataclysm of world war was less than a hundred years. The Reich that was to last a thousand years held up for barely twelve. The once-unchallenged superiority of the United States among the nations of the world is scarcely unchallenged today. Power cannot expand without a collapse. To someone who can take a long view of history, I think it must be clear that we are firmly in what Wendell Willkie called "one world or none," where no country can unilaterally pursue its own way without risking disaster for the whole globe.

अनेकचित्तविभ्रान्ता मोहजालसमावृताः ।
प्रसक्ताः कामभोगेषु पतन्ति नरके ऽशुचौ ॥ १६-१६ ॥

*16. Bound by their greed and entangled
in a web of delusion, whirled about by a
fragmented mind, they fall into a dark hell.*

"Hell" in the Gita does not refer to some place after the Last Judgment. Hell is a state of mind. Tamas *is* hell, and the indifference and utter insensitivity of the tamasic mind makes hell of life around it. Wrapped in itself, interested in nothing else, tamas is not touched by suffering even on a massive scale; it is barely even aware of it. We can see the extent of this apathy and indifference if we take a long-range look at the globe today: its colossal poverty, the pervasive contamination of its water, food, and air, and most of all the monumental cruelty of its wars.

The Vietnam war, I must tell you, put this country in a very different light for Third World nations that had looked to it for leadership. Christine and I returned to the United States from India shortly before American military involvement in Vietnam began in earnest, and I remember that within a few years you could scarcely pick up a periodical or turn on the evening news without learning of more casualties and destruction. The tragic toll of human life ran into two or three millions in the ten years before U.S. withdrawal. Many of these – perhaps most – must have been innocent civilians, women and children whose lives were sacrificed for no reason whatsoever.

Vietnam gives clues of what war has come to mean at the end of the twentieth century. In both instances, staggering numbers of sophisticated weapons were used primarily not to defeat armies but to destroy cities and civilians. No one pretended that these women, children, and aged were the enemy against whom war was originally intended. They were "incidental casualties." I doubt that they found the distinction of much comfort. They were killed essentially because the military mind, full of tamas, can approach a problem only in terms of killing. If killing doesn't work, as in the trenches of World War I or the bombing of Vietnam, it tries more killing – and today, with the progress of science so rapid and so diligently pursued, there are vastly more effective ways of killing than the military mind has any imagination to deal with. So it goes on doing what it understands: after all, the weapons are there to be used.

I mention Vietnam only because these tragedies stand out in my mind. Any war would prompt the same commentary on the colossal insensitiveness of this kind of violence, the fatal lack of imagination of those who plan and order the death and suffering of thousands or even millions of people for no other reason than to assuage the national ego. Few individual egos can become so bloated or be more callous. The national ego is full of tamas, which means it is riddled with fears, obsessed by revenge, and utterly insensitive to suffering. Tamas is the morphine of the spirit. It knocks out sensitivity to friend and foe alike, with the result that the national ego doesn't mind losing any number of lives as long as it ends up "winning."

Leon Wolff, after a detailed discussion of the Battle of Flanders, summarized World War I in a paragraph:

> It had meant nothing, solved nothing, and proved nothing, and in so doing had killed 8,538,315 men and variously wounded 21,219,452. Of 7,750,919 others taken prisoner or missing, well over a million were later presumed dead; thus the total deaths (not counting civilians) approach 10,000,000. . . .

"It had meant nothing, solved nothing, and proved nothing." That epitaph could stand for any war.

For me, as probably for thousands of other Americans, watching the withdrawal of U.S. troops from Vietnam brought a period of agonizing reflection. It brought home to every thoughtful observer the utter futility of war and the untold misery it causes. Yet the world has been sick of war countless times before, and as St. Francis liked to say, our knowledge is only as deep as our action.

I have heard that it was the women in this country who finally asserted themselves and brought the war in Korea to an end. With Vietnam, as I like to repeat with great appreciation, more than anyone else it was the young people who opened the eyes of the nation to the horror and stupidity of war. This was not accomplished by national leaders. The war was begun by national leaders; it was the people who brought it to an end. This is how it must be. I generally appreciate the sentiment in this country that we should not look to politicians to solve our problems; all too often they are the cause of them. Ultimately our problems are *our* problems, and it is we little people who can solve them if we join hands and keep our eyes on the welfare of all.

Human tragedy, as the Gita makes clear, is not inflicted on us by God. It is inflicted entirely by ourselves: if not actively, then by the gross insensitivity which enables human beings to close their eyes to the suffering around them. This too gives a precious clue: the most effective way to undo this fearful suffering is not to attack those who have caused it, but to work to open their eyes and soften their hearts until they become sensitive again.

As I write this, there are signs that for the first time in a generation citizens around the world are rejecting in impressive numbers the acceptability of a nuclear war. This holds tremendous promise. After decades of an overpowering sense of helplessness, people are beginning to believe that they can, after all, make a difference in the course of history. If we believe this, it *is* possible to abolish war. Only if we believe ourselves powerless would I say that war becomes inevitable.

I remember J. P. Kripalani, the distinguished historian who must have been on close terms with Gandhi for more than thirty years, describing how he first heard Gandhi talk about freeing India through nonviolent resistance. Kripalani was a young man then and a good intellectual, and he was shocked. He went up to Gandhi after the talk and said, "Gandhiji, you may know all about the Gita, but you don't know about history. Never before has a country been able to free itself without violence." "*You* don't know about history," Gandhi corrected him. "To say that something has never happened before does not mean it cannot happen in the future." This is why I think of our times not as the nuclear age but as the age of Gandhi.

आत्मसंभाविताः स्तब्धा धनमानमदान्विताः ।
यजन्ते नामयज्ञैस्ते दम्भेनाविधिपूर्वकम् ॥ १६-१७॥
अहंकारं बलं दर्पं कामं क्रोधं च संश्रिताः ।
मामात्मपरदेहेषु प्रद्विषन्तो ऽभ्यसूयकाः ॥ १६-१८॥
तानहं द्विषतः क्रूरान्संसारेषु नराधमान् ।
क्षिपाम्यजस्त्रमशुभानासुरीष्वेव योनिषु ॥ १६-१९॥
आसुरीं योनिमापन्ना मूढा जन्मनि जन्मनि ।
मामप्राप्यैव कौन्तेय ततो यान्त्यधमां गतिम् ॥ १६-२०॥

*17. Self-important, obstinate, swept away by the
pride of wealth, they ostentatiously perform
sacrifices without any regard for their purpose.
18. Egotistical, violent, arrogant, lustful, and angry,
envious of everyone, they abuse my presence within
their own bodies and in the bodies of others.
19. Life after life I cast those who are malicious,
hateful, cruel, and degraded into the wombs of
those with similar natures.
20. Birth after birth they find themselves with
demonic tendencies. Degraded in this way, Arjuna,
they fail to reach me and fall lower still.*

Someone has commented that in all the Hindu scriptures, there is no
place where the fate of those with negative tendencies seems more
hopeless than in these verses. We seem to have no way out. Nowhere
does Sri Krishna sound more like a wrathful, vengeful Lawgiver.

There are secular and even scientific versions of this judgment too:
schemes like astrology; theories that personality is written into our very
genes. Sri Krishna would not hesitate to call both of these superstitions.
I know people who believe that because their sun sign is such-and-so and
their good planets are all in squares while bad ones are in triangles, they
can never change. Some people even find this comfortable: it is arduous
to change yourself, and very easy to go on being what you are. "Well, you
know Leos," they say. "It's my nature to be dominating; what can I do?"

The Compassionate Buddha never used stronger language than when answering someone who spoke this way. "I *abhor* astrology," he said. He abhorred anything that binds the human mind. For the same reason, without differing with anything fundamental in modern biology, I think he would abhor the crippling belief that our problems are written hopelessly into our genes. I have had people tell me, "There's no point in my learning to meditate. What's the use? I'll always be like this. It's the way I am." One friend who was subject to very severe chronic depressions told me very earnestly, "You don't understand. Meditation can't do anything about this, because it's not a problem with my mind. The doctor says there is a particular chemical imbalance in the neurotransmitters of my brain." You can see why Sri Krishna, in an earlier verse, called this the path of greater and greater bondage. Nothing is more debilitating than a negative image of ourselves, and the voice that whispers "You're no good, you're no good" comes not from wisdom but from the ego-ventriloquist.

We should never succumb to this way of thinking. We should never conclude that our lives are hopeless, that we can never improve, that we are condemned by God or fate or chemistry or conditioning to repeat the same mistakes. We always have a choice. In fact, the verses which follow will affirm the glory of our human nature: not only that we can always choose a better path, but that someday we will. We can never alienate ourselves from our divine Self, and the whole force of evolution is pushing us towards this supreme goal.

Nevertheless, this reassuring picture is spread out over many lifetimes, and the way in which evolution urges us upward, if we do not learn quickly, is through suffering. I have seen a lot of literature recently about CAI, "computer assisted instruction." Life is PAI: we often learn through pain, through the consequences of our own mistakes. According to the Hindu and Buddhist mystics, if we insist on living selfishly, we will not only reap the suffering of selfishness as we go on; we will also carry that mental state into our next life.

Of course, this will require a suitable context. If we are going to develop our selfishness, we need selfish parents and a suitably self-centered culture and epoch. We have to go to the computerized birth-planning service in Bardo and spell out our needs precisely. "Wanted: One or two parents consistently interested in putting themselves first. Proof of deterioration of character required." A real devotee of sensory pleasure in ancient times, for example, might be born again in Nero's Rome, with social standing and wealth enough to indulge himself however he liked. Sri Krishna would wince at the thought, but he would say, "How else is the fellow going to learn?" Similarly, as I think Trotsky once implied, someone really violent might try the twentieth century. You can fairly well have your pick of countries and decades. Any real situation, of course, would be vastly more complicated; thousands of samskāras have to be accommodated. But this is the principle: we are what we are and where we are because of what we have been.

When I was living in Oakland, I remember some apartment houses going up across the street from us. I was alarmed to see how flimsy they were. You could hear everything going on in the next room, and when someone went up or down the stairs, the whole building shook. A friend of mine who knew the owner went and asked him why it was being built so insubstantially. His reply was irrelevant but rather significant: "You can't take it with you."

This is a common point of view. If you could take it with you, you should build things to last forever. But if you can't take it with you, what does it matter? Most of us, unfortunately, are working on things that we can't take with us: we can't take our houses, our cars, our swimming pools, our clothes, our work, anything. The Gita says simply, "Why not work on the things you *are* going to take: your own thoughts?" This is inescapable logic. Even if you don't want to take them, your thoughts are going to come along anyway; so you might as well make them the best thoughts possible.

In one of the odd similes in Hinduism and Buddhism, the passage from this life to the next is compared to a kind of boulevard, lined with trees on either side: *karmadāru,* trees of karma. And thoughts are like birds – or, more Buddhistic, like bats. When you leave this life, all these bats jump off and alight in the trees at the far end of the road, waiting for you to pass. Then, just when you are about to re-enter embodied life, they drop from the trees into your open knapsack. You have a new body, live in a new context, but you have the same old thoughts. That is what provides the continuity of our load of karma. When you change your thinking from selfish to selfless, learn to return good will for ill will, your thought load is different – which means your karma load has been changed too. This shows the supreme importance of working on our thoughts, which is ultimately the point of all spiritual disciplines.

Only after many years of preparation in sādhana do we enter the unconscious, which is where the real work on our deeper thoughts takes place. This can be a terribly unsettling revelation. Our real nature *is* light, but in each of us there is plenty of darkness too: dark continents of selfishness which we share with every other human being as part of our evolutionary heritage from the animal realms. Both sides, the divine and the nondivine, are at war in each of us, and the very basis of sādhana is to get into the unconscious and then fight your way out. There is no other way.

As I said, it is dreadfully disheartening to see so much that is selfish within oneself. Somebody once asked St. Francis of Sales, "I've been practicing spiritual disciplines all these years, and I see more in me that is sinful than I did when I began. Do you think I might actually be a worse person than before?" Francis replied with a smile, "No, you have always been like that. You're simply beginning to see what has always been present in the depths of your consciousness – in the consciousness of us all." Generally I am very careful to avoid striking a negative note, but a great deal of the unconscious is unpleasant and inhuman. Entering there is like walking into a forest: it is the nature of a forest to be infested by wild animals, and the nature of the unconscious to breed anger, fear, and greed.

To give a very personal example, I have to confess that I was never a very unkind person. My grandmother used to say I had more patience than she did, which was saying a good deal. So I always looked on myself as a relatively decent human being – that is, until one day in meditation when I looked into this forest for the first time. I was appalled. It took some time for me to realize that this is what everyone sees; for this is the human condition. That is why no illumined man or woman will ever scorn another person or criticize others' weaknesses or fail in compassion for any human error. In my eyes, it is the person who looks down on others who is on the lowest rung of the human ladder, not the person who occasionally slips and falls.

Fortunately, if you have been practicing all the disciplines sincerely and systematically, you cannot enter the unconscious until you have developed the capacity to grapple successfully with what you encounter there. This is a built-in safety mechanism in sādhana. So when you find yourself facing a samskāra, the very fact that you are face to face is a sign that you are ready for it. This is not to say that you will find the fight easy; just the opposite. These samskāras are huge and tough; anger, fear, and greed have been in training through millions of years of animal evolution. You can't expect to knock them out in the first round: in fact, you might as well prepare yourself to take a beating. You are likely to spend a lot of time on the ropes, especially in the early days; you may even find yourself looking up at a samskāra from the floor. That is the experience of even some of the greatest mystics, East or West.

In traditional language, these "powers of darkness" in the depths of consciousness are often referred to collectively as the Devil. There is a good deal of practical psychology behind this. "If you keep saying 'I'm a sinner, I'm a sinner,'" Sri Ramakrishna used to say, "you become a sinner." It is terribly debilitating to identify yourself with evil; it can tear you in two or drain all your will to fight. Call all that "Satan," the Christian mystics say, and identify with what is divine. Martin Luther, I understand, once threw his inkwell at the Devil to drive him away; he may have had a mess to clean up afterwards, but I'm sure the gesture had its effect. Nonetheless, in this age of psychology and science, people seem to understand more easily when instead of "Satan" and "soul," I talk about the ego and the Self. This makes it clear that both are in our consciousness, but that our real personality is divine.

"Don't be afraid," Sri Krishna tells Arjuna; "you have the qualities that lead to Self-realization." I want to make it very clear that all of us have these qualities in some measure, simply by virtue of our being human. Everyone can make the choices that improve personality; no one is compelled to remain at a lower level, whatever the mistakes and conditioning of the past. I sometimes read even experienced spiritual figures saying that in order to purify consciousness, you need to be born with a special kind of nervous system. I have to differ categorically: this is not necessary at all. I was born with the same kind of nervous system as everybody else – attracted by what is pleasant, repelled by what is unpleasant. Therefore I know from my own experience the truth of what every great mystic testifies, East and West alike: that you can remake yourself completely through the practice of meditation and the allied disciplines. That is the real glory of human nature; and that is why, though it may sound naive, I still tell Christine with a fresh sense of wonder, "There is nothing like meditation!"

त्रिविधं नरकस्येदं द्वारं नाशनमात्मनः ।
कामः क्रोधस्तथा लोभस्तस्मादेतत्त्रयं त्यजेत् ॥ १६-२१ ॥
एतैर्विमुक्तः कौन्तेय तमोद्वारैस्त्रिभिर्नरः ।
आचरत्यात्मनः श्रेयस्ततो याति परां गतिम् ॥ १६-२२ ॥

21. There are three gates to this self-destructive state: lust, anger, and greed. Renounce these.
22. Those who pass freely by these three gates of darkness, Arjuna, seek what is best and attain life's supreme goal.

When I was a college student I used to enjoy going down to the railway station to watch the trains. Nagpur Central was a terribly busy place; lines from all over India came together there. The vast, high-vaulted waiting room was as noisy as your Grand Central used to be, and out on the platforms tracks seemed to stretch as far as you could see. A huge board above the ticket area posted the Arrivals and Departures, some of which had quite colorful names: the Grand Trunk Express, the Malabar Express, the Deccan Queen. I liked to think you could walk in, pick your destination from the board as if from a menu, and travel anywhere in India you wanted to go.

It occurred to me the other day that in its deeper levels, the mind is very much like a huge, busy train station. Thoughts are coming and going almost all the time, day and night. Many of these are narrow-gauge distractions: the state of the economy, what to have for dinner, what Sarah said that night at the Bijou. But there comes a stage in meditation when you go right in to the central waiting room, where the major express trains ply. They are listed on the Arrivals and Departures board, but the mind offers very few lines. Sri Krishna lists the major ones here: Lust, Greed, and Anger; express service available twenty-four hours a day. But the choice of destinations, he tells Arjuna, is even more limited. You can line up at any of these gates, give the collector your ticket, and climb aboard; but though the routes are different, you will always end up in the same place, and it is not heaven.

The other day I was reading about Disneyland, which apparently is one of the places in the United States that visitors from other countries always want to see. Even former premier Nikita Khrushchev of the Soviet Union was fascinated by it. You can get a train there to take you into other "lands" – Jungleland, Adventureland, Fantasyland, Tomorrowland – where for a small fee you can be attacked by wild plastic hippos or weird bugaboos in a darkened cave. I tell friends from India, "Why bother? If you learn to meditate you can travel to all those lands in your own unconscious mind, and you'll have a much more thrilling time of it too." I am being lighthearted, but I am not exaggerating. The creatures in the unconscious are more jungly than anything you will find in Jungleland. Plastic hippos may look real enough to scare you, but they cannot hurt. Rage, resentment, anger, hostility, on the other hand, will beat you up and rob you of your prāna. If you stay on the ride, they will take you to the end of the line: a state of mind for which hell is the best name, though this is not a concept I even like to mention.

Looking around today, I have come to believe that the biggest of these three gates is anger. Our age has been called the age of anger; I would go further now and call it the age of rage. Newspapers could keep the same headline made up for most front-page stories: "Anger Erupts!" – in the home, on the street, at work, in the schools, between races, communities, nations, and even religions, most ridiculous and often most vicious of all. Books are written with little substance except anger. Magazines even praise it in the name of therapy. Films and television programs draw most of their action from angry characters, hostile language, and violent behavior. In a supermarket line, on the bus, walking along the city streets, I hear angry words at the slightest provocation.

After all I have said against lust and greed, it may seem surprising that I single out anger as the main gate to the land of sorrow. But there is a close relationship between lust and greed on the one hand and anger on the other – so close, in fact, that I would say you cannot play up lust or greed in any area of life without putting yourself on an express train to a chronically angry mind. "Angry" here, I should explain, is a comprehensive term. Angerland shelters all kinds of mental states which we may not recognize as belonging to the same family: fury, resentment, hostility, irritation, "righteous indignation," or simply going about "with a chip on your shoulder," spoiling for a fight.

Patanjali, the unexcelled teacher of meditation in ancient India, would explain this relationship in terms of the mind's dynamics. He is always clear and to the point. Lust and greed are not very different in the way they work, he would say. "Lust" does not refer only to sex – we speak of lust for wealth or power or fame – and "greed" need not refer to money; we can be greedy to have an experience, a particular pleasure, or power, or prestige, as well as to have a huge bank balance. To Patanjali, the scientist, the force is the same: selfish desire. Only the object of that force is different. When it gets fierce and swollen, there is tremendous power in the force of selfish desire. We *have* to have what we want, and if we cannot get it, we become angry, frustrated, or resentful; the power of the desire is expressed as anger.

Now, if it is just a single, momentary desire that gets thwarted – say, you have set your heart on seeing a particular movie and it is cancelled – Patanjali would say that first a wave of desire rises in the mind, then a wave of anger or irritation when the desire is blocked, and that is all. Anger that flares and dies immediately is not pleasant to anyone, but usually it does no serious damage. But look at what happens when a strong selfish desire becomes chronic. Then it is not just a single wave; it runs through our lives like a river, beneath every other passing state of consciousness. It becomes a basic drive in our lives. We live for money; we live for sex: in the deeper levels of the mind we may be thinking about them always.

In such a case, Patanjali would say, we are setting ourselves up for chronic frustration. Life, to put it mildly, cannot always deliver what we want. Here the very nature of the mind is a bit perverse. It wants fiercely to be made happy by getting a particular thing, a particular experience. Until it gets that, it lives in expectation – that is, in a kind of Neverland sometime in the future. Bliss is "just around the corner," but never here and now. And as the mind waits, there is a continuous, mounting, gnawing sense of irritation: life is failing to deliver. It is welching on its promises. We are being cheated. Everybody else is getting what they want; we can see that in the movies, on television, in the ads. Why can't we have what *we* want all the time too?

We don't usually verbalize this, of course. We know such expectations are unreasonable and absurd. But the unconscious is childish, and this is exactly the way it thinks. It wants its desires satisfied, preferably always, and it turns a deaf ear to philosophy. But perversely, when the mind *does* get what it wants, it feels pleased but also a little let down. A small voice inside always says, "Thanks, that was nice, but is that *all*?" Expectations have been swollen to impossible proportions, to which life cannot possibly be equal. So the desire gets fiercer – "Next time *has* to be better!" – and harder than ever to satisfy. The result is a chronic, mounting sense of frustration.

Of course, this is a simplified picture. Each personality is different, with many other intertwining samskāras in addition to these basic three. There may be positive forces at work in deeper consciousness which mitigate the expression of anger: a strain of patience, a measure of detachment. But in many people today, the essential pattern is the same. A kind of background of anger, fed by the feeling that our deep desires are not being fulfilled, is always bubbling away just beneath the surface of consciousness. It leaves a very low threshold of tolerance, so that often even a small, irrelevant irritation is enough to make us explode in anger.

Look around, Patanjali would say: doesn't this tally with our experience and our observation? On the one hand, if we look with some detachment, we see money and sex and material possessions played up everywhere. People expect them to be more accessible than ever: you can have as much as you want; that is the promise not only of Madison Avenue but of contemporary psychology. Yet on the other hand, who would say today that people are happier? What we see is people who seem angrier than ever, more frustrated, disillusioned, discontented, ready to snap at anyone or lash out in meaningless violence.

Dante had a big sign over these three gates: "All hope abandon, ye who enter here!" I would say no. Even if we have passed through the gates to sorrow a million times, we always have a choice the next time. Sri Krishna's advice is deceptively simple: "Pass each gate by, Arjuna. Don't even open them to take a look inside; you might be drawn in." Anger is a terribly fast train; lust is even faster. And greed for money or possessions can pick you up without your even knowing.

Avoiding these three requires not only will and patience but tremendous vigilance, especially in the climate of today. Everybody seems to be not only standing in line before the gates to sorrow but praising the states they lead to and trying to draw in their friends. Often here in the San Francisco Bay Area I see advertisements sponsored by the big casinos at nearby Lake Tahoe: "Come on, spend your weekend with us! We'll give you a free meal at our hotel and five dollars worth of chips; we'll even buy your gas!" They know they will get it back a hundredfold. Similarly, the gates of lust, anger, and greed have hawkers outside, offering us all kinds of promises and free tickets: heightened sense pleasures, therapeutic rage sessions, "trickle-down" theories of economics that tout the basic benevolence of greed. "Be warned, Arjuna," Sri Krishna says; "they're not going to fun-filled Tahoe. They'll take you to you-know-where."

The long-term consequences of saturating our society with these values are tragic beyond words. Particularly in the media, almost everything today seems to be tied to sex, violence, and the profit motive, as if schedulers and advertisers were convinced that these are the only things that will motivate us.

Yesterday afternoon I went to a friend's house to watch the finals of the U.S. Open tennis championship, broadcast live. I was grieved to see how dominant money had become in what I used to consider a truly fine game. Everything was valued first in dollars and only secondarily in terms of skill. Jimmy Connors was playing beautifully, but the commentator didn't have much to say about that; he kept repeating how much Connors was worth and how much was riding on the outcome of the match that day. Instead of saying "He has been playing brilliant tennis this season" it was "He has won thirty-five thousand dollars." This kind of talk leaves a bad taste in my mouth; it teaches us to put a price tag on everything. That is the conditioning we are subjected to today: a man is what his bank balance is; a woman's worth is her salary and possessions. The well-being of a community can be measured by the number of cars and TV antennas it has; a country's welfare can be measured by its GNP. All this is as ridiculous as it is common.

The broadcasting was interrupted for a while because of some satellite problem, so I took the opportunity to watch some of the other programs to see what people are taking in when they watch television today. I was horrified to see the continuous damage these programs are doing, breaking up social relationships, disrupting homes, exploiting and degrading the image of women (I would say of men too), playing man and woman, parents and children, off against each other, validating the attraction of addictive habits, revealing and appealing to the very worst in human nature.

We have become so used to programs like this that we seldom think of the culture and values they present. If you find a program tawdry, distasteful, or ridiculous, you simply change the channel. Millions on millions, however, do not change the channel. As much as a third of their waking hours may be spent absorbing the kind of thing I saw.

First was a "giveaway" program: something for nothing, usually money or toaster ovens, for anybody willing to do ridiculous things before an audience for half an hour. Doesn't everyone like to get something for nothing, even if it's something that nobody needs? There was also a so-called news program, though the events seemed to me to be selected more for entertainment value than for social significance. And of course there were the soap operas, in which you can learn, as someone has remarked, that almost everybody is secretly doing all the things you thought people didn't do because they shouldn't; so why shouldn't *you*?

But what disturbed me most was not one of the major studios' programs. It was a sexual liberation talk show on the educational channel. I couldn't believe my eyes and ears. Measuring life in terms of money was ridiculous enough, but here everybody was measuring by pleasure. Happiness and individual freedom were reduced to getting your share of sensation. How could anyone watch a program like that and not burst into laughter? The whole force of evolution is to lead us gradually to the realization that the body is not us, that life is not physical in its basis. In Hinduism this guiding force behind evolution is called *shakti,* creative power, and it is embodied and worshipped as the Divine Mother. Every woman is a source of this power. Every woman has immense spiritual potential, the capacity to regenerate society around a higher ideal. Because of that very power, it is a terrible tragedy for all of society if women start to line up as men have before the gates of lust, anger, and greed.

Over the years meditation enables us to enter the vast central waiting room of the mind, where thoughts are coming and going through these gates without our ordinarily knowing it. The difference is that now we are conscious in the unconscious, so we can actually begin to patrol these gates always. Even in our sleep we must learn to keep our vigilance at this deeper level, until we reach a state where these gates to negative consciousness do not open even in our dreams. Then, marvelously, they actually begin to rust shut. Flowering creepers grow over them as they do in India, when the encroaching jungle covers an abandoned temple. You cannot open those gates any longer; after a while, you cannot even find them. It may sound impossible, but in that state you cannot be angry or selfish even if you try; your consciousness will be full of love.

यः शास्त्रविधिमुत्सृज्य वर्तते कामकारतः ।
न स सिद्धिमवाप्नोति न सुखं न परां गतिम् ॥ १६-२३ ॥
तस्माच्छास्त्रं प्रमाणं ते कार्याकार्यव्यवस्थितौ ।
ज्ञात्वा शास्त्रविधानोक्तं कर्म कर्तुमिहार्हसि ॥ १६-२४ ॥

*23. Others disregard the teachings of the scriptures.
Driven by selfish desire, they miss the goal of
life, miss even happiness and prosperity.
24. Therefore let the scriptures be your guide in
what to do and what not to do. Understand their
teachings; then act in accordance with them.*

The Gita, I like to repeat, is not a book of commandments but a book of choices. Once this is understood, the Gita's presentation appeals greatly to the modern mind because it respects our freedom of choice completely.

My one quarrel with scholarly translations of the Gita is that because they are not concerned with putting teachings into practice, they often bury what is timeless and useful in the archaic language of rituals and a complex world view that Westerners do not share. Actually, Sri Krishna's approach is surprisingly current and terribly practical. He describes the forces operating in the mind and how they shape our actions, first on an individual scale, then finally in their global effect on the rest of life. Then he leaves it to us to decide how we want to act.

When I was a boy, I belonged for a time to the Boy Scouts of India. People in this country are sometimes surprised when I remind them that scouting is a British contribution, not American, and scouting in India followed Mr. Baden-Powell as closely as a different country and climate and so forth would allow. Our motto was "Be prepared." We used to ask our scoutmaster, "Be prepared for what?" He would just shrug and say, "How would I know?"

Still, he took his responsibilities seriously. When we were in the middle of some activity, he occasionally liked to surprise us by blowing his whistle and calling, "Fall in!" We would scurry into line and stand quizzically at attention. "Very good," he would say. "I just wanted to see if you were prepared. Fall out!"

Once we went on a camping trip into the dense forest that lay just beyond my village. The forest was full of wild animals in those days, and despite Hollywood's presentation, village children in India do not play in forests and jungles where they can be eaten. Therefore it was necessary to Become Prepared for the ways of the jungle.

Our scoutmaster briefed us carefully. "Beware of this and watch out for that," he said. "Do this, but don't do that. And follow my directions carefully." He drew a rough map on the ground. "This is the route I want you fellows to follow."

I had some cousins who disdained the safe and bland, wherever it might be. Danger was their cup of tea. "Sir," they said, "it looks more interesting to cross the river and go along *here*. We'd like to take that route."

"Better not," he said.

"Why not? What will happen?"

"If you take that route," he said seriously, "I will have to go back at the end of the day and report to your mothers that I have allowed their sons to be devoured by a tiger. That is highly embarrassing for a scoutmaster."

They were delighted. I need hardly say that they did cross the river and did get into trouble; and though they were not eaten, they did have to be rescued. "That should be a lesson to you," my scoutmaster said. I don't believe it was; they just liked to live dangerously.

Sri Krishna here is being a good scoutmaster. "Here is one route," he says, "and here is another. Every minute you're at a crossroads. This route seems like more fun, but it's full of wild animals. The path gets worse and worse as you go along – until you reach the end, which is unutterably horrible."

Arjuna shudders. "I'm a man of action," he admits. "I like danger, and I like challenges – but only if there's a purpose to it. Krishna, tell me the alternative."

And Sri Krishna smiles. "Just what I was about to do." That is the concluding two chapters of the Gita, and no one will be happier than I to return to verses that follow the upward rather than the downward path.

दैवासुरसम्पद्विभागयोगो नाम षोडशोऽध्यायः ॥ १६ ॥

CHAPTER SEVENTEEN

The Power of Faith

अर्जुन उवाच ।
ये शास्त्रविधिमुत्सृज्य यजन्ते श्रद्धयान्विताः ।
तेषां निष्ठा तु का कृष्ण सत्त्वमाहो रजस्तमः ॥ १७-१ ॥

ARJUNA:

1. O Krishna, what is the state of those who disregard the scriptures but still worship with faith? Do they act from sattva, rajas, or tamas?

"Faith" here is a not very adequate translation of *shraddhā,* which means much more. Literally, shraddhā is 'that which is placed in the heart': all the beliefs we hold so deeply that we never think to question them. It is the set of beliefs, values, prejudices, and prepossessions that colors our perceptions, governs our thinking, dictates our responses, and shapes our lives, generally without our even being aware of its presence and power.

This may sound philosophical, but shraddhā is not an intellectual abstraction. It is right at the bottom of our hearts. It is our very substance, Sri Krishna will say: it reflects all that we have made ourselves and points to what we will become.

And there is nothing passive about shraddhā. It would not be quite correct to call it a force; it is a mental state. But shraddhā is full of potency, for it prompts action, conditions behavior, and determines how we see and respond to the world around us.

When Norman Cousins talks about a "belief system" analogous to the body's organ systems, that is one aspect of shraddhā. He is referring to the power to heal or harm that is inherent in our ideas about ourselves. One person with a serious illness believes she has a contribution to make to the world and recovers; another believes her life is worthless, or that she has no hope, and she dies: that is the power of shraddhā.

Similarly, I would say, when psychologists talk about "self-image," they are often referring to one aspect of shraddhā. One person believes he will succeed in life, and despite overwhelming obstacles he does. Another, who believes he can do nothing, may be more gifted and face fewer difficulties, yet make very little of his life.

Yet shraddhā is not brute determination or self-confidence. It is a highly sensitive expression of our values: what we deem worth having, doing, attaining, being. The things we strive for show what we value; we back our shraddhā with our time, our energy, our very lives.

In fact, shraddhā literally determines our lives. In those tremendous verses from the Upanishads –

> We are what our deep, driving desire is.
> As our deep, driving desire is, so is our will.
> As our will is, so is our deed.
> As our deed is, so is our destiny –

that "deep, driving desire" is our shraddhā. When St. John says, "We are what we love," that word *love* could be translated by shraddhā. The Buddha gives us the explanation in the first verses of the Dhammapada: "All that we are is the result of what we have thought. We are made up of our thoughts; our lives are shaped by our thoughts." The Bible says simply, "As a man believeth in his heart, so is he."

In applying this chapter to the world today, therefore, I would interpret Arjuna's question very differently from the way it is usually understood. At the end of the last chapter, you remember, Sri Krishna enjoined Arjuna to follow the scriptures, since to do otherwise is to follow the downward course of rajas and tamas into sorrow. Now Arjuna wants to know about those who ignore spiritual laws but still "perform worship" out of some kind of faith. They do believe in something, he says, and they act according to their belief. What path are they on, upward or down? What kind of fruit can we expect from their actions?

The question, of course, is couched in the language of earlier times. If Arjuna were here today he might ask instead, "Our times are considered civilized and advanced. We have put our faith in science and technological growth, and we have achieved tremendous breakthroughs. Why is it that the problems we face are more menacing than anything faced in previous centuries?"

This is an excellent question. If scientific knowledge is the test of evolution, if technology is the standard by which to measure progress – if, in other words, we have put our shraddhā in the right place – then it stands to reason that with all our scientific progress, we should be more at peace with ourselves and with others. We should have banished sickness from both body and mind and banished violence from the earth.

Technology has become the faith of our fathers, yet we are finding the fruit of it often bitter. And we feel bewildered, like Arjuna. We did so much with science and industry, went so far. Why is the world more fraught than ever with alienation, hunger, and insensitivity, with violence so virulent that one or two individuals can hold whole cities hostage, with side effects of industrial growth that blight the planet?

This is not to belittle science and technology. I have a very high regard for science, and would be the first to acknowledge the debt we all owe to technology in making our world safer and more comfortable. But we need to remember that in other ways, technology has also made the world vastly more dangerous and less comfortable, often in the pursuit of goals that do not, in retrospect, seem worth the price. The problem is that science and technology make good servants but very poor masters – and we have let the servants take over the house, in the shraddhā that for every problem we face, every desire we want fulfilled, technology has the answer.

Let me take some illustrations from medicine, which has done so much to improve human welfare over the centuries. By and large, we are used to viewing medical history as a long series of triumphs against disease, particularly in the twentieth century. But there are disturbing signs that this trend has been reversed.

One example is the war on infectious diseases. When I was born, near the beginning of the twentieth century, most of the human race was still dying from diseases like smallpox, cholera, yellow fever, tuberculosis, influenza, and malaria, the same plagues that had haunted the world since ancient times. Smallpox was a daily threat while I was growing up. Fortunately, my village was particularly careful about sanitation, especially my grandmother; as a result, most of us in the village escaped when many around us died. Nevertheless, many of the boys in my school bore the scarred faces of those who contract the disease and survive.

Then vaccination came, one of Great Britain's most valuable contributions as a colonial power. At first it met with resistance, just as in the West. Nobody wanted to go to a far-off clinic to get stuck by a needle and perhaps even contract smallpox because of it. But the British government hit upon the clever idea of making the vaccinator a persistent domestic visitor. He came to your door without any notice, looking just like everyone else, and began making conversation. Then, while he was admiring the bangles on a little girl's wrist, he would pop the needle into her arm. It was over in a second, and it didn't really hurt. But still the vaccinator was not a popular figure. If a mother couldn't get her children to behave, all she had to do was say, "You know, the vaccinator is coming tomorrow." I don't suppose these dedicated efforts were ever popular, but as a result of them, smallpox began to disappear.

By the time I arrived in this country, in 1959, I was amazed at the nonchalance with which infectious diseases were regarded. With penicillin and the other miraculous antibiotics developed after World War II, the plagues I had grown up with were simply no longer taken seriously. They had been conquered in the West; soon they would be erased from the rest of the earth as well.

In 1959 the World Health Organization announced a daring plan to eliminate smallpox completely. Amazingly, the plan succeeded. After almost twenty years of heroic measures, the last person on the planet with smallpox was found, quarantined, and cured in 1977. On May 8, 1980, the World Health Assembly formally announced that "the world and all its peoples have won freedom from smallpox." Today the virus exists only in research laboratories in the United States and Russia, and there is pressure to destroy those cultures too.

For a while, it appeared that other infectious diseases would suffer the same fate. Tuberculosis, against which the nations of the world declared war in 1960, retreated dramatically in the developed countries for years. Malaria, carried by mosquitoes, seemed doomed by the pesticide DDT. By 1960, the Harvard School of Public Health had completely dropped malaria control from its curriculum. Not one case had been found in this country for years. Even in Sri Lanka, where cases had numbered one million in 1955, the incidence had dropped to a mere eighteen in 1963.

But by then, though very few realized it, the tide had turned. Through the natural mechanisms of evolution, the microbes were becoming resistant to the drugs being used against them. In the case of malaria, the new "supergerm" strains that resisted treatment were also being carried by mosquitoes that had developed resistance to DDT. Drug-resistant strains of tuberculosis quietly spread in the developed world until the *New York Times* announced grimly in 1992, "A Killer Returns." Frighteningly, the new strains have the capacity to activate another new lethal microbe, causing HIV infection to blossom into AIDS. One by one, the infectious diseases that plagued our past for thousands of years are returning, proving much more adaptable than science can ever be. AIDS itself symbolizes yet another variation: new strains of virus, like Ebola, for which no treatment is known, to which we now find ourselves exposed because of the very technological progress that enables human beings to invade ancient ecosystems and carry microbes around the world in twenty-four hours.

In the meantime, of course, we still face the same degenerative diseases which became epidemic in the developed world because of "life-style factors": things we do to ourselves, whether individually, nationally, or globally. Heart disease and cancer are still the biggest of these killers. Heart disease has begun to decline in this country, perhaps because of better diet and public education. Yet John Bailar, a statistician formerly with the National Cancer Institute, observed that "the cancer rate is holding steady and overall incidence is actually rising, even after adjusting for the effects of cigarette smoking" and longevity. "When you look at the whole picture," Bailar said, ". . . the progress essentially disappears."

Cancer, in fact, seems to be one of the diseases that can be traced in large part to industrial progress itself – to the contamination of our air, water, and food by substances like lead, asbestos, and a host of synthetic chemicals (from five hundred to a thousand new ones every year) to which all of us are exposed daily.

I think we have to be very careful, therefore, about boasting that we have made such incredible progress since the Middle Ages. Cancer was not a scourge in those days, you know. Heart disease was rare enough in the seventeenth century that Sir William Harvey noted it as a curiosity. Science has achieved great things, but it has also enabled us to magnify the consequences of our desires to such an extent that our ways of thinking are literally killing us, as prematurely and pervasively as a virulent disease.

Sri Krishna says later, "A person is what his shraddhā is." I would add that a nation is what its shraddhā is, too. This whole planet is what its shraddhā is. The Sanskrit word is *yugadharma,* the dharma of the times. Every age has its characteristic problems, and each epoch, each civilization, has its characteristic kinds of illness. Each, in a word, has its own karma – the often terrifying problems brought about by its beliefs and values and ways of thinking. In these last chapters of the Gita we see the full sweep of this magnificent insight, which lays the responsibility of our global situation at our own feet and then puts its solution in our hands.

श्रीभगवानुवाच ।
त्रिविधा भवति श्रद्धा देहिनां सा स्वभावजा ।
सात्त्विकी राजसी चैव तामसी चेति तां श्रृणु ॥ १७-२॥

SRI KRISHNA:

*2. Every creature is born with faith of some
kind, either sattvic, rajasic, or tamasic.
Listen, and I will describe each to you.*

We have spent some time looking at three stages in individual growth, corresponding to the gunas. Now I want to interpret the same stages on a much broader stage: global in breadth, thousands of years old in the evolution of human nature.

We can place individuals on this scale of development by the way in which they relate to their environment. Even more interesting, we can do the same with a society. This gives us a yardstick by which we can evaluate human progress and our contemporary civilization – its achievements, its values, its needs, and its potential for weal or woe.

The nearest Sanskrit equivalent for "environment" in this connection is *prakriti,* which adds a useful dimension because prakriti is not merely physical. In this volume I have been treating it as a continuum of matter, energy, and mind, rather like a lot of cosmic oatmeal. As *jīvas,* individuals, you and I are part of that oatmeal, even though we may think of ourselves as unique and separate. I have read several excellent books on what we are doing to the environment today, as if the environment is something different from us. It is not: we are an inseparable part of that continuum. What alters the environment alters us; the way we think and act alters the environment. So "environment" in this sense means not only physical surroundings, but the worlds within all of us as well – the aggregate of our thoughts, our hopes, our desires, our fears.

In answer to environmental problems, ecologists often propose that we simplify our lives. But we have to distinguish simple from primitive. On the physical level the two may seem similar – for example, neither may put much value in technology. But in terms of shraddhā, they are poles apart. Tamas is primitive; sattva means simplicity.

The kind of simple living the Gita would favor does not mean turning away from science, scrapping technology, and going back to the Stone Age. Some dedicated romantics get so disgusted with the trappings of modern materialism that they propose something very similar. In India after Independence, I remember, there was a faction that wanted to do away with all machines. At the other extreme were those who thought any machine was worthy of worship, never questioning the sense of replacing men with expensive machinery in a land where work was needed by millions and capital was costly and scarce. Between both extremes was Gandhi, often misunderstood, who gave a place to machines that were useful and beneficial to all, but asked simply that they not be used at the expense of India's unemployed millions or of village self-sufficiency. That is the approach of sattva, where nothing is valued that does not add to the welfare of the whole.

I want to emphasize again that science and technology are neither good nor bad. I am never critical of science. But I am often critical of the uses to which science is put, and deeply apprehensive of making it the basis of our civilization's shraddhā. Science, and particularly technology, makes a good servant but a most obnoxious master. But science can be put in its place. We want to arrive at that delicate balance where science will not deprive us of our humanity but will serve us with humaneness: where it will help us solve our problems rather than add to them or create new ones. This is a difficult balance to achieve, because technological progress is heady stuff. We can get swept away with it and lose our personal relationships, our sense of the unity of life, without ever being aware that we are losing anything at all.

Let me give a tongue-in-cheek sketch of human development from tamas into sattva, from primitive to simple. This is not an attempt at social science. I am not trying to illustrate the development of human institutions, but the evolution of the basic mental state of our species as it gropes toward full expression of the unity of life.

In some Indian languages today, *prakriti* not only means 'nature' but also 'primitive'. My grandmother used to tell us boys, "Don't act *prakratam*": that is, don't behave like a caveman. Caveman living is the earliest, crudest stage of human evolution, tamas. There the human being lives by what he can find. If it starts to rain and he sees a cave nearby, he gets in, just as a leopard might. But if he doesn't see one, he doesn't run around looking; he just gets wet. The idea of an umbrella is impossible; the thought of a raincoat is still in the womb of the future. That is tamas. Even little children are past that stage today: they may play in the rain for the fun of it, but if they don't want to get wet, they immediately put on their raincoats and boots. Yet there are throwbacks. When tamas lays hold of you – say, when you really feel depressed – rain may provoke no response at all. "Who cares if I get wet? What does it matter? Who cares about me at all?" My granny would say, "Don't be a caveman!"

At this stage in the evolution of consciousness, the thought that you can do something about a situation simply doesn't occur. A caveman can't worry about getting in out of the rain; it's hard enough just to get through the day. Food is the same. If you find an apple on the ground, you eat it. If you don't find one, you probably don't even wish for one. Tamas is inert; it takes everything for granted. It can't even connect an apple seed with a full-grown apple tree; how could it? If you told a caveman to cultivate an apple orchard of his own, he would think you meant to dig up a few acres with the trees intact and move the whole lot next to his cave.

This is not really a period in history. It is a stage in the development of consciousness, for which most of us have a time machine. We can travel back to our caveman days. In my university, for example, when a paper was due, there were always certain students who would not have anything to turn in. They had temporarily become cavemen. When I asked, "May I see your paper?" they would show me a stack of clean, white sheets unmarred by human hand. "I've been sitting here every day," they would tell me, "trying to receive some knowledge. But it doesn't come."

Another phenomenon is very common: you have something important to do, and you know you will feel reprehensible if you put it off. But you *have* to do something about that picture in the basement; it has been sitting there for months. Reason inquires, "Why not let it go on sitting?" But instead you spend a few hours picking out an acceptable frame, hanging it, rearranging the furniture to get everything right. I know people who will buy a crafts book and some special tools and make the frame themselves. This is taking a vacation from the here and now, climbing into a time machine and going back to the twentieth millennium B.C.

For a long while, in my professorial role, I thought it quite a poor show for students to indulge in this kind of procrastination. But gradually I began to see that effort *is* almost impossible when you are in tamas. Not being equal to any task is part of what tamas means. So I gradually learned to say, "Poor fellow! He's got caught in Stone Age living." It's like looking at a far-off star; you see it there before you, but you have to remember that you are actually looking fifty thousand years into the past. My problem as a teacher was how to get such students back to the present again. Instead of remonstrating with them, I used to search for ways to help them transform tamas into rajas, not only in schoolwork but in anything.

One characteristic of Tamas is that he doesn't feel tormented by problems, for the simple reason that he isn't aware of them. From a later stage, we can look back and say that tamas is nothing but problems. The mind is undeveloped; it is all darkness. But for that very reason it can't be aware of its benighted state. There comes a stage in evolution, therefore, when we have to develop the mind, even if it brings problems out in the open. We have to develop the art of thinking. Nobody comes into the world with a still mind. We have to be born with a troubled mind; only then can we learn to still it.

There is a close connection here with language. In Hinduism the faculty of eloquent speech is embodied as a goddess, Sarasvatī; that is how precious we deem it to be to the human being. When words are used for a great purpose, they have immense power to stir, support, inspire, and elevate us. If this marvelous capacity had not been developed through the world's great poets, writers, and speakers, civilization would be at a much lower level.

But in the Age of Tamas there are no words, only the kinds of sounds that animals make. The mind is raw. Nobody needs words, because nobody has anything to say. Why have a word for rain if you don't care if it rains? Why have a word for apple if you don't care if it's a turnip, or if you don't care if it's even there at all? You could say "eats" for everything, but why bother? And for those surges of feeling when thought must find expression, there is always "Me Tarzan, you Jane." Imagine what a wonderful relationship you could have if every day, when you couldn't contain yourself any longer, you came out with, "Me Tarzan! You Jane!"

Though it grieves me to say so, I sometimes think this is one area in which our whole culture is hurrying back to the Stone Age as fast as possible. I feel very grieved to see language losing its purity, literature losing its beauty, and communication being reduced almost to a mechanical level. If you want to express your opinion to your legislators today, you can send a note written for you by your lobbyists; after all, it will likely be answered by a computer anyway. If someone you love is in the hospital, why write? Send a get-well card; they have a dozen varieties at any supermarket, which couldn't be more convenient. The message may not be quite right, but all that really matters is that you not send a "dear nephew" card to your grandmother. And when I go to a movie, I feel rewarded if the hero and heroine can find any words at all to express their love. Everything is "I've got this special kind of thing for you, baby" or "Isn't this just *real?*" Soon, when Romeo wants to express his love for Juliet, he will be able to buy a videotape, send it to her, and say, "Watch this." It will be made by professionals, with the words already given and "certain portions prerecorded," as they say; how could Romeo do any better? When there is hardly any communication like this, we should not be surprised if relationships are very much on an animal level.

Speech mirrors thought, and when speech becomes tamasic, thought gradually sinks to the lowest available level. We can already see this happening with television, an utterly tamasic, utterly passive medium. Since about 1960, when television became virtually universal in American homes, millions of young people have grown up on five or six hours of television a day. In *Being There*, based on the novel by Jerzy Kozinsky, Peter Sellers gives a thoughtful portrayal of a man who has been fed a steady diet of television from infancy on. He talks solely in the clichés of soap operas and series dramas; in fact, the only ideas in his head have been supplied by television. Worst, and most startling, his feelings are sluggish. Like the language he lacks to express them, his emotional responses have been reduced to the most primitive kind. Usually he doesn't feel much at all, though he tries to follow his lines. But when something provokes him, his responses are on the animal level: rage, fear, hostility, hunger, raw desire. He watches a tragedy on his street with the same inertness he gives to the evening news: he feels nothing about it, can't say anything about it, and therefore is not likely to do anything about it. If he feels a pang of sensitivity at the time, it lasts as long as writing on water. We do not need to look far to recognize a state of mind in which millions of people live today.

From tamas we pass on to rajas, which I would say is the stage that civilization has reached today. In tamas, we are in a sense unaware of the environment in which we live. We don't know how to cooperate with it, and we don't know how to manipulate it to our advantage either. But in rajas we become aware of our environment and try to "master" it, which is not at all a negative development.

Rajas, for example, is the fellow who discovers fire. Tamas just sits there with the other rocks, but Rajas can't keep idle; he's too active. When he sees two stones, he *has* to strike them together. Suddenly he sees a flash, and the old gray matter starts working. "There must be something inside," he says. "Let's get it out and see what we can do with it." Rajas Prometheus has discovered fire, which means great things are around the corner.

It is the same with eating an apple. Tamas just tosses the core away, but Rajas has to do something with it, so he buries it. After a while he notices a little plant coming up. He is always observant, and always curious about how he can use what he observes. He thinks to himself, "Those leaves look like the ones on the tree where I got that thing to eat. I threw it here, covered it up, and now see what has happened!" Unlike Tamas, he has the capacity to think, to connect, to follow through. He gets more apples, eats them, and buries the cores; after a while he has a few more trees. It is only a matter of time before two-story harvesters are rolling across California's Imperial Valley by the light of the moon, churning up a thousand acres of tomatoes.

Here I would like to pay an overdue tribute to rajas, without which we would never have progressed out of prehistoric inertia. Rajas is a primary force behind the development of civilization. The problem is simply that we have become caught in it. Instead of harnessing its power we have let it run amuck, with the result that rajas, which has the power to solve all sorts of problems, has become the source of problems so terrible that they threaten to put civilization to an end. The crisis we face now is how to progress into the third stage, sattva, in which we learn that we and our environment are one and that the divinity within us is present also in every creature, every aspect of creation. Only when it enters this stage can we call a civilization mature.

When Rajas meets an obstacle, he has to figure out some way to overcome it. That is the secret of his progress. Tamas, by contrast, just gives up. Many, many little aspects of daily living that we take for granted are a kind of legacy to the human race bequeathed by rajas from the dawn of history.

Once in my childhood we went swimming with a boy who did not know how to swim. It didn't occur to us to ask if he knew or not; he said he wanted to come, so we took him along. He wasn't at all afraid of the water, either. We got to the river – seven of us, as I recall – and jumped in. Seven hit the water and went under, but only six came up. For probably a minute, we didn't notice anything. Then suddenly we realized he was missing, and I think that was the greatest fright of my life. We all dived together, and there was our friend somewhere near the river bottom. He gazed at us in a lackluster way without any panic, as if to say, "Why are you fellows in such a lather?" We hauled him up and told him point-blank, "Don't come with us again until you know how to swim!"

That is what happens to Tamas. Rajas fights; he doesn't want to die. He is too agitated to sit quietly waiting for death to take him, so he starts striking out, flailing away at the water; and he comes up. Again the gray matter starts to work: "Hey, if I do this with my arms and kick like that, I can move through the water!" He goes back and tells everybody in the cave, and pretty soon people are swimming.

This is Rajas's great contribution to the development of civilization: he doesn't take anything lying down; he has to fight back. Today, unfortunately, the same quality is his contribution to civilization's mortal problems also. We can harness all the fight of rajas to fight the war within, or we can go on fighting wars without, against nature and against each other: that is the crossroads at which we stand today. The first will take us into the Age of Sattva, the age of harmony, which is entirely within our reach. The second, needless to say, is leading us into disaster.

सत्त्वानुरूपा सर्वस्य श्रद्धा भवति भारत ।
श्रद्धामयो ऽयं पुरुषो यो यच्छ्रद्धः स एव सः ॥ १७-३ ॥

3. Our faith conforms to our nature, Arjuna. Human nature is made of faith. Indeed, a person is his faith.

Even the littlest child has shraddhā; I don't think anyone can function in life without it. It is right shraddhā when we function rightly, wrong shraddhā when we function wrongly; but everyone has shraddhā of some kind, and the whole message of this chapter is that even if your shraddhā is of the lowest kind, you can always elevate it. If your shraddhā is very selfish, you can change it to selfless. If it is violent, you can make it loving. This, to me, is the real glory of the human being: not intellectual achievements or prowess in science or any other external field, but the fact that there is no one on earth who cannot change the meanest shraddhā into the noblest.

Until I took to meditation, I had no idea that this could be done.

I had read that spiritual disciplines could transform the human personality, but this was knowledge 'placed in the head'; it did not affect what was placed in my heart. Like most people with a university education, if I may be permitted a terrible Sanskrit pun, my shraddhā was in *shirodhā*, 'that which is placed in the head' – in other words, in intellectual knowledge, mostly related to literature. That was what I believed in, and it shaped my life: when I had time, I used to spend it reading or going to plays or lectures.

Gradually, however, this faith began to weaken, even before I took to meditation. When a great literary figure came to my campus to speak, I would be seated right in the first row to take in everything he or she said. But when we began asking questions afterward, the answers such people gave seemed ordinary, immature, or misleading. I knew that if I asked my illiterate grandmother the same questions, the answers would be mature and helpful. How could that be? It was terribly unsettling, because though I loved my granny passionately, it was still not she but these literary figures that I wanted to emulate. To take their busts down from their pedestals and put them away in the attic after sixteen or seventeen years of worship was a shattering prospect. My shraddhā was changing, but the change did not come easily.

Yet as my discomfort grew more and more acute, I began to see that my grandmother embodied an entirely different shraddhā than all the other people I had come across. In her understanding of life she towered above every other person I knew, above every literary or intellectual figure I had heard or seen or read. That is the purpose served by a spiritual teacher. She showed me that a human being does not have to be caught in this shallow shraddhā that everything is physical; she taught me to question the very basis of life as it is generally lived.

A British biologist, Sir Peter Medawar, once advised a group of aspiring scientists, "You must feel in yourself an acute discomfort at incomprehension." That is a fine phrase. Most human beings take everything for granted. But there is a particular kind of person – the scientist-to-be, the philosopher, the mystic – who begins to feel increasingly dissatisfied with what the world accepts as real and to desire a deeper explanation, a prior cause. The budding mystic takes nothing for granted. He or she feels puzzled by life and human nature. What are we supposed to do here on earth? Is there a goal? If there is, how are we to attain it? Ordinary people dismiss such questions after a while, but for the mystic they acquire a driving, demanding urgency.

It is the same with changing to a higher shraddhā: it begins with an acute discomfort with the way things are around you. If you look upon yourself as physical and think of life as having no higher goal than the satisfaction of physical desires, you *should* feel uncomfortable. As Gandhi says, it is good not to feel well adjusted in a wrong situation. I think you can often see this in young people: the more sensitive they are, the more uncomfortable they become in today's society. They see no correspondence between the values professed by those around them and the way those people actually live; because of this acute discrepancy, they sometimes do rash or harmful things.

"You are what your shraddhā is." One line gives the secret of personality. Let me give one or two illustrations. For one, if you believe in your heart that by offending and retaliating against people you can "get even," that is what you are going to do. You can read all the books on psychology that you can find, go to any number of therapy sessions; if your shraddhā is "get even," you will act on it everywhere. The tragedy is that people who believe this only succeed in getting uneven, physically, emotionally, and spiritually. They avoid others, and others avoid them because they are so unpleasant. They have trouble working with others, enjoying life with others, sympathizing with others' suffering. How can their personal growth be anything but uneven? The gap between them and those around them will go on widening daily.

This is individual shraddhā. But we can speak of nations too as having a similar shraddhā, one deep-rooted example of which is expressed by that ridiculous proverb, "If you want peace, prepare for war." I think it is the Roman Empire that gave this preposterous shraddhā to the world, and all nations believe it today. It shows what little relationship there can be between what is "placed in the heart" and common sense. If you prepare for war, war is what you are going to get. To my knowledge, never in recorded history has there been a major arms race that did not erupt into war. If you have a gun in your home, you are likely to use it on someone when you are upset; if you do not have a gun, even if you get furious, you will probably just erupt with some unkind words and shut yourself in your bedroom. It is very much the same on an international scale. I read scientists and statesmen voicing the same warning about these massive nuclear arsenals: sooner or later, they are going to be used. But now look at the consequences of that shraddhā! It is horrible enough to have a Thirty Years War, when people lived out most of their lives knowing nothing but devastation, starvation, violence, and continuous social upheaval. That was the consequence of the biggest arms race of the time. Yet by 1914, technology had advanced to such a height that the suicidal arms race in Europe could wreak the same kind of destruction across the whole continent, and not in thirty years but in four. Such is progress that today, a single missile can destroy a city in minutes. In fact, at the end of the twentieth century, the threat of such a disaster may be higher than ever. Instead of two superpowers preparing for a nuclear exchange, we now have countries in the Middle East, Asia, and Africa – several of which are sworn enemies of others – in the "nuclear club." And the stockpiles of the former U.S.S.R. have not only not disappeared; they are negligently guarded and coveted by other nations. The chaos following even a limited nuclear exchange between such countries would make life in France during the Thirty Years War seem like heaven. Yet stockpiling these weapons is called preparing for peace! Gandhi's phrase was "the peace of the graveyard."

If you want peace, the Gita would say, prepare for peace. It should take no great spiritual awareness to see that. Particularly today, we cannot afford to go on selling arms to other countries, pumping weapons into both sides of a conflict for the sake of short-term profit. All this is just preparing for war, which we cannot expect to remain contained within borders on the other side of the globe. Coming from India, I am appealing to countries in Asia and Africa and South America not to purchase these weapons, not even to accept them as a gift, because they are going to be used. That is the shraddhā of weapons and its fruit.

Here is another modern shraddhā of individuals and nations: that life is physical. It leads us to evaluate everything on the basis of appearance. Rajas is typically impressed by size and fascinated by speed. Bigger and faster are always better. If it's good to be buried, it's better to be buried under a pile of rocks and best to be interred in a pyramid. Rajas the First builds the first pyramid-tomb in the world. Rajas the Second builds the biggest. Rajas the Third builds his on higher ground, so it looks biggest, and he gets it done in less time. Soon afterwards the pyramid game is played out and has to be abandoned, which probably brings more praise from the rank and file than any previous development. But Rajas has not learned anything; he is simply moving on to greener, bigger, faster pastures. In our times he finds a way to build tankers so big that their seams give from their own weight, tasteless oranges as big as grape-fruits, bombs that can incinerate thirty Hiroshimas at a tenth of the size it used to take to destroy only one.

Some people, if it takes twenty minutes to walk to town, have to find a way to get there in fifteen. If they cannot find a shortcut, they will design better shoes and find a faster way of walking. But walking is too much effort: one of the ironies of Rajas is that with all his energy, he is constantly obsessed with the idea of getting more and more out of less and less effort. So he thinks and thinks and comes up at last with the ten-speed bicycle, which I still think is one of his finest contributions to world civilization. And after a while comes the car. It's not perfect at first, so how does he improve it? He makes it bigger, and he makes it faster. If you ask, "Why bigger? Why faster?" he won't understand; he will look at you as if you are crazy. Today, coming from a bullock-cart village, I still have trouble believing that I travel to Berkeley or San Francisco at almost a mile a minute. It still seems incredible to me. Yet in this coun-try it seems so slow that some people feel they have to do seventy, eighty, ninety miles an hour. Within my lifetime, it was a miracle to cross the Atlantic by plane at all; now eight hours from New York to Paris seems so slow that you have to build planes that can travel a thousand miles an hour – just to do it, just because it can be done. You have nuclear missiles now that travel fifteen thousand miles per hour, so that a nuclear holo-caust can be over in an hour's time. It is a strange measure of progress.

The whole idea of unlimited progress rests on the prospect of unlim-ited resources. We are seeing that prospect dry up today, but many think it is only a matter of particular shortages: when we run out of oil we can use coal, and so on. But everything is limited, and we are gobbling the earth as if it were ours, all ours, to gobble. Nothing is ours. Nothing on earth belongs to us. We are tenants on earth, nothing more.

Imagine that I am going away for a few days and I ask my friend Bob to stay in my house while I am away. He is welcome to use everything, but when I come back I expect the furniture to be intact and to find something left in the refrigerator. That is exactly what Bob would do, being a good guest. But in this global house we are eating up everything, drinking up everything, and then planning to take the refrigerator to the flea market for sale.

To take just one example, it has taken three billion years for the world to accumulate its petroleum reserves and just one hundred years, in terms of what is economically feasible, to exhaust them. It is as if a man were to spend fifty years of his life amassing such an immense sum – say, ten million dollars – that he can will it to his son in the confidence that even if he makes a few bad investments at the outset, they won't make much of a dent. He gets the money, takes it to an enterprising commodities broker, and one week later he has lost what it took a lifetime to accumulate. That, you would say, is a truly prodigal son. You have to have genius to lose money that fast; you really have to work at wasting it. Yet that is just what a handful of nations have managed to do with the world's supply of economically available petroleum.

In fact, in terms of energy resources, it might be more appropriate to talk about the prodigal father. "There is always more in the future" translates very easily into "I can take whatever I want *now*." That is our shraddhā: *me*. "What do I care what happens in the future? What do I care what is left for my children and grandchildren? They'll think of something. Let them ride bicycles; it's good exercise. Why should I change my vacation plans, my lifestyle, just because of something that might happen thirty or forty years down the road?" That's really the meaning of this attitude, and we are beginning to reap the karma of it. It is lack of love. If we cared about those who come after us, we would not waste anything. If we had a different shraddhā, when petroleum was discovered we would have said, "All our successors are entitled to this – our children, their children, all succeeding generations." We would have used it very thriftily, so that they could do the same. But we do not see so clearly when the children are out of sight, perhaps in other countries. And when they are still unborn, how many of us remember that to consume the present is to steal from the children of the future?

King Faisal of Saudi Arabia, I think, in his spacious, luxurious palace, did not keep flowers on his desk. He kept a little flask of oil, "Allah's bounty," to remind him that all this comes from God. Petroleum does not belong to Aramco or Exxon or Royal Dutch Shell: "The earth is the Lord's, and the fullness thereof." It's not just for those who have the capital or political power or simply armed might to take it; it is for the peoples of the earth, all of them, present and future too. Let them enjoy it also. We don't want villagers in Burma to go hungry because our demand for oil pushes prices beyond what they can afford for fertilizers and machinery. We don't want families in the Soviet Union – or, for that matter, here in the United States – to shiver through the winter because scarce supply and high demand make it profitable for a few to speculate on exotic prices. And we don't want to tell our children, "Sorry, there's no more. While it was cheap we had a great fling with it; everybody did what they liked. You can have what's left: colder homes, restricted travel, oil spills, polluted air, radioactive wastes."

All this comes from the underlying shraddhā that life is essentially physical. From that it follows that the satisfactions of life are physical and external. To enjoy life we have to travel around, have a lot of things, do a lot of things, move, consume, get, hold, and hoard. Why? We cannot bear the thought of reducing, of wanting less, having less, going fewer places, looking inward for satisfaction instead of outward, even though all this is not only necessary now but beneficial. By simplifying our lives we would get more time and energy and interest for working with, loving, and serving other people. Our health would improve; depression, alienation, and boredom would shrink or disappear. If we could only see that, we wouldn't use the phrase "energy crisis" any more; we would speak of an energy opportunity.

Instead we look for other ways to shore up our accelerating consumption. I want you to see the sheer power of this shraddhā, how it is shaping lives and deaths, wars and bottlenecks and political entanglements, all over the globe. It is like a lemming; it *must* get to the sea to drown. Block its path in one place and it will go around or over or under; it will find some way to keep on going. Shraddhā can be just as persistent, just as heedless, just as blind. "Well," it says, "if oil's not easy to get any more, there's always coal. There's always nuclear power." These are the answers you still see in many books. Then they look at the pros and cons of coal, the way a lemming might look at a map and say, "Shall I take D Street to the river, or shall I go down by the quarry and jump in where the current is swifter?" It doesn't think to ask if there isn't something better to do than drown.

Shraddhā is what we believe in; when it changes, the world can be turned upside down. When you go to the store for a couple of loaves of bread, for example, and give a piece of old, green paper in exchange, the grocer accepts that paper out of shraddhā. He believes and trusts that the paper has a particular value; and because of that belief, he not only gives away a loaf of bread for it but gives away his time, his energy, his physical effort, and a lot of other things that are actually necessary or useful – vegetables, milk, cheese, paper towels – in order to accumulate similar pieces of paper, which in another kind of shraddhā he then gives away to a bank. He has shraddhā that the bank will be able to give the paper back when he wants it, though inquiry shows that even a conservative bank will owe many more pieces of paper than it has. And he has shraddhā that everybody else will have the same shraddhā in its value. That is a characteristic of shraddhā: it goes deep, so deep that it is shared by virtually everyone.

We know what happens when faith in even one bank is withdrawn, let alone faith in the banking system. If people start questioning, the system can collapse. Similarly, we know what can happen to a country when faith in its currency erodes: its economy collapses, because no one knows the value of anything. The same is true of shraddhā. When the whole world believes that God lives in every creature, people live and act accordingly; when that belief collapses, as we saw in the last chapter, the very basis of civilization is undermined.

It follows that shraddhā can be changed – upward or down, to use the language of the last chapter – and that when it is, the result is a revolution in outlook. Up to a few years ago, to take a trivial example, everybody believed that the four-minute mile was an inherent human limitation. It was a kind of invisible glass wall: you could approach it, but you could never actually reach it or get to the other side. And while everybody believed this, it was true. People resigned themselves to watching the world record creep up by hundredths of a second, harder and harder to beat as the magic wall got closer.

And then somebody who didn't believe in the wall ran faster. It was humanly possible! Belief in a four-minute wall collapsed, to such an extent that in today's craze for running, mothers and students go out in their spare time and break records that used to be regarded as written in stone by the finger of God. Today nobody is willing to set a limit to how fast a human being can run. There has to be some limit, but no one can find a physiological basis for setting it, and in the meantime records are broken every year.

This is tremendously encouraging. On the one hand, as I shall go on showing, the shraddhā of our times does have ruinous ramifications. But on the other hand, we can shed these ancient, imprisoning, disastrous superstitions as a snake sheds an old, constricting skin in order to grow. When we do so, we shall see such a revolution in human welfare and human happiness that we shall look back on today's civilization as the Dark Ages, despite its microchips and CAT scanners and its hard-won capacity to destroy itself several times over. No one knows to what heights the human being can soar. No one can set limits to what we can accomplish with the immense power for love, wisdom, and imaginative action inherent in us all. Only from a few great pioneers of the spirit – St. Francis, St. Teresa, Mahatma Gandhi – can we get a glimpse of what it means to realize our human potential.

यजन्ते सात्त्विका देवान्यक्षरक्षांसि राजसाः ।
प्रेतान्भूतगणांश्चान्ये यजन्ते तामसा जनाः ॥ १७-४ ॥

4. Those who are sattvic worship the forms of God;
those who are rajasic worship power and wealth.
Those who are tamasic worship spirits and ghosts.

We see life as we are, as our shraddhā is; and we worship the divine as we see it too. As shraddhā grows, therefore, how and what we worship changes also.

Physicists will confirm that the world we perceive through our senses is an apparent world, and dependent on the peculiarities of the senses and their limitations. When I take our dogs for a walk on the beach, for example, we don't really walk in the same world. We don't hear the same things; we don't see the same objects. I see occasional California poppies on the edge of the dunes, scattered among the purple lupine. Muka probably sees just one thing, a blob. Yet my beach is almost deserted, while Muka walks through a dense, rich jungle of separate smells. Neither of us is really walking on Stinson Beach; each walks in a world made by the mind.

It is the same with all the other senses. Here in Northern California, for example, wine tasting is an established profession. The wineries say, "You can blindfold our taster and give him a mouthful of one of our dozens of wines. Simply by holding it in his mouth, he will be able to tell you the wine and sometimes even the year." To me, you know, they all taste the same. I experience one substance; this taster experiences a hundred.

It is a subtle point, but even within the limits of the same five senses, what we perceive depends on who we are – depends, that is, upon our shraddhā. The more attention we give the senses, the more multiplicity we live in and the more separate we feel. But by learning to withdraw attention from the senses, we can discover a level of reality as wholly beyond the sense-world as Muka's world of smell is beyond my own.

This world that we perceive with the senses, then, has only a partial reality. It's not entirely unreal, just as the "solid" body you see with your eyes is not unreal. But the body an X-ray reveals is not at all solid, and that is an equally valid picture of reality. Similarly, when you rise above body-consciousness, the world you see is no longer the same. The world I saw as a student or in my early days as a professor was far, far different from the world I see today. It was not unreal, but I can see now that it had only a limited, partial reality. Then I saw the world; now I see into the world. I see the core of the divine Spirit that throbs at the very heart of life as the Ātman in all creatures – God immanent, as philosophers say – and Brahman, God transcendent. This is how everybody sees at the time of samādhi, and when we become established in samādhi, in the continuing vision of God, this is how we will see always.

This state is beyond the gunas completely. But the man or woman in whom sattva is predominant has some awareness of this divinity under-lying the perceptual world, and that is what the Gita means when it says "the sattvic person worships the forms of God."

First, to illustrate with individuals, let me take people in my village as an example. I am not saying that everyone in my village was established in sattva; not at all. But by and large, the way of life they have followed for centuries is characterized by sattva, and that culture shapes the lives of everyone in it, even those who are rajasic or tamasic.

Take the attitude toward water. Hinduism personifies all the elements and forces in nature, and Varuna is God immanent in water. A good Hindu may not know how to explain this in contemporary terms, but he or she always feels that water is sacred, something to be treated with invariable respect. In Hindu law, these aspects of God have legal personalities. If someone desecrates a temple, the presiding deity can file suit. By the same token, in this country, Varuna could file suit against the enterprises that polluted Lake Erie or Love Canal; that is the practical application of this attitude.

I don't say this is true all over India or that everyone shows the same sensitivity, but in Kerala, as far as I remember, the waters were always pure and clear. People would not foul them or pollute them, simply out of respect. I was pleased to read that an American who visited Kerala recently says this is still true today. The rivers are limpid, the lakes almost pristine in their purity; beaches like Kovalam, he says – I myself have never been there – are enchantingly beautiful and clean. That is what it means to worship the Lord in water: you don't waste it, and you keep it clean.

By contrast, rajas and tamas desecrate water in countless ways. I remember twenty years or so ago when Christine first took me to Cliff House in San Francisco, which looks out over the Pacific Ocean at the mouth of the Golden Gate. The view is magnificent, and I stood there for a long while with my back to the city, looking down the breakers along Ocean Beach and up past Land's End to the towers of the Golden Gate Bridge. Then, suddenly, the sound of the surf was broken by raucous, unearthly laughter. On the other side of the street was a so-called amusement park, from which a huge mechanical woman was broadcasting these chilling recorded sounds. I looked up at her and my heart sank. I recalled the words inscribed over the gate to hell in Dante's *Inferno*: "All hope abandon, ye who enter here." That is rajas, desecrating nature in the hopes of a little more cash.

Since then, I am glad to say, this mechanical monster has gone the way of all flesh. Varuna's vengeance. The whole of Playland was razed, and at the time even condominiums seemed a great improvement.

The sensitivity of sattva provides a way of looking at the world that has all but disappeared from contemporary culture. I read some years ago that ocean beaches in Long Island had to be closed because there was such a vast clutter of "floatable trash" – shredded styrofoam cups, plastic bottle caps, corks, balls, toys, cigar and cigarette tips, disposable diapers, and a variety of other decomposing items that drugstores tidily shelve under "personal hygiene." Similarly, the beaches where I used to walk are often littered with plastic bags, beer cans, broken glass, garbage, and oil. All this is desecration. So, in my eyes, are loud music, smoking, and drinking at the beach – and fishing. I take my walks well before breakfast now, before the crowds arrive with rods and pails: I know they are not cruel, merely insensitive, but it pains me to see people killing time by killing creatures. When you become sensitive to life around you, you will not enjoy even a motorboat in a wilderness area because of the terror and distress the noise brings to thousands of fish and waterfowl.

All forms of nature, the Gita would say, should be respected for the divinity in them. This is sattva, which looks on nature as something to be conserved, cherished, and drawn on thriftily for our needs, something not to be conquered but won over. The asuric attitude, by contrast, is to worship what you can get. Nature is to be conquered: even though, as I think Schumacher points out, nature includes *us*; if we conquer nature, we defeat ourselves. Nature is to be plundered, even though when we plunder nature, we impoverish ourselves.

One corollary of the "there-is-more-of-everything" shraddhā is "Waste what you want." When President Eisenhower was asked how citizens could help get the country out of an economic depression, he replied, "Buy anything." We get the same advice today. It is still a rare voice that suggests we have overgrown ourselves, or points out that we have based our industrial growth on unnecessary, wasteful production. What the economy needs, according to experts and advertisers alike, is for people to buy, buy, buy. Why should we, if we do not want what is offered, cannot benefit from it, or find it detrimental? Even in the case of goods that are useful and beneficial, the Gita would say, "If you don't need it, don't buy it. Leave it for someone else." This is love in action.

Last week, just among my personal friends, I counted five victims of cancer. It made it terribly personal, then, when I read that between seventy and ninety percent of all cancers can be attributed to things we are doing to ourselves, many of them related to unnecessary industrial production. Researchers keep looking for a cancer virus, yet in the last hundred years – mostly in the last forty – we have created some fifty thousand new organic chemicals. Into a global ecological balance developed over billions of years, we have abruptly dumped new substances with the same chemical basis as living tissue, without any idea of what they might do individually or together within an ecosystem or inside an organism like a human being.

The theory of progress held that wealth could go on growing forever, consuming the seemingly infinite resources of Africa, Asia, and South America. It seems not to have entered anybody's mind – except, of course, those of us in Africa, Asia, and South America – to leave those resources to be developed equably and at a reasonable pace. I suppose that as far as empire-builders were concerned, the rest of us were simply sitting on wealth that God had intended for those who knew how to take and use it. Nineteenth-century Europe proved itself well able to do both.

Land is one example I have not touched on. It was thought then that there was no end to it. You could do anything you wanted with it – build on it, cultivate it, graze it, mine it, raze it, erode it, bury waste in it, cover it with asphalt – there was always more. In places like our beautiful California, where resources are abundant, virtually nobody used to talk about limits. Waste didn't matter; it cost more to be thrifty than to be profligate.

Today, of course, it is plain that we are losing cropland on all sides. To me this is a clear signal that the time has come to reduce extravagant waste in the way land is used, and particularly to cultivate cropland with great care and a long-range vision. But these "no-limit-wallahs," as I would call them give a very different answer. *Wallah* is a Hindi word that can be added to other words to make a job title: somebody whose life and livelihood revolve around making, selling, hawking, touting, promoting, or exploiting something. It also has undertones of *chutzpah,* which makes it a very useful word indeed. A used-car salesman, for example, is a transportation-wallah. Encyclopedia publishers are knowledge-wallahs. And these big corporations and think-tank technocrats are no-limit-wallahs; that is their world. "With technology," they say, "you can always get more out of what you've got. Hype the soil with more chemicals; it'll double the yield. Next year you'll need to use more to get the same result, but by that time we'll have something stronger. Use more pesticides too; they work the same way. Get more machines so that you can get more out of cheap, discardable migrant labor. Keep your eyes on the bottom line. Who says we should cut back? When you're big, the only direction to go is up."

The karma for all this is extremely interesting. As so often in matters of ecology, it is just recently coming to light. Overuse of chemical fertilizers, it seems, is very much like abusing drugs: you get Mother Earth hooked. It does mean high yields the first few years, although natural ways have been developed of getting even higher yields. But each hit of phosphate fertilizers, though a shot in the arm for the crops, actually depletes the soil. The next time you need a stronger shot to get the same results, which of course depletes the soil further. Pesticides have similar problems: over a period of time, they actually make crops more vulnerable to pests. You get a kind of superpest that, as one writer puts it, "practically eats DDT for breakfast."

In the meantime, there is evidence that the pesticides are poisoning people, particularly those who work with them. The no-limit-wallahs – including many scientists, largely employed by other no-limit-wallahs – are still sanguine about this. We don't have clear proof yet that more than a few of these substances are poisonous, they say; why get alarmed? This is probably a safe question; it would take a long time to prove them wrong. Central nervous system disorders cannot easily be blamed on any one cause, nor can problems that result from intracellular damage: birth defects, sterility, immune system failure, cancer. By the time epidemiologists can describe convincing patterns – which took decades in the case of cigarette smoke, asbestos, coal dust, and X-rays – these experts will not have to worry about their reputations. If "fame is a food that dead men eat," so is blame. But karma is inescapable, and when one reads the accounts of sterility and birth defects among hired hands working on pesticide spraying operations in California's Imperial Valley, the only reasonable response to these profit-wallahs is to say, "The burden of proof is on *you*." If they can prove that these substances are safe to those who work with them, not to mention those who ingest them, then those substances can be used. But until then, there is no need to go on using people as guinea pigs simply because it produces a tidy figure on the bottom line.

अशास्त्रविहितं घोरं तप्यन्ते ये तपो जनाः ।
दम्भाहंकारसंयुक्ताः कामरागबलान्विताः ॥ १७-५ ॥
कर्शयन्तः शरीरस्थं भूतग्राममचेतसः ।
मां चैवान्तःशरीरस्थं तान्विद्ध्यासुरनिश्चयान् ॥ १७-६ ॥

5–6. Some invent harsh penances. Driven by their passions and consumed by selfish desire, they torture their innocent bodies and me who dwells within. Blinded by arrogance and pride, they act and think like demons.

"Demons" here is the word *asura* again: these are the now-familiar characteristics of Tamas and Rajas, Inc. In fact, these verses seem to have fallen out of the last chapter, which we thought we had done with.

There are two views of the human being, Sri Krishna says. One is the physical, which is the lowest. This view is not inaccurate, especially in the early stages of human evolution. But there is another view, not only held by the mystics but fully realized by them: that the human being is essentially spirit.

The Gita would not say it is wrong to look upon a person as physical, but it points out that this is only the beginning of understanding. Everybody *is* separate physically; that is why identification with the body leads to loneliness, insecurity, and a growing inability to maintain relationships. Ultimately it leads to violence, because physical consciousness on a large scale makes a world of antagonistic individuals, cultural adversaries, economic competitors, and opposing nations. So the physical view of life is not wrong; but it leads to terrible consequences. The higher shraddhā leads us to realize the highest in us; the lower shraddhā leads us lower and lower. Though it is not pleasant, it is perhaps necessary in these terrible times to remember Gandhi's observation that there is no limit to the human capacity for either degradation or exaltation.

If each guna has its characteristic "faith," each has its own ways of worship too. Sattva's is self-sacrifice – putting others first, serving the Lord in all. Rajas and Tamas, however, have a different style. In Arjuna's day, the "bizarre penances" Sri Krishna mentions referred to harsh practices performed in the name of religion, where the body was tormented for the sake of fulfilling some personal desire. This phenomenon has not disappeared, and it is not only in India that it lingers. But I would not hesitate to enlarge the scope of these words to make their application more contemporary, and I will give a couple of examples.

For one, it is not merely metaphor to call smoking an act of worship. The person who smokes is trying to propitiate a craving with the ritual consumption of a cigarette. Those who smoke heavily will tell you that it *is* a ritual. Not only are there particular gestures, but most of the satisfaction is in the performance rather than the smoke. No one really enjoys smoke in the lungs; the relief comes from temporarily getting the craving off your back. "Lady Nicotine, grant me peace of mind just for one hour!" This is what I hear from smokers themselves. If they can't actually light a cigarette, they can get some relief from simply holding one between their fingers or their lips. Such rituals, in the Gita's language, torture the body – and, as this verse adds terribly, the Lord within the body as well.

In the language of this verse, which is rather grim, this is worshipping disease. Instead of lighting incense at an altar, devotees light up tobacco. Their very example is missionary activity, teaching patients and children not to pay attention to the warnings of the surgeon general. We get horrified when we read about a primitive religion sacrificing animals or people, but if I may say so, what is the difference between that religion and this? They say the Aztecs used to toss maidens into wells for the sake of getting a good harvest. Today, being more enlightened, we sacrifice young people of both sexes. According to the World Health Organization, the global tobacco industry spends two billion dollars a year on advertising and promotion, mostly to sell enough young people on the habit to make up for the adults who are quitting. Isn't that sound marketing? Even if they still die prematurely, boys and girls will live longer than their elders; therefore they will potentially buy more cigarettes. Why concentrate your marketing efforts on men and women whose lives, and therefore purchasing power, may soon be cut short by your product? The karma for this kind of reasoning includes about a million deaths around the world each year that can be blamed on tobacco use. In the Gita's language, that is worshiping the demons. Two billion dollars a year spent on ruining people's health!

Adult smoking is still on the decline in the United States – a very promising trend for public health, but dismal news for domestic tobacco companies. Where are the losses to be made up? The women and children of this country are apparently not enough. To bolster the bottom line, cigarette manufacturers are pursuing a much more promising market: the Third World.

"It is in Asia," says John Hughes in the *Christian Science Monitor,* "that most growth for American tobacco companies is taking place. American tobacco exports to Asia were up more than 75 percent last year [1987], boosting sales by a billion dollars." The manufacturers argue that they are not trying to gain new smokers, but simply to get existing Third World smokers to switch to American brands. This should be simple, since everywhere in the media cigarettes are associated with Western progress, prosperity, status, and even sex appeal. But Asian men are already heavy smokers. "Aggressive marketing, the critics charge, may end up capturing a new Asian youth market, as well as women, who have traditionally not smoked."

It is impossible to convey the sense of outrage this kind of manipulation provokes in the Third World. Look at the shraddhā behind it. Health is poor enough in these countries. Life is already short; children are vulnerable from birth. And consumer protection is nonexistent. An earlier piece in the *Monitor* charged that "manufacturers are selling purported low-tar and filter cigarettes in poorer countries with four times as much tars as those sold under the same label in industrial countries." "There is an important moral question," Hughes concludes with understatement, "about browbeating Asian countries to accept American tobacco products which have been ruled harmful at home."

Unfortunately, all of us share some responsibility in these activities. Our tax money pays federal trade representatives to open up these markets, and even within the United States, while the Surgeon General tries to reduce smoking, the Department of Agriculture annually spends millions of taxpayer dollars in bolstering up the tobacco industry.

Of course, ours is not the only government to be involved so deeply. Three of the world's top four cigarette companies are actually public enterprises: the government monopolies of China, the Soviet Union, and Japan. (Rajas is no respecter of politics.) Two billion dollars a year is a lot of money – much of it, apparently, already in public trust. Why not spend it on agricultural assistance to the Third World instead? Corporations have plenty of room to make an honest profit without selling addiction to the poor on a global scale.

आहारस्त्वपि सर्वस्य त्रिविधो भवति प्रियः ।
यज्ञस्तपस्तथा दानं तेषां भेदमिमं शृणु ॥ १७-७ ॥
आयुःसत्त्वबलारोग्यसुखप्रीतिविवर्धनाः ।
रस्याः स्निग्धाः स्थिरा हृद्या आहाराः सात्त्विकप्रियाः ॥ १७-८ ॥
कट्वम्ललवणात्युष्णतीक्ष्णरूक्षविदाहिनः ।
आहारा राजसस्येष्टा दुःखशोकामयप्रदाः ॥ १७-९ ॥
यातयामं गतरसं पूति पर्युषितं च यत् ।
उच्छिष्टमपि चामेध्यं भोजनं तामसप्रियम् ॥ १७-१० ॥

7. The three kinds of faith express themselves in the habits of those who hold them: in the food they like, the work they do, the disciplines they practice, the gifts they give. Listen, and I will describe their different ways.
8. Sattvic people enjoy food that is mild, tasty, and nourishing, food that promotes health, strength, cheerfulness, and longevity.
9. Rajasic people like food that is salty or bitter, hot, sour, or spicy – food that promotes pain, discomfort, and disease.
10. Tamasic people like overcooked, stale, and impure food, food that has lost its taste and nutritional value.

In everything we do, we show our shraddhā. That is why, after some experience, a good spiritual teacher has only to observe for a minute or two to get a good idea of a person's mental state and character.

Likes and dislikes in food are one of the clearest indicators, because of the intimate connection between the sense of taste and the mind. Sattva likes food for what it offers naturally: its food value. What astonishes me is that there should be any other possibility. If food doesn't have food value, what value can it have? In addition it should be fresh, tasty in itself (as opposed to, say, because it is deep-fried and salted), and eaten in moderation.

Sri Krishna's criteria are really good. Sattvic food, he says, should increase our prāna – our energy, our vitality, our strength, our health. That is an excellent definition of nutrition, and a good clue as to how to enjoy eating too. Our shraddhā is that junk food adds to the pleasures of living; "health food," though we may appreciate it, is not widely looked on as one of life's joys. This shows how distorted our values have become. Junk food takes away from the pleasures of living. I have scarcely met anyone who could eat a ripe tomato just plucked from the vine without saying, "Now *there's* a tomato! Why don't they taste like that in the stores?" But when they want to indulge themselves, the same people do not go out and get a fresh tomato from their garden. They want fried, salted, months-old corn chips or some chemical candy with a name so ridiculous that we should be embarrassed to place it on the counter. All this is false shraddhā. When our taste buds are re-educated so that wrong thinking about food is changed, we will enjoy simple, natural foods, delicately prepared, much more than we think we now enjoy junk food. Not only that, we will find it impossible to enjoy "food" that is laden with salt or sugar, harmful, harsh-tasting, or made from petrochemicals. We will not be willing to put into our mouths anything that has been sitting unchanged for months on a grocery shelf.

So the spiritual life does not mean eating foods that are drab and tasteless; quite the contrary. Of course we should take taste into consideration, take into account what is enjoyable. But we should also cultivate a taste for what adds to our prāna, energy, health, and strength, and we should avoid eating something just because we have been conditioned to like it.

"Men and women of rajas," Sri Krishna continues, "like foods that are salty or bitter." The delicatessen is full of them. I do not want to step on any toes, but the reference includes a wide variety of almost universal favorites. Most of you, for example, take beer so much for granted that you may not realize how bitter it is. You may not remember how you had to cultivate a taste for it. In my early days as an English teacher, I once went with a friend into a British pub in India and ordered a big bottle of beer, which neither of us had ever tasted. English literature seemed to flow with beer and ale, and we naturally wondered what these heavenly beverages were like. The waiter really enjoyed the show. At first we couldn't open the bottle, and when we did, we couldn't manage to get anything into the glasses but foam. Finally I got a taste of the stuff, and I think that is when my hair started turning gray. Imagine six-packs of gall and wormwood brewed together!

In India, traditional cuisines include some of the most strongly-spiced dishes you will find anywhere. That is our conditioning: the hotter the food, the better. One great Indian physicist – C. V. Raman, who won the Nobel Prize – shocked us all when he pointed out as a scientist that the mouth is an open wound; we are applying hot chillies to an open wound and then saying while it burns, "How tasty!" This is so ingrained a taste that I have known very, very few Indians who could break away from it. Yet today, just because I have painstakingly re-educated my palate, my own tastes are utterly different. Today I enjoy, for example, asparagus just by itself, fresh from the garden, delicately prepared with the slightest touch of butter. Only sattva knows the real taste of food; rajas obliterates the taste with condiments and additives.

Rajas also enjoys foods that promote bad health. He actually goes after foods that burn and cause discomfort. We may say, "How perverse!" Perhaps, but not at all uncommon. The statistics, which can be borne out by our own observations, suggest that some forty percent eat to the point of discomfort regularly. We eat till we get heartburn, drop a couple of fizzy pills into a glass of water, and rest in front of the TV complaining, "I can't believe I ate the whole thing!" But the next night we do it again, because we think we like the taste so much that we pretend the consequences are not inevitable. If nothing else we put on weight and weaken the will; often we are courting serious diseases down the road as well.

Recently I read an article entitled something like "How to Kill Your Husband," the gist of which was that the salty, fatty "standard American diet" is a statistically effective way to do a man in without ever attracting attention. (It is also an effective way to do a woman in, though it may take longer.) How much of what we consume does *not* promote bad health? If we apply this criterion, considering the evidence that is accumulating against so many items in our national diet – food dyes, preservatives, artificial sweeteners and flavors, empty-calorie nonfoods, and over-the-counter drugs, to say nothing of sugar, salt, saturated fats, fad diets, and alcohol – I don't think anyone would deny that Rajas is a very big buyer in the food world.

And finally we come to Tamas, who, says the Gita, takes a perverse pleasure in foods which are overcooked, stale, or impure. Sri Krishna really knows how to lay it on thick. "Impure" today would include nonfood "foods" and other adulterated items, of which contemporary stores are so full. And "stale" I would extend to canned foods and other items prized for their long shelf life. Those canned tomatoes were not exactly picked this morning. Sattva has a kitchen garden; she goes out before dinner and picks what she needs for the evening's salad. Tamas, always ready for any situation with the lowest denominator of effort, pulls out a dusty can of tomato paste that he has kept handy since last Christmas. The supermarket had it for three months; the tomatoes were harvested and processed into long-lived pulp months before that. Sri Krishna says politely, "I wouldn't call that food." But Tamas says, "It's okay with me!"

Tamas, of course, is not merely the consumer of such foods; he is also the producer. "Convenience foods" are not nearly so convenient for the cook as they are for the manufacturer; their main virtues – that they ripen at the same time for mass harvesting, have thick skins to protect in transit, are uniform in size, color, and shape, and so on – are conveniences for the grower that translate directly into cash.

I have been reading a very entertaining essay by Philip Wylie, whom I used to know primarily as the author of *Generation of Vipers*. I had no idea he ventured into food until I encountered this piece reprinted in

Joan Gussow's excellent collection, *The Feeding Web*. I was interested to see that it was first published in 1954, when the problem he describes was small by the standards of today. Since then food technology has advanced so far as to go beyond food entirely.

"What America eats," Mr. Wylie says, is "handsomely packaged. It is usually clean and pure. It is excellently preserved. The only trouble with it is this: year by year, it grows less good to eat. It appeals increasingly to the eye, but who eats with his eyes?" This is the kind of question that Rajas and Tamas never ask. Sattvic food tastes good *and* looks good; tamasic food doesn't bother about either.

One of Mr. Wylie's illustrations that I appreciated was cheese. Real cheeses, he says, used to be made by many small, local factories, who sold directly to small, mostly local groceries. There were many variations in flavor, but these were enjoyed and even prized. Mr. Wylie doesn't take up the issue of scale directly – this was still in the fifties – but small is clearly beautiful in cheese-making too.

These old-fashioned cheeses, however, "didn't ship well enough." We should always remember to ask, Well enough for whom? Those who eat cheese, or those who make money from selling it? The only reason they had to be shipped great distances and stored for long times was to supply giant chain stores, and the only reason for chain stores is profit. Yet as Mr. Wylie says, "Scientific tests disclosed that the great majority of the people will buy a less good-tasting cheese if that's all they can get. Scientific marketing then took effect"– and scientific processing. Mr. Wylie blames all this on science, but science is neither bad nor good. I would lay the responsibility at the door of greed; science, or rather technology, is only the instrument. This is "science" at the beck and call of profit and "its motto is 'Give the people the least quality they'll stand for'" – which of course is our old friend tamas. If people will buy whatever is offered, then quality is clearly irrelevant. The underlying shraddhā is that the goal of making cheese is making money, which many people, I am sorry to say, would consider too obvious to be questioned. And if quality is irrelevant, then it is only reasonable to concentrate on the things that make a difference: durability, unit cost, uniformity.

"It is not possible to make the very best cheese in vast quantities at a low average cost," says Wylie. I would say it is not possible to make even decent cheese in vast quantities at a low average cost, especially if you want it to ship well and taste the same in Duluth in December as it does in Austin in August. "It *is* possible to turn out in quantity a bland, impersonal, practically imperishable substance, more or less resembling, say, cheese, at lower cost than cheese." In other words, you can't please everybody with one or two strong-tasting cheeses, but you can get almost everybody to accept one or two tasteless cheeses. They won't like them, but they won't be offended by them the way they would be by something with a pronounced flavor.

The identical product could be sold all over the country, and with energy costs not counted, it was so cheap and so much easier to obtain that it took over the market. Thus chain groceries took over the selling of cheese and many other foods, to the extent that independent family-style stores are rare today and real cheese can only be found in gourmet stores. This is the kind of activity that used to make Gandhi furious, and we who buy must carry some of the responsibility. By buying vegetable-gum substitutes, we are telling the marketing managers that we don't want cheese; what we are really interested in is cost and convenience. Who can blame them if they continue to produce this stuff? I think we should all support our small, local storekeepers if they stock things that are useful, even when it means a little extra cost and inconvenience.

Then Mr. Wylie takes on vegetables. "Agronomists and the like," he says, "have taken to breeding all sorts of vegetables and fruits – changing their original nature. This sounds wonderful and often is insane. For the scientists have not as a rule taken any interest whatsoever in the taste of the things they've tampered with! What they've done is to develop 'improved' strains of things for every purpose but eating. They work out, say, peas that will ripen all at once. The farmer can then harvest his peas and thresh them and be done with them. It is extremely profitable because it is efficient. What matter if such peas taste like boiled paper wads?"

In 1954 no one suspected that after twenty or thirty years of this kind of magical tinkering on a global scale, more would be involved than taste. Today farmers around the world have discovered to their cost that peas developed to ripen at once can be wiped out at once. Instead of a large, naturally diverse gene pool, with many different and well-evolved strains resistant to different diseases, we now have only a few hybrids for all the world's crops, controlled by relatively few seed companies. Where formerly only part of a harvest might fail, today a nation's crop can fail – perhaps a region that supplies a global market. Prices soar, small farmers and peasants can be ruined, and the poor can starve. As always, we are surprised at how far the consequences of an apparently beneficial breakthrough can go.

Wylie concludes with a very interesting point. "Of course," he says, "all this scientific 'food handling' tends to save money. It certainly preserves food longer. It reduces work at home. But these facts, and especially the last, imply that the first purpose of living is to avoid work – at home, anyhow." I would say "to avoid work" period. That is the underlying shraddhā of many consumers today, and all of us can name the guna by now.

"Without thinking," Wylie says, "we are making an important confession about ourselves as a nation. We are abandoning quality – even, to some extent, the quality of people. . . . If we apply to other attributes the criteria we apply these days to the appetite, . . . we would not want bright children any more; we'd merely want them to look bright – and get through school fast." And so on. This tamasic shraddhā corrodes our mental state; therefore it affects everything we do. That is the real issue, not taste. How many will understand when the Gita says that working together at home, eating together at home, doing the dishes together at home, are all opportunities for improving the quality of daily living? This is the purpose of work. It requires time, it requires effort, but its real meaning is to bring people together in love and respect.

अफलाकाङ्क्षिभिर्यज्ञो विधिदृष्टो य इज्यते ।
यष्टव्यमेवेति मनः समाधाय स सात्त्विकः ॥ १७-११ ॥
अभिसंधाय तु फलं दम्भार्थमपि चैव यत् ।
इज्यते भरतश्रेष्ठ तं यज्ञं विद्धि राजसम् ॥ १७-१२ ॥
विधिहीनमसृष्टान्नं मन्त्रहीनमदक्षिणम् ।
श्रद्धाविरहितं यज्ञं तामसं परिचक्षते ॥ १७-१३ ॥

> 11. *The sattvic perform sacrifices with their entire mind*
> *fixed on the purpose of the sacrifice. Without thought*
> *of reward, they follow the teachings of the scriptures.*
> 12. *The rajasic perform sacrifices for the sake*
> *of show and the good it will bring them.*
> 13. *The tamasic perform sacrifices ignoring both the*
> *letter and the spirit. They omit the proper prayers, the*
> *proper offerings, the proper food, and the proper faith.*

This word *yajna* is commonly used for the sacrificial offerings of formal worship. But the root *yaj* means simply 'worship,' which, in accord with the needs of the times, I interpret in a broader way. To me *yajna* means self-sacrifice, especially in selfless service, where we offer our time, energy, skills, and enthusiasm to a cause bigger than ourselves. This is the contemporary equivalent of the sacrifices to the Lord that were made in Arjuna's day, and it reveals the Gita's perspective on selfless service. Such work *is* an offering, and how we work and who we offer our service to cannot help but reveal the kind of person we are. These three verses, in fact, could be taught in business administration departments or corporate seminars, for they throw light on the mental states behind our work and actions.

Modern civilization is not particularly concerned with mental states. It is concerned with physical states, physical action, things that can be measured, preferably in dollars and cents. But the differences between this outlook and the Gita's are practical as much as spiritual. When you read in the paper, for example, that a firm has been successful, I don't have to tell you what the writer means: there is a tidy figure at the bottom line. But this is just a small part of the picture. If the firm has been successful by selling cigarettes, the Gita, taking a much longer view, would say it is an utter failure. The mental state behind those sales has to reap disaster, because of all the suffering it has gone to such lengths to sow. In this sense, the man to whom I sometimes go for a shoeshine when I am in San Francisco is a much more valuable member of society than the man or woman who participates in the selling or manufacture of cigarettes, liquor, or weapons.

Take medicine as an example. The very essence of the profession is healing; so we would expect medicine to be clearly a sattvic activity. Yet even here the Gita would say it is necessary to examine the mental state. For one, there are a lot of people in every profession for whom it is not the service offered, but the name of the profession itself that provides the primary motivation. I don't think anyone has ever become a garbage collector because of the name, even if it is changed to "sanitary engineer." Yet the garbage collector performs an essential service. Tagore has a beautiful poem praising the work of the sweepers in India as *yajna*, service of all. In most Indian views of caste, the sweeper is considered lowest; in the West too, I notice, the post is not exactly regarded as lofty. Yet the Gita would rate a sweeper's work very high – higher (here is the surprising side) than that of many professionals whose only interest in their profession is the profit or prestige it promises.

But it is not only motivation the Gita scrutinizes; the attitude with which a person works is equally essential. These are demanding criteria. If you prescribe a lot of drugs, taking the path of least resistance to deal with some symptoms whose cause you hope will go away, you are not practicing sattvic medicine. The name of the proper guna begins with a *T*. Two doctors from our University of California medical school charge that "irrational prescribing has led to tens of thousands of needless drug-caused deaths."

According to books and journals I have read, a lot of these unnecessary prescriptions are written because patients "put pressure on doctors." This makes no sense to me. If a patient puts pressure on you to do something harmful, or at best something wasteful, the answer is often to put more loving pressure on the patient. I know a number of doctors who do just that; they would not practice any other way. Their practice is sattvic. If the patient says, "I won't come to you again unless you give me more Valium," you do him a great disservice by writing the prescription. Not only that, you become known as a doctor who will yield to this kind of pressure. Once the word gets around, you find yourself compromising your ethics several times every day. Virtually everyone, doctors and patients alike, knows that tranquilizers are generally taken not to cure diseases but to mask problems. When doctors prescribe unnecessarily, they are participating in the problem rather than the cure.

What is even more frightful to me is a common attitude toward surgery. I certainly do not deny that surgery has a place in extreme circumstances. But even twenty years ago I used to maintain that most surgical operations are unnecessary, and I am glad to see this view shared today by more and more physicians and surgeons too. Surgery is severe trauma, an intentionally inflicted wound. To be warranted, it must be better than the alternative. Every good surgeon would agree to this, and yet we have to remember that we see what our shraddhā shows us. As I believe Abraham Maslow puts it, if your only tool is a hammer, you approach every problem as if it were a nail. A surgeon is a surgeon because he approaches disease in a particular way, following his bent, his training, and his experience. Where he recommends surgery, because that is how he always approaches this particular problem, an internist might insist on drugs – and I, in turn, might well maintain that neither approach would be as effective as going directly to the mind.

The doctor who uses the fewest drugs possible and recommends the least amount of surgery, within the framework of helping the body to heal itself, is a sattvic doctor. There is a third, related factor: the mental state of the patient, which is vitally affected by those to whom he goes for help. Norman Cousins comments from his own experience: "I've learned never to underestimate the capacity of the human mind and body to regenerate, even when the prospects seem most wretched." A sattvic nurse or physician has to have faith in this regenerative process, with which the body and mind are richly endowed. He or she will never write off a patient as hopeless. I have a long-held suspicion, based on personal observation, that it is even possible for nerves to regenerate themselves. I am not surprised at this, because what happens in the deeper stages of meditation has a far-reaching effect on releasing this regenerative capacity of the body and mind to heal themselves and recover their health and strength. But for this to take place, doctor and nurse have to support what is positive in the patient's own shraddhā and help to change what is negative, so that this healing capacity can be released.

Although this example is taken from medicine, the shraddhā it illustrates can be brought into any beneficial occupation or profession. William James said that human beings like to live far within self-imposed limits, which is very much what shraddhā does. We all have an invisible four-minute-mile kind of barrier in consciousness, setting stringent limitations on what we think we can do and be. I do not say that we have no limitations; to be human is to live in a world of limitations. But I am saying that we do not know what our real limitations are, even on the physical level. We cannot know until we try to push them outward. That is what the mystic can do. Meditation, the mantram, and the allied disciplines slowly expand every limitation that our old, surface-level shraddhā imposes on us. They don't get us out of the cage, but they make it larger and larger. When you go deep in meditation, you begin to see that so-called irreversible disease processes can sometimes be reversed, "ingrained" biological drives can be transformed. Even the aging process can be pushed far, far back. We cannot live forever; but no one, I would say, knows how long life can be extended by a man or woman who has got hold of the source of prāna and is leading a selfless life. In other words, there are tremendous possibilities inherent in the human being, in every human being, even on the physical level.

Mr. Cousins, I think, glimpses that the key to this is shraddhā, for he continues: "It is possible that these limits will recede when we respect more fully the natural drive of the human mind and body toward perfectibility." This natural drive is what the sattvic doctor and nurse try to harness, what the whole medical profession should try to harness. But it is not only a biological drive, and the same shraddhā – an unshakable faith in every human being's inalienable capacity to grow – is characteristic of the sattvic man and woman in all the helping professions. "No medication they could give their patients," says Mr. Cousins again of physicians, "is as potent as the state of mind that patient brings to her or his own illness. In this sense, the most valuable service a physician can provide for a patient is helping him to maximize his own recuperative and healing potentialities." Medicine is only one example; we could supply many more.

That is Sattva, who naturally thinks of work in terms of what he can give. Rajas, by contrast, thinks about what he can get. These strands are commonly mixed in each of us, and even a person with a good measure of sattva can have a dangerous element of rajas too. I have been reading a biography of Aldous Huxley, who had many factors favorable for a spiritual aspirant: a brilliant, searching intellect, a great cultural legacy, the Huxley family background, a keen interest in mysticism, a literary gift, and the opportunity of close association with a very good spiritual teacher, Swami Prabhavananda, whose own teacher was a direct disciple of Sri Ramakrishna. With books like *The Perennial Philosophy* and *Ends and Means*, Huxley did great service in presenting spiritual values to the West. But he also had a powerful rajasic element which led him to experiment with psychoactive drugs; and because he was so widely respected as an exponent of mysticism, his example encouraged a great many people to treat drugs as a route to instant enlightenment – a development whose fruits we are only beginning to see. When we have talents like this and the opportunity to influence people, we have to be particularly vigilant over everything we say and do. If we encourage others, even unintentionally, in ways that lead them or those around them into danger, part of their karma is ours.

Wherever rajas is present like this, the Gita says, action is tainted to that extent. But real trouble arises with work that is *primarily* rajasic, work undertaken solely for personal gain. We have had dozens of illustrations of this so far, and there are unfortunately many others to which attention should be called. The activities of what I have been calling Asuric Enterprises, such as dumping dangerous products on Third World markets – including nonfood "foods," hazardous drugs, tobacco products, weapons, and nuclear technology – fall into this category. In such cases, the element of rajas is compounded with tamas. We are in it for the profit, which is rajas. But it is tamas that makes us so insensitive that we do not care about, may not even notice, the human costs of what we do.

देवद्विजगुरुप्राज्ञपूजनं शौचमार्जवम् ।
ब्रह्मचर्यमहिंसा च शारीरं तप उच्यते ॥ १७-१४ ॥
अनुद्वेगकरं वाक्यं सत्यं प्रियहितं च यत् ।
स्वाध्यायाभ्यसनं चैव वाङ्मयं तप उच्यते ॥ १७-१५ ॥
मनःप्रसादः सौम्यत्वं मौनमात्मविनिग्रहः ।
भावसंशुद्धिरित्येतत्तपो मानसमुच्यते ॥ १७-१६ ॥

*14. Offering service to the gods, to the good, to
the wise, and to your spiritual teacher; purity,
honesty, continence, and nonviolence – these
are the disciplines of the body.*
*15. To offer soothing words, to speak truly,
kindly, and helpfully, and to study the
scriptures – these are the disciplines of speech.*
*16. Calmness, gentleness, silence, self-restraint, and
purity – these are the disciplines of the mind.*

Sri Krishna is about to speak of three kinds of spiritual aspirants, but
first he singles out three levels of sādhana: action, speech, and thought.
This is a useful distinction, but I want to stress that these three are separate only on the blackboard. In our lives, they have to be
practiced together.

Even in the first verse, which concentrates on the physical level
of sādhana, my emphasis is on the mind. Jesus and the Buddha too
emphasized that the mental state behind our speech and actions is
at least as important as what we say and do. Perhaps it is even more
important, since sooner or later every mental state has to bear fruit in
speech and action.

Pūja in the first verse usually means ritual worship, but the underlying meaning is deep reverence. The Gita is telling us what kind of people
deserve our love: that is, what kind can give us a model for living, a
shraddhā of human purpose higher than personal gain. I think this is
one of the greatest handicaps young people face today: very, very few
grow up with a living example of these timeless values. When we look
at the papers or at magazines or books, when we watch TV or go to the

movies, we see such an utter vacuum of ideals: no one whose life we can emulate, in whose footsteps we can follow. Entertainers, business leaders, politicians, and sports figures are often held up as models in the media. They attract attention in one small sphere of activity, so people want to be like them in everything. How seldom do we see anyone who has made his life itself a work of art! These are the men and women who truly deserve our love and emulation: those who know how to live with good will for all, how to work hard for the welfare of all, without being subject to selfish whims and caprices, resentments and personal vanities.

In my own life, though I had opportunity to meet many well-known figures, the one person who embodied all these principles of living for me was my granny. That is the vital role played by a spiritual teacher, who in a sense lives in a glass house. My grandmother did not sequester herself away; she chose to live right in the midst of people, participating in all their activities, sharing their joys and sorrows – the "tremendous trifles" of their lives, as Chesterton used to say – and in the midst of all that, to show them quietly how to live. There was an utterly natural artistry about this which I never saw fail her. As I became aware of it, I began to desire consciously to strive to become more and more like my teacher. That is why the Hindu tradition has emphasized for centuries that it is not enough for a spiritual teacher to preach spiritual values; he or she is expected to live them out, every moment of every day. Even if all the scriptures were lost, the tradition goes, we could reconstruct them from just one illumined man or woman's daily life.

श्रद्धया परया तप्तं तपस्तत्त्रिविधं नरैः ।
अफलाकाङ्क्षिभिर्युक्तैः सात्त्विकं परिचक्षते ॥ १७-१७॥
सत्कारमानपूजार्थं तपो दम्भेन चैव यत् ।
क्रियते तदिह प्रोक्तं राजसं चलमध्रुवम् ॥ १७-१८॥
मूढग्राहेणात्मनो यत्पीडया क्रियते तपः ।
परस्योत्सादनार्थं वा तत्तामसमुदाहृतम् ॥ १७-१९॥

17. When these three levels of self-discipline are practiced without attachment to the results, but in a spirit of great faith, the sages call this practice sattvic.

18. Disciplines practiced in order to gain respect,
honor, or admiration from the world are rajasic. They
are undependable and transitory in their effects.
19. Disciplines practiced to gain power over others, or
in the confused belief that to torture oneself is spiritual,
are tamasic.

Even among spiritual aspirants, Sri Krishna says, you will find three types, according to the dominant guna.

The lowest place on the ladder, of course, is reserved for Tamas, who may scarcely know why he is practicing spiritual disciplines at all. His understanding of them is mostly physical. Such misunderstandings can cause serious problems, particularly if an aspirant does not have a good, reliable, loving teacher to whom he or she gives undivided loyalty and respect. Those who are acutely aware of their physical existence, who live for the satisfactions of the senses, soon find that separateness becomes a compulsion, a kind of cult from which they cannot easily escape. Even so, by the draw of the spiritual teacher's love and personal example, a good teacher can often manage to instill a higher shrad-dhā – a self-image that is spiritual rather than physical.

The practical purpose of the theory of the three gunas is to show us how to change. Nobody is stuck in a negative state. Even to some-one who suffers from acute emotional paralysis, sunk in lethargy and unequal to any challenge, the Gita offers boundless hope. It does not play Pollyanna. "Sure," it agrees, "that is your present condition." The analysis is as precise as a doctor's diagnosis: "You are in the state of tamas; those are the signs and symptoms. You're a block of ice." Don't we say of someone who is emotionally paralyzed, "He's a very cold person"? Or of someone who can't form relationships, who can't find herself a place in life, "She's got an icy personality"? But the Gita not only gives the diagnosis, it also presents the cure. Just as a glacier can melt into a mighty river, tamas can thaw, turn into rajas, and be harnessed into sattva – by any of us, if we are willing to put in the effort it requires.

I have to repeat this reminder frequently, because we are so condi-tioned to believe we are stuck with the problems and personality we have today. Most of us are not emotionally disabled. But almost everyone experiences a kind of sporadic paralysis where it seems impossible to make an act of will and do something we dislike, especially when it is for someone else's benefit. We are, to coin a phrase, "tempoplegics," temporarily disabled. There is a kind of heat therapy for this problem, and the Sanskrit name for it in these verses is *tapas*. The word means 'heat' and also a fiery self-denial. Training the senses and putting other people first, going against your likes and dislikes, are all comparatively palatable forms of tapas in my presentation, and they generate great power. In this sense, meditation is a kind of electric blanket. When you feel lethargic, wrap it around you and turn it on; the ice will begin to melt. If you don't even care whether it melts or not, turn your meditation up higher. If your concentration is good, you *have* to have more energy; you may even feel the heat inside. That is transforming tamas into rajas.

These verses, with the previous three, give some very important instructions for entering the deeper stages of meditation. There is a significant difference between what I call the first half of sādhana and the second. In the first half, we have a wide margin for making mistakes. But in the second half, the margin becomes very narrow. What may seem a small mistake in the eyes of the world can then become quite large; and if we slip and fall, the suffering is that much greater because we are falling from a greater height.

In every tradition, mystics sound severe cautions to alert us to the danger of serious lapses in these latter stages of the journey. The point of these verses is to remind us to be vigilant about every aspect of our sādhana. Then, when the inevitable challenges come – challenges that will try us to the utmost – we will be able to keep our eyes on the goal and face them bravely without a slip or backward glance.

In the early years of meditation, most of our efforts are on the surface. We need to be regular, sincere, and enthusiastic, but whatever progress we achieve is still on the everyday level of consciousness, where the will does not operate much. This is true even of those who are intellectually trained or highly cultured. But after some years of immense effort, the rocky surface of the ego slowly begins to yield. At that time there are many symptoms in meditation – drowsiness, sleep, even blackouts – of which you may not be aware. But if you persist and break through the surface, you will be rewarded by a change in the level of consciousness on which you live. You will find you are a little more aware of the unity of life, a little less aware of the separateness in which you have been imprisoned. Without exaggeration this is a different world altogether. You have to learn all over again how to walk there, just as an infant learns to walk for the first time.

To facilitate this learning to walk, I usually give a number of practical suggestions. One, be sure you have enough selfless work to harness the energy released and channel it toward the welfare of all. A deeper level of consciousness brings more resources, more energy; if these are not utilized selflessly, they are going to cause trouble. The deeper your meditation, the harder you need to work. In fact, one of the simplest ways to assess your meditation is to look at your performance at work. How punctual are you? How concentrated? How harmoniously can you cooperate with your co-workers? Can you work with complete concentration, yet still drop your work at will when the time comes to drop it? The answers to questions like these tell a lot about interior progress.

Second, be sure to get adequate physical exercise. The deeper your interior life, the greater the need for vigorous physical activity. This is often forgotten. People sometimes fall into a kind of lethargy in the mistaken belief that this is what it means to work without tension, or even that it will benefit their sādhana. It is just the opposite. The body is our instrument of physical service, and it thrives on vigorous movement. If you are young or already in good condition, "vigorous" here means *vigorous*. Swimming, running, and fast-paced sports that require concentration are all excellent exercise. But unless you are in condition, please do not jump into such activities immediately. Work up to them gradually. If you are over thirty-five or have any particular physical problems, ask your doctor to start you on an exercise program.

Third, it is essential to be with other people. There is a widespread impression that to lead the spiritual life, you have to be a lone wolf. Again, the truth is just the opposite. Only when we have close relationships with other people can we reduce self-will in being more patient, forgiving, and kind, which is the very heart of sādhana.

Nutritious food, adequate sleep, and vigorous exercise are all important in sādhana. But even where such physical requirements are concerned, vitamin W – the will – is absolutely essential. Your body may be strong and resilient, you may be getting a perfect balance of amino acids and trace minerals, but if the will is not unified between the conscious and the unconscious, the latter stages of meditation can become too oppressive for the body to bear.

No example illustrates this more vividly than the transformation of sexual desire, which continues into the final phases of sādhana. The Sanskrit word for this transformation in these verses is *brahmacarya,* and although it is included here with the physical disciplines, it is essentially a matter of disciplining the mind. *Brahmacarya* is usually translated as 'sex control' or 'continence', but its literal meaning is 'conduct that enables us to move closer to the Lord.' Sex is sacred, a sacred source of power. The reason mystics everywhere place such emphasis on control of sexual desire is that the journey of sādhana is so arduous, so demanding, that we need to draw on every trace of its power to reach the goal. If you want to rise to your full height, if you want to love to your full depth, then try gradually to master sex. Try to harness it, not to strangle or suffocate it, so that this immense power is released to flow towards all in love. Every time you put someone else first, you draw on a little of this power and transform it. Tenderness, patience, selfless service, hard work for others without thought of personal reward – all these harness the raw energy of sexual desire and help to transform it, little by little, into an abiding flow of joy.

I need to repeat this over and over, because it is so foreign to our conditioning: If you feel strong sexual drives, congratulations. If you feel haunted by sex day and night, you are a person rich in resources. It's like striking oil in your backyard; you have a little Arabia to supply you with all the power you need. Just as with everybody else, it took me many years to understand this simple truth. I too was conditioned by the media, by poetry and drama and all the literature of romance. Only when I began to see how vast were the resources that the mastery of sex could release into my hands – to benefit everyone, to serve everyone, to lead a long, healthy, vigorous, creative life, always in security, always in joy, and never afraid of the challenges of life – only then did I begin to ask for my teacher's grace: "Make me like you!" It didn't happen naturally, and it certainly didn't come easily; it required years of valiant combat, ceaseless vigilance. It is terribly hard, almost impossible: that is its challenge. But it can be done; and when sex is transformed, the Hindu scriptures say, it is like fire transformed to light: every moment, every relationship, is suffused with joy.

दातव्यमिति यद्दानं दीयते ऽनुपकारिणे ।
देशे काले च पात्रे च तद्दानं सात्त्विकं स्मृतम् ॥ १७-२० ॥
यत्तु प्रत्युपकारार्थं फलमुद्दिश्य वा पुनः ।
दीयते च परिक्लिष्टं तद्दानं राजसं स्मृतम् ॥ १७-२१ ॥
अदेशकाले यद्दानमपात्रेभ्यश्च दीयते ।
असत्कृतमवज्ञातं तत्तामसमुदाहृतम् ॥ १७-२२ ॥

20. Giving simply because it is right to give, without thought of return, at a proper time, in proper circumstances, and to a worthy person, is sattvic giving.
21. Giving with regrets or in the expectation of getting something in return is rajasic.
22. Giving at an inappropriate time, in inappropriate circumstances, and to an unworthy person, without affection or understanding of what it means to give, is tamasic.

St. Francis tells us, "It is in giving that we receive." But the shraddhā of our times is that it is in grabbing that we receive. Very few people today, I think, believe that giving for the sake of giving is even possible for a human being, let alone desirable. Dr. Hans Selye, a good man determined as a biologist to be "realistic," finds nothing higher in human nature than "altruistic egoism": give your best so that you may receive the best from others. This is perhaps the highest view we can take when we believe that human nature is wholly physical. But the shraddhā of St. Francis reaches vastly higher, to show us our real human stature.

In these verses, therefore, I take the broadest view of giving. *Dāna* here does not mean only gifts that are wrapped in decorative paper and tied with ribbons and bows. It can also refer to giving support, love, time, attention, or skill. And though I shall begin by describing individual giving, the scope embraces business, charity, public aid, and all the service professions.

Sattva provides the standard. Sattvic giving, simply put, helps the other person to grow – which, of course, is something that cannot be clearly seen without detachment. As Sri Krishna says here, you must understand the time, the place, and the person to whom you are giving. The application is startling, for it often leads to just the opposite of what we would ordinarily do. To someone who is compulsively attached to money, for example, money is the last thing we should give. It would only strengthen the samskāra, deepen the compulsion. Similarly, to someone compulsively attracted to pleasure, opportunities to indulge that compulsion are not a sattvic gift; they would make that person more selfish.

This is easier to see with children than adults, perhaps because we can be more objective about child development than we can about adult development. When Christmas or birthdays come, a sattvic parent reflects on the effect a particular gift is likely to have on the child to whom it is given. If a child has a compulsive eating problem and we indulge that problem – giving special sweets, enrolling her in the Truffle-A-Day Club, making sure he gets acquainted with each of the hundred and thirty-seven flavors of ice cream at the store – then we are strengthening that compulsion, which to me is scarcely a sign of love.

In my own home, my grandmother was the only person who could discriminate so clearly that she never gave us children anything that would spoil us. I did not have many toys as a boy. I did not have many books, though I loved to read; I used the school library. I didn't have a bicycle until I went to college. For a long time I thought my granny was really ungenerous, perhaps even unaware of my needs. Only as I grew up did I realize that she was continuously giving me everything I truly needed to grow to my highest stature. Ultimately, hers was what the Buddha calls "the gift of dharma," which is the highest gift a human being can offer or receive. We get awed today when somebody gives a million dollars to endow a new performing arts center or a college library. But by the Buddha's standards, no gift is so precious or so permanent as the gift of living in accordance with the supreme law of life.

The right gift for a child, of course, varies very much from person to person. But I can make one or two general observations. I am not much of an admirer of giving children machines for toys; it does not help their creativity. An elaborate electric train, for example, is an electric train and nothing more; it will go round and round without any help from a child's imagination. The same is true for computers and computer games. There is plenty of time in life to learn to write your own program for balancing a checkbook, and not much is lost if you never get around to it, no matter what people say today. Childhood is the time for activities that foster imagination, not ingenuity; creativity, not cleverness: for broadening and deepening the faculties that enable us to identify readily with other people and other creatures, to sympathize and support and feel their joys and their suffering as our own. All these things are essential if a child is to grow up secure, loving, and loved. One of Gandhi's basic principles of education was that a child's hands should be taught as well as his head. I agree completely, but I would say "Head, hands, and heart."

If any return is expected when a gift is made – praise, prestige, a business favor, increased sales, a sense of obligation – that giving is not sattvic. More than twenty years ago, when the Blue Mountain Center of Meditation was founded, Christine and I decided we would never accept a gift that had strings attached. Time and circumstances have more than justified our stand. Of course we needed money as our activities expanded; we still need and value financial assistance today. But we always make sure that the person offering to help us is not prompted by any personal motive; otherwise it would not help that person to give it or us to accept.

Rajasic gifts, on the other hand, are "business gifts." You sit in closed session with the board and decide how much you can get by making a generous donation. Will it help your tax situation? Or, to use a good American expression, are there any kickbacks? (The word reminds me of a horse.) Are there favors that can be exchanged? Unfortunately there is no such thing as a free lunch anywhere in life, particularly for those who are interested only in personal pleasure or profit. Isn't it Walpole who says that all such men have their price? The price is karma. They may be honored with a statue or get their names engraved on cornerstones, but as far as karma goes they will receive no reward. The Karma Telegraph boy comes in singing, "He has given a thousand pounds, a thousand pounds, a thousand pounds, and so he expects to be knighted"; but that is all: Chitragupta, the Cosmic Auditor, doesn't so much as make an entry. To get good karma for giving, you must have no desire for personal benefit from it. Only then does it become *nish-kāma karma*, an act untainted by selfish desire.

More than that, Sri Krishna says, no one benefits from giving grudgingly. Suppose, for example, you are working in your garden, doing exactly what you like, and your neighbor comes over and says, "Can you help me get the spare bed down from the attic? Aunt Agatha's going to be here in two hours and I don't have anything ready." You wanted to finish watering before the sun gets too hot, and part of your mind says snippishly, "You've been expecting Aunt Agatha for a week! Why didn't you get the bed down earlier?" But you've been reading the Gita, so you say with half a will, "All right, if it won't take long." Sri Krishna says cheerfully, "Sorry, no credit for that either."

My granny understood these things intimately, though she did not know how to put them into words. When I was, say, reading *Ivanhoe*, which was much more important to me than helping my granny, she would call me and say, "Would you go to the bazaar and get a couple of coconuts for me to take to the temple?"

"Granny," I would say like any other boy "don't you see I'm reading?"

"Yes," she would say, "but this is more important."

"All right," I'd say, "I'll go." I would take the money and walk along slowly to the bazaar, and meet a couple of friends on the road and talk to them for a while, and stop to admire an elephant bathing in one of the village tanks, and all the time my granny would be waiting. When I finally got back, all she would say was, "That took you long enough." I didn't understand the satire. It was just a child's inability to understand another's needs, so that although I loved her, I didn't realize that my granny's needs *were* much more important than mine.

But later on, as I began to understand more, it dawned on me one day that I needn't wait for her to ask me; I could go to her first. The moment I understood something, I always liked to put it into practice. "Granny," I asked, "do you need anything for the temple today?"

"Aren't the boys playing soccer today?"

"Yes," I replied, "but I want to do your job first."

She said simply, "You've grown."

That was her way of teaching: letting me make my mistakes, showing me by her example how to avoid making the same mistake again, always keeping faith in my capacity to learn to read the unwritten lessons of her life.

Last Sri Krishna describes tamasic giving, and he covers all the bases: "things done at the wrong time, in the wrong place, in the wrong way, for the wrong person." Any way you look at it, Tamas can't win. To a nephew who has to have everything he sees, Uncle Tamas gives money; he doesn't want the boy ever to feel deprived. What lack of love! He might as well write on the greeting card, "I want you to stay crippled, so life will be more difficult when you grow up." His teenage children have a lot of irons in the fire, so he buys them each a car. "Why should I make them suffer?" he says. "I've got the money; let them enjoy themselves while they can." My grandmother would reply, "You're handicapping them. You're not helping them to grow. They need to learn to work; they need to learn to give. All you're helping them do is learn to take."

Even with small children, her way of playing with them was to let them participate in the work she was doing, which they enjoyed immensely. Children like to do real things. I remember nights before a big feast when she sat up at night cutting vegetables. She used to ask the little girls to come sit around her, and then she'd start them shelling peas. When you do this with children, you know, half the peas go into the bowl and the other half into little mouths. "That's all right," she would say. "We'll give you more peas." She wasn't trying to get the peas shelled faster; she was teaching them her own shraddhā of work. And in the book of karma, it is not written that Martha gave fifty units while Matilda gave only ten. All it says is "Martha gave; Matilda gave." What matters is shraddhā – the mental state behind the giving.

We can look at medicine too – in fact, at almost every human activity – through these verses; their application is sweeping if you know how to read between the lines. Medical care is a kind of giving, and all these criteria of Sri Krishna's provide interesting ways of evaluating what experts today are pleased to call "health care delivery." Overprescribing powerful drugs or resorting to unnecessary surgery, as I said earlier, is tamasic. People talk a lot about Medicare; they should worry more about Tamocare.

Rajas, on the other hand, is found where the physician or surgeon is motivated primarily by money, prestige, or a need for power. When I was still new to this country, I remember sitting in one of those tiny hospital rooms wearing nothing but a nice paper suit, waiting for probably half an hour. (Later I was told that in the drop-in clinic, people sometimes wait half a day.) Since I knew how to meditate, after a while I closed my eyes and just went in. When the doctor finally came, *he* had to wait, which he was not accustomed to doing. He gave me a few minutes, cleared his throat a few times, then scraped the chair back and forth and tapped his thermometer. I scarcely heard; my senses were all closed down. Finally I opened my eyes, and we got to talk about this problem of keeping people waiting. He actually said, though not in so many words, that it reassures him if he can make a patient wait; it puts the patient in his proper place. That one remark told me something about his mental state, how much security he actually had.

"You know," I said, "my way of reassuring myself is to turn up a little ahead of time whenever I can." He understood, and he saw the love behind it too. Keeping people waiting, especially when it is done deliberately, is another form of unkindness.

In any profession, building yourself up at someone else's expense is partly rajasic, partly tamasic: rajas contributes the insecurity, tamas the insensitivity. Many thousands of people, particularly those on lower incomes and the elderly, have to put up with this kind of treatment on a massive scale in getting health care today. I probably do not need to tell you that a child with a sore throat may mean hours of waiting in room after room, standing in line, waiting for forms to be found and filled out and filed again, waiting for the doctor, the nurse, the clerk, the pharmacist, one more faceless unit in the day's outpatient statistics. That is asuric health care on a terrible scale, with far-reaching effects on the wellness of the nation.

I don't by any means say that this is characteristic of doctors in general. But there are many who by their own confession go into the profession for the money it can bring or the prestige. That is Rajocare, and it need not be bad care either. If there is a lot of tamas mixed in also, you get the kind of doctor who keeps you coming back again and again while he palliates symptoms, or who orders unnecessary surgery just because it carries a big price tag or gives him a chance to show off his skill. But a purely rajasic doctor is not of this sort. He gives good care and attention, the best he can, to see that the patient really benefits, and he charges accordingly – he gets his time and money's worth too. A highly trained specialist may be like this. As long as he or she is good and the charge is reasonable, we can appreciate this kind of care.

But sattvic care is the highest. The sattvic doctor is interested in getting at the root of a health problem, not merely in treating the symptoms. If her patient has high blood pressure, she won't simply prescribe an antihypertensive. She will want to help him get his weight down, eat better, get more exercise; she may even encourage him to meditate, learn to manage stress, and change the wrong ways of thinking that contribute to chronic high blood pressure. This is the kind of care that I am interested in, and I hope someday to make a lasting contribution to it with the help of my medical friends.

Again, we can apply these verses to international assistance. Among tamasic gifts is the supply of armaments to other countries, often as a "token of friendship" or of "mutual alliance." One of the motives in tamas is to injure, and whatever the intentions may be, the result of giving arms as "aid" is that the recipient nation is injured instead of helped. In the Middle East, particularly, we have had several recent examples of how pumping arms into an area increases tension, heightens insecurity, and provokes so-called preventive wars with highly destructive weapons that bring suffering not merely to soldiers but to whole civilian populations.

For anyone looking at this kind of activity with detachment, the consequences can seem to involve a karmic justice. In my own lifetime, I have seen weapons that have been sold into some far corner of the world for defense purposes eventually find their way into another corner of the world where, in an unforeseen shift of alliances, they are used against one of the donor's allies or even against the donor itself.

Rajasic aid is a little better. It consists in selling goods or services in the donor's self-interest. What is sold may or may not be beneficial to the recipient, at least in the short run – rice, wheat, steel. But the purpose of the exchange is to benefit the donor: to make a profit or consolidate power or change the balance of trade or bolster a sagging regime. This kind of aid is tainted even when the goods or services are not harmful, because they are given in condescension and with an intent to increase the dependency of the recipient. Often the underlying motive is less than generous, and the net result less than beneficial.

In such activities there can be a large element of tamas as well, especially when foreign aid becomes an instrument of pressure or coercion as it did in Cold War conditions. The U.S. has used "gifts" of surplus grain this way, doling them out to countries most pliant to its perceived interests. During the drought of 1965, for example, when India planned to develop its own fertilizer industry so as not to be so dependent on imports, the American government responded by putting food shipments to India on a month-to-month basis. The *New York Times* commented, "Call them 'strings,' call them 'conditions,' or whatever one likes, India has very little choice but to agree to many of these terms."

In other cases, the United States has put pressure on a country to pay for its "gift" of wheat with a particular commodity – say, coffee – which forces agricultural production of that country to concentrate further on export crops at the expense of domestic foods. This too suits the interests of the donor, since it can sell such countries the food they do not grow for themselves. These are complicated issues, but rarely is the motivation what the Gita would call pure.

Sattvic aid, by contrast, furthers self-reliance. It may be skills or expertise or technical knowledge at an appropriate level of technology that helps the recipient nation to help itself. It carries no burdensome price tag; it depends on no burdensome supply of external resources like oil; it simply makes good use of what is locally available.

In this connection, I might point out that many Third World countries are as long on labor resources as they are short on capital and the elements of modern industrial technology. What sense does it make to build a big factory in Africa, financing a lot of expensive technology with years of debt, so that ten men can do the work of a hundred in turning out products for foreign exchange? Why not give the hundred men jobs, even if they actually do the work by hand, and produce things that are needed locally, made from local materials?

These are not criticisms of the United States. All great powers tend toward rajasic "giving." I chose these illustrations simply because they lie within my own personal experience. I am not pointing a finger at the problems of any country. Every country has a dark side, and every country has a bright side too. We should be aware of the dark side, the Gita would say; otherwise we cannot see problems at all. But it is essential to keep our focus always on the bright side, for that is the side which is real. If we lose sight of what is positive, we have no way to change.

ओं तत्सदिति निर्देशो ब्रह्मणस्त्रिविधः स्मृतः ।
ब्राह्मणास्तेन वेदाश्च यज्ञाश्च विहिताः पुरा ॥ १७-२३ ॥
तस्मादोमित्युदाहृत्य यज्ञदानतपःक्रियाः ।
प्रवर्तन्ते विधानोक्ताः सततं ब्रह्मवादिनाम् ॥ १७-२४ ॥
तदित्यनभिसंधाय फलं यज्ञतपःक्रियाः ।
दानक्रियाश्च विविधाः क्रियन्ते मोक्षकाङ्क्षिभिः ॥ १७-२५ ॥
सद्भावे साधुभावे च सदित्येतत्प्रयुज्यते ।
प्रशस्ते कर्मणि तथा सच्छब्दः पार्थ युज्यते ॥ १७-२६ ॥

23. 'Om Tat Sat': these three words represent Brahman, from which come priests and scriptures and sacrifice.
24. Those who follow the Vedas, therefore, always repeat the word 'Om' when offering sacrifices, performing spiritual disciplines, or giving gifts.
25. Those seeking liberation and not any personal benefit add the word 'Tat' when performing these acts of worship.
26. The word 'Sat' means 'that which is'; it also indicates goodness. Therefore it is used to describe a worthy deed.

Om stands for the mantram. *Tat*, literally 'That,' stands for Brahman, the pure Godhead, which cannot be described in word or thought. And *sat* means literally 'that which is real' – real in the sense of what is abiding, changeless, everlasting. From *sat* comes *satya*, 'truth,' which was Mahatma Gandhi's definition of God. Evil, Gandhi said, has no reality of its own; it is real only insofar as we support it. Goodness, by contrast, cannot be extinguished; it can only be hidden. "I do dimly perceive,"

Gandhiji once said in memorable words,

> that whilst everything around me is ever-changing, ever dying,
> there is underlying all that change a living Power that is changeless,
> that holds all together, that creates, dissolves, and recreates. That
> informing Power or Spirit is God. And since nothing else I see
> merely through the senses can or will persist, He alone is. . . . I can
> see that in the midst of death life persists, in the midst of untruth
> truth persists, in the midst of darkness light persists. Hence I
> gather that God is Life, Truth, Light.

This is not merely philosophy; there you see Gandhi's real genius.
War, for example, has no reality of its own. It is not a "necessary evil";
no evil is necessary. War takes place only so long as we support it. If
more and more people refuse to support it, as thousands of women
did some years or so ago in a full-page ad in the *New York Times,* we
could see an end to war. When we truly do not want war on earth any
more, we can establish everlasting peace; nobody makes war but we
ourselves.

यज्ञे तपसि दाने च स्थितिः सदिति चोच्यते ।
कर्म चैव तदर्थीयं सदित्येवाभिधीयते ॥ १७-२७॥
अश्रद्धया हुतं दत्तं तपस्तसं कृतं च यत् ।
असदित्युच्यते पार्थ न च तत्प्रेत्य नो इह ॥ १७-२८॥

27. To understand the meaning of self-sacrifice,
self-discipline, and giving is 'sat.' To act in
accordance with these three is 'sat' indeed.
28. To engage in sacrifice, self-discipline, and giving
without good faith is 'asat,' without either worth
or goodness. Nothing worthwhile can come from
such action, either in this life or in the next.

Wherever wrong attitudes are present, Sri Krishna says, the result is
asat – literally, 'unreal.' When we work halfheartedly, with reservations,
with ill will or without concentration or respect, in the long run what

we do will have no lasting benefit.

It is often assumed that beneficial ends justify any means. As you say in this country, "anything goes." The Gita would say, "'Anything goes' means nothing will come of it." Mahatma Gandhi declared with his life that wrong means can never bring about right ends – just as, in the long run, right means cannot help but bring about right ends.

In my language, there is no difference between ends and means. I look on my day's work not only as the means to an end, but also as an end in itself. When you give your time and effort to selfless work without reservation, the work itself is the end.

The main reason we have not been able to establish peace in the world today, Gandhi would say, is that we have been using wrong means. The very theory of the balance of power – or, as it was called during the Cold War, the balance of terror – contradicts the unity of life. You try to frighten me more, I try to frighten you more, and we call it peace if neither side attacks! Economic sanctions, manipulating other countries' food supply, selling arms, undermining the freedom of other people to lead their own lives – all these are wrong means, whatever end we intend to achieve by them. Therefore, Sri Krishna says, they are *asat:* their results are tainted, as transient as writing on water. The next time you go to the beach, try writing *peace, peace, peace* on the water; see how long it will last.

Yesterday at the beach I saw an elaborate castle made of sand, standing in proud dignity near the curl of the tide. When we returned after a long, brisk walk, the waves had washed everything away. That is what happens to even the best efforts to bring peace to the world when we do not use right means: understanding, sympathy, education, respect. This applies in all human situations, at all levels from individual to international. The words "self-sacrifice, self-discipline, and giving" in these verses refer to any kind of help or charity.

I want to tell you a story to illustrate how even good work undertaken with arrogance or lack of compassion can bring about more harm. The story is "Rain," one of the great short stories of the twentieth century, written by W. Somerset Maugham. Although it is about individuals, you can read between the lines to apply it even to corporate benevolence and foreign aid. It was originally published in a collection called

The Trembling of a Leaf, which took its title from a significant epigram by Sainte-Beuve: "There is only the trembling of a leaf between happiness and despair."

The background of "Rain" makes an interesting story in itself. It seems that in December, 1916 – shortly before the story was first published – Somerset Maugham sailed on a Sydney-bound steamer called *Sonoma.* Scholars playing detective recently managed to find the passenger list of that voyage and were rewarded to discover not only the names of Mr. Maugham and his secretary but also of one "Miss Thompson"; Maugham hadn't even bothered to change her name. Encouraged, they tracked down everyone they could find who had sailed on the *Sonoma* in 1916 and asked them what this Miss Thompson looked like. "Coarsely pretty," the survivors recalled. "Flashy. A little plump. Full of animal vitality."

Many of the young men on board naturally began following Miss Thompson around, just as in Maugham's story. Her luggage included a phonograph which she played in her cabin throughout the night, while these men sat talking and singing and drinking with her. Maugham's cabin was two doors away, and he became quite interested in this scene. As he says, everybody was "copy" to him; everyone was a potential story. Just as a mystic can see deep into the positive side of human nature, Maugham saw deep into the negative side, and he could be ruthless in describing it too.

The "Reverend Davidson" – Maugham *did* change his name – was on the ship as well. He was a medical missionary, and Maugham describes him in his journal: "A tall thin man. . . . He had hollow cheeks and high cheek bones, his fine, large, dark eyes were deep in their sockets, he had full sensual lips, a cadaverous air and a look of suppressed fire." His wife, Maugham records, was from New England, which I suppose implies that she was inclined to judge people's failings without remembering the compassionate theory of the three gunas. Maugham noted with relish that she loved to decry in detail the depraved marriage customs of the local natives. We can imagine her opinion of Miss Thompson.

Davidson was genuinely concerned, if not about Miss Thompson herself, at least about her moral situation. I remember Walter Huston in the movie role, pacing up and down and cracking his knuckles, terribly upset because this woman was leading so many young men astray. But instead of compassion, his attitude was one of condemnation. "If the tree is rotten," he exclaims, "it shall be cut down and fed into the flames." Motives like these are *asat*; therefore, the Gita would say, they cannot escape bringing harm to everybody involved.

As Maugham's story picks up, the steamer is delayed at Pago-Pago for a fortnight because of quarantine. Sadie Thompson has a field day. There is uproarious merrymaking in her room day and night, which does not endear her to her missionary friends. Davidson does some sleuthing and learns that she is originally from San Francisco and has escaped a raid on the red-light district in Honolulu; now she is on her way to Sydney in search of a job as a barmaid. Clearly she could use a fresh start. But Davidson is not interested in finding some way to help her; he is only trying to have his way. He goes to the authorities and asks them to deport her.

What happens afterwards to the real Miss Thompson I do not know. But in Maugham's story Davidson goes on like this, using any self-righteous means he can think of to plunge her into an even lower shraddhā of herself than she already has. For a long time he is not particularly successful. But he is determined to "save her soul," to bring her around to his own view of her, and slowly he breaks her down. She begins to see herself as a fallen woman and learns to feel ashamed. He finds out that she is fleeing a three-year jail sentence in San Francisco, and he threatens her continually; he is determined to get her to go back and pay for her sins. Finally she becomes cringing and dependent. The phonograph is silenced. She begins dressing plainly, stops wearing makeup and perfume, lets Davidson read the Bible to her, and confides in him at length about her past sins. She believes she has met a man unlike the rest: someone of real moral stature, who is not after her physical attractions but is truly concerned for her soul.

To accomplish this "miracle," however, Davidson is obliged to spend a good deal of time with her – talking to her, listening to her, reading to her, reasoning with her. And as she responds to him, though he does not realize it, he begins to respond to her too. The wheel of karma has begun to roll. He has had no sympathy or understanding for this woman or for the men so driven by compulsive desire; these are not emotions that he recognizes. But Sadie Thompson was "coarsely pretty." She and Davidson spend long hours talking to each other, often well into the night, and slowly she begins to come up in his dreams. What he has been judging in others is happening to him, and not because of Sadie: the same samskāra he condemns so vehemently in others is acting now in his own consciousness.

Finally comes a long, long spell of continuous, monotonous monsoon rains. Davidson is already obsessed with Sadie, though he cannot allow himself to realize it, and the ceaseless drill of the rain begins to pound in his head, his heart, his veins. On the night before she is to sail back to San Francisco, unable to control his pent-up desires, he enters her room and does not leave until two.

The following morning the rain has ceased, and Davidson is not to be found. Eventually his body is discovered washed up on the beach. He has committed suicide; the fierce samskāra of judgment has turned on him. Sadie is her defiant self again, dressed and made up as before, and her phonograph is going full blast. "You men!" she says derisively to the doctor who represents Maugham. "You're all the same, all of you!"

There is a ray of sunshine around this story. Maugham was in Hollywood soon after it was written, and late one night another writer called John Colton came to his hotel room and said, "I can't sleep. Do you have anything good to read?" Maugham said, "I have the proofs of a short story I've written. You may read those if you like." Colton might have wanted some more sensational Hollywood stuff, but he had to get to sleep somehow. Maugham's story kept him up all night, and the next morning he went back and said, "I've got to make a play out of this!" That is how "Rain" came to be presented on Broadway in 1922. It sold out for some eighteen months, and every actress around wanted to play the part of Sadie. It shows that people's hearts are still with the under-dog, which is a very appealing facet of human nature.

You can see, reading between the lines, that Davidson's shrad-dhā applies to a much wider picture than the relationship between a repressed missionary and a lady "full of animal vitality." Any attempt to help another person – or community, or nation – that is tainted by disdain, condescension, or a judgmental or "holier than thou" attitude is *asat*. I want to repeat that nations and charities can fall victim to this too. When "help" is defined by conformance to our own ideas of what is right – or, worse, by our own self-interest – the results are poisoned by our shraddhā. Sooner or later, they have to turn against us.

By contrast, for the way of love, we have only to remember the example the Reverend Davidson professed to follow. Jesus was at supper in a Pharisee's house when a woman "whose sins were many" – according to tradition, Mary Magdalene – stole in behind him and knelt for a long while weeping at his feet. A great Malayalam poet gives her thoughts in beautiful words: "You who walked on water, rescue me also from the ocean of my tears." Everyone at the table is shocked that Jesus should allow such behavior from such a woman. But Jesus explains simply, "She loves much because so much has been forgiven." And to Mary he repeats, "Your sins are forgiven. Go in peace."

Asat is another way of defining ignorance. We can guess from this how many efforts to help other people, other races, and other countries are *asat*. They are based on the conviction that if we can have our way, things will improve for everyone – a kind of "my-way-only" shraddhā which often shapes economic policy and most foreign policy, including foreign aid.

Emerson, I believe, pointed out that the ancestor of every negative action, every negative decision, is a negative thought. That is the power of *asat*: evil has reality only insofar as we support it with negative thinking. We do not have to be afraid of negative thoughts if we do not welcome them. They are in the air, and they may knock at anyone's door; but if we do not embrace them, ask them in, and make them our own, they can have no power over us. Evil draws its support from the welcome mat we spread in front of our door. There is no need to go in for the strong language that orthodox religions occasionally use, of hellfire and brimstone and things like that: it is enough to say that we must be acutely vigilant about every thought we entertain.

In Berkeley, particularly in the sixties, University Avenue was often lined with hitchhikers. Many carried signs: "Vancouver," "Mexico," "L.A." One said in simple desperation, "Anywhere!" Thoughts are hitchhikers too and we can pick them up or pass them by. Negative thoughts carry signs, but usually we see only one side, the side with all the promises. The back of the sign tells their true destination: *duhkha*, sickness of body, mind, and spirit. Suffering to ourselves and others originates in picking up these hitchhikers, which nobody is obliged to do. No matter what our conditioning, each of us has the freedom to drive past without even giving negative thoughts a glance. If we do not stop and let them in, they cannot go anywhere; they are not real.

Hindu and Buddhist mystics offer a dazzling theory to explain this. Just as we live in a physical atmosphere, they say, we are surrounded also by a mental atmosphere, called *sukshmākāsha* in Sanskrit. The air we breathe is full of billions of atoms and ions of different substances, some beneficial, others poisonous, some natural, others man-made. Our mental atmosphere too can be polluted to a grievous extent. "You have standards about automobile emissions," these mystics would say, "to protect the purity of the air. Don't you think you should have equally stringent standards about polluting the mental atmosphere with negative thoughts?" We can actually teach the mind to breathe selectively, so that we can go safely through an atmosphere full of poisonous ideas and not be seriously affected by them. This is actually adding positive thoughts, which benefits everybody.

The other day our children were telling me about the importance of trees. If they were not always releasing oxygen, they explained, life on earth would perish. A person whose mind is free from negative thinking spreads life-giving oxygen in much the same way. On a smoggy day in California, the trees along the freeway look gray and drab in the haze; they do not seem to add anything valuable to the landscape. Yet if they were gone, our big cities would suffocate from their own activity. In the same way, although a selfless man or woman may seem to go through the day doing nothing extraordinary, such people are life-giving. Without them, nothing would revitalize the atmosphere in which we think. By being very vigilant, trying never to support or encourage negative thoughts, all of us can play a part in this vital service, which benefits everybody around us.

Ākāsha is usually translated as 'space,' but it is more than physical. I read that in a sense, physical space contains not only objects but a kind of record of events in the realms of energy. From outer space, physicists say, we can even pick up a faint echo of the "Big Bang" of creation. Similarly, like a vast library, ākāsha contains records of past thoughts and actions. They are there on the shelves, positive and negative alike, and we can check them out, take them home, and assimilate them or we can leave them where they are. The law of gravity has been present since the beginning of time; Newton, so to say, merely found the right wavelength to pick it up. Similarly, the mystics say, there is sympathy in the world; pick it up. There is antipathy in the world; don't pick it up. There is love in the world; pick it up. There is hatred; don't pick it up. Hatred destroys – individuals, families, nations, life itself. Love heals.

If we go on supporting negative thoughts, these verses remind us, what we do cannot be beneficial, even if we try to aim for a better world. But if we give ourselves wholeheartedly to selfless work without any desire for recognition or praise, power or remuneration, then our actions are *sat*. They cannot help bearing good fruit, not only in the world but in our own lives, by removing obstacles to our sādhana.

श्रद्धात्रयविभागयोगो नाम सप्तदशोऽध्यायः ॥ १७ ॥

CHAPTER EIGHTEEN
Love in Action

अर्जुन उवाच ।
संन्यासस्य महाबाहो तत्त्वमिच्छामि वेदितुम् ।
त्यागस्य च हृषीकेश पृथक्केशिनिषूदन ॥ १८-१ ॥

श्रीभगवानुवाच ।
काम्यानां कर्मणां न्यासं संन्यासं कवयो विदुः ।
सर्वकर्मफलत्यागं प्राहुस्त्यागं विचक्षणाः ॥ १८-२ ॥

ARJUNA:

1. *O Krishna, destroyer of evil, please explain to me how one kind of renunciation differs from another.*

SRI KRISHNA:

2. *To refrain from selfish acts is one kind of renunciation; to renounce the fruit of action is another.*

This morning our children came to me with a newfound treasure. From a distance, I thought the oldest had a live snake in his outstretched hands. Kerala is full of snakes, some of which are deadly, and everyone who grows up there quickly learns to jump first and pull out the field identification manual later. Even now, though I haven't seen any poisonous creature for more than twenty years, my first response is to draw back. The children must have seen this, for they smiled. "Don't worry, Uncle," they said. "It's not alive. It's just a snake's skin." It lay there as fragile as medieval parchment, delicately burst at the seams.

I had been reading an interview with Albert Szent-Györgyi, one of the most distinguished scientists of our time, who won the Nobel Prize in 1937 for his discovery of vitamin C. "Snakes can grow," he says, "only by bursting their skins. Molting has to be a painful process, and should it fail the snake would die. Mankind grows by bursting the outgrown skin of antiquated ideas, thinking, and institutions." The Gita would agree, and from its point of view we, *Homo sapiens,* stand clearly at the crossroads today. Whatever purpose it may have served in the past, the constricting skin of self-interest – national and individual alike – has to be sloughed. Otherwise, as Szent-Györgyi implies, we shall certainly perish.

Often it is just when old ideas are ready to burst that we feel they will last forever. When I was born, the heights of progress were supposed to be contained in the eleventh edition of the *Encyclopaedia Britannica,* the last great attempt to wrap up what the race had learned on every subject from physics (pre-atomic, of course) to the making of horse-drawn carriages. The authors seem never to have questioned that they sat at the zenith of civilization. Every article is written with implacable authority. Yet the whole is a compendium of outworn ideas, the constricting skins of modern industrial thought – about races, about empires, about the nature of the physical world, about progress and the nature of the human being. There is no hint of suspicion that this might be the end of an era. In the entry "War," a British expert observes that with the new kinds of military technology, "losses in battle . . . are almost insignificant when compared with the fearful carnage wrought by sword and spear." This just six years before the Battle of the Somme! "I cannot help seeing a parallel," Hans Koning commented in the *New Yorker,* "for we in our time seem as little able to really think through the meaning of our nuclear ordnance as these men – with their eight pack animals and their Napoleonic cantonments – understood the meaning of their 16.25-inch projectiles."

Old ideas, the Gita would say, are not sloughed by government decisions or in the boardrooms of corporations. They are given up by individuals, who go on to influence other individuals. Because the problems we face look so immense, it is easy to lose faith in this. I always try to remind people that though we are small, the power that can be released in us is anything but small. Despite appearances it is we, the ordinary people of the world – each of us individually – who have the power to change the circumstances of our lives. We do not often assert that power to choose; therefore we may not believe we truly have it. But it is a tragic misunderstanding to think that human destiny is made by anything other than individuals. We shape history together, all of us, by the total of our desires.

One poignant quote from Szent-Györgyi still lingers in my mind: "Here we stand now on our tragically shrunken globe with our ruined economy, with these terrific weapons in our hands and fear and distrust in our hearts." The Gita opens on just such a scene. No one thrust those weapons into our hands; we have gone to great lengths to accumulate them, pawned our national economies and our intellectual resources for them, piled up more than we could ever use, given them away, sold them in ridiculous numbers for the profit of it: if we had tried systematically to make the globe as dangerous as possible, we could not have done a better job. As for the fear and mistrust in our hearts, where have they come from? Have we tried to dispel them throughout this century, or have we stirred them up? The law of karma may grind slowly, but it grinds exceeding small.

Yet this law is not some relentless, irreversible force of destiny. It represents the consequences of our choices – choices that are still being made today, will be made tomorrow, by people like you and me. No matter how massive our arsenals, how extensive the pollution of our environment, how violent our relationships, or how irreversible our direction may seem, we can change all these things by the choices we make from now on. And karma is not a punitive force. Its purpose in evolution is not to punish us for past mistakes but to teach us to make wise choices in the future, to teach us to live in harmony with the unity of all life. In this sense all our problems have a spiritual purpose: to enable us to evolve, by pushing and prodding and encouraging us toward the goal of life.

There are two levels to this: one individual, the other global. In this more comprehensive view, all the successes and failures of our humanity serve this same purpose of trying to guide and urge and chastise us into living in harmony.

War, pollution, and the growing poverty of perhaps two thirds of the globe are the collective karma of wrong ideas people have pursued in the past, in the belief that they would bring peace and prosperity to those who pursued them and eventually, ideally, to all. There is no point in berating ourselves for following these ideas, which are the basic values of industrial civilization: they made heady promises which it was only natural to pursue. Yet today we should be able to see that even on the material level, industrial civilization has not been able to make good those promises. This was a stage through which we had to pass; now it is time to learn from our limitations and move on. We are, as Szent-Györgyi says, at a turning point in the history of civilization, where we must slough our outmoded habits of thinking, break out of old institutions, or die.

In the last chapter, I spoke of three stages in the growth of civilization. Tamas, the first stage, is primitive in its simplicity; wants are few, because it takes almost all our prāna just to stay alive. In this stage, the human being lives at the mercy of nature, dictated to by physical circumstances. We are now at the crest – perhaps even a little past the crest – of rajasic civilization, which thrives on complication. Rajasic progress, which begins by trying to satisfy human needs, ends in endlessly multiplying desires. The more problems it solves, the more problems its solutions create. In this stage, so intent on not living at the mercy of circumstance, we live increasingly at the mercy of our own nature. We produce in order to be producing, consume for the sake of consumption, desire to desire to desire.

This skin of rajasic thinking is what we have to slough if we are to progress safely into civilization's third stage, that of sattva. Here, instead of multiplying human wants, we begin to reduce them voluntarily. Sattva is a return to simple living: not primitive simplicity, but the artistic simplicity of a life that includes only what gives most meaning and value. Sattvic civilization is not poor, not even in a material sense. It has a place for every material thing that enhances human life. But it has no place for things that are at the expense of life, or that sap vital resources – including time, most vital of all. It renounces so as to leave life freer for the things that matter most.

In espousing material values, the Gita would say, we were only striving for happiness. That happiness can be attained, even on a global scale, but not by satisfying material values. It can be attained only by satisfying the whole human being, who is essentially spiritual. I am not talking of a Neverland where sorrow does not enter; there is no such place. Nor am I speaking of Utopia. But it is possible, even without the world filling up with saints, for ordinary people like you and me to live in such a way that this very earth becomes heaven. This does not require that everybody take to the spiritual life; but it does require a higher view of the human being – in other words, a return to spiritual values in our relationships, our work, our education, even our politics and economics.

The Gita embraces both these goals: the one of global fulfillment, with profound material consequences; the other individual. This last chapter, which sums up the way for both, is the full flowering of the Gita's message for our times. It gives the secret of effective action, the secret of full, victorious living – karma yoga, perfectly exemplified in the life of Mahatma Gandhi.

In Sanskrit, the chapter is titled "Freedom through Renunciation." I have called it instead "Love in Action," which I feel gives a much better idea of its meaning. Renunciation sounds terribly drab. Who would want it? But as Sri Krishna explains, it leads to freedom: that is, to full health, rich relationships, a heightened capacity to love; to a world of harmony, a world without want, a world without war. For renunciation means giving up selfish living and thinking. Therefore it means the release of love, which is not just a force in individual relations; it expresses itself in putting the welfare of the whole first in all affairs. Love means placing human values above material. It means not trying to build the happiness of a few on the exploitation of many. It means that food for people comes before food for profit. An entire society can be built with love as its foundation, with plenty of room for every legitimate human need and activity.

The material view of life, the Gita would say, is not evil. It is simply based on the lowest possible view of the human being. In the Christian tradition this is the state of the Fall, characterized by original sin. The Gita does not disagree about the sin, but instead it emphasizes original innocence, original love: not the Fall but our native state before the Fall, to which it is our purpose to return. The mirror of love, the mystics say, is always present in the depths of consciousness. It is present in everyone, in every society, whatever problems we face, whatever the karma of the times. All we have to do is to remove the dust that covers it.

त्याज्यं दोषवदित्येके कर्म प्राहुर्मनीषिणः ।
यज्ञदानतपःकर्म न त्याज्यमिति चापरे ॥ १८-३ ॥
निश्चयं शृणु मे तत्र त्यागे भरतसत्तम ।
त्यागो हि पुरुषव्याघ्र त्रिविधः संप्रकीर्तितः ॥ १८-४ ॥

*3. Among the wise, some say that all action
should be renounced as evil. Others say that
certain kinds of action – self-sacrifice, giving,
and self-discipline – should be continued.
4. Listen, O Bhārata, and I will explain three kinds of
renunciation and the central truth underlying them.*

There are people in the spiritual traditions of both East and West who hold that any kind of worldly activity taints us, getting us embroiled in self-centered activities and relationships. Trying to find ways to remove the threat of war, to help deal with the problems of poverty and hunger, to make our neighborhoods safe from violence again – all these agitate the mind and make it difficult to concentrate on spiritual disciplines. Why not forget about the state of the world, retire into the mountains somewhere, and lead a life of simple tranquility?

One of the most cogent arguments against this is that it doesn't work. Anybody's mind can calm down, at least on the surface level, when there is nobody around to contradict you. But left on its own, the mind goes on dwelling on itself; the ego becomes bloated. If somebody says something critical – asks, perhaps, what your way of life is contributing to the world – you blow up. Just beneath the surface of the mind, every samskāra is still there. What progress has been made? The mind, with all its same old problems, is busier than ever.

Today, to avoid the problems of stress and tension, we are advised to "let go" and "take it easy." Even experts sometimes say, "What does it matter? Go with the flow." By now I don't suppose I have to name the guna. Recently I was surprised to read the advice of a prominent physician on how to deal with stress: "Rule Number 1 is, don't sweat the small stuff. Rule Number 2 is, it's all small stuff." To me, this is a most depressing view of life and of human capabilities. Such attitudes are often considered spiritual, but this is a gross misunderstanding. Not only the Gita but Jesus and the Compassionate Buddha too teach a message of active love and selfless service. There is no conflict between what Christian mystics call the active and the contemplative lives, between meditation and selfless action; they go together as naturally as breathing out and breathing in. "What a person takes in by contemplation," Eckhart says, "he pours forth in love."

The Buddha approaches this problem from another angle. He would ask, "What about the law of karma?" All of us have accounts which have to be balanced somehow. I can illustrate this from bank accounting practices in British India. In those days, the agent of the Imperial Bank of India – British, of course – used to live on the bank premises upstairs, and as a rule none of the clerks, who were Indian, were allowed to leave until the books were balanced. I remember my friends in the bank occasionally coming home at midnight. The bank agent could afford to take his time. He could go upstairs, have a leisurely dinner, and then saunter down again to see how his staff were doing. And as soon as debits and credits were balanced, the doors were unlocked and everybody was released to go home.

It is the same with karma. All of us are here on earth because we have made many mistakes in the past, often in ignorance of the unity of life. But ignorant or not, the entries of unfavorable karma are there in our ledger books; we are operating in the red. We have a tremendous debt to pay the rest of life, and until that debt is paid and our accounts balanced by entries of good karma, we cannot be released from the bondage of conditioned action and reaction. Even on a global scale, until we learn to live with the welfare of the whole in mind, we will be entangled in the terrible web of karma that I have been describing in previous chapters. We will go on making the same mistakes that lead to a poisoned environment, dangerous neighborhoods, broken homes, and a planet at war.

If "balancing the books of karma" sounds occult, I can assure you it is terribly practical. When two people have been at loggerheads, for example – disliking each other, thinking resentful thoughts about each other over and over and over – their enmity takes a toll on their health and vitality and peace of mind, especially when they have to work together or sit down at the same dinner table. Not only that, there is a subtler toll paid in strengthening negative samskāras like resentment, so that the ill effects will spread to other relationships as well. The law of karma says clearly, "Balance your books." Your heart will be at peace; your health will be good; you will have more energy; your relationships will be sound; you will not be plagued by past incidents or be fearful of future ones. All these improve concentration and help to strengthen detachment, which in turn benefits meditation. Past a certain point, unless we have ample opportunity for selfless activity right in the midst of life, side by side with other people, it is not possible to make spiritual progress.

Before we take to meditation, most of us have no way of getting hold of a samskāra and turning it around. It is only natural that our earlier entries are mostly in red – karmic debts we have to repay. The purpose of selfless action is to tot up entries in the black. This is not merely a matter of accumulating "good deed" entries for physical actions done and kind words said. When the motivation comes from the heart, we are not just doing one good action; we are changing our mental state, from which future words and actions will spring. In this way a change in consciousness can actually write off old debts, so that the karma to be repaid becomes minimal.

My granny used to illustrate this with a frightening example. If, she would say, you fought with someone – perhaps even in a previous life – and caused that person to lose an eye, the law of karma requires that somehow, someday, you too must lose an eye. That is the orthodox Hindu interpretation, and I should add that the penalty need not be exacted in a fight; it might be in an accident. But if you have changed your consciousness, my granny would add, and are sincerely trying to base your life on nonviolence in deed, word, and thought, you have already learned the lesson that karma had to teach. Then the law will still take its payment, but the debt will be immensely reduced: instead of losing your eye, she would say, you might only singe an eyelash.

Hindus personify the inner auditor who keeps the books of karma within each one of us as a kind of CPA – Chitragupta, our Cosmic

Personal Accountant. When you feel insecure, that is Chitragupta looking at the liabilities side of the ledger and musing, "What a lot of entries!"
When you feel secure, that is Chitragupta doing a favorable audit. All
of us have both kinds of entries, assets and liabilities. But make more
and more entries on the right side of the ledger, the Gita advises, and
one day your life will be entirely in the black. Then you can throw your
bottle of red ink away. You can no longer have negative entries, because
the nexus with karma has been cut; you have paid your debts and are
free and clear. Imagine if you could operate a business like that, where
once you broke even, you could never slip into the red again! In terms
of karma, this can happen even with ordinary people like you and
me. You become naturally loving, naturally kind: even if you tried, you
would not be able to do anything at the expense of any other creature.

यज्ञदानतपःकर्म न त्याज्यं कार्यमेव तत् ।
यज्ञो दानं तपश्चैव पावनानि मनीषिणाम् ॥ १८-५ ॥

*5. Self-sacrifice, giving, and self-discipline should
not be renounced, for they purify one in wisdom.*

"Self-sacrifice, giving, and self-discipline" are the three kinds of *yajna*
or sacrifice presented in the last chapter. The Gita is offering a very
interesting concept: meditation is essentially a process of purification.
So are its related disciplines in my eight-point program, from repeating the mantram to putting others first. Everything we do – meals, work,
relationships, recreation, even sleep – is viewed not from the mundane
point of view but in reference to the supreme goal.

This is a very practical perspective. We know what strenuous disciplines a championship athlete has to undergo to win an Olympic gold
medal. A great gymnast doesn't keep her body supple and lithe for the
sake of beauty, although I don't suppose she minds being beautiful:
she does it because a lithe, supple body is essential for a world-class
gymnast. Similarly, Sri Krishna is lifting the disciplines of sādhana out
of the realm of good and bad, right and wrong, into the dynamics of
championship living. Putting others first, giving of ourselves gener-
ously, and hard, selfless work are not simply morally desirable. They are

exercises that we must practice regularly if we want to win life's highest prize. We may not think about it in these words, but all of us appreciate unselfishness, generosity, and self-discipline in others, and all of us have our moments of these virtues too. Sādhana simply means practicing them not just when it is convenient or when we are feeling good, but like a championship athlete: every day, systematically, eagerly, and with sustained enthusiasm.

Yet "purification" is not exactly a word that catches the aspirations of modern times. It has Victorian overtones, which is perhaps the worst fate that can befall a word today. My beatnik friends in the early sixties felt particularly sensitive to this. "People who tell you to have a pure mind," one of them told me bluntly, "are usually hiding their 'unclean' thoughts under a rug. They have the same kind of desires I do; they just repress them. That's not only dangerous, it's dishonest."

"The Gita is not talking about repression," I said. "This is a matter of optics." I still wasn't accustomed to this phobia of Victorian thought, but I had learned the appeal of scientific images. "According to Patanjali," I said, "the mind is like a clear crystal; it has simply got covered with dirt. If you want to see life clearly, you have to wash all the dirt off."

"And what do you mean by 'dirt'?" he asked. From the look on his face, as if he had just bitten into a sour apple, I could tell he still thought I was in Sunday school. The Gita's answer took him by surprise.

"Thinking about yourself," I said. "That is the worst kind of smog. A person who thinks only of himself is like one of those old cars that drives around filling the air with dark, oily fumes. He is really polluting the atmosphere."

On a smoggy day in Los Angeles, I am told, you can wash your windows in the morning and find a thin film of grime on them by the end of the afternoon. That is how self-will builds up on the crystal of the mind. It takes a long time, of course, for the crystal to become so dirty that you can't see through it. But we have been allowing self-will to accumulate since childhood – the Hindu and Buddhist mystics would say for many lifetimes. It is only natural that all of us have cleaning to do.

To me yajna does not mean ritualistic sacrifice, although that is how it is usually understood. It refers essentially to the sacrifice of self-will, which means putting other people first. When you work harmoniously at a job you do not like, that is yajna; you are sacrificing self-will. When you return patience for hostility, you are sacrificing self-will. When you refuse to act on a strong selfish desire or sense-craving, you are sacrificing self-will. Just as an Olympic athlete has exercises for reducing excess weight, these are exercises for trimming down our excessive burden of karma. If you want to make steady progress in sādhana, therefore, you cannot afford self-will. The less self-will you have, the less your karma-burden and the faster you will make progress; the more self-will you have, the heavier your karma and the slower you will make progress. That is the main reason for differences in how individuals' consciousness evolves.

Yajna is not just a matter for individuals; it should have a preeminent place in international relations. For some reason, people often think that love is fine on a person-to-person basis but no foundation for a sensible policy of domestic or foreign affairs. As Gandhiji pointed out, historians pay little attention to good will, love, and nonviolent resolution of conflict; enmity and war are much more interesting. But this only shows that peace, harmony, and prosperity are the standard of normalcy; what we write about are the disruptions.

Yet history does tell of one particularly glorious experiment in government by love. Though there have been others, none is more dear to me personally or illustrates better how everyone benefits when yajna is practiced on a national scale.

Emperor Ashoka ascended his throne in 268 B.C., some fifty years after Alexander the Great turned back at the gates of India. Ashoka's grandfather had driven out the garrison established by Alexander, and Ashoka inherited an empire that extended from central India up into Central Asia. However, empires never seem to be big enough, and nine years into his reign Ashoka launched a massive campaign to acquire the rest of the Indian subcontinent.

The land of Kalinga lay immediately to the south. Despite fierce resistance, it was finally subdued. Victorious, young Emperor Ashoka walked through the battlefield among the mutilated, dead, and dying of both sides. History must have seen countless similar scenes of slaughter since then: Carthage, Culloden, Gettysburg, Flanders, Stalingrad. Other victorious generals and rulers – we are told it of Alexander – must have been moved by the sight of the suffering their victories had cost. Yet they continued to wage war; Ashoka did not. At the height of his military power, he was so stricken by the human cost of war that he renounced violence entirely and devoted the rest of his reign to the welfare of his people. The southernmost corner of India, which would have been easy to subdue, remained; Ashoka retreated from its borders and gave it his protection. As H. G. Wells says in his *Outline of History,* we have no record of any other ruler renouncing war like this in the hour of victory.

What was the result of this change of heart? Surely this pacifist's kingdom fell prey to wolves? It did not; it prospered. Ashoka became a follower of the Compassionate Buddha and lived his life *bahujana-sukhāya, bahujanahitāya:* 'for the happiness of all, for the welfare of all.' He built roads throughout his kingdom, with way stations for travelers; he planted forests; he established universities and monasteries. He built hospitals not only for people but for animals, too. He made laws that are still exemplary for their humanity, and established a state policy of mutual respect for all religions. His foreign policy, even toward traditional enemies, was based on friendship; free trade and cultural exchange were encouraged with all countries.

The result was that Ashoka's people prospered, trade and culture flourished, and friendly relations with surrounding nations were enjoyed for the thirty remaining years of Ashoka's reign. In relating his horror after the conquest of Kalinga, Ashoka comments – the words are almost the Buddha's own – that no one can truly be conquered except by love: and he adds, in a new kind of royal pride, that he has already made many such conquests, not only in his own land but in other lands as well. "Amidst the tens of thousands of names of monarchs that crowd the columns of history," says H. G. Wells,

> . . . the name of Ashoka shines, and shines almost alone, a star. From the Volga to Japan his name is still honoured. . . . More living men cherish his memory today than have ever heard the names of Constantine or Charlemagne.

Why shouldn't nations follow Ashoka's principles today? It could still be done. For many years, throughout the Cold War, I appealed to the United States and the Soviet Union to renounce their enmity and assume such leadership together. It would have served the self-interest of both countries much better than the "balance of terror" policies pursued for so many years. This kind of mutual respect seemed impossible, but friendly relations with Red China were considered impossible and even immoral not many years ago. All that vanished overnight. Our rigid fear of the Soviet Union could have been sloughed just as easily if we had glimpsed the potential of a different kind of statesmanship.

At that time, the U.S. and the U.S.S.R. commanded the lion's share of the world's resources. In science, technology, medicine, they led the world. What might not have been accomplished if they had joined hands? Khrushchev once proposed to John F. Kennedy, "Let's go to the moon together." Why not replenish the earth together? Neither would have lost by it. The manipulations of the Cold War badly tarnished the reputations of both superpowers throughout the rest of the world. If they had joined hands against some of the environmental problems that face us all, they might have left a joint legacy that would make the whole globe rejoice.

I am not saying that problems and conflicts of interest would have vanished, of course. We have conflicts of interest even between states of the union. But how much more promising the future would have been! And how much more promising it would have been to have begun to solve some of these immense problems, working together with such a pool of resources, instead of adding the burden of a vast former empire in collapse.

This is not idealistic talk. It is much more realistic than the conventional *Realpolitik*. If it no longer applies to two global superpowers – and I suspect it will again, in time – it still makes good sense in every part of the world held hostage by the military rivalry between two countries. The example of India and Pakistan is particularly close for me, but there are other examples around the globe.

It may prove to be the smaller nations that show the world how to work together. They have the motivation: the biggest problem threatening their survival, too, is this kind of military rivalry between bigger neighbors. The great powers need more than the material and human resources of smaller countries; they also need their friendship and cooperation. With all my heart, I would appeal to developing nations to follow Gandhi's way and not cooperate with the manipulations of other countries trying to gain influence against one another. They should not accept "gifts" of arms or act as pawns in balance-of-power games. They need not mortgage their future with loans and trade deficits to industrialize along Western lines. They can cooperate with each other to solve their problems whenever help from the big powers is offered with strings attached. Even if political differences divide them, they are much better off learning to help each other than trying to play one foreign power against another.

एतान्यपि तु कर्माणि सङ्गं त्यक्ता फलानि च ।
कर्तव्यानीति मे पार्थ निश्चितं मतमुत्तमम् ॥ १८-६ ॥

6. Yet even these, Arjuna, should be performed without desire for selfish rewards. This is essential.

In orthodox circles, this powerful word *yajna* is often confined to a very restricted field of human activity connected with religious rituals. I do respect the place that these traditional rituals can have in the lives of those who respond to them deeply. But I belong to the most ancient of traditions in India, represented by the Upanishads, which say that by themselves, rituals are a very frail boat for crossing the sea of life and death. Here the dangers are so great and the challenges so overpowering that all of us ordinary human beings require the tremendous spiritual disciplines that have been handed down by the mystics of all the world's great religions. It is these disciplines – also denoted by the word *yajna* – that alone can deepen our consciousness and make our will indomitable, our discrimination infallible, our loyalty all-consuming.

In practical terms, I would say that whatever we do for the welfare of all – not just for our own family, not just for a few restricted people, but for the welfare of all – without any hankering after prestige or profit, working in cheerful harmony with everybody else involved, that is yajna. When we can work like this, the miracle of yajna is that such work contains within itself the secret of success. However hard we work, however dedicated our contribution, it is not we who make selfless work succeed. The secret of its success is contained in its very concept. Wherever you find the earnest, loving, concentrated desire to bring people and resources together to improve the welfare of others, the Lord may be said to live in that desire.

This is not really as exotic as it might seem. In personal life, for example, we often say that we teach our children not so much by what we say or what we talk about but essentially by what we are. Similarly, when we work together in a loving manner for the benefit of others, cheerfully giving our very best at a job we are privileged to do in the service of the Lord without ever asking about our own personal reward or recognition, then our very example is going to influence others to help us attain our selfless goal.

Yajna is measured on a sliding scale. As our understanding deepens, we see how more and more of our thought and activities can become an offering. Any act prompted by selfish desire is tainted to the extent of that desire; but the same act without self-centered motivation can be an offering that purifies the mind.

In a small way, I can illustrate this from my own sādhana. As a young man, my interests were mostly literary. I wanted to be a good writer and an eloquent speaker. These are rather harmless desires, but I have to confess that they had nothing to do with benefiting other people; they were wholly personal aspirations.

I tried to launch my literary career in high school. My teachers had been telling me that I should take to writing, my friends used to enjoy my stories, and so one day I took it into my head to send a short story to the *Illustrated Weekly of India,* which was then publishing stories and essays by important English writers. It was a little like a high school student trying to get his first story published alongside the big names in the *New Yorker*, except that of course this was still British India, with the *Illustrated Weekly* under an English editor and almost exclusively the province of British writers. But I hadn't considered any of this. My friends had said, "You should write that down," and I had simply believed them.

I told my intentions to my high school English teacher, my uncle. "When you want to submit a story for publication," he explained, "it has to be typewritten. Otherwise the editor won't even look at it." I didn't even know that. I had never learned to type, of course; in fact, so far as I knew, nobody in our village had a typewriter. But in the next town there was a typing school where students did job work. I went there and told them I needed to have a story typed for the *Illustrated Weekly.*

"Where is your story?" the man asked.

"I haven't written it yet," I said. "But if you give me some paper, I'll write it out for you here."

He was genuinely impressed, which didn't displease me. I wrote out my story in high confidence, all unfounded, and when I was finished he announced to his typing students, "Look at this! This boy comes in and wants us to type a story he hasn't even written and then writes it on the spot, and it's not bad either. Listen." He read it aloud and everybody seemed pleased. I mailed it.

It came back promptly. I've never seen such promptness, though you know the British are noted for it. Enclosed was a little note set in type under the *Illustrated Weekly's* crest: "The Editor of the *Illustrated Weekly of India* presents his compliments and regrets his inability to make use of your valued contribution."

That was the beginning of my career. I must say my friends stood by me loyally. "What does it matter if the editor likes it or not?" they asked. "You can read us your stories any time."

I kept on trying. My pile of rejection slips grew, and I began to appreciate how gracious that first one was. I came to think of them as dejection slips. One manuscript came back with no explanation except two words written in the margin: "No use." That hurt me deeply. Many years later, when a student of mine came up after class and complained that her story had been rejected, I brandished my collection of these notes and said, "You've just begun!"

Then one day the miracle happened. One of the best papers in India – the Madras *Hindu*, which I still read – published a story I had sent them. I showed it to everybody I knew. "Read this!" They would get to the end and then exclaim, "Hey, that's your name!" "Of course," I would reply. "Otherwise, why would I show it to you?" And at the end of the month, a check came. I had never received a check before, so I showed it to my granny. She couldn't read Malayalam, let alone English. "What does it say?" she asked.

"It says 'Pay to the order,' Granny."

"Well, you go to the bank right away and order them to pay you." But before I went, she took the check and showed it to everybody she could find. "That's my boy, the writer."

After that I slowly began to be published regularly. The editor of *The Times of India* accepted a piece and wrote back, "From now on, whatever you write, please send it to me first." I became rather well known in certain circles, which was not at all displeasing.

Once, I remember, I was invited to the home of a distinguished government official whose daughter had been following my articles closely. I felt very flattered to hear her say how much she and her classmates enjoyed them. Then she asked a question that every established author likes to hear: "What is the secret of your writing?" I imagine I came up with all kinds of learned nonsense, but the truth was I didn't have any idea what the secret of my writing was, or if it had any secret at all. My host came to my rescue. "It's not what he writes about," he said, "or even the way he writes it. It's the way he looks at life." "Hey," I said, "that's right!" That is how simple I could be. But there was truth in that man's observation: in the way I was looking at people and events around me, I was already trying to convey the unity I could see dimly beneath the apparent diversity of the human scene.

I am trying to show you how human personal desires can be. After all, wanting to be a writer is a harmless desire, and being pleased if one succeeds is a very harmless, understandable kind of pleasure. My motives were quite innocent. I loved literature and the drama of the lives I saw around me, and I wanted to share what gave me joy. But none of this is yajna. I wasn't writing to benefit anybody; I was simply writing for the love of writing.

It was the same with public speaking. There too I achieved some degree of notoriety, largely because I worked on my skills assiduously from college on. But I wasn't trying to help anybody; I simply wanted to become a good speaker.

On one occasion, however, the local head of the Ramakrishna Order happened to ask me to deliver the keynote address for the celebration of Sri Ramakrishna's birthday. I was floored. Here was a dedicated monk, highly placed in one of the most prestigious monastic orders in India, asking a householder to speak to a great gathering on the subject of their founder! I was uncomfortably aware of my position as I took my place on the stage. But once I began speaking, my deep love for Sri Ramakrishna welled up. I became completely absorbed, just as I do today, and forgot all about my notes. The rhetorical effects I used to rehearse so carefully came to me spontaneously. I felt afterwards a little like a magician who keeps reaching into his hat to see what will come forth next; my talk was as new to me as it was to my audience. They appreciated it, but I don't think anyone appreciated it more than I did.

That occasion gave me a glimpse of unsuspected resources, which I could tap by reaching for a higher purpose. I began to see that I could use my literary training not merely for entertaining an audience, but for enriching other people's lives. That was yajna, and it can happen with virtually any skill. In those days I used to have to prepare for every talk I gave. Now I simply sit down and begin to speak; every day of my life is my preparation.

नियतस्य तु संन्यासः कर्मणो नोपपद्यते ।
मोहात्तस्य परित्यागस्तामसः परिकीर्तितः ॥ १८-७ ॥
दुःखमित्येव यत्कर्म कायक्लेशभयात्त्यजेत् ।
स कृत्वा राजसं त्यागं नैव त्यागफलं लभेत् ॥ १८-८ ॥
कार्यमित्येव यत्कर्म नियतं क्रियते ऽर्जुन ।
सङ्गं त्यक्त्वा फलं चैव स त्यागः सात्त्विको मतः ॥ १८-९ ॥
न द्वेष्ट्यकुशलं कर्म कुशले नानुषज्जते ।
त्यागी सत्त्वसमाविष्टो मेधावी छिन्नसंशयः ॥ १८-१० ॥

*7. To renounce one's responsibilities is ignorance.
The wise call such renunciation tamasic.
8. To avoid action from fear of difficulty or physical discomfort is rajasic. There is no reward in such renunciation.
9. But to fulfill your responsibilities knowing that they are obligatory, while at the same time desiring nothing for yourself – this is sattvic renunciation.*

10. Those endowed with sattva clearly understand
the meaning of renunciation and do not waver.
They are not intimidated by unpleasant work,
nor do they seek a job because it is pleasant.

Sri Krishna is trying over and over to make it clear that renunciation is essentially a mental state. We cannot free ourselves of the tremendous backlog of human conditioning by packing up belongings and giving them to the Salvation Army. I have had people come to me and say, "Yesterday I was reading about St. Francis, and I decided to renounce my stamp collection and give it to the newspaper boy." This may or may not be a good idea, depending on individual circumstances. But in any case, the renunciation is often only a sporadic impulse. Afterwards the person either suffers regrets or gets attached to something else. Attachment is a samskāra, a living force in the mind. If you take away its stamp collection, it will grope around for something else to grab and hold: houseplants, art nouveau, classic cars, French wines, chess openings; the possibilities are endless. What makes the difference, Sri Krishna says, is the motivation behind the act of renunciation. And as usual, he comes up with three kinds of motivation.

Tamas is great at renouncing responsibilities. Halfway through college, or when he has a family to support, he decides that the time has come to give up worldly life with all its problems and devote his time to contemplation, gardening, writing poetry, or enjoying the simple life. "I'm not causing anybody any harm," he says, and on the surface it may seem true. But the mental state says point-blank, "I don't care. What matters is that I do what I like."

This, of course, is not simply a matter of individuals. Bureaucratic bodies can be severely afflicted with tamas, as they come to reflect the lowest common measure of sensitiveness among those they comprise. Their very size creates torpor. We see this so frequently that I doubt if there is any need for examples. Governments and corporations defaulting on their responsibilities will tell you that onerous obligations such as public health were never properly theirs to begin with.

Rajas, by contrast, gives things up when he is forced to, usually by pain. If he renounces martinis, it is not because he has got hold of his desire and turned it around; it is because he has developed an ulcer and drinking martinis *hurts*. He gives up smoking because his cough has become too painful, because it is difficult even to breathe.

Let me be very clear: I applaud everyone who gives up smoking, whatever the motivation. It is the purpose of pain to prod us into making such changes, and though the experience is unpleasant, it is much better to learn from pain than not to learn at all. But here we have to look at the mental state and see how much it contributes to freedom. I know people who, though they have given up cigarettes, cannot watch someone light up after dinner without a stab of envy or deprivation. I appreciate their willpower; but at the same time, as they would be first to admit, they are not free from the compulsion of that desire in the mind. There is neither joy nor freedom in this kind of renunciation; the mind is still clamoring. Therefore, the Gita says, there is no spiritual reward in it either: that is, no reduction of unfavorable karma. All that can be said is that no more harm is being done on the physical level.

My granny did not at all appreciate this kind of motivation. She just didn't like the idea of life pushing her into a corner and saying, "Now stick 'em up and give me all you've got!" She used to tell me, "Little Lamp, *you* be in control. If you see that something is bad for you, give it up freely, in the pride of your strength. Then you can tell life cheerfully, 'Do what you like. I'm free.'" There is a gallant courage about this that appealed to me deeply, long before I was able to follow it in my own life.

The mental state behind rajasic renunciation is fascinating. Rajas simply can't let go of something he wants, even when he is forced to. If he has to give up oranges, he grabs on to apples; when apples are taken away, he takes up bananas. On a larger scale, these quirks are fraught with danger. Rajas finds it painful to be dependent on oil, but instead of lowering energy consumption, he embraces nuclear power. He gets embroiled in a war to "protect" some imagined interest, finds his involvement catastrophic, and finally pulls out; then a few years later he gets into the same kind of war somewhere else. In all such cases, what has to be renounced is the underlying selfish attachment, the compulsive desire to have a particular thing whatever it costs. When that desire is removed, any problem can be solved.

The word the Gita uses for "pain" in these verses was a favorite of the Buddha's: *duhkha*. It stands for anything from physical suffering to anxiety and alienation. The whole anguish of our age, virtually all its social and environmental problems, is duhkha, the prime symptom of epidemic selfish attachment. This is a deadly diagnosis, to which we cannot safely respond piecemeal. Banning a particular fluorocarbon or negotiating a treaty over one kind of weapon is an important step; but this is the way of Rajas, who wants to eat his cake and have it too. It does not get at the underlying cause.

One last point: on the spiritual path, you sometimes find people who say, "I have renounced work; I don't want to get involved in making money. I don't even want to touch money." I touch money; on the whole, I find it rather useful in carrying on selfless work in the twentieth century. Mahatma Gandhi must have had millions of rupees pass through his hands, and he not only suffered them to pass, he solicited them from everybody. He was a tirelessly imaginative fundraiser. If a woman with gold bangles came to touch his garment and get his blessing, he would tell her, "Why don't you give me those bangles to sell for the poor? You'll look so beautiful without them. Your arms will feel much lighter, and so will your heart." Many people gave, and the more they gave the more he asked. Enormous amounts of money were needed to fund the rural uplift work in India's seven hundred thousand villages, and Gandhi reminded us that it was everyone's privilege to give. We should thank the poor, he told us, for giving us the opportunity to undo some of our karma.

We are all sent into life for one task: to enrich the lives of others. Anybody who takes from life without giving to others in return, Sri Krishna says earlier, is a thief. Calcutta used to have a place called Thieves' Bazaar, where if someone had stolen your wristwatch, you could usually buy it back the following morning from a middleman for only half the original cost. If you complain, the man will shrug. "It's cheap! You'd have to pay twice that much to replace it new." Those who live for their own profit and pleasure, Sri Krishna says, are holding their own Thieves' Bazaar: stolen time, stolen energy, stolen education, stolen talent, stolen prāna.

न हि देहभृता शक्यं त्यक्तुं कर्माण्यशेषतः ।
यस्तु कर्मफलत्यागी स त्यागीत्यभिधीयते ॥ १८-११ ॥

*11. As long as one has a body, one cannot
renounce action altogether. True renunciation
is giving up all desire for personal reward.*

The other day I overheard one of our āshram children, who is about
five, making a philosophical point to his mother. "I've had a bad day
today, mommy," he said. "Tomorrow I'm going to stay in bed with my
bear and my blanket and not go out at all."

"I don't think so," his mother said cheerfully. "Your stomach will make
you go out. In the middle of the night it will start growling, and you'll
wake up and find yourself on your way to the kitchen."

Even physically, she was saying, it is impossible to avoid action. To
be human is to be active, not only physically but essentially in the mind.
Even if you could keep yourself in bed twenty-four hours a day, your
mind would run on nonstop. As Dr. Hans Selye says, work is a biological necessity. Once we enter the rajasic stage of human evolution, we
have to be active; that is our nature. But though we cannot choose to
be inactive, we can choose the kind of action and our motivation for
it. Working only for ourselves tightens the ties of our conditioning,
but learning to work without selfish attachment gradually elevates our
consciousness and purifies it of selfish motives.

There is another dimension to these verses, which has broad implications: "action" here means karma in all senses of the word. Even
if you confine yourself to bed, you are still accumulating karma. You
may remember my earlier quotation from Lord Mountbatten: "If you're
doing nothing, you're doing wrong." Doing nothing creates karma too,
because it reflects a choice; and to do nothing in a wrong situation can
be bad karma indeed. We cannot go before the karma court, for example, and say, "I never worked on atomic weapons! I'm not responsible if
a lot of generals and politicians built up those ridiculous arsenals." The
judge will ask, "What did you do to undo the situation through peaceful, persuasive means?" If we did everything we could, the judge will
say, "No unfavorable karma."

The same argument holds for all sorts of other activities. I remember reading in the Oakland papers a few years ago that ten people had been killed that week over cocaine deals in the Bay Area. Everybody who shows approval of drugs – even "beautiful people," or those who write the articles and produce and sell the accoutrements that make drug use a fashionable fad – has a karmic role in tragedies like these.

Life needs the contribution of every one of us. Until there is no trace of selfish motives in our consciousness, we cannot avoid being involved in karma; merely to be alive is to be part of its net. So the Gita draws a very practical conclusion: since action is unavoidable as long as we are alive, why not make the best of it and work hard and selflessly, accumulating good karma by contributing to the welfare of others?

अनिष्टमिष्टं मिश्रं च त्रिविधं कर्मणः फलम् ।
भवत्यत्यागिनां प्रेत्य न तु संन्यासिनां क्व चित् ॥ १८-१२ ॥

12. *Those who are attached to personal reward*
will reap the consequences of their actions: some
pleasant, some unpleasant, some mixed. But
those who renounce every desire for personal
reward go beyond the reach of karma.

This "mixed karma" shows Sri Krishna's dry sense of humor. Partly you like what you get from life, partly you don't: sometimes you're happy, sometimes you're not; sometimes you can be loving, sometimes you cannot. This is a very popular kind of karma, always on sale. It makes a perfect formula for romance.

To me karma is not some mystic theory; it is a force that blows through the world like a wind. Nobody can escape it, just as nobody can live without air. Each of us therefore is expected to learn from karma the consequences of certain actions, just as we learn from gravity. We have to apply the concept to our lives and ask ourselves the crucial questions: How kind am I? How often do I indulge in unkind language? Do I tend to ride roughshod over other people, or manipulate them to suit my needs? These are not pleasant questions, but their purpose is not to make us feel guilty. They are intended to help us see what to look for and what to change in order to lift the burden of sorrow from our lives.

According to the Hindu and Buddhist mystics, of course, karma and reincarnation go hand in hand. This life then becomes not an isolated, chance event but a link in a continuous chain of life, broken only on the physical level by a succession of births and deaths. At some point, ready to learn from all this, we finally begin to suspect that it is we ourselves who forge this chain by our own karma, our thought and action. Then, as Swami Vivekananda says beautifully, we "turn from the temporal to the eternal." This is what happened to me halfway in life, through my teacher's grace.

Vivekananda gives one of the clearest formulations of the law of karma that I have ever come across:

> Every thought that we think, every deed that we do, after a certain time becomes fine, goes into seed form, so to speak, and lives in the subtle body in a potential form, and after a time it emerges again and bears its results. These results condition the life of man. Thus the human being molds his own life. Man is not bound by any other laws excepting those which he makes for himself.

He concludes succinctly: "Once we set in motion a certain power, we have to take the full consequences. That is the law of karma." This is a very far-reaching statement. I have tried to fill this book with examples, yet I have scarcely begun to illustrate the extent of the law of karma.

I like to present karma as part of cosmic education, a kind of teaching assistant whose job is to dispel our ignorance and issue our diploma into wisdom. Since karma is often unpleasant, a sensitive person can fall into the belief that this is a school of suffering. There is truth to this, but I always like to present the positive side also. In the Sanskrit scriptures this world in which we live – of birth and death, good and evil, right and wrong, unity and disunity – is called *karmabhūmi,* the land of karma, the land of work. When you feel oppressed by the burden of the world and the tragedies enacted on it, please remind yourself that it is only here, where we find the choice between the best and the worst, that the human being can discover the unity of life. Strangely, it is in this utter darkness that we begin to grope for light; it is in the midst of utter violence that we begin to yearn for love.

For animals, evolution is a natural process; for human beings, it is a matter of choice. Animals do not have to make any effort, resolve their conflicts, or transform their passions in order to evolve. When our dog Muka gives me a pitying look, I sometimes imagine he is thinking, "Poor fellow! You have to work hard every day for what we dogs can do just by being dogs." I would say, "Touché." Being human is a danger-ously free adventure. Chitragupta, our cosmic accountant, tells each of us cheerfully, "If you like, you can live in the dark." And he adds, "Of course, if you prefer, you can walk toward the light. Night or light. You choose." I like this kind of talk. Nobody ever forced me to meditate, you know. Nobody, not even my teacher, ever asked me to transform my passions. Just understanding the laws of life – that I can remake myself, change my samskāras, change my future completely – was enough to make me want to be king of my own life.

This choice is offered to every one of us. There is no privilege involved, no prerogative we can invoke. If we are giving our very best in sādhana, trying our hardest to transform our passions and curb our self-will, we have Sri Krishna's promise that he will not allow the consequences of our mistakes to undo our progress. But if we are working half-heartedly or disharmoniously or indulging our self-will, karma has to follow sooner or later.

The *Mahābhārata* uses a homely image to describe this. When you do something unkind, it says, you are giving birth to a little calf of karma which immediately sets out to find its mother. "As a calf recog-nizes and seeks out its mother in the midst of a thousand cows," the *Mahābhārata* says "so the effects of past deeds do not fail to recognize and seek out the doer in his new life." Here you are, looking differ-ent from the last time around, feeling different; you yourself have no memory of any previous existence; and just as you are walking down Telegraph Avenue, minding your own business, this calf comes nuzzling up to you out of nowhere. It has been wandering, looking, sniffing every passerby – "Nope, not him; nope, not her" – and then suddenly, "Hey, *here's* the one I belong to!" It jumps on you like a friendly pup and starts licking your face. And you wonder, "Why does this happen to me? Why is life so unfair?"

Once you learn to treat others with respect, however, the calf comes of age. After a calf grows up, you know, its mother is just another member of the herd. Similarly, your deeds will come, sniff at you, and wander on: "You're not my owner! I'm going to rejoin the herd." The relationship with your past is ended.

In a sense, you see, you are *not* that calf's owner any longer. Whatever was done in the past applies to the person that did it – selfish, insecure, vindictive, self-willed. Karma says, "This creep has asked for everything the law can give." Many years later, after sincere sādhana, when you come before the bench for trial, the judge puts on his black cap to give the creep his due. But the defense protests, "Your Honor, there has been a mistake. This is not the same person as the accused; this is a different person from top to bottom. Every thought is loving; every act is kind."

The prosecutor objects. "I demand the highest penalty under the law!"

"Overruled," the judge says. "Mistaken identity. Case dismissed with costs."

Let me repeat: nothing is gained by bemoaning the mistakes of the past. What is important is to change today. Then we can stand on Sri Krishna's promise and say, "My past has fallen away. Now please do your part, and lift the burden of karma from my shoulders."

पञ्चैतानि महाबाहो कारणानि निबोध मे ।
सांख्ये कृतान्ते प्रोक्तानि सिद्धये सर्वकर्मणाम् ॥ १८-१३ ॥

13. Listen, Arjuna, and I will explain the five elements necessary for the accomplishment of every action, as taught by the wisdom of sānkhya.

The purpose of work is the attainment of wisdom. Modern civilization hasn't caught up with this idea, which turns economics upside-down. It is meant literally; and it is not at all impractical, as it may sound. From the spiritual perspective, which I would say includes even material well-being, the purpose of work is not to make money, nor to feed oneself and one's family, nor to achieve any kind of personal fulfillment, nor even to provide the goods and services that society needs. It is to remove the obstacles to living in harmony with the unity of life: in a word, to remove the obstacles to love.

All these verses become clearer if you remember that "work" is a translation of *karma*. For "work" you can fill in "action"; and of course you can fill in "karma" too, which makes for a very big picture. In practical terms, all work – everything we do – is for one supreme purpose: to undo the unfavorable karma that we have accumulated in the past. After all, it is in our relationships with others that we have accumulated this wrong karma. It follows that there is no way to undo this karma except in our relationships: by being patient, being kind, working in harmony, never failing in respect or trying to have your own way.

Yesterday a friend asked me a good question: "How can work help to slow down the mind?" On the one hand, the Gita has been telling us that the very purpose of work is to undo karma and still the mind. But on the other hand, as everyone with some self-knowledge knows, the usual effect of work is to get us speeded up and personally entangled in how the work turns out.

The key is simple to understand but difficult to practice: Sri Krishna is talking about *selfless* work. In this sense, the purpose of work is to learn to work hard without any ego-involvement at all. Stilling the mind is simply another way of expressing this, for nothing stirs up the mind except the ego.

"Stilling the mind" is a very abstract concept, and "renouncing the ego" is worse. It may be impossible to understand these things until a person has some way of practicing them. That is one function of work in sādhana: to bring abstract ideals down to earth. Many of the disciplines in my eight-point program are ways to still the mind through work. When you are working with one-pointed attention, for example, that in itself helps to slow the mind. When you do not gauge what you do by what you like or dislike, you are turning your back on the ego, which will make it easier to steady your mind.

When people tell me they would like a job that is more interesting or more intellectually challenging, they sometimes mean only that they want more personal recognition, perhaps even a little more power: not much, you know; just one step higher on the ladder, two or three more employees to supervise, a position a little closer to the boss's ear. These are very human foibles, but indulging them is the opposite of work's real purpose. Instead of weakening the ego, this strengthens it. The idea of "*I am the doer*" – "It is *I* who do this action, *I* who decide it, *I* who am responsible for its success or failure" – arises from the desire for personal attention. When that desire goes, personal conflicts disappear.

अधिष्ठानं तथा कर्ता करणं च पृथग्विधम् ।
विविधाश्च पृथक्वेष्टा दैवं चैवात्र पञ्चमम् ॥ १८-१४ ॥
शरीरवाङ्मनोभिर्यत्कर्म प्रारभते नरः ।
न्याय्यं वा विपरीतं वा पञ्चैते तस्य हेतवः ॥ १८-१५ ॥
तत्रैवं सति कर्तारमात्मानं केवलं तु यः ।
पश्यत्यकृतबुद्धित्वान्न स पश्यति दुर्मतिः ॥ १८-१६ ॥

*14–15. The body, the means, the ego, the
performance of the act, and the karma involved:
these are the five factors in all actions, right
or wrong, in thought, word, or deed.
16. Those who do not understand this think of
themselves as separate agents. With their eyes
clouded by ignorance, they fail to see the truth.*

The word I have translated as 'ego' here is *kartā*, literally 'doer.' Virtually all of us would say, "This is a reference to *me*. Of course I am the doer of my actions; who else could be?" Actually, Sri Krishna reminds us, all action is performed by prakriti; the Self, our real personality, has little to do with it. The ego which decides to act, the body which carries out that action, the means, and the activity itself are all elements of the same field – made, in a sense, of the same stuff. So too is *daivam,* the karma of that action. *Daivam* could be translated as 'fate' or 'destiny,' but this is misleading, for in the Gita's presentation nothing is foreordained and nothing happens by chance. We choose our own destiny, because consequences are a part of every action. So is the volition behind it, in the way that a seed, its nutrients, the soil it is in, and the climate are all part of the environment that makes the seed grow into a tree. Hindu and Buddhist scriptures emphasize that karma is actually contained in the action itself, and only needs time and the proper conditions to become manifest.

None of this, Sri Krishna says, involves the Self, who belongs to a higher order of being. Until we realize the Self, however, we can't go through life doing what we like and saying, "I'm not the doer; I'm not responsible." To live is to be responsible. As long as we are present in the body, it is necessary to be responsible for our actions, for the plain reason that we are going to incur the karma whether we feel responsible or not.

Karanam refers to the means involved in the doing of any action. To a large extent, these determine the karma that results. For right results, right means are essential. Wrong means can never lead to a right end, any more than thistle seed can yield a harvest of apples. However good the desired end may be, however sincerely it is desired, wrong means bring wrong ends simply because they are prompted by self-will, which always provokes more self-will: opposition, ill will, anger, and the stubborn insistence on having one's own way. Everything becomes tainted in this kind of atmosphere, even in the best of circumstances.

Every action has stages, phases of development. If you look only at the first phase or the third and do not look at the goal, you are likely to get caught in what you are doing. Then you get entangled, and burn out or lose hope. You may even get so personally involved that you begin resorting to any expeditious way of getting things done the way you see them, which in the long run can only weaken your effort and turn results against you.

I can give a personal illustration from the way the Blue Mountain Center of Meditation has grown. When I began teaching in this country, almost twenty-five years ago, I once took the advice of enthusiastic friends and rented a hall in Oakland for a public talk. "That's the way these things are done in the United States," I was told. "You've got to think big." I was willing. We put up some posters, probably on telephone poles, and a hospitable friend offered to open a coffee bar at the hall and to provide a lot of cookies, which she felt sure would draw a crowd.

We turned up early, and I expected a large gathering. There were three: myself, Christine, and our friend, who was standing there at the coffee bar and drinking up the coffee herself. "Would you like some?" she asked. "There are a lot of cookies for you, too."

The rest of the crowd arrived later: a young fellow and his brother, who I decided later must have been coaxed into coming. As soon as I started speaking, he fell asleep.

Imagine: you rent a hall, set up a coffee bar, draw an audience of four with your wife included, and one of the four falls asleep! You can see why Sri Krishna says that if you want to do important work, you can't afford to have your ego involved: if you do, you are bound to get agitated and hurt and be tempted to do all kinds of things to keep it from happening again.

Instead of being bothered on that occasion, I watched my mind and was pleased to discover that it wasn't agitated in the least. Events like this belong to the first phase of selfless work. If I had forgotten that first phases are followed by second phases, I might have given up and concluded that I would never be able to reach great numbers of Americans about the value of meditation. But those incidents were not the whole. I was seeing only the first act, perhaps only the first scene. To put it another way, this was simply the first in a long series of steps. I was learning to walk, so to speak, being tested, being trained. I told Christine, "We don't have to worry about the number of people. We just have to give our best." I gave the same enthusiastic talk to those four that I would have given to a packed hall, and within a few weeks Sri Krishna saw to it that I was speaking on meditation at the University of California campus to an audience of almost four hundred students. I didn't let myself get elated: if I had, I would have been leaving myself open to depression when the next turn of ill fortune came.

Whatever you are doing, don't think in terms of prestige or personal power or profit, all of which can be terribly insidious. As long as the work is beneficial, it doesn't matter whether the part you play is large or small; what matters is that the work be done. Every role is important. At Nilgiri Press, where my books are published with the help of many dedicated friends, I always remind them that collating and stuffing envelopes are as important as editing or typesetting. If the collating is off, we get the kind of letter I once got: "Pages 33 through 64 were very inspiring, but did you need to put them in twice?"

All this has a direct bearing on the fifth element in action that Sri Krishna mentions: the karma involved. In no job, no activity, should we forget the law of karma, which often works in hidden and seemingly contrary ways.

I remember asking my granny about this when I was still young, long before I had any grasp of karma's inner meaning. Like all Hindu children, I grew up with the stories of the *Mahābhārata*. The Pandavas were universal "good guys" and the Kauravas universal "baddies." What I could never understand was that the Kauravas lived in air-conditioned palaces, ate sumptuous cuisine, went about in special chariots with beautiful damsels, and generally (at least till the end) got their way in everything, whereas the Pandavas had a very thin time.

"Granny," I asked, "the Pandavas were devoted to Krishna, but the Kauravas weren't. The good guys should have had the best of times and the Kauravas the worst. Why did it happen otherwise?" She replied, "You're looking at it from the point of view of worldly enjoyment, as if that were the point of living. I look at it from the point of view of spiritual growth." The law of karma often puts us in difficult situations so we can take advantage of those situations to grow spiritually, just as the Pandavas did. We need such situations to work out unfavorable karma we have accumulated, and without such tests and trials, growth is not possible.

यस्य नाहंकृतो भावो बुद्धिर्यस्य न लिप्यते ।
हत्वापि स इमांल्लोकान्न हन्ति न निबध्यते ॥ १८-१७॥
ज्ञानं ज्ञेयं परिज्ञाता त्रिविधा कर्मचोदना ।
करणं कर्म कर्तेति त्रिविधः कर्मसंग्रहः ॥ १८-१८॥

17. The person who is free from ego has attained purity of heart. Though violence surrounds him, he is free from violence.

18. Knowledge, the thing to be known, and the knower: these three promote action. The means, the act itself, and the doer: these three are the totality of action.

All of us have committed mistakes, and all of us face significant obstacles in our sādhana and our personal growth. We find it easy to get angry, for example, and very difficult to be selfless. Here the Gita combines profundity with practicality. It does not say, "You're perfect; you're pure; it's not really you that causes these problems." It recognizes our present inadequacies, yet at the same time it offers a permanent solution: a set of disciplines by which we can learn to identify with our real Self, which is not touched by any of these inadequacies at all.

We carry an immense burden of karma on our shoulders, and it is this burden that prevents us from going deeper in meditation. That is perhaps the most frightening penalty of the law of karma, and it terrifies all sincere spiritual aspirants. Where there is a big load of karma, your mind has to be agitated; that is probably the single most important cause for lack of progress in meditation.

No matter how heavy this load of personal karma is, however, we can always cope with it. It may be too heavy to be easily dissolved, but it is never more than we can deal with. People sometimes ask me about karma, but their questions are not always very useful. The only really practical question to ask about karma is, "How can I remove its burden?" And the most practical answer is: Put those around you first every day, even when they are difficult, and don't insist on having your own way. If I had to reduce going beyond karma to a single formula, I would quote the simple advice of a Christian mystic: "Be kind, be kind, be kind." You don't have to understand how karma works or make checklists of what specific karma needs to be undone. It is enough to be kind to everyone, every day, as much as you possibly can – in fact, I would say, a little more than you can. Working like this draws on every human faculty – body, senses, mind, intellect – to take us beyond the law of karma into a state of undivided love.

On the other hand, as long as we live under the sway of personal likes and dislikes, and especially of resentments and hostilities, our load of karma will grow heavier and heavier. An active ego cannot help producing karma because it is the very source of negative thinking, which eventually gets expressed in destructive speech and action. Over the years, this adds up to a terribly heavy burden.

We are seldom directly aware of this burden because we are physically oriented. All we know about is physical loads. If we see someone trudging down the street with a packing crate on his shoulder, we don't ask why he is hunched over and seems to have such difficulty in walking; we are painfully aware of the weight he is carrying. Yet every day we see people bowed down under the weight of karma and we never suspect the reason. They too may trudge along, their eyes dull; it may challenge them just to get through the day. We shrug and say, "That's how they are." If our eyes could see below the physical level, we might see huge loads of karma riding on their shoulders.

Some time ago, while delivering an unusually heavy shipment of books to the post office, one of my friends drove too close to a soft shoulder and slipped into the water control ditch by the side of the road. We had to call a tow truck to pull him out. Without the weight of those books, he told me later, the shoulder of the road would probably not have crumbled. Everyone understands this explanation because physical burdens can be felt and seen; but if I say I see people fall into the ditch because they have so much karma in their trunk, it sounds occult. Yet I am not exaggerating. Everybody's unconscious has a million harsh words, a thousand neglected opportunities to put others first. Even if each is small, the weight adds up, and it is all that weight that impedes our spiritual progress. Empty your trunk of self-will, the mystics say, and you will find that karma no longer oppresses you. Once the trunk is emptied, it is closed and locked; for without self-will, there is no karma. All your actions are prompted by love, and the good karma that selfless actions produce goes to benefit others.

Recently I read about a diligent bank clerk who managed to break the necessary codes so that as far as the bank computer was concerned, a particular account was inactive. The computer would go on sending out the proper statements, but whatever credits should have been posted to that account got credited to some special accounts set up by this clerk instead. Karma accounts work a little like this too, only instead of embezzlement, it is fulfillment. After your karma account is closed, credits for good karma keep coming; but they cannot go to your account because it has been erased. So your banker says, "To whom shall I credit this?" And you can choose. All the beneficial karma that you naturally accumulate after illumination can actually be directed to others' accounts, lifting a good deal of their burden.

ज्ञानं कर्म च कर्ता च त्रिधैव गुणभेदतः ।
प्रोच्यते गुणसंख्याने यथावच्छृणु तान्यपि ॥ १८-१९ ॥
सर्वभूतेषु येनैकं भावमव्ययमीक्षते ।
अविभक्तं विभक्तेषु तज्ज्ञानं विद्धि सात्त्विकम् ॥ १८-२० ॥
पृथक्त्वेन तु यज्ज्ञानं नानाभावान्पृथग्विधान् ।
वेत्ति सर्वेषु भूतेषु तज्ज्ञानं विद्धि राजसम् ॥ १८-२१ ॥
यत्तु कृत्स्नवदेकस्मिन्कार्ये सक्तमहैतुकम् ।
अतत्त्वार्थवदल्पं च तत्तामसमुदाहृतम् ॥ १८-२२ ॥

*19. Knowledge, action, and the reasons for action
can be described according to the gunas. Listen,
and I will explain their distinctions to you.
20. Sattvic knowledge recognizes the one
indestructible Being in all beings, the divine
unity underlying the multiplicity of creation.
21. Rajasic knowledge sees all things and creatures
as separate and distinct.
22. Tamasic knowledge, without any sense of
perspective, sees one small part and mistakes it
for the whole.*

We can take these verses as a commentary on science, the midwife of our modern civilization.

Tamasic science, the Gita says, sees only its own small corner of life and thinks that is the world. Once this might have been a matter for small concern, but today it is likely to be disastrous. Most weapons research is conducted in large labs where each person is working on one part of a weapons system – a guidance mechanism, say – without having to think about what the whole system will do. It is just a job, an elaborate technical problem. When he solves such a problem, as a good scientist he feels the same satisfaction that he might feel after a game of chess. In such isolation, what makes him stop to think about how the weapon might be used, what it might do, whom it might be used on? What prompts him to reflect that soon the innovation he has been working on will be part of every major nation's arsenal, so that it threatens *him*, his family and friends, and he has to race toward something even more destructive? There are hundreds of thousands of such scientists today, in every country that can afford them, doing their best, in their ignorance of the whole, to increase the devastation that can be wrought by stockpiles of weapons capable of killing every person on earth many times over. I feel sure that the vast majority of these men and women of science are good people, educated and cultured, enjoyable to know. But they have no sensitivity beyond the surface of life, because their intellect mistakes the part for the whole.

In Sanskrit the word for science, *vidyā*, implies a deep, intimate understanding of a subject's inner nature. That is characteristic of sattvic science, represented by towering figures like Newton and Einstein. Our modern civilization has contributed a remarkable number of such figures, men and women for whom science meant a lifelong, all-absorbing search for truth. But the cornerstone of our times is not sattvic but rajasic science, whose purpose is not to learn from nature but to exploit it. Rajasic science has an amazing genius for making money out of natural laws. On its lab walls are two guiding mottoes: "If it can be discovered, it can be sold" and "If it can be made, make it!"

I don't think anybody illustrates this kind of genius better than Thomas Edison. Sattvic science, by Edison's time, had predicted the unity of electric and magnetic fields; the problem facing rajas was how to turn those abstract equations into patents. Edison solved the scientific, industrial, and commercial problems together, which means the goal in his mind was more than simply scientific. His new generator was designed not only to produce electric power, but to do so at a highly competitive price. When he patented his incandescent electric lamp, he also patented an electric meter for billing potential customers. That is the genius of rajas. In ten years the Edison "package" was producing power and making money in countries all around the world.

Edison's success, incidentally, also launched a key institution of rajasic science: the research lab. Sattvic science is characteristically pursued by individuals, but individual research is too idiosyncratic and too slow. Rajas wants fast results, and he needs results that pay. So he puts a lot of people together and proceeds to do research the way pin factories in

Adam Smith's day made pins: one person fashioning the head, a second the shaft, a third putting them together, and so on. It is an effective approach; the Manhattan Project is probably its greatest monument. There some of the greatest physicists in history came together to turn airy theories about the nature of matter into a bomb of incomparable power. They did so in just a couple of years, pursuing two or three different approaches at once – men and women from all kinds of backgrounds, with all kinds of temperaments, working together in harmony and efficiency. The Manhattan Project made a deep impression on the asuric mind: it showed that profit and the power to destroy can be gleaned from even the most abstruse thinking in search of truth.

I have been enjoying a personal perspective on this period in a book called *Disturbing the Universe,* written by an English physicist named Freeman Dyson who came to Cornell University after the war to join Hans Bethe and the other great physicists who had followed him from Los Alamos. Reading Dyson, I began to form my own ideas of why the Manhattan Project had been so successful. The physics department at Cornell, he says, hummed with creative activity in those years – a constellation of brilliant scientists, working together day and night without thought of personal gain to achieve something really big. Even when the goal is destructive, I still respond to this kind of atmosphere where dedicated individuals forget their differences in working for a great cause. This is one of life's greatest joys. Every one of us can work better in a selfless project if we remember the joy these scientists shared in their work:

> It was youth, it was exuberance, it was informality, it was a shared
> ambition to do great things together in science without any
> personal jealousies or squabbles over credit. Many years later they
> received well-deserved Nobel prizes, but nobody at Cornell was
> grabbing for prizes.

This is the spirit of sattvic science, yet at Los Alamos it allowed itself to be harnessed by rajas for an unimaginably destructive end. There is a tragic element of blindness to consequences in this, a fatal lack of imagination. Still, the Manhattan Project demonstrates what a small band of dedicated, selfless people can achieve. The men and women who made the atomic bomb were a very gifted lot. But I want to call your attention to another gifted lot – a group that includes you and me. We too are connected with the Manhattan Project, only what they built up, we can demolish. And we can do it in much the same way: with the same resourcefulness, the same daring, the same dedication, and the same harmonious effort.

One man who particularly caught my attention in Dyson's story was Richard Feynman, a brilliant, intuitive, unorthodox young physicist who solved problems with a creative leap of the imagination that these other great scientists sometimes found difficult to follow. Dyson recalls that when Feynman spoke to a gathering of distinguished physicists, struggling to put his vision into words, his theories were rejected out of hand – and this by perhaps the greatest assemblage of genius that science had seen for generations. Feynman pursued his ideas against this tide of learned opinion for some five years before they gained acceptance. All of us should remember this if we want to do original work, which cannot help running counter to the conventional wisdom. "What I saw of Dick," Dyson says, "reminded me of what I heard Keynes say of Sir Isaac Newton six years earlier: 'His peculiar gift was the power of holding continuously in his mind a purely mental problem until he had seen straight through it.'" This capacity is necessary for achieving great things, and the Gita reminds us that it is available to everyone who reaches beyond his or her private, personal self for a higher purpose.

Here I want to put in an enthusiastic word for the ordinary people of the world. I consider myself a very ordinary person, and I presume that by and large my readers are ordinary also. That, to me, is our glory. But even ordinary people like you and me, when we harness our personal desires to achieve a selfless goal, can do extraordinary things. In that sense ordinary people do become extraordinary. You remember Gandhi's assurance: "I have not the slightest doubt that any man or woman can achieve what I have, if he or she would make the same effort and cultivate the same hope and faith." Like Gandhiji, if we draw on meditation to ally our personal efforts with the forces of truth, love, and unity, we *can* help to reverse the disastrous trends we see around us, even if we ourselves are very small.

नियतं सङ्गरहितमरागद्वेषतः कृतम् ।
अफलप्रेप्सुना कर्म यत्तत्सात्त्विकमुच्यते ॥ १८-२३ ॥
यत्तु कामेप्सुना कर्म साहंकारेण वा पुनः ।
क्रियते बहुलायासं तद्राजसमुदाहृतम् ॥ १८-२४ ॥
अनुबन्धं क्षयं हिंसामनपेक्ष्य च पौरुषम् ।
मोहादारभ्यते कर्म यत्तत्तामसमुच्यते ॥ १८-२५ ॥

*23. Work performed to fulfill one's obligations,
without thought of personal reward or of whether
the job is pleasant or unpleasant, is sattvic.
24. Work prompted by selfish desire or self-will,
full of stress, is rajasic.
25. Work that is undertaken blindly, without any
consideration of consequences, waste, injury to
others, or one's own capacities, is tamasic.*

No translation can do justice to the precision of these terms, which are
deadly in Sanskrit. "Work" here is still *karma*, any human action or
activity. But I want to apply it specifically in the sense of employment,
in order to get the Gita's view of economics.

We can begin with asuric economics: Tamas and Rajas, Inc. Tamas,
the Gita says, does everything blindly, wrapped in a thick fog of *moha*,
the blindness of self-will. He can see just one thing, the only thing he
is interested in: himself. Because of this blindness, he pays no attention
to the cost of anything he does – neither in money, nor in resources,
nor in harm to other people. Tamas is wasteful of everything, even
lives. The word Sri Krishna uses is *kshaya*, which means not only waste
but decay, corruption, consumption. The Sanskrit name for tuberculosis comes from this word; it carries the connotation of wasting away.
Tamasic work drains prāna, consumes vitality. A person whose personality has been invaded by tamas wastes time, wastes effort, wastes life
itself. Tamasic economics does the same.

Tamasic work is work that harms people, work that inflicts injury or
death on other creatures. This is the lowest kind of human occupation.

Yet if you ask him about it, Tamas will shrug and reply, "It's just a job." One employee of a major weapons contractor explained in the paper recently, "It's just like any other job, really. I don't feel like what I'm doing has anything to do with death and destruction. We come to work, we do some paper work, and we go out for a beer afterward." His plant builds missile-launching systems. No job is "just a job," the Gita would say. Every job is karma: it carries costs. Each of us has the responsibility to assess the consequences of our work, for we will share in the karma of it whether we think about consequences or not.

Some years ago the *New Yorker* carried a profile of a man who, upon graduating from college in physics, proved to be a brilliant designer of nuclear weapons. What intrigued me was that he was a gentle, peace-loving young man; he merely happened to have a genius for making bombs. As a young physicist in the heady early years of the Atomic Age, he found himself tantalized by the challenge of ballistics problems no one else could solve. He couldn't let a second-rate bomb design lie around without improving on it, even when an "elegant solution" meant a smaller, simpler bomb that could kill more people. "The worst invention in physical history," he admits, "was also the most interesting." And he adds a very illuminating observation: "The theorist's world is a world of the best people and the worst of possible results." That is what moha does.

This is a talented, sensitive person, who I am glad to say has turned to more constructive activities. He gives us a clue to how rajas can be transformed. Given intellectual challenge and support, the same scientists can harness the same ingenuity, imagination, and dedication to achieve a beneficial goal. The rajasic researcher is not cruel. What satisfies him in defense work is not being destructive, but the things that make any kind of scientific work rewarding: intellectual challenge, professional respect, the satisfaction of solving problems skillfully, pride when a job is well done.

It is the same, I believe, with other defense-related work. Most people hold these jobs because they need work, and this is where jobs are. They would be happy doing something more beneficial, and all of us share the responsibility to shift toward an economy that makes more beneficial work available. Just as each of us has to ask about "right occupation," everybody should ask about "right economics," which is based on caring and sharing. How does our present economy use its resources, human as well as material? What are its costs – again, human as well as material? Finally, whom does it benefit? What things are included in its "bottom line"?

The arms industry makes a good place to begin. What are its real costs, and what does it contribute? Most people, I think, believe that big spending on war and weapons can buy a country into prosperity. In the United States, wasn't it full-scale war production that pulled the economy out of the Great Depression and made this the richest country on earth? "Everyone knows war is good for business," says Tamas. He is not strong in analytical thinking; he likes to fall back on formulas. "Defense spending is a shot in the arm for the whole economy."

Sattva would agree with the analogy: a defense economy becomes addicted to high spending very much the way a person becomes addicted to drugs. Each new contract stimulates the economy a little less, and more money is required to get the same boost the next time. The arms industry, in fact, is a powerful engine of inflation. Nothing puts a ceiling on its costs. As in other industries where a few companies control the market – oil, the grain trade – prices tend to "float free" of real expenses. And however high the price tag, governments always seem to be willing to buy more weapons. A few industries do get an immediate "shot in the arm" from all this public spending, but everybody gets higher prices, higher taxes, and a cheaper dollar later on.

Inflation is deadly for those who live on fixed incomes. Hundreds of thousands of older people today cannot afford what you or I would call minimum food, heat, clothing, and rent, the costs of which continue to rise. But defense spending does more harm than merely fueling inflation. It usurps resources which should be benefiting people and their work: skills, training, talent, natural resources, even capital. In a sattvic economy, a sound economy, resources go to produce goods and services that people need and can use. An arms economy pours human and material resources into a black hole. Nobody benefits from what is produced, and in fact we benefit most if it is not used at all. Defense spending seems to have a stimulating effect, but over a period of time the economy wastes away from inside. It is producing nothing of use, and eating up a country's potential in the process.

"Nonsense," Tamas would object. "Defense spending isn't barren; it creates jobs." How many jobs, and what kind? Leslie Nulty, assistant to the president of the machinists and aerospace workers union, stated that "a dollar spent virtually anywhere else in our economy creates more jobs than a dollar devoted to military procurement." One billion dollars spent on defense creates, directly and indirectly, some 28,000 new jobs. The same amount of money would create 32,000 jobs if spent in public transit and 71,000 if spent in education.

Defense spending may actually even cost jobs because of the cuts in social spending it requires. In California, a state agency has concluded that although the current increase in military spending will create some 670,000 new jobs, it will eliminate almost a million jobs that people are now holding.

Further, a good deal of new defense money goes to specialists, not to the local electricians, carpenters, building contractors, and unskilled laborers who swell unemployment rolls. "Economists," I read in the *San Francisco Examiner*, "worry that the nation's brightest engineers are designing supersonic fighters and electronic warfare systems instead of fuel-efficient cars and reliable color television sets that can compete with well-made imports." An asuric economy pours more and more of its resources into a contracting sector, while much of its labor force idles and critical parts of its industrial capacity may grow obsolete. Finally it begins to ask why it is falling behind other nations, which are supplying more and more of its goods.

These are large issues. What is at stake is not merely a destructive industry, but the profit motive itself. An asuric economy would be built on waste and exploitation even if the question of arms spending could be set aside. The story of what Tamas and Rajas, Inc., do to a nation's economy would make a fascinating book. All I can do in a few paragraphs is raise questions, but that is enough to suggest the Gita's perspective.

A sattvic economy focuses on the welfare of all, which leaves room for everybody to make a reasonable profit in producing and selling goods and services that people need. In an asuric economy, however, an industry does not exist for the sake of producing something useful. It exists to make money, which may or may not involve producing something, useful or otherwise. Other costs or benefits are essentially irrelevant. Rajas makes his business decisions on the basis of "maximizing the bottom line," no matter what the consequences elsewhere. He measures averages and aggregates. If corporate profits are up, then the economy is "recovering," even if the higher profits have been gained by firing large numbers of people and a record number of businesses have failed. If GNP is rising, he concludes that the economy is getting stronger, although as Richard Barnet points out, many activities counted in the gross national product – "the automobile accident industry, the cancer economy, the costs of pollution, crime, and welfare – though they put money in a lot of pockets, [make] the economy poorer, not richer."

Sattvic economics, to borrow Mr. Schumacher's subtitle, is "economics as if people mattered." It counts human costs as well as material ones, and its bottom line measures the whole rather than the benefit to a few. Asuric economics, by contrast, is *essentially* wasteful. Its very nature is to be careless of the whole. It doesn't intend to waste resources; it doesn't want to put the health of workers and consumers at risk or to despoil the environment. It only wants to go on making more money. But wealth has to come from somewhere, and in a limited world, unlimited profits cannot be had without someone paying the costs. This is crucial, because it means that we cannot pursue the welfare of the whole globe with the traditional motivations of greed and growth.

Rajas tends to consume resources at a prodigious rate – and not only natural resources; I am speaking also of human beings. In the early days of the industrial revolution, workers were used up as carelessly as any other plentiful commodity, for the same reason: they were cheap, and the profit motive required that they stay cheap. This was dictated by an Iron Law of Wages, which Rajas found it convenient to consider as inexorable as the law of gravity: when you can buy a man (or a woman, or a child) for a dollar a day, Market Forces will not allow you to pay a dollar ten. Today, of course, this looks more like an Iron Law of Greed. Yet many people still believe in it. It has helped to create a central paradox of industrial civilization: unheard-of prosperity side by side with intolerable poverty and despair.

This paradox has not disappeared with industrial growth; it has spread. In Dickens's day, the industrial slums of a prosperous city might be as close as the other side of the tracks; today they are often on the other side of the world. In a world of global markets, poverty has become a global problem. Asuric Enterprises can buy labor wherever it pleases, and it has the economic power to dictate its terms to nations that can supply labor cheap. The same forces which made slums of cities now keep whole populations poor – not out of anyone's cruelty, I repeat, but simply to ensure a decent bottom line. This may be good business for big business, and it makes the GNP soar; but I don't think any country benefits by encouraging it. Poorer countries are kept poor, and even in wealthier countries we see poverty increasing as labor is purchased elsewhere or supplied by itinerant immigrants.

Let me give some illustrations, first from the Third World. Rajas's formula for economic development is to encourage the profit motive. Wasn't that what made the industrialized nations rich? He looks at a country like Brazil, a showcase for his theories, and observes with puzzlement, "This is the country of the Economic Miracle: massive foreign investment, a booming GNP, a wealthy elite and a middle class that, if small, is slowly growing. Why is inflation out of control, and why are the poor poorer than ever? Why do so many in the middle class feel economically threatened instead of more secure?"

The "economic miracle" that Brazil represents is financed by attracting large amounts of foreign capital, which is a little like inviting the fox in to build hen houses. International businesses have profited immensely from "developing" Brazil. Natural resources have been taken from the country instead of being used for local development, at the cost of waste, depletion, and destruction. Jobs *are* created by such activities, but local workers are still employed at local wage levels: if they were not so cheap, development would not be so attractive. Skilled labor is often brought in by outside contractors; so no skilled local work force is being trained. The money that does flow back into the country does not usually go where it can buy corn and beans; it goes to investors – wealthy individuals, large domestic businesses, banks, multinational corporations. Now, nothing keeps a domestic bank, business, or citizen from reinvesting profits at home. But generally it is more profitable to put the money somewhere else, where it does no domestic good – in a U.S. or Swiss bank, in Japanese stocks, in gold, or even in a foreign investment corporation that wants to "develop" some other country. The GNP may soar, but who benefits? The assets that should be developing local economies and businesses, building locally-owned factories, training domestic workers, raising food for self-sufficiency, are flowing out – benefiting a few, but actually making the nation poorer.

Wasting away under the cover of a rising GNP is not a disease of developing economies only. Even in this country, I have been noticing how deftly profit can be made to grow without productive activity. Here Rajas's ingenuity really shines. "Why break your head," he asks, "competing in a world where labor, materials, and capital are expensive and markets glutted? Instead of improving production or cutting costs, you can show growth by acquiring another company and merging the balance sheets." This has actually been a popular corporate activity. Similarly, immense amounts of money which could be invested in beneficial work are invested elsewhere for the sake of short-term profits. Much of it goes into money-lending – the "money market," buying and selling million-dollar IOUs. Who would want to tie up capital in retooling a factory for only a possible long-term profit when he can lend it out at ten or fifteen percent with scarcely any risk or effort? A lot of money can be made in this way, but the activity is sterile. The economy is continually draining its resources and going nowhere. One statesman has even observed that the U.S. is slipping into the status of a colonized country, supplying the world with raw materials and foodstuffs and importing most of its finished goods.

To his surprise, Rajas is beginning to discover that unlimited growth, instead of being a panacea, can be a kind of economic cancer. Asuric Enterprises' activity, aiming continually at short-term profit instead of taking a long view of "care and share," ends with consuming its own sources of vitality.

Any economics based on separateness, the Gita would say, cannot help failing in the long run. Rajas would have us believe that the free pursuit of profit, which obviously is of immediate benefit to a few, will eventually benefit everybody. This is an outworn idea; it cannot be sustained by a global view, which observes that around the world, in many countries both developed and developing, the gap between rich and poor is widening and the numbers increasing of those who live in poverty. We live on one small planet, where everything is interconnected; unlimited growth cannot be pursued for some without costs that will eventually be paid by all. A sattvic economics, a twenty-first century economics of caring and sharing, is not a luxury but a necessity.

मुक्तसङ्गो ऽनहंवादी धृत्युत्साहसमन्वितः ।
सिद्ध्यसिद्ध्योर्निर्विकारः कर्ता सात्त्विक उच्यते ॥१८-२६॥
रागी कर्मफलप्रेप्सुर्लुब्धो हिंसात्मको ऽशुचिः ।
हर्षशोकान्वितः कर्ता राजसः परिकीर्तितः ॥१८-२७॥
अयुक्तः प्राकृतः स्तब्धः शठो नैकृतिको ऽलसः ।
विषादी दीर्घसूत्री च कर्ता तामस उच्यते ॥१८-२८॥

*26. A sattvic worker is free from egotism and
selfish attachments, full of enthusiasm and
fortitude in success and failure alike.
27. A rajasic worker has strong personal
desires and craves rewards for his actions.
Covetous, impure, and destructive, he is easily
swept away by fortune good or bad.
28. The tamasic worker is inattentive, vulgar,
arrogant, deceitful, malicious, and lazy. He is
easily depressed and prone to procrastination.*

The word *kartā* means literally 'one who does', so these verses really
refer to the character we show in all our actions, the mental states
behind behavior. Nevertheless, the side of ourselves we show during
work can be particularly revealing of our state of mind.

The other day I saw a devastating film about war, *A Bridge Too Far*.
One scene still haunts me: the vision of thousands of paratroopers literally darkening the sky. That is what can happen in selfish attachment,
when a person is invaded by rajasic and tamasic thoughts: the mind
becomes blotted out with negative obsessions, and night descends on
consciousness. Such people live in darkness, and the tragedy is that they
have no idea of it; they think everything is light. Not seeing clearly, they
are liable to do disastrous things. Where there is no danger, they are
suspicious; where they should be wary, they rush in blindly. For this
reason it is not wise to give responsible jobs to those who lack detachment: even if their intentions are good, their judgment cannot be trusted.

Sattva, by contrast, has a clear sense of priorities. This is not really a matter of efficiency. It reflects a mental state in which life has a unified purpose, making every day precious. The other day someone was telling me that a friend of hers did not have long to live. I had to remind her that none of us have long to live. Sattva remembers this always, reminding us to make the most of every day as an opportunity to give.

In fairness, I think all of us understand and respond to this ideal deep in our hearts. But most people have never had the experience of giving simply and purely, for no other reason than love. They have been conditioned to evaluate even an act of charity in terms of the admiration or status it brings; they have not had the opportunity of working with others for a great cause without expecting even a thank you. How could they know that this selfless giving of resources, time, or talents can release us from tension and competition?

I began to learn this lesson when I was a freshman in college. In those days I wanted to be a writer, so naturally I wanted to see more of life. That summer I persuaded my grandmother to let me spend my vacation traveling among some of the villages in the neighboring state of Tamil Nadu.

Soon I came across a village very different from the one where I grew up. Our village was prosperous and literate, but this Tamil village was so poor that it didn't have a school, and most of these villagers did not know how to read or write. They were simple, hard-working farmers; that was all.

But they had a strong desire to learn. They asked me to stay and be their teacher, not only of the children but of the adults too. What would I charge? They had never had a teacher in the village before, they explained, and they had no money with which to pay. But they could provide me with food, each family taking turns, and I could stay with one of the better-off households as if I were their own son. All this moved me deeply. I was only a freshman, after all; most of these villagers were old enough to be my parents. And I had only three months of vacation. How much can you teach in three months to people who had scarcely had a day's schooling in their lives, who knew nothing but crops and soils?

"What do you want to learn?" I asked.

"We'd like to know arithmetic," they said, "for buying and selling. We'd like to learn how to read, so we could read the stories in the scriptures.

And we'd like to know how to write, so we could write letters to our relatives and friends."

"That's a lot," I said.

They smiled. "We have all summer. Of course, we can't come during the day; we have to work in the fields. But we can come at night."

That kind of desire really impressed me. "Do you have a building where we could meet?"

"No," someone said. "But we can make one."

In my mind the three months began to shrink into two. "How long would it take?" I asked.

They grinned enthusiastically. "We can do it tonight."

I couldn't believe my ears.

"Sure," they said. "It's a full moon. We'll start after dinner. You have your meal and then come and select the site; we'll do the rest."

That was my first glimpse of the real strength of India's villagers, the millions of peasants who hold the country together. I selected a pleasant site on a gentle hill, from which you could see the river running close by. And after dinner, probably about eight o'clock in the evening, a man turned up from every hut in the village. These were men who had been up before dawn, worked hard in the hot fields with just a couple of hours rest when the sun was at its zenith. I was so profoundly impressed that I insisted on working alongside them, though I probably only slowed them down; they had to teach me everything. But by the time the sun came up the next morning, we had a one-room school – mud walls, thatched roof, sand from the riverbank for a floor, even a slate to write on and a piece of railing for a bell. As far as we were concerned, it was perfect.

I taught throughout that summer, and though attendance was a little irregular, by and large someone from every household was there faithfully every evening at eight when class began. None of us had a watch, so we used to end the lesson when we heard the whistle and clatter of the Blue Mountain Express chugging its way up the hills. Sometimes I would get so absorbed that when I heard a train and stopped, they would laugh and say, "The Blue Mountain Express went by an hour ago. That's the Malabar Express; it must be eleven o'clock." By the end of the summer we didn't go home till we heard the Cochin Express go by at midnight.

By that time they could read, write, and reckon, which must have felt like the greatest achievement of their lives. Yet I felt I had learned much more. I never received a penny for my work, though in their simple affection my students used to bring me all kinds of things they had grown or made: mangoes, coconuts, bananas, grass mats, a pair of handmade sandals. But I received much more than I gave. From those simple villagers, who had just the bare minimum of material possessions, I learned to understand the words of St. Francis: "It is in giving that we receive."

बुद्धेर्भेदं धृतेश्चैव गुणतस्त्रिविधं शृणु ।
प्रोच्यमानमशेषेण पृथक्त्वेन धनंजय ॥ १८-२९॥
प्रवृत्तिं च निवृत्तिं च कार्याकार्ये भयाभये ।
बन्धं मोक्षं च या वेत्ति बुद्धिः सा पार्थ सात्त्विकी ॥ १८-३०॥
यया धर्ममधर्मं च कार्यं चाकार्यमेव च ।
अयथावत्प्रजानाति बुद्धिः सा पार्थ राजसी ॥ १८-३१॥
अधर्मं धर्ममिति या मन्यते तमसावृता ।
सर्वार्थान्विपरीतांश्च बुद्धिः सा पार्थ तामसी ॥ १८-३२॥

*29. Listen, Arjuna, as I describe the three
types of understanding and will.
30. To know what to do and what to refrain from doing,
what is right action and what is wrong, what brings
security and what insecurity, what brings freedom and
what bondage: these are the signs of a sattvic intellect.
31. The rajasic intellect confuses right and wrong
actions, distorting dharma and adharma.
32. The tamasic intellect is shrouded in darkness,
utterly reversing right and wrong wherever it turns.*

The subject of these verses is *buddhi,* which is not just intelligence but discriminating intelligence – not merely seeing, but seeing into. It is not enough to see the physical side of life, Sri Krishna says; we have to see into its heart. It is not enough to see people as physical creatures; we have to see the Self in them. It is not enough to see the world; we have to see into its underlying unity. Otherwise nothing makes sense, nothing holds together, and we are left with no way of judging wise choices from foolish ones.

The tamasic intellect, the Gita says, is shrouded in darkness; it thinks wrong is right and right is wrong. This applies not only to the Big Issues of ethics. When you are unkind to someone, that is tamas; your intellect is telling you that wrong is right. On a national level, if you want to see sophisticated explanations of why right is wrong and wrong is right, you can read the state papers of almost any country – or, for that matter, the front page of almost any newspaper.

The rajasic intellect, by contrast, is mixed: sometimes clear, but muddied wherever self-interest comes into play. Throughout the work of our meditation center I have met many men and women who were outstanding in their professions. I was often surprised to discover later that in situations where they were emotionally entangled, the same experts could be foolish and even childish. That is rajasic understanding, and I think it is saddest in education and science, where the very basis of the profession should be sattvic knowledge, without any selfish motive.

When Tamas and Rajas incorporate themselves in science, the combination is disastrous: one can't tell what is right and what is wrong, and the other doesn't care. Genetic engineering is a good example. Some years ago scientists announced that they had finally learned how to put individual microorganisms to work – a truly numerous labor force! "A microorganism," one spokesman for the new industry said, "is basically a little chemical factory." It takes in substances and produces other substances without wages, downtime, or labor disputes, an industrialist's dream. By changing the right gene in certain bacteria, for example, the bacteria will then actually produce the substance you desire, in great quantities and at low cost, simply by growing and reproducing. There *is* promise in this, but not, I would say, unless the mental state behind it changes. Any approach to life as basically something to exploit *has* to backfire, because that attitude infects every application. It is tamasic through and through.

"What we have been able to do," this spokesman explains, "is speed up evolution, if you will. We can literally now get our hands on the genetic makeup of microorganisms and pick the characteristics we want." Unfortunately, the very things that make this technology so powerful – the fact that microorganisms grow very rapidly and reproduce on their own – give it immense potential for getting out of control. But long-term problems pale next to short-term profits, which have been stupendous. These are developments that have thrilled Wall Street.

Predictably, however, others find them disturbing. As with nuclear power in the early days, one senses that the technology has taken a life of its own. It is natural, I think, to feel mistrustful when one learns that an agency of one's own government – the National Institutes of Health – has patented the genes of indigenous human beings on the other side of the globe. Behind such actions lies a mental state that can only be viewed with alarm.

Professor Liebe Cavalieri of the Cornell medical school summed the situation up well in an opinion piece contributed to the *Christian Science Monitor*. "One might ask," he commented drily, whether the same human beings whose ignorance of the whole has brought the world to its present state "could generate the fullness of vision needed to redesign a better system." And he concluded, "Rearranging our genes is not likely to provide the solutions we so desperately need."

The lure of profit in genetic engineering has even infected education. Of course, universities have been entangled in business through weapons, food, and pharmaceutical research since World War II, so that a student of the sciences now goes through college taking for granted that the nature of his or her profession is not merely to understand the physical world, but to help exploit it for some vested institution. With bioengineering, however, the "big money" got really big. Some university biologists have resolved the dilemma by dropping out of teaching and opening commercial labs of their own. Many who remain have been able to eat their cake and have it too, as prestigious universities find profitable ways to share their faculty and facilities with big business. I would not call such people scientists any longer; they are businesspeople, teaching a little on the side. I have no quarrel with anyone who does not want to teach; but as a former teacher, I feel qualified to plead that teaching and extreme self-interest do not mix. I am not saying that teachers should be underpaid. I am talking about getting caught, deeply caught, in personal gain. These are people who should embody the highest values in scientific research. They cannot afford to be indebted to profit-oriented corporations that need to manipulate the public for the sake of growth and market share.

The federal government contributes 46 percent of our "total R&D spending." Industry contributes 51 percent. In practice, I would estimate, this means that almost all of the money spent on scientific research is tied to one of two major purposes: making new profits in consumer markets and increasing the effectiveness of weapons of war. Since that is where the money is, that is where fresh scientific talent is attracted. So we are talking about the bulk of our scientific resources, not only financial but intellectual as well.

You may remember Toynbee's comment that if our civilization has made great strides in technology, it is because so many people have given their best to technology. Isn't it time that we gave our best to peace, and to finding decent solutions to the problems of human health and welfare? If we fail in these areas, no historian is going to praise us for our skill in designing microchips.

धृत्या यया धारयते मनःप्राणेन्द्रियक्रियाः ।
योगेनाव्यभिचारिण्या धृतिः सा पार्थ सात्त्विकी ॥ १८-३३ ॥
यया तु धर्मकामार्थान्धृत्या धारयते ऽर्जुन ।
प्रसङ्गेन फलाकाङ्क्षी धृतिः सा पार्थ राजसी ॥ १८-३४ ॥
यया स्वप्नं भयं शोकं विषादं मदमेव च ।
न विमुञ्चति दुर्मेधा धृतिः सा पार्थ तामसी ॥ १८-३५ ॥

33. The sattvic will, developed through meditation, keeps prāna, mind, and senses in vital harmony.
34. The rajasic will, conditioned by selfish desire, pursues wealth, pleasure, and fame.
35. The tamasic will shows itself in obstinate ignorance, sloth, fear, grief, depression, and conceit.

We have been looking at the human being in terms of the intellect; these three verses make the same kind of evaluation in terms of the will. This is a highly interesting approach, because normally it is only the intellect that gets attention. Even in my high school, boys who were unruffled by opprobrious names felt crushed if you said they had a small IQ. But if you tell someone his Will Quotient can be counted in one digit, how much do you think he will care?

In fact, the intellect is overrated. Even when coupled with a high IQ – perhaps especially when coupled with a high IQ – a weak will is a terrible handicap in every walk of life. When the will is flaccid, its weakness begins to affect decisions from the moment the alarm goes off in the morning. Five-thirty, time for meditation – well, why not make it six? Six arrives and the weak will observes, "A quarter after is just the same." It is not only meditation that suffers; you are undermining your whole day.

The Sanskrit word for 'will' here is *dhriti,* from the same root as *dharma*: *dhri,* 'to support.' The will is what supports us, what holds all our faculties together in harmony, vitality, and strength. "Strength," Gandhi said, "does not come from physical capacity. It comes from an indomitable will." In times of trial and turmoil, when fortune frowns and friends forsake you, if your will is strong you will never lose heart or feel abandoned. You can look at the life of Gandhi and see what this means: he faced the bitterest opposition, calumny, and betrayal over and over, up to the last moment of his life. So did Teresa of Ávila; so did St. Francis. Where will you find more vibrant, cheerful, hopeful, beneficial lives?

For these reasons, the Gita offers rather surprising advice: if you want to be secure and self-reliant, if you want to become loving, if you want friends who will stand by you, then do everything you can to strengthen your will; don't do anything that undermines it. Even a midnight snack can undermine the will, though you conscientiously work off the calories the very next day. In the early days, of course, training the will requires effort and vigilance. It is not so simple or easy as it may seem. But the rewards will amaze you; and in the end, reassuringly enough, everything you had to work at becomes spontaneous and natural. Then you are free.

The sattvic will, Sri Krishna says, maintains an even flow of prāna among all our human faculties: the various parts of the body, the senses, and the faculties of the mind. I could write a book on this one observation, for it gives the secret of perfect health on every level, physical, emotional, and spiritual. Prāna is consumed by desires, so to conserve prāna, we need to develop a strong will and a clear sense of discrimination. The mind has right desires, which may be satis-fied, and wrong desires, which are to be defied. "Wrong desires" means those that are selfish: desires for things that benefit nobody, including ourselves. When a wrong desire is defied, there are rich dividends in prāna. Recently the newspaper has been carrying compelling graphs which show how retirement accounts grow: you put in a thousand or so every year and by the time you retire, due to the magic of compound interest, those thousands have turned into half a million. In the same way, by not spending prāna on wrong desires, our vitality account can compound a millionfold.

This is not an exaggeration. I have been reading about Gandhi's daily schedule when he was in his sixties, and the only way I can describe him is to say that this is human capacity multiplied a million times. Here is one day, not uncommon, where he gets up at three in the morn-ing to start answering correspondence; he confers with Indian leaders through the day, gives press interviews, has his prayer meeting and walk after dinner, and then goes at eight in the evening for another four-hour session with the English Viceroy of India. The fate of our country depended on the outcome of those talks; he should have been bowed under the burden. Instead, at midnight, he walks home discuss-ing the meeting with colleagues, lies down to sleep at one, and gets his secretary up at three to start the next day! This kind of life went on for months at a time, and it is a thrilling confession when he tells us that he throve on it. A life without challenges, he said – a life when you are not being stretched to the utmost – simply is not worth living. It shows what capacities we all have, if we can only remove the crust of self-centered living that prevents them from coming into play.

सुखं बिदानीं त्रिविधं शृणु मे भरतर्षभ ।
अभ्यासाद्रमते यत्र दुःखान्तं च निगच्छति ॥ १८-३६ ॥
यत्तदग्रे विषमिव परिणामे ऽमृतोपमम् ।
तत्सुखं साचिकं प्रोक्तमात्मबुद्धिप्रसादजम् ॥ १८-३७ ॥
विषयेन्द्रियसंयोगाद्यत्तदग्रे ऽमृतोपमम् ।
परिणामे विषमिव तत्सुखं राजसं स्मृतम् ॥ १८-३८ ॥
यदग्रे चानुबन्धे च सुखं मोहनमात्मनः ।
निद्रालस्यप्रमादोत्थं तत्तामसमुदाहृतम् ॥ १८-३९ ॥

*36. Now listen, Arjuna: there are also three
kinds of happiness. By sustained effort,
one comes to the end of sorrow.
37. The spiritual life seems like poison at first,
but tastes like nectar in the end. This is the joy
of sattva, born of a mind at peace with itself.
38. Pleasure from the senses seems like nectar at
first, but it is bitter as poison in the end. This is
the kind of happiness that comes to the rajasic.
39. Those who are tamasic draw their pleasures
from sleep, indolence, and intoxication.*

These are particularly potent verses, because they deal with the ever-popular subject of pleasure. Before I go into a practical commentary, therefore, I think the subject calls for a sobering reminder: that all of us are born to die. This puts pleasure into rather clear perspective.

I am proud to tell you that to my teacher, the very thought that I would die someday was something her limitless love could not tolerate. She *had* to take me beyond the reach of death, to that state of Self-realization which she herself had attained; her love made this the major focus of her life. Similarly, we know that the Buddha was impelled into the search for immortality when he looked on his lovely wife and newborn son lying asleep and realized that their youth and beauty could not escape the ravages of time and death. His love was so immense that that moment of insight burst in his consciousness like a bomb; after that, nothing would satisfy him until he had secured the secret of immortality and could teach it to everyone who would hear. Of course, it is natural for a man to love his family, natural for a grandmother to love her grandson. But the love I am talking about is something much higher than normal: it shapes your entire life around the desire to rescue those you love from the suffering of self-centered living and the agony of death.

To realize your immortal Self, you have to remember your physical mortality always. Very few of us can do this, but it provides a perfect perspective for evaluating life around us. Every day we move closer to the great change called death, not only those of us who are older but those who are young as well. Even when I was a boy, my grandmother used to remind me that life flies fast for everybody, and I loved her so much that her words went deep into my heart and remained there to keep me sensitive to the transience of time. Even before I took to meditation, I remember looking out across my freshman class and seeing suddenly that all those bright, beautiful faces would someday fade away. And I would recall those lines of Housman:

> With rue my heart is laden
> For golden friends I had,
> For many a rose-lipt maiden
> And many a lightfoot lad.
>
> By brooks too broad for leaping
> The lightfoot boys are laid;
> The rose-lipt girls are sleeping
> In fields where roses fade.

These were not morbid reflections. They released such tenderness that even if a student offended me or let me down, I always remembered how short life is: too short not to love, too short not to care.

That is the practical side, you see. People who are selfish have simply forgotten their mortality. People who are unkind have forgotten how quickly the play will all be over. And people who measure life in terms of pleasure forget that every pleasant experience, even the most rarefied, lasts such a short while; nothing remains of it that we can hold or build our lives on. When you remember that life is fleeting, you will have no time to be unkind, no time to quarrel, no time for anything but to give. Even those who do not meditate, if they can remember this, will find that it gives them access to a deeper level of consciousness.

When you feel like indulging your senses unduly or giving free rein to your self-will, I would suggest you remind yourself that set against a longer perspective, these indulgences are going to amount to very, very little. Our short span of life is over so soon. There isn't going to be anyone to be attached to, anyone to quarrel with, anyone to be jealous of, anyone to resent. Every older person is dimly aware of this, but by that time most of us are trapped in habits of mind that we find difficult to change. Now, while you have strength and vigor and determination, you can draw on this haunting recollection of mortality every day to strengthen your will, reduce your self-will, train your senses, and not let anything get in the way of your meditation.

These verses seem to call for poetry, so let me conclude with some lines from Robert Frost. I first became acquainted with them when I learned that Jawaharlal Nehru, our first prime minister, used to keep them on his desk as a constant reminder. They are the conclusion of a poem called "Stopping by Woods on a Snowy Evening":

> The woods are lovely, dark and deep,
> But I have promises to keep,
> And miles to go before I sleep,
> And miles to go before I sleep.

The forests of desire too are dark and deep, thick with unfulfilled desires. It is only human to feel tempted, to want to stray into them and take our time returning. But all of us have promises to keep, and miles to go, many miles, before we reach our home.

न तदस्ति पृथिव्यां वा दिवि देवेषु वा पुनः ।
सत्त्वं प्रकृतिजैर्मुक्तं यदेभिः स्यात्त्रिभिर्गुणैः ॥१८-४०॥

ब्राह्मणक्षत्रियविशां शूद्राणां च परंतप ।
कर्माणि प्रविभक्तानि स्वभावप्रभवैर्गुणैः ॥१८-४१॥

शमो दमस्तपः शौचं क्षान्तिरार्जवमेव च ।
ज्ञानं विज्ञानमास्तिक्यं ब्रह्मकर्म स्वभावजम् ॥१८-४२॥

शौर्यं तेजो धृतिर्दाक्ष्यं युद्धे चाप्यपलायनम् ।
दानमीश्वरभावश्च क्षत्रकर्म स्वभावजम् ॥१८-४३॥

कृषिगोरक्ष्यवाणिज्यं वैश्यकर्म स्वभावजम् ।
परिचर्यात्मकं कर्म शूद्रस्यापि स्वभावजम् ॥१८-४४॥

40. No creature, whether born on earth or among the gods in heaven, is free from the conditioning of the three gunas.
41. The different responsibilities found in the social order, Arjuna, have their roots in this conditioning.
42. The responsibilities to which a brahmin is born, based on his nature, are self-control in body and mind, purity of heart, patience, humility, learning, wisdom, and faith.
43. The qualities of a kshatriya, based on his nature, are courage, strength, fortitude, dexterity, generosity, leadership, and the firm resolve never to retreat from battle.
44. The occupations suitable for a vaishya are agriculture, dairying, and trade. The proper work of a shudra is service.

These verses refer to the caste system, about which there is a good deal of misunderstanding. Over many centuries these ideas of caste became a terribly rigid and oppressive mold, particularly with respect to the millions of outcaste Indians whom Gandhi called Harijans, 'children of God.' It is one of the greatest chapters in Gandhi's life when he begins to take on the ruthless exploitation of these people, who had been relegated to the lowest conceivable position in society.

At the same time, many people do not understand that although Gandhi was utterly opposed to the caste system as an instrument of exploitation, he was not opposed to the idea of caste itself. He wanted its rigidity dissolved, he wanted the very idea of "outcaste" Hindus to disappear from our hearts, but at the same time he wanted to preserve certain good qualities in this kind of social organization. This needs some explanation because it seems so contradictory. How can a man like Gandhi, so completely dedicated to the inalienable dignity in every human being, find anything to praise in a system that places individuals into different categories by birth?

First let me explain briefly what the caste system was like in ancient India, when it had certain virtues which can still be appreciated today. The original purpose of the four *varnas,* to use the Sanskrit word, was to facilitate living in the world. *Varnas* were something like roles, although much more comprehensive. The categories are: *brahmins,* priests and certain other professionals such as physicians and teachers (branches of knowledge were considered sacred in ancient India); *kshatriyas,* rather like the nobility of medieval Europe; *vaishyas,* the farmers, craftsmen, and merchants; and *shudras,* largely unskilled laborers.

These were not originally rigid categories, in which people were trapped by birth. Just as today a plumber's son might open his own hardware shop and make a name for himself in the world of business, a shudra was once able to become a vaishya, a craftsman or merchant. Similarly, though it is regarded as rather unseemly – meditation and sacred learning are considered to be their proper province – we find brahmins in the *Mahābhārata* who are highly skilled in the martial arts. Perhaps most important, caste was no bar to seeking and attaining Self-realization. I am speaking here of historical fact, not denying that there were prejudices to the contrary. The Buddha, himself born a kshatriya, drew great disciples from the so-called lower castes. So did Sri Ramakrishna, who was born into a very pure brahmin family just a little over a hundred years ago. The same holds true today. Mahatma Gandhi came from a vaishya or merchant community; the word *gandhi* means 'grocer'. And my grandmother's family, Eknath, are kshatriyas.

There are very practical reasons for traditions like these, which help to explain why the caste system has endured for probably three thousand years or more. First, we are talking here about culture – perhaps a hundred generations in which the families in a particular varna shaped their lives around the same habits, values, and standards, passed from parent to children. Because India embraces so many regions, languages, and traditions, you can find wide variations even within the same caste; brahmins in Kerala, for example, will have different habits from brahmins in Bengal. To take just one illustration, though my ancestral family are kshatriyas, we have been strict vegetarians for many generations. Every vegetarian, I think, can appreciate how difficult it is for a vegetarian to cook for a nonvegetarian, or even to share the same kitchen. Similarly, though they are not brahmins, men and women in my ancestral family are raised in an atmosphere that assumes the very highest spiritual ideals, which again is a characteristic of the ideal brahmin family. For these and many other similar reasons, our women generally married – as Granny and my mother did – men from a nearby brahmin community with lofty, pure values.

If you extend these illustrations to all the other values and habits of daily life, you will see how natural it is for an Indian man or woman to marry someone from a similar family background. The essential purpose of caste organization was to group people not so much by their occupation as by their values, their whole way of life. Again, however, I want to emphasize that I am talking about ideals, not trying to describe or defend how caste is followed in India today. I simply want to illustrate the truths behind these verses of the Gita, which might otherwise be lost in misunderstanding.

At its best, varna represents society as a collection of individuals with different aspirations, all evolving toward the one supreme goal of life, Self-realization. Life *is* evolving in this direction, it says in effect, yet not everyone desires the goal. People desire various things in life, according to their dominant gunas. Each, therefore, is born into the class where those accumulated personal desires can be fulfilled and the lessons of karma learned.

In other words, this ideal society is based on the assumption that life's highest activity is not the pursuit of wealth or power but renunciation. Most people have other goals, and they lead their lives accordingly; yet everybody reveres renunciation as the highest of ideals, and everybody expects the brahmin to live up to this ideal too. So arose a kind of spiritual *noblesse oblige*. In ancient India, the kshatriya had a very demanding code of honor, somewhat like the codes of chivalry in the West. A warrior was expected never to take unfair advantage of an enemy, not even to save his own life; and I have mentioned that he was expected never to turn his back in battle, not against any odds. If he gave his word, he was bound to it; and so on. Yet he was permitted the very human failings of the passions, on which the brahmin was expected to have turned his back.

In my granny's eyes, the same high standards apply to everyone who tries to lead the spiritual life, even ordinary people like you and me. This is a great responsibility. After we have been meditating for some time, though they may not say so, those who live and work with us develop certain expectations. If we burst out in anger, they feel surprised: even if everybody else gets angry daily, they expect something more of us. In a quiet way, our struggle to transform ourselves represents a very hopeful capacity in every human being; when we slip, they feel somehow that we have let them down. The more a person is capable of, my granny would say, the greater the responsibility to live up to those capacities.

The word *brahmin* means literally one who aspires to realize Brahman. The Buddha tells us what this means:

> Him I call a brahmin
> Who is never angry,
> Never causes harm to others
> Even when he is harmed by them.
>
> Him I call a brahmin
> Who clings not to pleasure. . . .
> Who does not hurt others
> With unkind acts, words, or thoughts.

Anyone who bases his or her life on these ideals, the Buddha is saying, *is* a brahmin, whatever the circumstances of his birth or the conditioning of her personality. Even a person who is selfish, or greedy, or full of anger or fear, can rise from tamas through rajas to sattva, and eventually pass beyond even the conditioning of sattva to attain Self-realization.

That is the power of meditation; do you see the sheer immensity of it? I am not speaking figuratively at all. We talk about the power of the sun, so immense that we can grasp it only when someone says that the sun converts billions of tons of hydrogen into helium every second and still has enough to go on burning for billions of years; then something sinks in, and still we have only a clue. It is the same with meditation. The Gita tells us that all our anger, all our fear, all our greed can be transformed into pure love, a force that will go on working even after we shed this physical body: we can't grasp it, but we know the power of these negative forces, which make us act in ways we do not choose; we know the terrible power such forces can have over whole societies; and we have the example of Gandhi, a little man of our own times, who managed to transform these awesome forces into a love that has altered history. Just as hydrogen can be transformed into helium, self-will can be transformed into love. The most angry person on earth can become the most loving; the most fearful can become the most fearless; the weakest can become the strongest. All this is the power of meditation.

स्वे स्वे कर्मण्यभिरतः संसिद्धिं लभते नरः ।
स्वकर्मनिरतः सिद्धिं यथा विन्दति तच्छृणु ॥ १८-४५॥
यतः प्रवृत्तिर्भूतानां येन सर्वमिदं ततम् ।
स्वकर्मणा तमभ्यर्च्य सिद्धिं विन्दति मानवः ॥ १८-४६॥
श्रेयान्स्वधर्मो विगुणः परधर्मात्स्वनुष्ठितात् ।
स्वभावनियतं कर्म कुर्वन्नाप्नोति किल्बिषम् ॥ १८-४७॥
सहजं कर्म कौन्तेय सदोषमपि न त्यजेत् ।
सर्वारम्भा हि दोषेण धूमेनाग्निरिवावृताः ॥ १८-४८॥

45. By devotion to one's own particular duty, everyone can attain perfection. Let me tell you how.
46. By performing work selflessly, a person worships the Creator who dwells in every creature. Such worship brings that person to fulfillment.
47. It is better to perform one's own duties imperfectly than to master the duties of another. By fulfilling

the obligations he is born with, a person never
comes to grief.
48. No one should abandon duties because he sees
defects in them. Every action, every activity, is
surrounded by defects as a fire is surrounded by smoke.

It is in our work and our relationships that we contribute to the rest of
the world. It is not enough, therefore, to make progress in meditation;
we also have to be sure that we share the fruits of meditation with those
we work and live with, primarily through our personal example. This
is the only way in which our personal karma can be undone. After all,
Sri Krishna asks drily, if we don't work out our own karma, who is going
to do it for us? Nothing is more important.

Sri Krishna is trying to make it clear here that how we work is as
important as what we do. Spiritual values are not so much taught as
caught, from the lives of those who embody them. Your job may be
nothing more glamorous than janitor in a hospital, but if you are practicing sādhana sincerely, you *will* be contributing to other people's lives,
even though you may not see it happening. These are spiritual laws.
I have friends who have come back from a stay in the hospital and told
me that the person who gave them most support and cheerful encour-
agement was an aide who was particularly thoughtful, or the night
nurse who always had a smile and something cheerful to say.

Every one of us can enrich his sādhana, improve her contribution
to the world, by giving the utmost concentration to the job at hand
in a spirit of detachment. Both these are necessary: concentration
and detachment. When they are present together, it is enough to go
on giving our best in fulfilling the responsibilities with which we are
entrusted. As sādhana deepens, new opportunities will open up to suit
our growing needs and capacities.

"Duties" here is *karma* again, and the word gives some valuable clues.
We don't have to envy others because the jobs they do seem to be more
prestigious or creative, or because other people seem to have more
skill; we are where we are, doing what we are doing, because we have
something to learn from that particular context. Our karma – what we
have thought, done, and desired – brought us to that job and to those

co-workers, because this is just the situation to work out the mistakes we made in dealing with others in the past. As that karma is worked out, we grow. Soon we may need a new context to work in, new people, new challenges, greater opportunities for service.

Last, Sri Krishna reminds us gently, is there any job that is one hundred percent perfect? Is there any position where you do only what you think you should, where your employer gives you meditation hours and mantram breaks and allows you to tell him how to conduct his business according to your interpretation of the eternal verities? Every job has its requirements that are not ours. Very few jobs are pure. No occupation is free from conflict; no task guarantees to protect us from stressful situations or from people with different views. And no job is free from drudgery; every line of work has a certain amount of routine. Sri Krishna says, Don't ask if you like the work, if it is creative, if it always offers something new. Ask if you are part of work that benefits people. If it does, give it your best attention. In that spirit every beneficial job can become a spiritual offering.

असक्तबुद्धिः सर्वत्र जितात्मा विगतस्पृहः ।
नैष्कर्म्यसिद्धिं परमां संन्यासेनाधिगच्छति ॥ १८-४९ ॥
सिद्धिं प्राप्तो यथा ब्रह्म तथाप्नोति निबोध मे ।
समासेनैव कौन्तेय निष्ठा ज्ञानस्य या परा ॥ १८-५० ॥

49. He who is free from selfish attachments,
who has mastered his senses and passions,
acts not, but is acted through by the Lord.
50. Listen to me now, Arjuna, how one who has
become an instrument in the hands of the Lord attains
Brahman, the supreme consummation of wisdom.

These verses begin Sri Krishna's last great description of the man or woman who has attained Self-realization – one of the most memorable passages in the Gita, which I highly recommend for use in meditation.

What does it mean to become "an instrument in the hands of the Lord"? One explanation is that we become an instrument of our own

Self, no longer moved by emotional and physical conditioning but motivated solely by love. To do this, we have to quiet the mind completely, for the mind is the place where conditioning lives – in fact, the mind *is* our conditioning. We live our lives within the narrow confines of the mind, never suspecting that there is anywhere else to live. But beyond the mind is a much vaster place, the Self, which mystics call the land of love, our soul's true home.

To find our Self, then, we have to look somewhere other than our feelings and opinions. No idea could be more confusing today. If we are not what we feel and think, what can we be? This confusion is compounded by misunderstandings about the word love. We are told that our nature is *love*; but isn't love a feeling, the most powerful of human emotions? The mystics say no: it is a state of being, an infinite force, the draw of unity. Our emotional states – liking, disliking, hoping, fearing, and so on – cover our native state of love. When the mind is completely still, we become love itself: we live in love; love is the spring of all our action.

No one can give an eyewitness account of the land beyond the mind, but all of us have a passionate nostalgia for it deep in our hearts. As we go deeper in meditation we begin to feel we are exiles here, tourists, wandering about and saying as tourists do, "Back home . . ." This world of change is not our native place. When we sense this and nostalgia begins to haunt us, all the thousand and one desires of the mind start to merge in the desire to return home. It is in this unification of desires that the mind is slowly dissolved.

The mind is a tumultuous place, a riot of thoughts; there are demonstrations on every side. It's very much like Berkeley used to be in the sixties. Today people sometimes ask me in awe, "You mean you were there during the Free Speech Movement? You went to Vietnam Day, got tear gas in your eyes, watched the troop caravans roll down the streets to protect People's Park from the people?" I reply, "Of course. For a while I lived right off Telegraph Avenue." But that was nothing. If you really want to see where the action is, look inside the mind: restaurants, movies, street theater, record stores, booksellers, craftspeople, all kinds of sights, sounds, smells, and hits. Whatever you want, you can get it from a vendor on Mind Street.

We don't know our own mind. In fairness, I have to admit that it is an extremely interesting place to learn to know. Nowhere on earth is more fascinating. But the better you get to know the mind, the more you will feel out of place there. Like so many dropouts from the sixties, you get tired of the Avenue. When every day is a demonstration, you know, after a while you get tired of demonstrations. You get tired of sampling the smorgasbord of sensations. "It's not like the old days," you tell your friends. "Maybe we should move to Mendocino." And at last comes a great desire to leave this town forever. Like a traveler who grows weary of foreign lands, like an expatriate who has been away too long, you get detachment from the once-enticing sights and sounds and think more and more of going home.

The mind is not stilled forcibly. You part with it over a long, long period, with good will. But when in the end it falls away from the horizon, you shed no tears. This was the source of all your turmoil, the distorter of your vision, the disrupter of your relationships. It does not need your sympathy. We feel sorry for the mind only as long as we identify with it. Once we see we are not the mind, we mourn its passing no more than we would mourn an old TV set when it blows its last transistor.

Simply to hear about men and women who have done this is inspiring. Then we know that it can be done; we can see the results in the glory of their lives. Afterward, they tell us, there is no movement in the mind. Therefore there is no anger, no fear, no greed, no separateness. When you attain this state, all sorrow falls away.

In the deeper stages of meditation, there are moments when the mind puts up a little sign: "Back in Two Minutes." Mr. Mind gets up, puts on his hat, and steps out for a turn around the block, taking his staff of problems with him. While they are gone, things are so blissful you can't help saying, "This is heaven!" It is. In those two minutes all your problems are temporarily suspended. Not solved, of course; they will return when the mind starts up again. But for two minutes you have a flash of heaven here on earth, and an intense nostalgia wells up in your heart. "*That's* where I belong!" you exclaim. "That's where I come from! Here's my passport; remember? That's what it says." And you wonder, "Why am I wandering around here?"

In this sense we are all searching from door to door to find our home. We knock at the house of Pleasure, but when she answers, her old man, Depression, is right there by her side. Knock at the next door and out comes Profit. "Is this home?" we ask. "Can't say," he replies. "But I can offer you a hot deal on some unsecured notes. Got a pen?" "We're not looking for a deal," we tell him. "We're trying to find our way home." He shuts the door, and we realize he has kept our pen. But it could be worse: if we go inside, pleasure or profit can slam the door and lock us in. That is perhaps the greatest tragedy in the latter part of life, when habits become rigid and we lose the will, the initiative, and the imagination to extricate ourselves from the wrong place. We pretend we have just what we wanted: we hang pictures on the wall, cultivate some African violets, buy a lacquered wooden sign from the five-and-ten that says, "No place like home!" But I don't think the heart is fooled. When we feel frustrated, insecure, not at peace with ourselves or others, we are admitting to ourselves, "This isn't home. I *want* to be fooled, but I'm really an alien here."

When this realization comes, you may get even more restless. You might leave your old haunts and habits and go to New Orleans for a while, Paris, Molokai, Kathmandu. You're looking for your own place, which is a sure sign that you are not where you belong. It's as if you are always in somebody else's house: the tables are all the wrong height, you reach for the soap and find your hand in the ashtray; everything is different, everything is off. Where you expect love you find hatred, where you expect appreciation you get deprecation, where you expect security you find nothing. The world is topsy-turvy, just the opposite of what it appears.

The Sanskrit word for this is *Māyā*: the illusion of separateness, personified as the cosmic magician who has made the world the way it seems. "Presto!" She takes reality, turns it into a big jigsaw puzzle, and throws the pieces into the air. Then she challenges us. "Hey, Gale! Come on, John! Who can put these back together?" That is what we have come into life to do. We get hold of a few pieces and put them together our own way. "That's reality," we explain. It's a modern work of art: two eyes inside an ear, say, on top of the neck of a giraffe. Māyā laughs and laughs.

Māyā's magic works with two wands, tamas and rajas. With tamas she covers up the Self – our home, our native state. She wraps it in such a dense blanket of unconsciousness that we cannot see inside. Then with rajas she throws out all the bright, dazzling pieces of this world-puzzle before our eyes. We cannot put this puzzle together by searching through the pieces of life outside us. We have to turn inward, have to put the pieces of ourselves together inside. When we have made ourselves whole, we see the world as whole; we see life as it really is. All the pieces of life fall into their proper places. Then, when we act, it is not as a separate fragment of life. We act in accordance with the cosmic forces that hold the world together – unity, truth, love – and all our actions are imbued with their power. We seem to act, but it would be more accurate to say that these cosmic forces act through us: or, as the Gita puts it, that we are "acted through by the Lord." "From age to age," Sri Krishna says earlier, "whenever violence threatens to engulf the world, I come to life in a human heart" – in Gandhi, St. Francis, St. Teresa, Mīrā – "to help show the world a way out of darkness into light." In a small way this can happen to any one of us, if we empty ourselves of ourselves: we can become "an instrument in the hands of the Lord," an instrument of his peace.

बुद्ध्या विशुद्धया युक्तो धृत्यात्मानं नियम्य च ।
शब्दादीन्विषयांस्त्यक्ता रागद्वेषौ व्युदस्य च ॥ १८-५१ ॥
विविक्तसेवी लघ्वाशी यतवाक्कायमानसः ।
ध्यानयोगपरो नित्यं वैराग्यं समुपाश्रितः ॥ १८-५२ ॥

51–52. Unerring in his discrimination, sovereign of his senses and passions, free from the clamor of likes and dislikes, he leads a simple, self-reliant life based on meditation, using his speech, body, and mind to serve the Lord of Love.

There are four obstacles to realizing the Self: obsessive identification with the body and senses, the mind, the intellect, and the ego. These verses describe what results when these obstacles are overcome.

We can think of these as layers covering the Self, which we have to learn to peel away as easily as a pullover. The sensory level is the outermost region of personality, nearest to the physical level. Next comes the mind, our emotions and feelings. After that comes the intellect, our judgments and opinions; and beyond that, nearest to the Self, comes the domain of the ego, the sense of 'I.' All our attachment to the satisfactions of these regions has to be left behind level by level in our inward search for the Self.

In leaving these attachments behind, nothing is lost. The senses do not atrophy; they become vital, vibrant, responsive, and obedient. The mind becomes calm and the intellect lucid and penetrating, because there is no longer any selfish attachment to agitate the mind and cloud judgment. Nothing is lost, and everything is gained. That is why John of the Cross says so cryptically, "If you would possess everything, desire to possess nothing."

We begin to enjoy everything by loosening our attachment to the senses. This, of course, runs counter to the current of our times, which urges us all to cultivate sensory attachments as the key to happiness. Many years ago, if a waiter asked what you would like for dessert, he might offer three or four choices, one of which would be ice cream – not chocolate ice cream or vanilla, just ice cream. You got what they had. Today, thanks to modern technology and our pursuit of pleasure, a waiter can show you a board with one hundred thirty-seven flavors. You have to study the combinations for a quarter of an hour to make a serious selection: "Do I want chocolate? If I do, should it be mixed or straight? For straight chocolate there is Dutch, milk chocolate, bittersweet, and fudge; if I want it mixed, should I get rocky road, fudge swirl, mocha, or chocolate mint?" The next time I ask for Dutch chocolate ice cream, I am afraid the clerk will stare at me as if I had stepped out of a time machine. "You can't just say 'Dutch chocolate'! What *kind* of Dutch chocolate? Utrecht? Amsterdam? Rotterdam Rich?" When you are going constantly after sensations, your world fills up with sensations. That is what being a connoisseur often means.

The trouble with refining and extending the senses this way is that it moves us away from the center of our personality. At first the senses are only a few yards off; they know to whom they belong. Then they go as far as the corner: they can still keep us in view, but they are forgetting to look. They wander off after some promising sensation until finally, like little children, they are out of sight and far away. If you find them on the street corner and ask, "To whom do you belong?" they do not know; they have been cut off from their real personality. In other words, we are actually living in our senses, identifying with them completely. This is the beginning of alienation and confusion.

Meditation begins to recall the prāna that has been caught in the senses. In this way we draw them closer and closer again, until they start to remember: "Oh, yeah, I belong to Steve!" They form working relationships with their boss again, stray less, come back when they are called. One sign of this is that the senses become clear and strong. Another sign is a feeling of deepening security, of an intimate, comfortable relationship with our own selves.

Learning to do this is a matter of reversing our conditioning. Tastes, for example, are not dictated by our genes; they are habits we acquire through practice. The first time the taste buds get something pleasant, there is only a mild response; not much prāna is vested there. But the next time they perk up and say, "Hmm." After that they keep a little extra prāna ready for enjoying, and the next time the sensation comes along, they smack their lips and exclaim in satisfaction, "Ahh!" We can decondition ourselves in the same way. The first time we have to give up something we crave, the senses roar in protest. The second time, they mutter in resignation. And the third time they say "Ahh!" again: they have got the taste of freedom.

Meditation can be described as a kind of spiritual screwdriver, intended for loosening identification with the body. Before you can use a screwdriver, of course, you have to locate the screw, and most of us do not know where the screws to the body are. There are five: the senses, which we have grown used to tightening at every opportunity. Finally they get tightened down so hard that something breaks; then we wonder why we feel tense. In meditation you can slowly get your screwdriver onto each screw, fit it carefully into the slot, and begin to loosen up your mind. You cannot twist the senses out at once, as "instant mysticism" claims. You go on loosening gently for a long, long time, until finally the senses become so responsive that you can slip them in and out without effort.

All the five senses can be unscrewed like this through meditation. When there is no tightness in the senses, no clamor from them, tension is gone. Then the question of resisting a sensory temptation – to steal into the kitchen at midnight, for example, and eat up all the cookies – does not even arise. No resistance or effort is necessary. The cookies are in the kitchen, you are here in your bed; where is the conflict? This is our natural state. Far from it taking the joy out of life, joy is exactly what we gain.

Below the level of the senses is the mind. The senses draw their sustenance, their prāna, from the mind: when it relaxes, the senses relax; when it gets tense, the senses are stimulated, and so are the vital organs. Everything takes its cue from the mind. To attain real physical health and a resilient nervous system, therefore, it is not enough to work on the body; you have to train the mind to be calm and kind. As the mind relaxes in meditation, conflicts are resolved, turmoil is quieted, and the senses grow clear and alert.

Detachment from your emotions is important even to survive in today's world of stress, but it is essential for anyone who wants to try to do some good in the world. Only a detached person can jump into a crisis and help; an attached person just gets sucked in. Many years ago, when I was traveling on a train in India, a fight broke out between two people in my compartment. One of the onlookers was also from Kerala, and I have to tell you that people from Kerala have a reputation throughout India for being what you call feisty. This man watched the quarrel turn into a fight, and as he watched he became more and more excited. Finally he lost his self-control and jumped to his feet. "I don't care who's right or wrong," he exclaimed to me in Malayalam. "I just want to join in!" That is exactly what happens with strong attachments.

Detachment from the mind brings the capacity to sit back and not act automatically on every emotion that comes along. I can illustrate this from a little incident last week, when I was returning from Berkeley late at night and had to wait at a railroad crossing while a long freight train rattled by. It was a familiar sight which I still enjoy: the crossing gates were down, red lights were flashing, and the bell kept ringing even after the caboose had passed to make sure that we didn't drive onto the tracks before they were clear.

I could easily imagine a similar scene within the mind, perhaps hundreds of times each day. When you come to a samskāra crossing, if you know you are not your mind, you have all these safeguards: gates, bells, lights, even a brakeman with a red warning lantern. But if you identify with your mind, you have nothing. People who get angry easily, or who frequently feel insecure or greedy over people or things, have no bell or gates at their mental crossings and no brake on their minds. When a samskāra is steaming down, they hurtle forward at a hundred miles per hour, and the samskāra scoops them up on the cowcatcher and drops them off at the other end of the line.

On the other hand, when you get some detachment from your mind, you can look on your emotions with a kind of creative aloofness and a sense of mastery. For a long time, of course, the trains will still come. But when a big one, Santa Fe Anger, roars into view, you will hear the bell and see the red lights flashing long before it reaches the crossing, giving you plenty of time to stop. Then you can sit back, turn off the engine to save fuel, loosen your seat belt, and watch the piggyback resentments and rusty hostilities pass one by one; there is no connection with you at all. Your engine is turned off, the hand brake is set, and you are safe – in the midst of tremendous anger, fear, or lust, which no longer have any power over you. Then you ask yourself in wonder, "Why did I always get caught in those accidents?" There is no need. After all, no law says that when you see a train, you have to lie down on the tracks.

अहंकारं बलं दर्पं कामं क्रोधं परिग्रहम् ।
विमुच्य निर्ममः शान्तो ब्रह्मभूयाय कल्पते ॥ १८-५३ ॥

53. Free from self-will, aggressiveness, arrogance, and the lust to possess people or things, he is at peace with himself and others and enters into the unitive state.

Even in our most intimate relationships, each of us with some self-knowledge would have to admit that we live largely in private worlds. It is a devastating admission. Two people may say honestly that they love each other, that they can't get on without each other, yet each lives in a private mental apartment with its own particular furniture – memories, expectations, hopes, fears, desires, prejudices – that no one else in the world has seen. Even that person knows very little of it. "Judge not," says Jesus, "that ye be not judged." We should never criticize another person; we haven't entered the apartment where he or she lives. In the best of close relationships – between man and woman, parent and child, friend and friend – all we can usually do is stand on tiptoe and peek in through a window to see the furniture in the front room. Only with someone like Gandhiji do we encounter an open world, where anybody can walk in and see how he lives, how he thinks, what his motivation is. That is the world of love.

When you love one person, while there *is* a selfless element, it is good to remember that by the very fact of saying "one," we are limiting our love physically. A good part of a one-to-one relationship is physical. Over and over, Sri Krishna has warned us of the danger of physical relationships: like all physical things, it is their nature to change. Desires are transients; they can never make permanent tenants. They will come in the morning and say, "We're going to stay here all the time. We'll sign a ten-year lease. When you go on vacation we'll still be here to look after the house and water your African violets." And we believe them. "Long lease," we say. The following Sunday morning we go over to invite them for brunch: the bed hasn't been slept in, the African violets are dry, the cats are mewing, and the desires have gone. Every sensory desire is like that: as long as we don't have it, we want it; as soon as we get it, we don't want it any more – at least, not for a while, not until the desire arises again in a slightly different form. The Buddha's description is perfect: "Not having what you want is suffering; having what you do not want is suffering."

Selfish desire stirs up the mind, and any movement in the mind, even what we call pleasant excitement, lessens joy, undermines security, and moves us a little further away from the Self. It *is* pleasant, granted. The Gita does not say that pleasure is painful. It merely adds that pleasure comes and goes: and that when it goes, it leaves deprivation, frustration, and depression. Pleasure and pain are not separate; they are Siamese twins. If you want the one, you get both.

My granny had her own ways of opening my eyes to this. "Sri Krishna doesn't say not to go after pleasure," she would begin.

"He doesn't? Granny, he's the right teacher for me!"

"He says, 'If you want to go after pleasure, go ahead.'"

I couldn't believe my ears. That is when I fell in love with the Bhagavad Gita, which really knew the way to a boy's heart.

"But," Granny continued, "he says if you go after pleasure, you shouldn't cry if you meet pain along the way."

Later – much later – I had opportunities to talk to people who had gone after pleasure systematically. Those with some self-knowledge confided to me candidly, "I had the money, I had the leisure, and I went after everything I enjoyed most. And mostly I got what I wanted. But I could never make it last, and the more I tried, the less I seemed to get. In fact, many of the same things that I sought for pleasure actually led me into sorrow."

I needed a long, long period of experimentation to learn this – many years of making the same kind of mistakes that every human being makes. When finally I caught on, I went to my granny and said, "Guess what! You know what you were telling me all those years ago about pleasure? I found out you were right." I felt I would burst with love when she put her hand on my head and replied simply, "You're a bright boy." Never a word about why it should have taken so long. Some people never learn; that's what she was trying to say. So don't get depressed or distraught if it takes you years to make this discovery, as it has taken almost every spiritual aspirant East and West. But don't go placing yourself in situations where desires can stir you up; it will impede your spiritual growth. Stirring brings up all the sediments of the mind from past experiences, all sorts of emotionally charged memories both pleasant and unpleasant, and it will take a long time for them to settle down again.

There is joy, great joy, in going against strong personal attachments for the sake of a higher goal. There is immense satisfaction in knowing that you are making a contribution to the world in which you live. "This is the true joy in life," says Shaw:

> the being used for a purpose recognized by yourself as a mighty one; . . . the being a force of Nature instead of a feverish selfish little clod of ailments and grievances complaining that the world will not devote itself to making you happy.

That is rather strong language, but it puts the glory of renunciation into terms that can stir us all. Instead of "being a force of Nature" with a capital N, of course, the Gita talks of becoming an instrument in the hands of the Lord; but that is the only difference. Shaw is choosing his words very carefully. A selfless life *is* a force. Its contribution does not die; it continues in the stream of consciousness.

Translated into orthodox language, this is why our lives are said to belong not to ourselves but to the Lord. I was not a particularly devotional boy, but I found this a useful, personal reminder in my younger days, when I sometimes felt tempted to do something which, though not harmful, was not exactly for the benefit of all. When this motivation sinks deep, you will find it easy to go against self-will, just as a mother finds it easy to miss a movie or a few hours' sleep for the sake of her child. It is when you spend your time dwelling on yourself, unprepared to sit back and look at the needs of a larger world, that motivation fails.

We can look at this from another perspective: that of prāna. To enjoy life completely, prāna *has* to be consolidated, harnessed, and conserved, because this is the very power of enjoyment.

Farmers in this country, I understand, often have their own gas tanks; they cannot afford to be dependent on an outside source. Similarly, every one of us has a personal tank of prāna in reserve. There is no electric pump for this tank, only a manual pump with very stiff action, which we have to prime for a long time before we can bring prāna reserves up where they can be used. But the tank *is* there. Just as a baby is protected in the mother's womb, the Upanishads say, our prāna reserves are protected against our own mistakes. We can squander our personal prāna on sensory pleasures, but those deeper reserves cannot be drawn on until we take to meditation. That is why a human being can turn toward a higher goal, choose a higher path, at any time; the capacity is never lost.

However, like gasoline, prāna is dangerously flammable. Just as gas stations post signs warning us not to smoke around the pumps, the sign on our reserve prāna tank says "Danger! No Self-will." Self-will is so incendiary that it can destroy not only us but our home and even our community, when prāna intended for spiritual growth is ignited for selfish ends.

Prāna can be understood as the capacity of the will to govern the senses and passions and to resolve conflicts, not only within personality but between oneself and others. This is a very creative faculty, and it is not coincidental that prāna is closely connected with sex. In spiritual psychology, sex is not a physical desire. It is creative energy, the deep yearning for complete Self-integration; what we call sex is simply its potent, most physical expression. The more we think of ourselves as physical creatures, the more we feel compelled to satisfy this yearning in physical ways. But its roots go deep into the mind, and its highest purpose is to provide the power for realizing the Self.

I always try to make it clear that sex has a beautiful, natural place in a completely loyal and loving relationship, where it expresses the mutual desire of two people for lasting union. But even there, I would say, sex is not merely physical; it is a force. When you begin to master physical desires for the sake of moving closer to someone you love, you will find that your relationship gains immensely in tenderness, security, depth, and joy. Giving up something for a person you love, learning to change habits in yourself which brought that person sorrow, working shoulder to shoulder in a selfless cause: all these bring a lasting sense of joy to which no sensory pleasure, however acute, can be compared. This does not rule out any of life's innocent enjoyments; it merely reminds us that we are here for something vastly higher.

Strong sexual desires, therefore, are a sign that prāna is plentiful. This is the capital of vitality, and a man or woman with strong desires is a prāna millionaire in the making. I used to say this often in Berkeley in the early days, and it was very popular. But I realized later that I was occasionally being misunderstood. There were people who heard that if they had strong sexual desires, they could go far on the spiritual path; so they thought it might be helpful to cultivate those desires – which, if I may say so, is scarcely necessary. Not only that, it is as dangerous as smoking next to a petrol tank. If a person with strong physical passions of any kind can learn to harness them, they will provide a lot of power for spiritual growth. But if they are not harnessed, there is no doubt that these passions will harness us. They will slip a bit into our mouth, fasten on a bridle, climb on our back, and ride us into situations where we can satisfy those desires, whatever the cost to others and to ourselves. So on the one hand, don't ever think negatively about yourself if you have passions too strong to be easily harnessed: they are power rising, power that you will need for spiritual growth. But remember too that this power has to be transformed – through selfless work and patient, tender, selfless personal relations.

Now and then, I should add, someone comes to me and complains, "I don't have strong sexual desires. Does that mean I don't have enough prāna to make it to the goal?" Self-will, I assure them, makes a more than adequate substitute. The Gita has something for everybody.

The technical name for these prāna reserves is kundalinī – evolutionary energy. You can imagine kundalinī as a tremendous, tightly-coiled spring, a coil of vitality that has been twisted and compressed a million times in the course of evolution. To release the energy packed into this spring you have to start uncoiling it with your own hands, which is an almost impossible task. When someone tells me, "I'm not making any progress. Thoughts of sex haunt me continuously," I reply, "The spring has been coiled for millennia, with all the power of evolution behind it. Now you're trying to uncoil it with your bare hands, and you want it to happen overnight?"

Finally, after many years of sincere sādhana, the great day comes when you become aware that kundalinī is uncoiling. This awareness usually comes in sleep – not really in the dreaming state, though mystics often describe the experience as a dream, but in what the Upanishads call dreamless sleep – the deepest state of ordinary consciousness, where the mind-process rests and only a veil of the unconscious mind separates us from the Self. In that state you can peek behind the conscious mind and see, even feel, the spring uncoiling just a little. This brings a strange sense of exhilaration, but at the same time, it means that even bigger challenges are coming. Immense amounts of power are being released into your life, and you have to be very vigilant to see that they are used in selfless work.

Imagine trying to get a powerful spring to uncoil. You have opened it up a little, but the tension is tremendous; it keeps straining to snap back to its original state. Not only do you have to go on trying to make it uncoil further, you have to hang on continuously just to keep it from coiling back up again. If you lose your vigilance, even for a moment, the spring may snap back and you will have to start all over. These are terribly difficult times. The fatigue and exhaustion this effort brings is much more than physical. It cannot be borne without a loving teacher, as I can testify from my own experience. The struggle continues even when you go to sleep, you see. How long can you hold on? There are limits to everybody's personal will, everybody's personal endurance. But when you have been doing your utmost for probably many years, just when you think that you cannot hold on any longer, your teacher may come and release the spring one turn with a deft touch. Then you know that as long as you go on trying, your personal will is allied with a much deeper will that cannot be broken.

When our āshram children were small I used to see them riding behind the wheel of the family car, seated on a parent's lap and driving very slowly around the block. The mother or father seemed to steer effortlessly, where the child had to pull on the wheel as hard as he could to avoid running into a tree. A good spiritual teacher has the same light touch. When you are doing everything possible to get yourself off the shoulder of the road and into an attractive ditch, he can keep you going in the right direction with a touch on the wheel so deft that you may not even notice it.

We have a long drainage ditch that runs alongside our access road, hidden from view much of the year by the high grass. It looks like a very commonplace ditch, but it has witnessed great adventures. It has seen proud men fall and brave women panic, and watched sleek Cadillacs rescued without ceremony by a lowly tractor. Accidents like these can happen in sādhana too, and this is one of the most serious dangers in the latter stage of meditation. The mind is so powerful that anybody who loses vigilance can end up in a ditch, and it is not enough to be hauled out. The body cannot afford to lose the vitality it needs to face these crises; the nervous system cannot afford to lose resilience. Ultimately, all the disciplines we practice from the earliest days of meditation are meant for keeping us alert and in control in these critical stages, with both hands on the wheel.

I can give you a shining hope to look forward to. As you near the end of the journey, weeks and months will pass when you have been doing your best continuously to get kundalinī to uncoil. You go to sleep exhausted, sure that nothing will ever happen, and while you are in dreamless sleep the Lord comes leisurely and gives the spring an expert touch. One turn of kundalinī uncoils with a whiplash whirl so powerful that it jolts your whole body; every cell feels the impact. These are very difficult experiences for the body to pass through, for it is channeling forces much greater than a human being is ordinarily able to bear. But even while your body feels the stress of it, your consciousness is flooded with joy.

ब्रह्मभूतः प्रसन्नात्मा न शोचति न काङ्क्षति ।
समः सर्वेषु भूतेषु मद्भक्तिं लभते पराम् ॥ १८-५४ ॥
भक्त्या मामभिजानाति यावान्यश्चास्मि तत्त्वतः ।
ततो मां तत्त्वतो ज्ञात्वा विशते तदनन्तरम् ॥ १८-५५ ॥
सर्वकर्माण्यपि सदा कुर्वाणो मद्व्यपाश्रयः ।
मत्प्रसादादवाप्नोति शाश्वतं पदमव्ययम् ॥ १८-५६ ॥

*54. United with the Lord, ever joyful, beyond the reach
of self-will and sorrow, he serves me in every living
creature and attains supreme devotion to me.
55. By loving me he shares in my glory and enters into
my boundless being.
56. All his acts are performed in my service, and
through my grace he wins eternal life.*

This promise of eternal life is the essence of the mystics' message everywhere. It is not rhetoric, but a literal statement of fact.

In the West the study of death is considered eschatological, the study
of "last things." In Hinduism, however, death is like a gate. Just north of
the Golden Gate Bridge is a tunnel called the Rainbow Tunnel, through
which Highway 101 passes on its way to and from San Francisco – four
lanes in, four lanes out. The gate of life and death is like that: coming
from one direction we are born; passing in the other we die.

Now, the other day on the way to San Francisco I looked up and saw
a helicopter flying over; it didn't have to pass through the tunnel at all.
That is what you can do once you attain samādhi: you can go through
that tunnel without any break in consciousness; and you can come back
again, which is an experience beyond what words can convey. With a
person who is dying, you can go down that road with him almost to
the end and relieve much of the burden of the fear of death.

At the mouth of this tunnel, the threshold of individual awareness,
you understand what death means: the conscious jīva, the separate
personality, is withdrawn completely into the fathomless depths of the
unconscious. Words are terribly elusive here, and what I mean by "the
unconscious" is not quite what most psychologists mean. But I know of

no better word in English. This is a deep stratum of undivided, universal consciousness underlying the individual personality, which none of us is ordinarily able to enter as a conscious individual. When you can reach this level in your meditation, you are withdrawing conscious awareness into the depths of the unconscious – waking up in the unconscious, if you like. This is parallel to what takes place in dying, but in meditation it is done intentionally, in full awareness. Then you know that death is not the end of the story: if it were, there would be no awareness in that state; you would not be able to return to tell the tale.

On this seabed of consciousness there is no passage of time, no past or future, because there is nobody to think about past or future. To experience time, you have to have a mind that can think of past and future, and at that level the mind-process is completely still. For the same reason, nothing "happens" in this state; things can happen only where there is time. I have to fall back on the language of traditional mysticism and say this is pure being. This is how mystics come up with those answers that drive logicians to tear out their hair. If you ask me, "Is there such a thing as time?" I would have to answer, "There is, and then again there isn't." The Buddha used to smile at such questions and say nothing, because any answer would be misleading.

You can see why it is not possible to enter such a state if the mind is divided. In the Hindu tradition they say that if even a single ray of desire slips away from the focus of your meditation, you cannot enter samādhi. When Gandhi says that this requires the patience of a man trying to empty the sea with a blade of grass, I can attest to it with my own experience. You can be right on the threshold, even see the door opening, but you will not be able to go in; that slight stray desire will hold you back. I had a good deal of patience even in those days, and I was prepared to go on trying as long as might be required. But my intellect, which was well trained to look at things objectively, surveyed the situation I was in and reported, "That's it, boss. You've gone as far as you can go." That brought me immense grief. I remembered the moment in Sri Ramakrishna's sādhana when he takes up a sword, falls at the feet of the Divine Mother, and cries out in the desperation of love, "If you don't reveal yourself to me, I'll put an end to this body!" That is the stage I am referring to. It is as if you have finally managed to open the door an inch or two, so that you can catch a glimpse of what is on the other side, but no amount of effort can open it wider so you can slip through. There is an essential paradox: how can the ego throw itself out? It's like trying to lift yourself by your own bootstraps.

This is where the teacher comes to your rescue. Except for my teacher, I can tell you candidly that the door to samādhi would never have opened for me: I had one foot inside, but I could not have gone further through my own personal effort.

Once you can go in and out of that door freely, however, you can travel with a dying person across the threshold of life and death, from the far side of which no separate individual can return in this same life. If the dying person has a deep bond of love for you, that love is a channel through which you can communicate your personal realization: that death is not the end of the story but only a door, a gate, a bridge, through which we pass to rest a while before we come back to pick up our evolution where we left off. To somebody who understands this, death loses its terrors. There may even be a certain eagerness to take on a new body and start afresh.

चेतसा सर्वकर्माणि मयि संन्यस्य मत्परः ।
बुद्धियोगमुपाश्रित्य मच्चित्तः सततं भव ॥ १८-५७ ॥

57. Make every act an offering to me; regard
me as your only protector. Make every thought
an offering to me; meditate on me always.

Sri Krishna is coming to the end of his instruction to Arjuna. Now he is saying over and over again in different ways, "From now on, let there be no more reservations or qualifications in your mind. Let your pledge be 'Everything I have.'"

This is no more than we should expect from love. I remember a popular singer's perceptive remark: "I love to fall in love, but I know it will only last six months." When personal relationships are based on physical attraction, I think six months is an optimistic estimate. But what Sri Krishna says, what the Buddha says, what Jesus says, is very different: "You can be in love always – when you can love me with all your heart, all your mind, all your spirit, and all your strength."

People sometimes ask, "What does it mean to remember the Lord always?" That is a fair question, for this is not an intellectual recollection. One way to answer is to say what it means *not* to remember: anger, hostility, resentment, irritation, impatience, all these and a hundred other unpleasant states of mind. When you remember God in your heart, unkindness cannot arise, because God is love.

I wish you could see through my eyes the little quarrels I witness every day – in people's homes, on the bus, in stores and restaurants. They look so ridiculous when you remember how little time we have here, even those of us who are young, and how much remains to do to attain the goal. To the mystic, a whole lifetime consists of evanescent days, a garland of nows that are gone too soon. There is no time to quarrel, no time to be selfish, no time to waste on any activity that does not take us closer to the goal.

This does not rule out any of the innocent joys of life. I always remind people to look at my own example. Though I am only a mini-mystic, through the grace of my teacher I now live in a state where I never forget Sri Krishna; even in my sleep I am aware of him always. Yet anyone should be able to see that I enjoy life to the fullest. I eat good food; I have many rich, lasting relationships; I enjoy long walks on the beach every day; I read widely; I go to movies and concerts and the theater regularly. I haven't given up anything of enjoyment that I value. But I don't live for the enjoyment of these things; that is the point. I enjoy life *because* I live for the joy of others, and everything I do is arranged around that one overriding priority.

I want you to know that reordering my priorities was as difficult for me as it is for everyone else. Nothing less is required than the single-minded dedication with which an artist pursues his art, and although I had this capacity even in high school, I gave my devotion to other goals. In those days I could not imagine living in a world without literature, music, sports and games, and all the other amenities I loved. Only after I turned to meditation did I begin to see that if I wanted to give all my love to Sri Krishna, I would have to withdraw the love that was caught in these harmless pleasures. It wasn't that they were harmful in themselves, you see, only that they had caught and held my love.

It was the hardest struggle for me to detach myself from these pursuits. For a long time I did not think I would be able to do it, and my intellect kept asking, "Is this really necessary? After all, where's the harm in these aesthetic delights?" I began to free myself from attachment to these innocent pleasures the day I realized that even if I became a great poet and won the Nobel Prize, I would still die unfulfilled. After that, everything in the arts became a distraction. Now nothing is a distraction; I can enjoy all these things in freedom. At the outset, renouncing them seemed like a loss; today I can see it has been an infinite gain.

This is not abandon. "Make every act an offering to me" means the abandonment of self-will, not of self-control. It is very important on the spiritual path not to let yourself be coaxed out of the driver's seat, especially during meditation. You are tapping resources below the surface level of awareness, and the unconscious has powerful forces which can take the wheel without your knowledge.

It requires many years of strenuous training to learn to stay in the driver's seat always. Much later, tremendous insights may come which will sweep you up out of yourself miles high in consciousness. I can give you a thrilling example from the life of St. Teresa of Ávila. She was absorbed in contemplation, she relates, when suddenly she felt as if a great eagle had swooped down on her and lifted her high in the air, so that she felt she had left her body behind. "Yet I was not afraid," she says, "because of my love." Teresa had many such experiences, yet this great genius possessed such control that when the Lord swept her up like this while she was frying an egg, her nuns tell us that her hand never lost its grip on the skillet! That is my granny's way too, and it can save an aspirant from many pitfalls.

If the mind has been allowed to swing wildly when a dramatic experience comes, however, that very abandon can close the door. Instead of ecstasy, tantalizing moments come which mystics often describe in metaphor. "I heard the Lord's footsteps," they will say, "coming to the garden of my heart, and I grew so terribly excited that I heard him turn and tiptoe away." This is why I say to stay in the driver's seat; don't let any emotion sweep you away. Excitement has to be followed by depression, and the depression that can follow a near visit from your divine Beloved, St. Teresa says, is perhaps the heaviest anguish the heart can bear. In Christian mysticism this is known as the Dark Night of the

Soul, and it is sometimes considered to be a necessary part of spiritual growth. On the basis of my own experience, however, as well as the experience of others, I can say categorically that almost all such black depressions can be avoided, if we begin today to train the mind not to get excited. But the time to begin is now.

Every wave in the mind – every desire, every fear – has a force in it. Even a small desire has power, and anger, fear, and greed can be like hurricanes that sweep away every obstacle in their path. Even if we sincerely want to unify our desires, how can we deal with these typhoons of the mind? They keep blowing in every human being; no one can escape them. But they can be turned around. Meditation and the mantram can build a kind of miraculous wind tunnel in consciousness so that when anger blows in at a hundred miles an hour, it is turned around, to blow out as compassion – still at a hundred miles an hour, but wholly in the other direction. Greed going in at a gale comes out as a gale of love for all. There is no loss of force. I can't imagine what such a wind tunnel might look like, but I know what it feels like when these storms of passion blow up inside and are whipped around in the other direction into hurricanes of positive power. If you want to see the extent to which it can go, look at the life of Gandhi.

The power of the mantram to turn a gale of anger around is dependent on the depth at which you can repeat the mantram. On the surface of consciousness, which is as deep as anybody can get at the beginning, there is very little power in the repetition. You will note that I did not say "very little power in the mantram"; the holy name is full of power. All that is wrong is that you haven't driven the mantram in deeply enough, which can only be done through repetition – that is, hard work.

Sometimes I get letters saying, "The mantram hasn't been working." In my old days as an English professor I would have written in the margin, "Wrong word. *You* haven't been working." The mantram always works, but if you want it to do impossible things like turn around a hundred-mile-an-hour storm of anger, you have to get it down to the level of the mind where those storms arise, and that is done by repeating it over and over at every possible opportunity.

I have been using the mantram for many, many years with a diligence that still astonishes even me. I use every minute I get. Even on campus, in the midst of an extremely busy schedule, if I had a few minutes I used to sit in our crowded beehive of a faculty lounge, close my eyes, and repeat my mantram. "E.E. must have been burning the midnight oil again," my colleagues said. "He's catching forty winks." I was catching forty mantrams.

At the beginning, I should add, I was not able to do this with deep devotion. Many Indians have a deep vein of devotion for their Chosen Ideal, the form of God they love and worship in the mantram – usually Rāma, Krishna, Shiva, or the Divine Mother. This is a great asset, but I have to confess to you that I did not have it when I began, just as most of you will not have it: this kind of devotion is increasingly rare in the modern industrialized world, East as well as West. I repeated my mantram with such diligence essentially out of love for my granny, and as my meditation deepened, I found to my delighted surprise that I had begun to tap a deep, unsuspected, overwhelming love for Sri Krishna in and through my teacher, which the mantram called forth.

For a long, long time, repetition of the mantram *is* mechanical. But as meditation deepens, your repetition acquires more power, for with deepening meditation comes deepening devotion. I repeated my mantram with a kind of tenacity that most people cannot imagine, making use of every possible moment, lying awake sometimes for hours at night and keeping at it, all to attain the state called *ajapajapam*, where the mantram goes on continuously without any conscious effort. This is how Christian mystics explain St. Paul's injunction, "Pray without ceasing," and it is how I would explain this verse: "Make every thought an offering to me." Today the mantram is with me always, at the deepest level of consciousness, and I would not hesitate to call its power limitless. Now and then, in dreamless sleep, I hear it reverberating through consciousness and my whole body vibrates with the power of it. It is as if I were holding on to a pneumatic drill, except that this is not noise but an unheard sound more thrilling than the sweetest music.

मच्चित्तः सर्वदुर्गाणि मत्प्रसादात्तरिष्यसि ।
अथ चेत्त्वमहंकारान्न श्रोष्यसि विनङ्क्ष्यसि ॥ १८-५८ ॥

58. Drawing upon your deepest resources,
you shall overcome all difficulties through
my grace. But if you will not heed me in
your self-will, nothing will avail you.

Sometimes my granny used to say in front of my friends or acquaintances, "Little Lamp, you're not going to be like anybody else." It used to bother and embarrass me deeply. "Granny," I complained, "you shouldn't say things like that. Lots of boys I know do well in school."

"That's not what I mean," she said.

"Your love is making you blind," I protested. "You don't know me. I have lots of faults."

"You don't know yourself," she corrected. "I know you have faults."

I gulped. "You do?"

"Of course. I know faults you don't know I know. I even know faults that *you* don't know." (I have to admit that took me aback.) "But, Little Lamp, you also don't know what your real capabilities are. I know that too."

I have said before that Granny wasn't good with words, and I never could get her to explain any further. I didn't understand, and I did not agree; I *was* a very ordinary boy. Only much later did I remember her words and realize that she was talking about immense capabilities which lie unsuspected in every one of us – the limitless inner resources of the Ātman.

Some years ago, when the "Treasures of Tutankhamen" exhibit came to San Francisco from the museum at Cairo, I read a little about how these treasures were discovered. It has all the ingredients for a great short story. After six years of fruitless digging, the English archaeologist Howard Carter was routinely checking an unpromising plot of land in the Valley of the Kings when he uncovered stone stairs leading down to a secret tunnel. The passage showed the familiar signs of tomb-robbers breaking in and departing in haste. But at the far end, barely visible in the darkness, was a sealed door. Breathlessly Carter managed to make enough of a hole to admit a candle. As the flame flared up, its light glinted off gold and jewels: the little room was full of the treasures of a king. Beyond he would discover other rooms with even more dazzling riches, the greatest treasure trove in Egyptian archaeology.

When you finally reach a certain deep level in meditation, you feel much the way Carter must have felt when he first peered through that door, which had not been touched for three thousand years. As I said, I was not aware I had any tremendous latent capacities; no one is. But after many years of meditation, when I finally gained access to this treasury in consciousness, I couldn't believe what I found. Until then, I had thought I had at most a little piggy bank, full of nickels and dimes of prāna that I'd been able to pick up. On special occasions – usually when I wanted to answer some urgent personal call – I could turn the piggy upside down and shake out enough small change to satisfy my desires. All the while, my granny had been trying to tell me I was a millionaire. Living in a piggy world, what can we understand of the realms of Rockefellers and Mellons and Du Ponts? Who would suspect that he or she has a Fort Knox within, when most of us feel lucky just to be able to pay our bills? That's why I say that everyone is ordinary until he or she begins to tap these resources; yet everyone is extraordinary when these resources are realized.

As long as we live on the surface level of life, our difficulties will be superficial also. If they seem big, it is because we have so little of our deeper resources at our command. But as we learn to function at a deeper level, the demands naturally become more challenging. I can assure you from my own long years of sādhana that these demands will never become more than you can handle or more oppressive than you can bear. To believe we are unequal to the challenges of spiritual growth is wrong shraddhā, piggy-bank shraddhā, the result of a lower image of ourselves. I want to correct that shraddhā by pointing out that these challenges are natural and necessary as meditation deepens, and everyone has the resources to deal with them. In my own sādhana, when I found myself plunging into deeper consciousness at a speed I was not prepared for, I made a very heartening discovery: however difficult the problems I faced, I could always turn inwards, go deeper, and bring up a little more capacity for solving them. This discovery comes to everyone who perseveres, and once it comes, the wrong shraddhā of defeatism and diffidence begins to be set right.

In other words, whether or not we feel personally worthy or personally capable of superhuman effort is not the issue in sādhana. The great mystics of East and West have given us their assurance, based on experience, that no one achieves Self-realization through personal effort; it is always a supreme gift of grace. All we can do is give our very best continually: follow every discipline to the best of our ability, pick ourselves up when we slip, and strive continuously to unify our desires. I tell my friends, "If you strive as I have striven, you will overcome all obstacles. That is Sri Krishna's promise."

Yet there is another side to this verse too, a second half, which I do not want to dwell on but which is vitally necessary to understand: this wholehearted personal effort is absolutely essential. It is not sufficient, but it *is* essential. Unless we throw all our personal weight on the side of sādhana, that weight is going to fall on the side of self-will: and as Sri Krishna says here, "If you will not heed me in your self-will, if you will not try your best, there is no way I can help you." This is not a matter of the Lord withholding his love and support; these can never be withdrawn. It is simply a matter of spiritual dynamics.

I want to be very clear here, because to me these are very reassuring verses. All of us begin sādhana with doubts and reservations; if we did not have doubts and reservations, we would not be here as human beings. Some of these are relatively superficial and fall away as our meditation deepens. But others, whose roots go terribly deep in personality, may actually appear more acute when we reach a level of awareness where we see them more clearly. It is easy to get despondent at this point, to throw up our hands and say, "What can I do? The Gita says I need wholehearted devotion to go further, and I'm split in two." This is only natural. After all, we are trying to do away with the ego; we can't expect it to go quietly. It pulls in one direction; the Self pulls in another. Throw the weight of your personal choices and desires on the side of the Self, the Lord entreats; he will do the rest. "If we will do what we can," says Augustine, "He can do as he wills."

The unconscious is a vast undiscovered land, trackless, endless. On the face of it, bringing light to these limitless regions is impossible; the very word "unconscious" tells us that this part of the mind is not subject to conscious regulation. Yet the mystics say with humility but great daring, "Yes, it *is* impossible. Nevertheless, we have done it; therefore we know that it can be done." Compared to this stupendous mastery, I don't think any earthly achievement can be mentioned in the same breath.

यदहंकारमाश्रित्य न योत्स्य इति मन्यसे ।
मिथ्यैष व्यवसायस्ते प्रकृतिस्त्वां नियोक्ष्यति ॥ १८-५९ ॥
स्वभावजेन कौन्तेय निबद्धः स्वेन कर्मणा ।
कर्तुं नेच्छसि यन्मोहात्करिष्यस्यवशो ऽपि तत् ॥ १८-६० ॥

59. If you say, "I will not fight this battle,"
your own nature will drive you into it.
60. If you will not fight the battle of life, your
own karma will drive you into it.

Two forces pervade human life, the mystics say: the upward surge of evolution and the downward pull of our evolutionary past. Yet ultimately, everything in human experience, every side of human nature, has a supreme evolutionary purpose: of leading, pushing, cajoling, forcing us towards the goal of life.

This is a very reassuring point, so I would like to illustrate a little. It means that every problem we face, every trial we endure, offers the opportunity to take us closer to our goal. I mean this without exception; there is no hit and miss in life. When Gandhi, in his early twenties, buffeted by failure in India, snapped at the offer of a low-paying job in South Africa because it meant a change of scene, that proved to be a door opening onto the circumstances he needed to begin his sādhana and transform his character. But it might equally have been a door to further failure. The Lord did not give him a ticket to Self-realization, guaranteed passage. He gave him hardships, and Gandhi used those hardships to begin living for others rather than himself. How many Indians had been ill-treated in South Africa? Surely tens of thousands. Of them, this one man was touched so deeply by injustice that he learned its lesson: to fight it not on one's own behalf, but on behalf of all.

Similarly, every apparent liability has a purpose, a role to play in spiritual growth. When I find someone who is rebellious, for example, I try to show that we have developed this capacity for a reason: to reach the goal of life, we have to rebel against our own selfishness and self-will. What you read in the lives of the great mystics is nothing other than the capacity for rebellion used wisely. Take St. Teresa of Ávila: if ever there was a born rebel in those days of the Inquisition, it was she. Her biographers tell us that she was a fiery girl with a will of her own, who dreamed as a child of stealing off to the Crusades. She drew on that fiery temperament when she turned to Jesus, rebelling with such instinctive genius against everything that kept her from union with him that she overcame her separateness and won him completely. She was such a revolutionary that having her self-will violated became a treat, because she knew it took her closer to her goal. When people criticized her, abused her, spread scandalous stories about her, even brought charges against her, she became sweeter as she got tougher, bringing up deeper resources, trying harder than ever to win her opponents' hearts. These are the capacities of a great spiritual genius, and they came to her because she marshalled every trace of a fierce fighting spirit to remove the obstacles on her path.

Finally, every mistake we make has a purpose. Made because of karma, it offers an opportunity for some of that karma to be undone. This is the battle of life, and it is good to be aware that below the surface, it has already been joined. Restlessness, dissatisfaction with life on the superficial level, even a nagging conscience, are all signs that the upward and downward forces of evolution are struggling deep within. If the struggle is not pleasant, we should remember that merely to be aware of it means that we have reached a point where we are ready to take our evolution into our hands.

If we think of our negative samskāras as hurricanes in the mind, the human personality is a storm center – not one strong wind but hundreds. When I go to the beach for a walk, I sometimes encounter strong winds blowing off the Pacific. Going downwind can be refreshing; the wind at my back seems to help carry me along. But once I turn around and start to walk back, the same wind is not at all pleasant. It blows sand in my face and makes it difficult to walk, so that I sometimes have to lean into the wind to keep from being blown backwards.

We get this kind of wind from the mind too. It blows us in the direction of our conditioning: towards what is pleasant, away from what is unpleasant. If we turn around and try to retrace our steps, we find ourselves walking against the onrush of millions of conditioned thoughts, which blow grit into our eyes and make it difficult to see clearly. Our natural tendency is to keep our eyes on the ground in front of us and plod along, one foot after another, which is a good way to lose one's sense of direction. In a strong wind, you can also get disheartened this way and feel you are getting nowhere. Even when the wind is full in your face, I would say, keep on going forward and don't lower your eyes from the goal. Sri Krishna says, "Keep your eyes on me always": with our desires focused on him, every difficulty and obstacle can be overcome.

There are those who say, "I don't want to walk against the wind of my samskāras. I'm not going to let the wind blow sand in my face." This too is a natural response. But the Gita's reply is terrible in its implications. If you refuse to face into the wind, the Lord says, your samskāras themselves will eventually turn you around and push you forward. That is what sorrow and suffering do. There is a limit to what a person can suffer; and when you lose your peace of mind, when your nights become unbearable, when your relationships wither and your health deteriorates – then, Sri Krishna says, "your need for me will be so desperate, so driving, that the very weight of your suffering will force you to turn and walk against the wind." But the longer we put this off, of course, the farther down the beach we will be, and the more sand and wind we will have to endure on the way back. Sri Krishna's heartfelt appeal is very real to me: "Don't wait until you can scarcely walk, until sandstorms are raging all around you; turn around and face your samskāras *now*."

There are a rare few who have only to hear this appeal to turn. They are the stuff of which great mystics are made. But most of us need some prodding. In this perspective every event, every activity we engage in, has one supreme purpose: to make us dissatisfied with everything that is finite, so that eventually we turn inward to discover our real Self.

This need not come as a sudden decision to take to the spiritual life. I am not referring only to the kind of dramatic change of heart that we read about in the lives of great figures like St. Francis of Assisi, who goes along in life seeming like the rest of us until something opens his eyes, a veil falls, and immediately he turns to God. An ordinary person burdened by a self-centered, separate life might not say "I'm seeking God" but "I'm seeking a better way of life. I've got to have peace of mind, better relationships; I want to be able to sleep at night." This is quite enough for a beginning. Your mind is driving you to distraction, you want to sleep well, and after you have tried the late show and hot toddies and sleeping pills and found that nothing works, you say, "All right, maybe I'll try this meditation." Ultimately, Sri Krishna says, all the drugs will fail; every external effort will fail. That is the nature of life: that is its purpose.

When I began speaking out against smoking in this country, in 1959, very few people considered tobacco a serious health hazard. Friends told me that I was giving too much attention to a trivial issue. I would never get people to stop smoking, they said, and in the meantime I was putting off many in my audience who had come to hear not about cigarettes but about spiritual values. Cigarettes were everywhere in those days: in every movie, on television, in all the ads. Public money was spent supplying planeloads of free cigarettes to "our boys" overseas, so systematically that the program looks now like a government plan for seeding cancer. In those years, the idea that cigarette smoking might be forbidden in public places sounded absurd, impossible.

But the hazards of smoking became more apparent. You could hear individuals express the desire to stop, though often they did not know how. Eventually, with some, the suffering becomes too great; then it is not "I want to stop smoking" but "I've got to stop – now!" That desire is wrenched up from a much deeper level than the craving to smoke, so it draws a lot of will. If it arises while a person can still change, an amazing amount of damage can be undone.

In the same way a whole society can change. One by one, in person after person, a habit is reversed by the goading of experience, until presently you can see that habit being reversed across a nation. This is happening today with smoking, and it can happen with any other kind of habit, even habitual ways of thinking. Not very long ago, in some of the most civilized nations on earth, there was an addiction to profit which took it for granted that children should work in factories fifty or sixty hours a week to keep the Industrial Revolution going. This was scarcely questioned by many good people; it was theologically defended in churches. Yet although the addiction to profit persists, it is no longer unmitigated. When the scale in which suffering is weighed sinks lower, the desire for change arises; the heavier the weight of suffering, the more that desire will rise. Everywhere it is the same: with smoking, with prejudice, with exploitation, with pollution, with war. When the price becomes more than we can pay, we say, "All right, doc. I'm ready to put myself in your hands."

Halfway in sādhana, once meditation is well below the surface level, we reach a critical juncture. The ego realizes that it is embattled for its life, and then it really begins to fight back in all kinds of subtle, insidious ways. The ego is a very shrewd customer. He knows just where we are weakest – different people have different places – and that is where he strikes. Most of the time, he keeps a low profile. He sits with dark glasses in the back of a chauffeured car, parked discreetly across the street, and issues orders to his henchmen: our samskāras, senses, feelings, fears. If we are strongly attached to sensory pleasures, he comes up with excellent reasons why we ought to enjoy life a little more; after all, didn't the Buddha himself say not to go to ascetic extremes? If we are restless, he might stir that samskāra up with talk of travel or a new career. Or he may strike at the intellect: "Why go to extremes? You're a good person; your likes and dislikes are reasonable enough. It's all right to work on your liabilities, but why torment yourself in trying to become something you are not?" Or, more direct: "Who do you think you are, St. Francis? What makes you think you can do what only one person in a million has done?" There are many, many scripts like this, all supporting something which part of us wants desperately to believe: that we have no choice but to remain our petty, separate selves.

This development should not surprise us. We have been trying to blaze a trail into the dark forests of the unconscious: now that we are inside, we find that the same trail is a path for the wild creatures that roam there to get out. In other words, we have pushed our conscious world to the edge of the unconscious, which means that once-hidden samskāras are just beyond the frontier of our day. This is necessary, because otherwise we would not be able to take them on. Once they are in the open, however, if we do *not* take them on, they will take us over. It is not pleasant to face them, I agree; but it is even more unpleasant to be taken over by them. We have no choice but to fight.

At this stage, the wise man or woman becomes acutely vigilant. Sensory desires and self-will can be so powerful that even a dedicated aspirant can be swept away. If you do not resist a samskāra at this stage, it may creep up on the will without your notice. Then suddenly you find that will and desire are running side by side, which means conflicts everywhere. You manage to keep your senses at bay for five days, say; then suddenly you find yourself making up for lost time. After a day or two of indulgence you manage to stop again, but the struggle is more painful than ever, and you need more effort to keep from falling back again. The same can happen with self-will: just when you think you can relax a little, a morning comes when your mind erupts because you cannot have your way. These are critical developments, for if you let compulsive desires or self-will grow stronger, they can break away from the will and pull out ahead, leaving the will to trail along feebly like a shadow.

In the beginning of the Gita, you remember, Arjuna asks Sri Krishna to drive his chariot between the two armies on the morning before battle is joined. He looks at the forces arrayed against him, face after familiar face, and tells Sri Krishna, "These are my relatives, my friends! How can I fight them? It would tear me in two." This is how everyone feels for a while. We look at our ego, our selfish desires, our samskāras, and we feel, "This is who we are!" We can't bring ourselves to fight these forces; it is like asking us to destroy our very selves. In plain language, we do not want to go through with it. We do not want to give up these desires, and our will to fight is sapped at the very root.

All this is because we have not yet seen anything of our higher Self; we are still identifying with our lower, physically oriented personality. We ask, like Arjuna, "Wouldn't it be better not to fight at all?" Arjuna, you remember, throws down his bow, as if he is about to give up. His head is swimming; he doesn't know what to do. That is how the Gita opens, and the whole of this magnificent scripture is an answer to his question. Now, in the final chapter, Sri Krishna will soon leave it to Arjuna to choose: to fight, or to run away.

As a boy, I remember being puzzled by an expression in English literature: "Hobson's choice." "Who is this Mr. Hobson," I asked my teacher, "and what was his choice?" My teacher, who was my uncle, shrugged. "How should I know?" Later, so that I could tell my own students, I found out: Thomas Hobson, a carrier in Cambridge, was immortalized by Milton for no better reason than telling everybody who came to rent a carriage from him, "Take any horse you like, so long as it's the one closest to the door."

As far as being in this battle goes, Sri Krishna says, we have Hobson's choice: that is, no choice at all. We cannot help being attacked by our samskāras; we have no way of avoiding the karma of our nature. Simply by being alive, we are standing in the middle of the fight. "But," Sri Krishna always adds, "you do have a choice in which direction you face. You can face the fight squarely, or you can turn around and give up."

It is good to remember here that Arjuna is a *kshatriya,* a warrior. The mark of a true kshatriya in ancient India was simple: his chest would be scarred from weapons, but on his back there would not be a single mark, because a kshatriya never turns from battle. That is the tradition from which Arjuna came; and I don't mind telling you that though of course she never wielded a weapon, my granny was made of the very same stuff. So too was Gandhiji, once he had remade himself through these powerful spiritual disciplines. Through meditation and its allied disciplines, everyone can develop the capacity to fight this battle and never to yield or run away. All our aggressiveness, all our anger, all our pride, all our determination, have been given to us just for this purpose.

Sri Krishna says, "Your very nature will force you to change." We are caught in our nature like a fish in a net, but this is a net we have made ourselves. For a long time, we don't want to escape from it. As Sri Ramakrishna says, we want to snuggle up in it and feel secure. "I like it here," we say. "I like being tangled. I like the fisherman coming and poking bait into me." Even so, Sri Krishna says, nature itself – the upsurge of evolution – will eventually force you to work free. Aren't there creatures which, if you place them in utter darkness, have to seek the slightest ray of light? That is how we human beings are. Our modern civilization may protest, "No, darkness is comfortable; we should learn to live with it": in the end it is of no avail, because our need is for universal light.

ईश्वरः सर्वभूतानां हृद्देशे ऽर्जुन तिष्ठति ।
भ्रामयन्सर्वभूतानि यन्त्रारूढानि मायया ॥ १८-६१ ॥
तमेव शरणं गच्छ सर्वभावेन भारत ।
तत्प्रसादात्परां शान्तिं स्थानं प्राप्स्यसि शाश्वतम् ॥ १८-६२ ॥

*61. The Lord dwells in the hearts of all creatures
and whirls them round upon the wheel of time.
62. Run to him for refuge with all your strength, and
peace profound will be yours through his grace.*

Generations ago my ancestors made provision for a potter and his family to live in our village not far from our ancestral home. He and his sons made most of our family's pots, and most of those for the rest of the village too. We children used to go and watch him at his work. He went down to the river every morning to fetch a particular kind of clay, which he brought back to mix and knead until it was ready. Then, while all of us watched admiringly, he sat down in front of his potter's wheel, took a lump of clay, and effortlessly began to shape it into what he wanted: a pot, a bowl, a drinking cup, a little oil lamp.

That wheel fascinated me. It wasn't turned by a treadle, as I have seen here; it was worked by the potter's son, who was expected to learn the craft at his father's knee and carry on the family occupation. I used to marvel at the way the wet, shapeless clay came to life when the wheel began to spin; it seemed to grow and blossom like a flower under the deft touch of the father's hands.

In a wonderful image, Sri Krishna says to stand back from evolution now and look at ourselves from a vantage point that can embrace five billion years: we shall see the jīva, the individual personality, shaped under the fingers of karma from life to life while it spins on the wheel of time. That spinning and shaping is Māyā. Our life in the human context starts as a lump of clay, neither good nor bad, neither selfish nor selfless. And we are the potter. If we turn out a pot that is unsymmetrical, we can't return it and demand our money back. Sri Krishna would ask, "From whom?"

On the other hand, there is plenty of clay. If one pot is unsymmetrical, we can put on more clay and try again; and if the first pot is not perfect, it can still be of use to other people. In other words, even our liabilities can be turned into assets when we start living for others rather than ourselves. In this way we undo our negative karma.

As karma is undone, an interesting thing happens to the mind: it begins to quiet down. That is the dynamics of the mind. Karma arises from our selfish desires; the more selfish desires we have and the more active they are, the more negative karma we produce by thinking and acting in response to those desires. As we undo our negative karma, by being kind and not acting on our samskāras, selfish desires subside and the potter's wheel of the mind slows down. Finally there comes a state when we are detached from our desires and do not act on them. If a samskāra starts to rise in the mind, the mantram switches it off, which means that we are no longer producing unfavorable karma. But there is still a lot of unfavorable karma from previous mistakes waiting to be worked out through good karma: this is the purpose of work and even of personal relationships.

Finally the pot we have been shaping is perfected. All that is negative in personality has been removed; we have reshaped ourselves in the highest image of the human being. But as Shankara says, even after we have finished our pot, taken it off the wheel, and left the potting shed, the wheel goes on spinning by itself for a while because of its own momentum. In other words, even in the last stages of sādhana the mind may still have a few negative feelings and personal desires, simply from the force of all our previous conditioning. But then we no longer identify with them, not in the slightest. They have no power to compel us to act on them.

In my early days in Berkeley, I remember being taken for a drive in a friend's old car when the sky clouded over and drops of rain began to fall. My friend turned a switch and the windshield wiper in front of him went on – in front of him, but not in front of me. "That one's broken," he explained cheerfully. "The wiper arm came off." All the way home the little stub of a housing went *click-click*ing back and forth, acting just like a real windshield wiper but accomplishing nothing at all. That is what a burned-out samskāra is like. Some situation comes, some stimulus that used to require a response, and you just sit back and watch it. It switches back and forth, you comment "Very interesting," and then you turn it off; there is no sense of deprivation.

Here I have to confess that I belong to a very realistic tradition which recognizes that all the conditioning we have received over thirty or forty or fifty years, even if you want to talk only of one lifetime, is not going to be completely erased from the human mind. Everyone is likely to face times when the wheel of the mind seems to start up again. There is no need to get apprehensive or despondent when this happens: all that is necessary is to be sure that we don't pick up more clay, throw it on the wheel, and sit down to make compulsive images of it. That is where the danger lies. When the wheel is spinning, don't buy clay, even if it is on sale. And if you have the clay, don't make pots: that is, don't brood over your desires, talk about them, feed them, or fantasize about their fulfillment. Then, when a strong desire comes, you will not associate yourself with it. It will dart across the clear sky of your mind like a bird and vanish, with no disturbance, no call to action, no connection whatever between it and you.

All this time concentration is deepening, and many far-reaching physiological changes are taking place in addition to what is happening in the mind. As concentration deepens, the mind slows down, and with it all other biological processes. When absorption is profound, the breathing rate may fall from sixteen per minute to three or four; finally it may be suspended for a minute or two. This is a tremendously exhilarating experience. The mind has temporarily closed up shop; the ego has gone on a two-minute vacation.

One way to describe this situation is to say that for those two minutes, there is nobody home. This is the negative side, which Catholic mystics call the Divine Desert, the Void. The positive side is that all the mind's unruly customers have departed, leaving an utter stillness that cannot even be dreamed of until we experience it. It is healing and life-giving. Just two minutes, but once you get a taste, those two minutes count for more than anything else in the world. Afterwards, faced with even the most tantalizing sensory experience, you remember that stillness and say, "No. If I indulge now, it will stir up my mind and block my progress. I'll do anything, forego anything, to taste those two minutes again."

You become acutely vigilant: training your senses, going against your self-will, willingly doing things you used to abhor, everything possible to quiet the mind.

Here the Gita gives us precious counsel in a verse that has comforted seekers for many centuries: "Run to Him for refuge with all your strength, and peace profound will be yours through his grace." This is not running away; it is running home: *sthānam shāshvatam,* to your real home. Take refuge in your Self, Sri Krishna says; dive deep to the shelter in the depths of consciousness where the Self abides; take refuge in the kingdom of heaven within. There is no time, space, or causality at these depths; it is no exaggeration to call them eternal. And there is no agitation; these are realms of "peace profound." If a storm is blowing on the surface of consciousness, at this depth you can actually say, "Be still!" and it will be still.

In the final stages of sādhana, mornings come when your meditation is so deep that if a parrot were to come and sit on your head, you wouldn't know it. Your body would be so still that the parrot would think it was sitting on a rock. Yet the mind may not stop that morning, nor the next, nor the next. You go on doing everything possible, waiting with a kind of quiet eagerness, an impatient patience, expecting every day to hear a knock inside so you can say, "Come in!" But nothing happens. You may hear a few steps coming toward the door, but they retreat; your absorption is not yet complete.

Yet inside a tremendous unification is taking place. All your other desires are dissolving in this one desire to open that door. Every desire has to be consumed; otherwise the wheel of the mind can start up again and begin generating more karma. Finally, after many days, weeks, even months of this delectable torture, your accounts are clear; your mind is utterly calm. One morning in meditation the door opens without any knock or warning, and the Lord swoops down like an eagle, as St. Teresa of Ávila says, to lift you out of yourself into the unitive state.

This tremendous experience is not something we can force. We cannot demand, "I'm ready *now.* Give me illumination or else!" All we can do is say humbly, "I have emptied my mind to the best of my ability. My self-will is reduced as far as I can go. I'm content to wait now; I can wait as long as you like." This period of waiting can be a great test; but when the Lord finally reveals himself to us, we know that this revelation is a supreme gift of grace which can come in no other way.

There is a quiet but tremendous statement in the Katha Upanishad: "The Self reveals itself to whom it chooses." No one who has experienced this can get over the wonder of it. There is no rhyme or reason about it that we can see. Through no human effort can the mind be stilled or the ego completely erased; when we have done everything we can right down to the unconscious level of the mind, our separate, personal will lies down and says, "There is nothing more I can do." Then it is that the miracle takes place: to the great Catholic mystics, through a saint or through Jesus the Christ; in the Hindu tradition, through our spiritual teacher. That is why every morning and evening I begin my meditation with love and devotion to my grandmother, because I can find no other explanation than her grace of how a little fellow like me could have been enabled to attain this unitive state.

इति ते ज्ञानमाख्यातं गुह्याद्गुह्यतरं मया ।
विमृश्यैतदशेषेण यथेच्छसि तथा कुरु ॥ १८-६३ ॥
सर्वगुह्यतमं भूयः श्रृणु मे परमं वचः ।
इष्टो ऽसि मे दृढमिति ततो वक्ष्यामि ते हितम् ॥ १८-६४ ॥

63. I give you these precious words of wisdom;
reflect on them and then choose what is best.
64. These are the last words I shall speak to
you, dear one, for your spiritual fulfillment.

These precious words of the Gita are *guhyād guhyataram*: the best-hidden secret on earth. It is not that they are physically hidden; you can walk into the supermarket or a Greyhound bus depot and buy a copy of the Gita or *The Imitation of Christ* for less than the price of a sandwich. But their wisdom is hidden until we desire to find it, when we encounter someone who can open the inner meaning of their words from the depths of personal experience.

"Arjuna," Sri Krishna says, "I have given you wisdom that you can't get anywhere else. Now I want you to reflect on it. Think it over deeply. Test it everywhere, in every situation. Then *yathecchasi, tathā kuru*: do what you like." These daring words are Sri Krishna at his greatest. He doesn't say, "If you don't do what I say, you're going to be in hell for a trillion years." He pays us the highest tribute: "You are rational, thoughtful people; you know now what is beneficial and what is harmful, what is health and what is illness, what is love and what is hatred. Now you can choose." This is the glory of the Gita: no threats, no intimidation, complete respect.

There is an artistry in this way of teaching which appeals to me deeply. Hindu aesthetics places great emphasis on a principle called *dhvani*, 'suggestion': the artist just plays two or three notes, so to speak, and then expects us to fill in the melody. This is a high tribute to our imagination, and in fact dhvani expects a great deal of the audience. Even a very cultured Westerner can find its touches difficult to catch, for the ear has to be trained to catch all kinds of echoes.

My freshman students in English literature used to find this difficult – especially science students, who were required to take freshman English and wanted everything spelled out in black and white. It was painful for them to sit through a class listening to poetry, and one of them told me point-blank: "I don't understand it, and I can't use it either." When I saw their point of view, I began to explain how to look for dhvani in a poem, how to catch and appreciate the echoes of an unstruck sound. Then they began to enjoy themselves. After a while, even students who had already passed their English requirement came to sit in on my class. It was a great delight to me to see their eyes light up as they caught something the first time; they were looking into a whole new world.

Kālidasa, a great poet and playwright whose stature rivalled Shakespeare's, provided marvelous examples; he had dhvani in every line. I would recite a verse to my students – "His love had set like the sun" – and the freshman girls would look downcast. "Why are you sad?" I would ask. "When the sun sets, don't you know it's going to rise again?" Their eyes would open, and they would gasp with insight and expectation. Then I would explain dhvani: how with one deft image, a great poet can suggest volumes.

My teacher was that kind of artist; she had dhvani in everything she said and did. Each little thing was a quiet lesson, not spelled out, but left with boundless respect for my love and imagination to reach out and grasp. She might tell me an incident from the *Mahābhārata*, something that Arjuna did, and not draw any moral or conclusion; but she knew that my love for her would take her words deep and turn them over and over in my mind, trying to see how I could apply that incident to my own life. She spoke seldom and never tried to explain, but that only enflamed my love to reach out farther. There is infinite respect in this way of teaching, infinite love, infinite trust, just the opposite of rigid rules and proscriptions. The teacher touches a few keys, then leaves it to us to make out the melody in our own lives.

मन्मना भव मद्भक्तो मद्याजी मां नमस्कुरु ।
मामेवैष्यसि सत्यं ते प्रतिजाने प्रियो ऽसि मे ॥१८-६५॥
सर्वधर्मान्परित्यज्य मामेकं शरणं व्रज ।
अहं वा सर्वपापेभ्यो मोक्षयिष्यामि मा शुचः ॥१८-६६॥

65. Be aware of me always, adore me,
make every act an offering to me, and you
shall come to me; this I promise.
66. Abandon all supports and look to me
for protection. I shall purify you from
the sins of the past; do not grieve.

"Abandon all supports." This is terribly difficult advice, because it means not to hold on to anything on earth – any material thing, any person, any source of satisfaction. If we are trying to hold on to anything external, we cannot hold on wholly to the Self. But it is only human nature to prefer diversified investments. We want a balanced portfolio of props in life, just in case one or two fall through. I see advertisements today for investment packages that promise to protect you against anything the future might bring: flat inflation, runaway inflation, deflation, depression, "stagflation," even chaos. "This may work with money," Sri Krishna says, "but it won't work with me. If you want to invest in me, mortgage everything you have – all your passions, all your emotions, all your desires."

Arjuna is still the slightest bit dubious. "Krishna," he asks his friend, "what if it doesn't work?"

Krishna smiles sweetly and replies, "Then you lose." No promises.

My granny used to talk this way too: in fact, it is the language of mystics everywhere. Gandhi, I think, was once asked a clever question: "Why can't the Lord give us fulfillment first? Then it would be easy to renounce personal profit and pleasure." Gandhi replied in effect, "That is not love; that's a contract." He was a lawyer, you know. The real lover of God says, "Take everything I have, everything I am; I don't ask for any favor in return. It is enough just to love you." That is the acme of love, and it is one of life's great ironies that we can't learn it from the annals of romance; we have to get it from the mystics, who have renounced everything the world offers. As John of the Cross says, they ask for nothing; so they get everything.

Only the very rarest of mystics can renounce everything at once. Most of the rest of us try for some time to keep a firm grip on the sense world, which is an age-old instinct. Pediatricians test a reflex called the Babinski: if you stroke the soles of an infant's feet in a certain way, the toes curl downward as if to grasp. The response must have been developed millions of years ago, when we were carefree monkeys playing about on the branches of trees. Just as our feet have been conditioned to grasp at branches, the mind has been conditioned over an even longer period to grasp at the experience of the senses. Now we have to learn to let go and grasp at what seems like nothing, in what John of the Cross calls "the dark night of the senses." You can see how impossible the challenge is.

In the language of Western psychology, we are trying to enter the unconscious, trying to trace our fundamental samskāras into the depths where these incredibly powerful forces arise. The mind has no bridges from one level of awareness to the next; there are not even any roads. How we can descend consciously into deeper levels is therefore beyond any physical feat, beyond what reason can understand.

On the surface, for example, a samskāra like jealousy looks no bigger than our little finger. It is not too difficult to get your mind off it – by going to a movie, or eating a pizza, or diverting your attention with some other kind of activity. But as meditation deepens and you trace the samskāra into lower levels, that little finger becomes a wrist, unexpectedly thicker and stronger. By strengthening your will, you can still manage to wrist-wrestle that samskāra; you may even believe for a while that you have it under control. But in the unconscious, you see that your samskāra continues on down to become a big, burly arm. At a deeper level, it is with you always. At night it may come out and pummel you in dreams. That is what an obsession is, and however attached we may be to it, no obsession is anything but torture. You long to free yourself from it, to draw that immense power into your control.

In the film version of *The Old Man and the Sea*, I believe, there is a long wrist-wrestling sequence where it takes Spencer Tracy many, many hours (and a certain amount of rum) to bring his opponent's arm to the table. Similarly, it takes a great deal of time and effort to build up your will until it can bend down a negative samskāra. You will find it so strong, so firmly fixed, that for a long while you can only hold on and go through the motions. You don't know what to do. Every morning in meditation you go deep into consciousness and find your samskāra seated at the frontier with its sleeves rolled up, saying, "Come on, I'm ready." You grip its huge hand and find that your will has turned to custard.

This is a very elusive experience, but I can try to explain it intellectually: when you are in the unconscious, how can you make a conscious effort? The question is absurd, because you have lost your conscious will. Even if you sit down with a mighty resolution – "I'm going to make my muscles so strong that I can bend this fellow's wrist right to the table" – when you get below the surface, there is no will to carry out your orders. You might as well be writing on water. It is most exasperating: you are seated at the table like Spencer Tracy, facing this muscular samskāra while everybody stands around watching; you try to flex your arm, and your muscles melt.

Here I have to change the metaphor, because conscious effort can do nothing in such cases. There is nothing to do but let go and make a giant leap to a deeper level, which in traditional language is the entrance of grace. I can shed some light on this from my own personal experience. As a young man I had plenty of dedication and stamina, plenty of capacity for hard, sustained effort. I gave myself to my pursuits completely: I lived wholly in a world of literature, and I wanted nothing else from life. In other words, most of my prāna was already unified, which meant that I entered the spiritual life with a well-developed singleness of purpose. Naturally, when I began to meditate, I was hopeful that this capacity for dedicated, determined, sustained effort would enable me to break through any obstacle. For a while it all went smoothly. Through sheer persistence I was able to go on deepening my concentration, because my concentration was already good. I was able to resist sleep and similar obstacles in meditation and to exercise reasonable restraint over my senses, because I was already used to subordinating activities to an overriding goal. But when I came to my first frontier in consciousness, I found myself utterly at a loss.

I read many books at that point to find out what others had done – that, as I said earlier, was my intellectual shraddhā, to look for answers in books. But no answers came. I consulted many people, and it shows how catholic a good Hindu can be that I went to men and women of all religions who were trying sincerely to live out spiritual teachings in their daily lives. None of them could give me practical advice. Some said simply, "We haven't reached that point, so we cannot guide you."

I was so completely focused on my goal that when I began to suspect I might not be able to go further, the torture was excruciating. The fear haunted me. Often I would dream in Hindu imagery of leaping across a river and falling into the torrent, or of trying to leap a canyon and plummeting into an abyss. But finally, in very deep meditation, I received the kind of help that comes from a source beyond oneself. In the Hindu tradition, this help comes from your spiritual teacher, who can ally his will with yours at a deep level; and the will of a person established in Self-realization is a will that cannot be broken. This tremendous alliance, however, is a joint effort. The teacher cannot change levels for us; our part is to let go.

These are some of the great adventures in deepening meditation. We are halfway across the sea of birth and death, out of sight of land, and everything is dark and uncertain. We cannot see the other shore; yet we have left this shore for good: if anyone at this stage were to abandon spiritual disciplines, he or she would find life empty; the world of ordinary satisfactions would soon seem a desert. At this time, even a dedicated aspirant can feel lost. Not a single light beckons you; not a gull comes to herald that land lies ahead. You look back on the shore you have left, with its familiar landmarks, and you heave a great sigh of attachment and affection. "I'm leaving all those sandpipers! I'll never be able to play with sand castles again." That is the time to stop looking back and throw everything you have into reaching the other side. Whether you cross the sea or not, the time when you could be satisfied with sand castles is past.

As far as my experience goes, this is where love is indispensable: the kind of love that Mīrā has, that St. Teresa has, who gives everything – all her love, all her passion, all her loyalty – to the Lord, saying, "Even if I lose everything, I will love you and you alone; I shall pursue no other goal." Nothing but that kind of passion is powerful enough to carry us forward when it seems that everything else must be left behind.

"When you can give yourself like this," Sri Krishna promises, "I shall release you from all your karma, the burden of all your mistakes" – in orthodox language, from all sin. This is the ultimate mystery of grace, but it can be explained to some extent in terms of the dynamics of the mind. To give yourself completely, your mind has to become still; every selfish desire must be extinguished. Otherwise you will still be hanging on in some closet of the mind. When you let go of every selfish attachment, the mind-process stops; it has no more selfish desires. How can it produce more karma? Whatever we may have done in the past, its stigma on our consciousness has been erased; the residue of karma has been dissolved in our love for the Lord. After that our consciousness is pure. We have the example of great saints, East and West, who led very reckless lives before they took to the spiritual path. When someone asks them afterward, "Did you really do those things?" they smile and reply, "That was a dream; it happened long ago. I *was* that person once, but that person died: the body is the same, but in it is someone wholly different from before." Like a story with which you identify until done, like a movie that absorbed you while it lasted, your past no longer applies to you; it has left no more stain than the light of the film left on the screen.

इदं ते नातपस्काय नाभक्ताय कदा चन ।
न चाशुश्रूषवे वाच्यं न च मां यो ऽभ्यसूयति ॥ १८-६७॥

*67. Do not share this wisdom with anyone
who lacks in devotion or self-control, lacks
the desire to learn, or scoffs at me.*

This friendly advice is just good teaching. To people who are receptive, who listen with an open heart and a willingness to test what they hear, the words of a scripture like the Gita are precious; they give the keys to the mastery of life and death. But there is very little point in talking about them to a person who does not wish to hear. No one benefits, not on either side.

The vision each of us has of the world, the mystics would explain, is dependent upon the level of consciousness on which we stand. In simpler language, we see life as we are. This is a revolutionary statement, because we are conditioned to believe that we see life as it is. This is the basis of our daily behavior, and it is appalling how much unkindness, misunderstanding, and intolerance are due to inadequate perception.

As I write this, our dog Muka is waiting outside the door. If I could go and tell him, "The sky is blue, and this rose is red," he would cock his head and say abruptly, "I don't think so." He takes it for granted that the world is black and white; I take it for granted that the world has colors. Yet how many colors? A good artist, with the same sensory equipment, will see different colors where I only see blue. An extraterrestrial might see a much wider spectrum; his world might even be framed in extra dimensions. Whose world is real? In this sense Muka and I do not live in the same world, and for us to argue about what color the sky "really" is would be a waste of time.

Similarly, when I go to San Francisco, in a sense I am not in the same world as the joggers and sightseers who share the Marina with me. We live in the world our mind experiences, and all I can say is that I live today in a wholly different world from the one I lived in as a young man. I don't see people as objects that please or threaten me; I see the Lord in many disguises, wearing warmup jackets and three-piece suits. I do not so much see faces as *into* faces, into states of mind. Most important,

I see a world of meaning, shaped by forces we can learn to harness and understand: love, unity, and the forces of the mind, held together in the law of karma. I live in a world whose pieces form a pattern, where nothing happens by chance; I see choices everywhere. But if someone objects he sees nothing but blind forces, helpless conditioning, meaningless events, a world without options, how can I object? We will agree on surface details, such as how to get to Cliff House, but beyond that we live in different worlds.

In the same way, this verse reminds us, we should not judge harshly those who scoff at spiritual realities. We might as well condemn Muka for not believing in colors. But at the same time, very little is gained in trying to convey these truths to those who are, at best, merely curious. There is a kind of window in consciousness that must be opened in order to grasp interior realities, and unless that window is opened, even the most persuasive words pass in one ear and out the other without anything happening in between.

य इदं परमं गुह्यं मद्भक्तेष्वभिधास्यति ।
भक्तिं मयि परां कृत्वा मामेवैष्यत्यसंशयः ॥ १८-६८ ॥
न च तस्मान्मनुष्येषु कश्चिन्मे प्रियकृत्तमः ।
भविता न च मे तस्मादन्यः प्रियतरो भुवि ॥ १८-६९ ॥

68. He who teaches this supreme mystery of the Gita to all those who love me will come to me without doubt.
69. No one can render me more devoted service;
no one on earth can be more dear to me.

All of us qualify for these verses to the extent that we are trying sincerely to translate the teachings of the Gita into our everyday lives. It is good to remember that everyone is a teacher, for good or ill, teaching others through actions and behavior. When we base our lives on spiritual values, we are teaching them much more effectively than if we were to bring a little blackboard to work every day and give noon lectures on humility.

With so many urgent physical problems – poverty, pollution, the threat of nuclear war – even good people sometimes wonder if teaching meditation isn't a luxury. After all, physical problems are easily seen, while meditation works so quietly that it may seem to have no connection with everyday problems. "It may lower your blood pressure," they say, "but how does it help the world?"

Meditation, I tell them, is a tool. Anyone can use it for releasing tremendous inner resources, and these resources cannot help flowing into loving service. The whole message of the Gita is to show how to release our full human potential into selfless, skillful action. The kind of action, of course, will vary from person to person, and its scope will widen as a person grows. The job of meditation is simply to release the resources. Nothing is more worth teaching, Sri Krishna says; for wherever these resources are released, in whatever field, they throw light on how pressing human problems can be solved. That is why the Buddha, like the Gita here, states emphatically that no one does the world greater service than those who show us how to drive out anger, fear, and greed from the human heart.

In a world that seems without options, such people offer boundless hope. Nowhere will you find anyone more hopeful than the mystics, nowhere such a glorification of the human being. Their emphasis is always on our essential goodness, our innate love, our inalienable divinity. Every human being, they remind us, can realize this innate love. And they do not merely remind us; if we are willing, they show us how, guiding us safely through the dangers along the way. There is no need for a spiritual teacher to add anything; the love is already present. I must have said this a million times, yet it is so simple that I suspect most people who hear me have not guessed how tremendous are its implications. It means that we don't have to stuff good will into the mind; we only have to remove ill will. We don't have to acquire a loving nature; we only have to remove what covers it. This brings the solution to every human problem within reach, for as William Law says, all problems arise from the lack of love.

अध्येष्यते च य इमं धर्म्यं संवादमावयोः ।
ज्ञानयज्ञेन तेनाहमिष्टः स्यामिति मे मतिः ॥ १८-७० ॥
श्रद्धावाननसूयश्च श्रृणुयादपि यो नरः ।
सो ऽपि मुक्तः शुभांल्लोकान्प्राप्नुयात्पुण्यकर्मणाम् ॥ १८-७१ ॥

70. Those who meditate on these holy words
worship me with wisdom and devotion.
71. Even those who listen to them with faith,
free from doubts, will find a happier world.

In the traditional interpretation, this "happier world" is a plane of consciousness after death. Scholars are inclined to smile at such assertions, as at the idea that merely listening to the Gita a prescribed number of times can ensure a particular heaven. Yet there is a certain truth in these simple beliefs. Even without meditation, the words of a scripture do have power to purify consciousness to some extent when they are read or listened to systematically, with faith and an open heart. Then the perennial truths of life go in, and the more they fill our consciousness, the more naturally they will affect our action. We should not find this difficult to believe. All of us know the power of the media – movies, television, popular songs – to fill our minds and occupy our thoughts; and what our thoughts are, we become. This verse only states the positive side.

But I like to apply these words to life here and now. "Those who read these words with faith," Sri Krishna promises, "will find a happier world." This is not blind faith. *Shraddhāvān* means 'those who have shraddhā': those who believe the human being is more than a physical creature, that there is more to life than the physical, chemical level. This is enough to open a window of understanding. Such people may say honestly that they do not know what the human being is or what life is. They may tell you they are still searching. But if the heart is willing, that is enough. When they read these words sincerely, testing them against their own experience, they will find that the Gita and the other great scriptures open onto a world of infinite hope.

Sri Krishna does not promise that they will find a more pleasant world. They will see problems all the more clearly: a world threatened by war, poverty, and pollution, communities poisoned by hatred, families at odds, individuals imprisoned in self-will. But instead of a world without options, they will see choices opening everywhere. They will know that their lives count, that they can make a contribution; and they will have the tools – meditation and the allied disciplines – for releasing all the resources they need. Such people, Sri Krishna says, "will find a happier world." I would say, "They will *make* a happier world." In the midst of sorrow, they will find the great joy of being able to help.

The Hindu scriptures tell the story of a great king, Vipashcit, who, like Ashoka, devoted his reign to improving the welfare of his people, who came to love and revere him as a saint more than a king. When he died, it is said, Sri Krishna appeared before him to escort him into heaven. But King Vipashcit had an unusual request. "Lord," he said, "before I enter eternal bliss, may I see the suffering of those in hell?"

Sri Krishna must have been a little surprised by this, but he agreed, promising an angel to accompany and protect him. So, like Dante, King Vipashcit passed with his immortal guide into another plane of consciousness. But what he saw puzzled him. Wherever he passed, he saw only happy faces. People ran to greet him and to receive his blessing, but the tears in their eyes were tears of joy. Now, a saintly king is still a king, accustomed to having his requests taken seriously, and there must have been a note of hurt in his voice as he turned to his escort and asked, "Why have you brought me here directly? I wanted to visit the other place first."

"Your majesty," his angel replied respectfully, "this *is* the other place."

"I don't understand. I expected hell to be full of suffering. Why is it that every face I see is shining with joy?"

"This world *is* full of suffering: behind you, beyond you, wherever you cannot see. It is being close to you that fills these people with joy."

"Then," said Vipashcit, "I need go no further. I have found my heaven."

कच्चिदेतच्छुतं पार्थ त्वयैकाग्रेण चेतसा ।
कच्चिदज्ञानसंमोहः प्रनष्टस्ते धनंजय ॥ १८-७२ ॥
अर्जुन उवाच ।
नष्टो मोहः स्मृतिर्लब्धा त्वत्प्रसादान्मयाच्युत ।
स्थितो ऽस्मि गतसंदेहः करिष्ये वचनं तव ॥ १८-७३ ॥

*72. Have you fully understood my message? Are
you free from your doubts and delusions?*

ARJUNA:

*73. You have dispelled my doubts and delusions,
and made me ready to fight this battle. My
faith is firm now, and I will do your will.*

Arjuna's reply is the real end of the Gita, the conclusion of his dialogue
with Sri Krishna. The instruction is over; the fight is about to begin. But
Arjuna's will is undivided now, which means that it is one with the
divine will; victory is only a matter of time. His spirit is caught by those
marvelous lines of William Blake:

> Bring me my bow of burning gold!
> 　Bring me my arrows of desire!
> Bring me my spear! O clouds, unfold!
> 　Bring me my chariot of fire!
> I will not cease from mental fight,
> 　Nor shall my sword sleep in my hand
> Till we have built Jerusalem
> 　In England's green and pleasant land.

To those in the thick of this battle, the Gita gives two watchwords:
fight and faith. Give your very best against your samskāras, never give
up; then have faith for the rest. Remember Augustine's assurance: "If
we will do what we can, He can do as He wills."

Arjuna says literally, *Smritir labdhā*: "I have my memory back.
I remember now who I am." We can imagine him looking back over the
long travail of evolution through which each of us has passed and shaking his head in wonder. "How could I have forgotten?" Our present state
is a kind of prolonged amnesia: we have forgotten our divine nature, the

unity from which we came. When a person has amnesia, don't friends try to awaken his memory with reminders, once-familiar objects, the faces or voices of those who once were dear? All this happens as we begin to wake up from this spiritual amnesia and recall: we are not a separate, isolated creature but a prince, a princess, with a kingdom to return to and a mission to discharge when we return.

Arjuna is at his full stature now, every inch the warrior. You remember the insignia: no wounds on the back; no retreating. That is the mark of the lover too: no retaliating, no retreating. The forces are gathered, and Sri Krishna has thrown down a very personal challenge to us all: If you can forgive, if you can learn to return kindness for unkindness, love for hatred, you are on the side of light. But if you cannot forgive, if you prefer to meet violence with violence, then you are on the other side, whatever goal you may have in view. Therefore, the Gita says, the fate of the world is in your hands. By our choices, each of us helps to shape the destiny of us all.

For years, we will not have the remotest idea of what a ferocious enemy we have to deal with. Our aggressive instincts, our militancy and rebelliousness, the daredevil desires that make a person sail around the world alone or climb an unclimbed mountain, have all been given to us so that we can fight self-will to the end. Nothing is more difficult, no fight more fierce. But when the battle is won, the dark regions of the unconscious where anger, fear, and greed used to roam like wild animals will be fully conscious and flooded with light. Jacopone da Todi, with the understatement of a great lover and a brave warrior, tells us in words so simple that I like to quote the original Italian:

> *La guerra è terminata:*
> *de la virtu battaglia,*
> *de la mente travaglia*
> *cosa nulla contende.*

> The war is over.
> In the battle of virtue,
> the struggle of spirit,
> all is at peace.

Then, the Upanishads say, we pass here and now from the unreal to the real, from darkness to light, from death to immortality.

संजय उवाच ।
इत्यहं वासुदेवस्य पार्थस्य च महात्मनः ।
संवादमिममश्रौषमद्भुतं रोमहर्षणम् ॥ १८-७४ ॥
व्यासप्रसादाच्छुतवानेतद्गुह्यमहं परम् ।
योगं योगेश्वरात्कृष्णात्साक्षात्कथयतः स्वयम् ॥ १८-७५ ॥
राजन्संस्मृत्य संस्मृत्य संवादमिममद्भुतम् ।
केशवार्जुनयोः पुण्यं हृष्यामि च मुहुर्मुहुः ॥ १८-७६ ॥
तच्च संस्मृत्य संस्मृत्य रूपमत्यद्भुतं हरेः ।
विस्मयो मे महान्राजन्हृष्यामि च पुनः पुनः ॥ १८-७७ ॥
यत्र योगेश्वरः कृष्णो यत्र पार्थो धनुर्धरः ।
तत्र श्रीर्विजयो भूतिर्ध्रुवा नीतिर्मतिर्मम ॥ १८-७८ ॥

SANJAYA:

74. *This is the dialogue I heard between Krishna, the son of Vasudeva, and Arjuna, the greathearted son of Pritha. The wonder of it makes my hair stand on end!*
75. *Through Vyasa's grace, I have heard the supreme secret of spiritual union directly from the Lord himself.*
76. *Whenever I remember these wonderful, holy words between Krishna and Arjuna, I am filled with joy.*
77. *And when I remember the breathtaking form of Krishna, my joy overflows.*
78. *Wherever the divine Krishna and the mighty Arjuna are found, there will be prosperity, victory, happiness, and unshakable wisdom. Of this I am sure!*

We have reached the end of what is to me the most marvelous document in the world, and I do not mind telling you that I could begin it all again. I must have read the Gita dozens of times, but each time it offers fresh insight, inspiration, and wisdom.

"Wherever we find Krishna and Arjuna" – that is, wherever there are men and women who turn to these timeless truths for guidance – the Gita assures us that the forces of light will be victorious. Life is not a blind area where blind forces are at work. Just as there are physical laws that govern the universe, there are equally operative spiritual laws which derive from the unity of life. When we violate this unity, negative consequences follow; we have seen many examples in this volume. In the same way, when we act in harmony with this unity, the very nature of the universe supports us. We may feel insignificant, but we have the invisible but inexorable support of cosmic forces behind us. Mahatma Gandhi's life gives a perfect illustration, and we have his quiet but precise testimony that these are laws that can be verified as thoroughly as the law of gravity:

> The claim that I have made is neither extraordinary nor exclusive. God will rule the lives of all those who will surrender themselves without reservation to Him. In the language of the Gita, God acts through those who have acquired complete detachment, that is, self-effacement. Here is no question of hallucination. I have stated a simple scientific truth to be tested by all those who have the will and patience to acquire the necessary qualifications, which are again incredibly simple to understand and easy enough to acquire where there is determination.

Gandhi is much, much more than the father of the Indian nation, much bigger even than the political history the world presents. His greatest significance is to show us the true potential of the individual human being, who, though physically limited, can become an instrument of divine forces that can change the world in some measure.

I have often said that to understand Gandhi, we have to understand the Gita. But the reverse is also true: to grasp the Gita, it is a great help to understand Gandhi. One of his most revolutionary contributions is that evil has no lasting reality. What *is* real is the underlying unity we call God, because it cannot be erased, cannot be altered, cannot be taken away. Here is the practical application: evil is real only insofar as we support it. If you stand in front of the sun, don't you cast a shadow? There *is* darkness on the path; yet the sun still shines, and if you remove the obstruction to its light, the shadow disappears. Evil is a kind of shadow, the absence of light. It can disappear when what obstructs the light is removed. Each person who says or does or even connives at evil, therefore, bears a terrible responsibility: for the time being, he or she is helping to make that unreal evil real. As we withdraw our support – of unkindness, injustice, violence, exploitation, war – these evils will cease to exist.

From this perspective, every problem in the world has its final solution in withdrawing our personal support. Here Gandhi comes home to every one of us. We don't have to look to presidents or prime ministers to solve these problems; we don't have to look to leaders or experts in any sphere. We look to ourselves. If, in my own life, I can withdraw support from everything that violates the unity of life, I have reduced evil by one measure. This is much more than a negative contribution. It releases a tremendous positive force which finds expression in our work, our relationships, and our priorities. As that force spreads, it begins to change the lives of those around us.

This is where Gandhi really glorifies the individual. Truth, he maintained, does not need strength of numbers. Too many followers can actually be a hindrance; a crowd or a majority can be swept away. If only one person can turn from evil completely, in action, word, and even thought, he or she alone can change the world. Toward the end of his life, Gandhi was sometimes asked how he had managed to bring down the greatest empire the world had known. Gandhi replied in effect, "What makes you say *I* did it? I was only an instrument." He was trying to tell us that God – truth, love, unity – is always present. By emptying himself of himself, he became a vehicle through which these forces could work. Wherever this happens, though it may take time, other hearts cannot help but respond. The Lord dwells in every one of us, and "deep calleth unto deep."

When we look at the forces arrayed against us, it is only natural to ask how our small contribution can work against these impossible odds. Sri Krishna would object, "What makes you think that you are working alone?" Just as physical forces like gravitation are always operating, love, truth, and compassion operate everywhere, under all circumstances. Gravitation is not something added to the world; it is part of its very fabric. Similarly, love and unity are part of the fabric of life, part of its very nature. Just as we respond to these forces, others too will respond. We see only a tiny part of the stage: one corner in space, moment by moment in time. We can act, the Gita reminds us over and over, but we cannot dictate the fruits of our action. "Just do your best," Sri Krishna says; "then leave the results to me."

Even in our own sādhana, this brings immense reassurance. Spiritual disciplines are terribly difficult, and illumination almost impossible for an ordinary human being – I would say, even for a remarkable human being. The main reason why it can be achieved, even by little people like us, is that these cosmic forces are at work, helping everybody who undertakes this heroic task. Without these forces, there would be no future for the world.

In these dark times, therefore, I would like every one of you to remember this: we are not alone. This is not a world of chance, with "neither joy, nor love, nor light, nor certitude, nor peace, nor help for pain." We are surrounded by creative powers, as surrounded as we are by air and light and gravitation. It is only when we fail to ally ourselves with the forces of light that they are unable to support us. If we give our wholehearted support, love *will* triumph. This remembrance brings faith; it brings hope; it brings the certitude of victory.

मोक्षसंन्यासयोगो नाम अष्टादशोऽध्यायः ॥ १८ ॥

So ends the Bhagavad Gita.
May the Lord of Love, enshrined in the hearts of all,
inspire every one of us to live to make our world a land
of peace and joy, love and wisdom.
Om shānti shānti shānti

Be Aware of Me Always

SRI KRISHNA:

Those who are free from selfish attachments,
Who have mastered the senses and passions,
Act not, but are acted through by the Lord.
Listen to me now, O son of Kunti,
How one who has become an instrument
In the hands of the Lord attains Brahman,
The supreme consummation of wisdom.

Unerring in discrimination,
Sovereign of the senses and passions,
Free from the clamor of likes and dislikes,
They lead a simple, self-reliant life
Based on meditation, using speech,
Body, and mind to serve the Lord of Love.

Free from self-will, aggressiveness, arrogance,
From the lust to possess people or things,
They are at peace with themselves and others
And enter into the unitive state.

United with the Lord, ever joyful,
Beyond the reach of self-will and sorrow,
They serve me in every living creature
And attain supreme devotion to me.
By loving me they share in my glory
And enter into my boundless being.

All their acts are performed in my service,
And through my grace they win eternal life.

Make every act an offering to me;
Regard me as your only protector.
Make every thought an offering to me;
Meditate on me always.

Drawing upon your deepest resources,
You shall overcome all difficulties
Through my grace. But if you will not heed me
In your self-will, nothing will avail you.

If you say, "I will not fight this battle,"
Your own nature will drive you into it.
If you will not fight the battle of life,
Your own karma will drive you into it.

The Lord dwells in the hearts of all creatures,
And he whirls them round on the wheel of time.
Run to him for refuge with all your strength
And peace profound will be yours through his grace.

I give you these precious words of wisdom;
Reflect on them and then choose what is best.
These are the last words I shall speak to you,
Dear one, for your spiritual fulfillment.

Be aware of me always, adore me,
Make every act an offering to me,
And you shall come to me;
This I promise, for you are dear to me.

Leave all other support, and look to me
For protection. I shall purify you
From the sins of the past. Do not grieve.

Do not share this wisdom with anyone
Who lacks in devotion or self-control,
Lacks the desire to learn, or who scoffs at me.

Those who teach this supreme mystery
Of the Gita to all those who love me
Will come to me without doubt. No one
Can render me more devoted service;
No one on earth can be more dear to me.

Those who meditate on these holy words
Worship me with wisdom and devotion.
Even those who listen to them with faith,
Free from doubts, will find a happier world.

Have you fully understood my message?
Are you free from your doubts and delusions?

ARJUNA:

You have dispelled my doubts and delusions
And made me ready to fight this battle.
My faith is firm now, and I will do your will.

Glossary & Guide
to Sanskrit Pronunciation

GUIDE TO THE PRONUNCIATION OF SANSKRIT WORDS

Consonants. Consonants are generally pronounced as in English, but there are some differences. Sanskrit has many so-called aspirated consonants, that is, consonants pronounced with a slight *h* sound. For example, the consonant *ph* is pronounced as English *p* followed by an *h* as in ha*ph*azard. The *bh* is as in a*bh*or. The aspirated consonants are *kh, gh, ch, jh, th, dh, ph, bh.*

c as in *c*hurch	*g* as in *g*old
h as in *h*ome	*j* as in *J*une

The other consonants are approximately as in English.

Vowels. Every Sanskrit vowel has two forms, one short and one long. The long form is pronounced twice as long as the short. In the English transliteration the long vowels are marked with a bar (ˉ). The diphthongs – *e, ai, o, au* – are also pronounced twice as long as the short vowels. Thus, in the words *nīla* 'blue' and *gopa* 'cowherd,' the first syllable is held twice as long as the second.

a as in *u*p	*ri* as in w*ri*tten
ā as in f*a*ther	*e* as in th*ey*
i as in g*i*ve	*ai* as in *ai*sle
ī as in s*ee*	*o* as in g*o*
u as in p*u*t	*au* as in c*ow*
ū as in r*u*le	

SPELLING OF SANSKRIT WORDS

To simplify the spelling of Sanskrit words we have used a minimum of diacritical marks, retaining only the long mark (ˉ) for the long vowels and omitting the other diacritics which are sometimes used in rendering Sanskrit words into English.

abhyāsa Regular practice.

adharma ['not dharma'] Injustice, evil, anything which goes against moral laws.

advaita ['not two'] Having no duality; the supreme Reality, which is the "One without a second." The word *advaita* is especially used in Vedānta philosophy, which stresses the unity of the Self (Ātman) and Brahman.

ahamkāra [*aham* 'I'; *kāra* 'maker'] Self-will, separateness.

ahimsā [*a* 'not'; *himsā* 'violence'] Nonviolence, doing no injury, wishing no harm.

ajapajapam The holy name (*mantram*) repeating itself in the mind of the user without conscious effort on his part.

ākāsha Space, sky; the most subtle of the traditional elements (ether).

Ananta The cosmic serpent that Vishnu rests upon.

apara ['not transcendent'] Lower knowledge; intellectual knowledge.

Arjuna One of the five Pandava brothers, and an important figure in Indian epic and legend. He is Sri Krishna's beloved disciple and friend in the Bhagavad Gita.

asat [*a* 'not'; *sat* 'truth, goodness'] Untruth; anything unreal, untrue, or lacking in goodness.

āshram [Skt *āshrama*'] A spiritual community, where meditation and spiritual disciplines are practiced.

asura In Hindu myth, a demon; figuratively, a being with an evil nature. The adjective *asurika* or asuric means evil, base, or demonic.

āsurī [Belonging to the demons or *asuras*] Demonic, evil, not tending to spiritual welfare.

Ātman The Self; the innermost soul in every creature, which is divine.

avatāra [*ava* 'down'; *tri* 'to cross'] The descent of God to earth; the incarnation of the Lord on earth; the birth of divine consciousness in the heart of any being.

avidyā [*a* 'not'; *vidyā* 'wisdom'] Ignorance, lack of wisdom, want of knowledge.

aviveka [*a* 'not'; *viveka* 'discrimination, judgment'] Want of judgment, lack of discernment.

avyaya The eternal, the changeless.

Bardo [Tibetan *bar* 'between'; *do* 'two'] In Tibetan mysticism, the state between two lives in which the soul awaits a proper body and context for rebirth.

Bhagavad Gītā [*Bhagavat* 'Lord'; *gītā* 'song'] "The Song of the Lord," name of a Hindu scripture which contains the instructions of Sri Krishna.

bhakti Devotion, worship, love.

bhakti yoga The Way of Love.

Bhārata India; a person who lives in India; a descendant of King Bharata.

Bhīshma A revered elder of the Kaurava dynasty who allows himself to be killed by Arjuna in the *Mahābhārata* battle.

Brahmā The god of creation. Brahmā, the Creator, Vishnu, the Preserver, and Shiva, the Dissolver, make up the Hindu Trinity. *Brahma*, a word with masculine gender, should not be confused with Brahman, which has neuter gender. (See next entry.)

Brahman The supreme Reality underlying all life, the Divine Ground of
   existence, the impersonal Godhead.

brahmin [Skt. *brāhmana*] A person who strives to know Brahman; in
   traditional Hindu society, a person of the priestly or learned class.

Buddha [from *budh* 'to wake up'] "The Awakened One." An enlightened being;
   the title given to the sage Siddhārtha Gautama Shākyamuni after he
   obtained complete illumination. The Buddha lived and taught in North
   India during the sixth century B.C.

buddhi Understanding, intelligence; right idea.

Chitragupta "The Hidden Accountant;" the recorder of each individual's karmic
   record.

chitta Mind, the substratum of mental activity.

daivam God's will; destiny.

daivī [Belonging to the gods or devas] Divine, spiritual.

deva A divine being, a god.

devī A divine being, a goddess.

dharma Law, duty; the universal spiritual Law that holds all things together in
   a unity.

dhvani Sound, note; allusion; a subtly suggested meaning.

Drona A general of the Kaurava army. He was a learned brahmin who became
   a warrior. The preceptor of the royal princes, he taught the heroes of the
   Mahābhārata the skills of war.

duhkha Pain, suffering, sorrow.

Ganges [Skt. *gangā*] A great river of northern India, looked upon as a sacred
   symbol.

Gītā "The Song," a shorter title for the Bhagavad Gita.

guna Quality. Specifically, the three qualities which make up the phenomenal
   world: *sattva*, law; *rajas*, energy; and *tamas*, inertia.

Harijan [*Hari* 'God'; *jan* 'born of'] Child of God; Gandhi's name for the so-
   called untouchable classes of India.

Himālaya [*hima* 'snow'; *ālaya* 'abode'] "The Home of Snow," the great mountain
   range which stretches across the northern border of India.

jīva Living being; the living soul; the individual soul that is identified with
   separate existence.

jnāna Wisdom; the knowledge acquired through meditation and spiritual
   disciplines.

jnāna yoga The Way of Wisdom.

Kālidāsa Name of a celebrated poet of ancient India.

kāma Selfish desire, greed; sensual desire.

karma [*kri* 'to do'] Action; former actions which will lead to certain results in a
   cause and effect relationship.

Katha Upanishad An early Hindu scripture that contains the teachings of the
   god of death concerning the immortal soul.

Kauravas "The sons of *Kuru,*" usually refers to Duryodhana and his brothers, who are the enemies of the Pandava brothers. The Kauravas are the evil geniuses of the *Mahābhārata.*

Keshava "He who has long, beautiful hair," a name of Krishna.

Krishna ['black'; or from *krish* 'to draw, to attract to oneself'] "The Dark One" or "He who draws us to Himself;" name of an incarnation of Vishnu. Vishnu, the cosmic force of goodness, comes to earth as Krishna to reestablish dharma, or law. Krishna is the friend and advisor of the Pandava brothers, especially Arjuna, to whom he reveals the teachings of the Bhagavad Gita. Krishna is the inner Lord, who personifies spiritual love and lives in the hearts of all beings.

kshatriya A warrior or prince; the ruling class of traditional Hindu society.

kshetra A field; a place; a sacred place or temple.

kundalinī "The serpent power," spiritual or evolutionary energy.

Kurukshetra "The field of the Kurus," where the *Mahābhārata* battle takes place.

līlā Game; the divine game of God, who creates the worlds in play.

Mahābhārata The great epic of India, composed in about the ninth century B C. Vyāsa is traditionally considered to be the author of this epic, which tells of the war between the sons of Pandu (the forces of goodness) and the sons of Dhritarāshtra (the forces of darkness).

mahātma "Great Soul;" a title of respect and reverence.

manas The mind; more specifically, the faculty which registers and stores sensory impressions.

mantram [or *mantra*] A holy name or phrase; a spiritual formula.

Māyā Illusion; appearance, as contrasted with divine Reality; God's creative power. Through Māyā the Godhead creates the world, and through Māyā the Godhead is hidden.

Mīrā A woman saint of medieval India remembered for her songs to her beloved Krishna.

Nachiketa The youth who learns of death and immortality in the Katha Upanishad.

nirvāna [*nir* 'out'; *vāna* 'to blow'] The complete quietening of self-will; realization of the unity of life.

ojas Strength, vitality, energy.

Om [or *Aum*] The cosmic sound, heard in deep meditation; the Holy Word which signifies Brahman or the Godhead. This is probably the oldest Hindu mantram.

Pāndavas "The sons of Pandu," a collective name for Arjuna and his four brothers – Yudhishthira, Bhīma, Nakula, and Sahadeva.

para Transcendental knowledge, wisdom.

Patanjali The author of the *Yogasutras,* an ancient text on meditation. He lived around the second century B.C., and his method of meditation is sometimes referred to as *rāja yoga.*

prāna Breath; vital force.

Prithā The name of Arjuna's mother (she is also called Kuntī). Arjuna is called Pārtha, "son of Prithā."

pūjā Worship, especially a ritual worship with an offering of fruits and flowers.

Purusha "Person," the inner soul or spiritual core of a person. In the Gita, the terms *Ātman* and *Purusha* are roughly interchangeable.

Purushottama "Highest Person," Supreme Being, God.

Raghuvamsha The name of a classical epic which tells of the great dynasty of the Raghus, in which Prince *Rāma* was born.

rāja yoga The Royal Path, the way of meditation taught by Patanjali.

rajas Passion; energy; the second of the three qualities (*gunas*).

Rāma [from *ram* 'to rejoice'] The Lord of Joy; spiritual joy; name of the prince who was Vishnu's incarnation.

sādhana A body of disciplines which is followed to attain the goal of Self-realization.

sādhu Good person; a holy sage.

sahaja A natural or established state of spiritual awareness.

samādhi Union with God; a state of intense concentration in which consciousness is totally unified.

samsāra The world of change; the round of birth, death, and rebirth.

samskāra A personality trait conditioned over many lives or one life; a tendency within the mind which will show itself when given the opportunity.

Sanjaya The mystic who divinely perceives the Gita and narrates it to the blind king Dhitarāshtra.

Sānkhya One of the six branches of Hindu philosophy. The goal of sānkhya is to liberate the individual *Purusha* (spirit) from *prakriti* (mind and matter).

sat [from *as* 'to be'] The Real; truth; goodness.

sattva Goodness, purity, law; the highest of the three qualities (*gunas*).

satya Truth, truthful; good, the Good.

satyāgraha [*satya* 'truth'; *āgraha* 'grasping'] Gandhi's term for a moral struggle that would never resort to violence.

Shakti Power; God's feminine aspect.

Shankara Name of Shiva. A Hindu philosopher of the sixth century A.D. who taught the doctrine of Advaita Vedānta; he wrote a commentary on the Bhagavad Gita.

Shiva A major deity of the Hindu pantheon. He is the third god of the Hindu Trinity– the Great Lord who brings about the death of the worlds, and who takes his devotee beyond death.

Shrī or *Srī* A title of respect originally meaning "Lord" or "Holy"; in modern times, simply a respectful form of address.

shraddhā Faith.

shūdra The fourth Hindu caste; a worker or servant.

sthūlasharīra The physical body.

sūkshmasharīra The subtle body, which follows the soul after death.

tamas Inertia, ignorance, darkness; the lowest of the three qualities or *gunas*.

tapas Austerity, control of the senses; the vitality acquired through self-control.

tat "That," Brahman, the impersonal godhead.

tejas Splendor, inner power, radiant vitality.

Upanishads Ancient scriptures that emphasize mystical experience. They form the final portions of the Veda.

varna Caste, class, the four general classes recognized in traditional Hindu society.

Varuna God of waters and the ocean. In the Veda, the moral overseer of the world.

Veda [*vid* 'to know'] "Knowledge"; the name of the most ancient Sanskrit scriptures, thought to be a direct revelation from God to the mystics of the past.

vidyā Knowledge, wisdom; a science or branch of study.

Vishnu The great sustaining god of the Hindu pantheon. He is the second god of the Hindu Trinity; the Preserver who incarnates himself in age after age for the welfare of all creatures.

yajna Offering, sacrifice, worship.

Yudhishthira Arjuna's older brother, the leader of the Pandava faction. He becomes king of all North India after the victory of the Pandavas at Kurukshetra. He is known for his justice and love of dharma.

yugadharma The "dharma of the age," what is appropriate for the times.

yoga [from *yuj* 'to unite'] Union with God; a path or discipline that leads to total integration of consciousness.

Index

END

MORE BOOKS BY EKNATH EASWARAN

The Bhagavad Gita for Daily Living:
A Verse-By-Verse Commentary

Volume 1: Chapters 1–6 The End of Sorrow

These opening chapters explore the concept of the innermost Self and source of wisdom in all of us. Easwaran explains how we can begin to transform ourselves, even as householders engaged in busy lives.

Volume 2: Chapters 7–12 Like a Thousand Suns

These chapters go beyond the individual Self to explore the Supreme Reality underlying all creation. Easwaran builds a bridge across the seeming divide between scientific knowledge and spiritual wisdom and explains how the concept of the unity of life can help us in all our relationships.

Volume 3: Chapters 13–18 To Love Is to Know Me

Global in scope, these final chapters make an urgent appeal for us to see that all of us are one – to make the connection between the Self within and the Reality underlying all creation. Easwaran shows how the Gita can guide us to make wiser choices, to heal our environment and establish peace in our world.

The Bhagavad Gita, The Upanishads, The Dhammapada
Classics of Indian Spirituality Series

These best-selling translations each include a comprehensive, accessible introduction explaining the cultural background and core concepts of the scripture.

MORE BOOKS BY EKNATH EASWARAN

Passage Meditation: A Complete Spiritual Practice
Train your mind and find a life that fulfills

This classic manual presents Easwaran's universal method of passage meditation. It is a unique source of practical support for new and experienced meditators, offering all the instruction needed to establish a vibrant meditation practice and keep it going.

Essence of the Bhagavad Gita: A Contemporary Guide to Yoga, Meditation, and Indian Philosophy

Based on talks given in the later years of Easwaran's life, this book is his in-depth exploration of the key themes of the Gita: the nature of reality, the meaning of yoga, and the unity of life. It complements Easwaran's other writings on the Gita, offering further insights into this much-loved scripture.

Essence of the Upanishads: A Key to Indian Spirituality

Easwaran shows how the Katha Upanishad, another ancient wisdom text, embraces all the key ideas of Indian mysticism and presents them in the context of a mythic quest – the story of a young hero who ventures into the land of death in search of immortality.

Gandhi the Man: How One Man Changed Himself to Change the World

Easwaran, who grew up in Gandhi's India, gives a moving account of the turning points and choices in Gandhi's life that made him not just a great political leader but also a timeless icon of nonviolence in the world today. This book includes more than 70 photographs and a chronology.

**☧ Blue Mountain
Center of Meditation**

The Blue Mountain Center of Meditation publishes
Eknath Easwaran's books, videos, and audio recordings,
and offers retreats and online programs on his
eight-point program of passage meditation.

For more information and resources, please visit:
www.bmcm.org

The Blue Mountain Center of Meditation
Box 256, Tomales, California 94971 USA
Telephone: +1 707 878 2369
Toll-free in the US: 800 475 2369
Email: info@bmcm.org